beowulf

widsith

the fight at finnesburg

HƿÆT ƿE GARDE

na in gear dagum þeod cyninga
þrym ge frunon hu ða æþelingas ellen
fremedon. Oft scyld scefing sceaþe(na)
þreatum monegū mægþum meodo setla
of teah egsode eorl syððan ærest ƿear(ð)
fea sceaft funden he þæs frofre geba(d)
ƿeox under ƿolcnum ƿeorð myndum þah
oð ꝥ him æghƿylc þara ymb sittendra
ofer hron rade hyran scolde gomban
gyldan ꝥ ƿæs god cyning. ðæm eafera ƿæs
æfter cenned geong in geardum þone god
sende folce to frofre fyren ðearfe on
geat ꝥ hie ær drugon aldor(le)ase. lange
hƿile him þæs lif frea ƿuldres ƿealdend
ƿorold are for geaf. beoƿulf ƿæs breme
blæd ƿide sprang scyldes eafera scede
landum in. Sƿa sceal (geong g)uma gode
ge ƿyrcean fromum feoh giftum on fæder

BEOWULF

TOGETHER WITH

WIDSITH

AND

THE FIGHT AT FINNESBURG

IN THE

Benjamin Thorpe Transcription

AND

Word-for-Word Translation

WITH AN INTRODUCTION BY

Vincent F. Hopper

BARRON'S EDUCATIONAL SERIES

GREAT NECK, NEW YORK

All inquiries should be addressed to
Barron's Educational Series, Inc.
343 Great Neck Road
Great Neck, New York

PRINTED IN THE UNITED STATES OF AMERICA

Library of Congress Catalog Card No. 62–18764

CONTENTS

INTRODUCTION

Benjamin Thorpe was one of the outstanding pioneer editors and translators of *Beowulf;* many of the now widely accepted readings of the manuscript were first proposed by him. In his preface to the work which is here reprinted, he describes the condition of the only extant *Beowulf* manuscript: "All manuscripts of Anglo-Saxon poetry are deplorably inaccurate, evincing, in almost every page, the ignorance of an illiterate scribe, frequently (as was the monastic custom) copying from dictation; but of all Anglo-Saxon manuscripts that of *Beowulf* may, I believe, be conscientiously pronounced the worst, independently of its present lamentable condition, in consequence of the fire at Cotton House in 1731, whereby it was seriously injured, being partially rendered as friable as touchwood."

The first printed transcript of the Cotton manuscript was prepared by the Icelandic scholar G. K. Thorkelin in 1815. A second followed in 1833, done by John M. Kemble who also did a translation in 1837 and added many suggested readings which have become commonly accepted. Thorpe collated the text of the Thorkelin edition with the original manuscript in 1830, by which time many of the words transcribed by Thorkelin had become faded or obliterated in the manuscript. Then, taking cognizance of the later suggestions of Kemble, he produced his combined edition and translation in 1855. His general method was to include emendations in the text when they seemed unquestionable, consigning to footnotes the corresponding readings in the manuscript. When there was doubt about an emendation, however, he retained the manuscript version in the text and suggested the correction at the foot of the page. His word-for-word translation was intended to be as literal as was "consistent with perspicuity."

This edition is therefore of great interest not only because of the device of printing both text and translation on the same page but also because it makes vivid the extraordinary difficulties attendant upon the reading of the *Beowulf* manuscript. Thorpe also added the texts and translations of "The Scop or Gleeman's Tale" (now usually known as "Widsith") and the fragment of "The Fight at Finnesburg" because of the cross reference materials of both of these poems to passages in *Beowulf*.

BEOWULF

Although there is still much doubt about the origin of this heroic poem, it appears to have been an Anglian poem composed in Northumbria (or possibly Mercia) during the first half of the eighth century. It presupposes an aristocratic Christian audience whose Germanic background and ancestry included the knowledge of Scandinavian and all of Germanic tradition and folk-lore of which the stories of Beowulf's three battles were a part, stories which were transmitted to England during the Anglo-Saxon invasions. Consequently, the pagan *Wyrd* or fate blends somewhat uncertainly with the implication of a Christian God as all-ruler of the universe. Beowulf himself is unknown to recorded Germanic history, but it is reasonable to assume that an actual heroic Beowulf did indeed live and that the accounts of his prowess described in this poem were among the legends that were woven about him.

CONCERNING SCYLD THE SHEAF-CHILD. The poem opens with a prefatory section which gives the ancestry of the Danish king Hrothgar whose mead-hall is the scene of the first adventure of the poem. The founder of the line is Scyld Scefing, or Scyld Sheaf-Child, so named because of the tradition that as a child he had drifted, lying on a sheaf of wheat, in a boat filled with arms until the boat landed on the island of Skaney. From this frail child there developed a mighty king who ruled valiantly and well, respected by his own people and feared by his tribute-giving neighbors. After many years a son was born to him named Beowulf (probably the scribe's confused rendering of Beow or Beowa of the Anglo-Saxon genealogies and not the Beowulf of this poem). After mentioning the fame of this child, the preface concludes with an account of the death and elaborate funeral of Scyld, describing how he was laid in a ship loaded with parting gifts of arms and treasures and the ship set adrift on the waters which had borne him to the country's shores as a child.

I. The genealogy continues with a reiteration of the fame of Scefing's son Beowulf, his son Healfdene, and Healfdene's four sons Heorogar, Hrothgar, Halga, and Ela. Heorogar, as is implied later, ruled for a time but then turned over the government to his brother Hrothgar who built the great hall Heorot, a symbol of his fame and glory. But tragedy lurked in the darkness where the demon Grendel, one of the evil descendants of Cain, listened to the gleeman chanting lays of the glory of God.

II. Filled with rage, Grendel comes at night to Heorot, kills the thirty thanes sleeping there, and returns home with their slaughtered corpses. Daybreak brings woe to the ruler and his people upon their discovery of the monster's vengeance. The next night Grendel returns, the hall soon stands deserted (at night), and for twelve years, refusing to parley or to make peace, the demon prowls over the fen, raiding and destroying. The tale is soon noised abroad by the gleemen.

III. News of this calamity reaches the Jute Beowulf, a nephew of Hygelac, king of the opposite territory of West Gothland. Strongest and boldest of men, Beowulf chooses a band of fifteen heroic followers and with them sails to Hrothgar's realm where he is challenged by the Scylding coast-guard who is stationed on a cliff to keep watch.

IV. Beowulf identifies himself as the son of Ecgtheow

and describes his followers as Goths and hearth-companions of Hygelac. His mission, he says, is to assist Hrothgar, lord of the Danes, in overcoming his demon-foe. The coast-guard welcomes them, promises to guard their ship, and speeds them on their way to King Hrothgar.

V. Up the stone-paved street march Beowulf and his men. Arriving at the hall they are greeted with admiration by a noble Dane Wulfgar who asks them who they are. Beowulf again identifies himself, Wulfgar goes to Hrothgar, and, in courtly fashion, asks a hearing for the strangers.

VI. Hrothgar recalls that he had known Beowulf as a child and that he has heard of Beowulf's matchless strength. He bids Wulfgar to welcome the strangers and bid them approach. Beowulf introduces himself to King Hrothgar, explains his mission, and, as evidence of his capability, mentions his night of wrestling with the sea-monsters. If he loses his battle with Grendel, he remarks, there will be no need to bury his body or to feed him longer.

VII. Hrothgar continues to reminisce about Beowulf's father and his great feat, while apparently a warrior with the Wylfings, of killing Heatholaf. This account is followed by an obscure passage concerning his own settling of a quarrel with the Wylfings. He then turns abruptly to a description of the ravages wrought by Grendel and then, with equal abruptness, invites Beowulf to speak his own mind and welcomes Beowulf and his company as guests. The ale flows and the minstrel sings.

VIII. Hunferth, jealous of Beowulf's glory, asks Beowulf if he is the one who was defeated by Breca, prince of the Brondings, in a swimming contest and dares him to spend a night in the vicinity of Heorot. Beowulf angrily replies with his own version of that youthful exploit, telling how, with naked swords to defend themselves from the sea-monsters, they swam together for five nights in the icy waters, then became parted, and Beowulf was attacked by a monster who dragged him to the bottom of the sea where Beowulf dispatched him with his sword.

IX. Continuing the story Beowulf describes successive slaughters until he killed nine of the monsters whose bodies were washed to the shore. He himself, fatigued by battle, was borne by the tide to the land of the Finns. Breca, he boasts, never achieved the equal of this feat. He rails at Hunferth as a murderer of his own brothers and as helpless before the fury of Grendel. He concludes by boasting that he will rid Heorot of the monster. Amidst the ensuing revelry Wealtheow, Hrothgar's queen, passes the cup first to her lord and then to all the people. Giving the cup to Beowulf she thanks God for his arrival. Beowulf's reply that he will conquer or die pleases the queen. The celebration continues until Beowulf begs leave to retire. They all leave Beowulf alone in the hall after a parting speech by Hrothgar expressing his confidence in the hero.

X. Beowulf removes his armor and gives his sword to his thane, boasting that he will meet the unarmed monster on its own terms. He then lies down to sleep with his companions around him, none of whom expected to see home again. From afar in the night Grendel approaches.

XI. Grendel smashes open the door, bites and swallows one of the thanes, and springs at Beowulf who seizes the monster's arm. Grendel, never having felt such a grip, attempts to flee to the fen. The mead-hall barely withstands the vibration caused by his struggle to escape. The Danes are smitten with terror at Grendel's wail of defeat.

XII. Beowulf's companions draw their weapons and hack at the monster with their blades without effect. Finally, the monster's arm is wrenched from its socket. Bleeding to death Grendel escapes over the moor to his lair. Beowulf fastens the arm high up near the roof of the hall.

XIII. The next morning warriors gather from far and near to applaud the victory and to trace the monster's footprints across the moor to a blood-stained pool. The valor of Beowulf is praised by all. One of the thanes introduces a tale from the Nibelungen legend, recounting how Sigmund the Volsung with his son and nephew slew wild beasts in the forests and how, thereafter, when the nephew Fitela was not with him, Sigmund destroyed a great dragon with his sword and gained a great treasure. When this story is concluded all return to Heorot to view the wonder, the king and his queen with her maidens joining them there.

XIV. Hrothgar praises Beowulf's achievement and gives glory to God. He promises to cherish Beowulf hereafter as his own child. Beowulf responds by acknowledging his chagrin that the dead body of Grendel is not in the hall, says that he had intended to hold his arm until his other hand could strangle him, regrets that he broke away, but expresses his agreement that the monster could not escape his doom by ripping loose his arm. Hunferth is silent as all declare that no weapon could perform what Beowulf has done with his bare hands.

XV. The hall is cleansed, repaired, and refurnished with new golden tapestries. A great feast is held, and Hrothgar bestows a banner, breast-plate, and helmet upon Beowulf. After Beowulf drinks the king's health, eight stallions are brought into the hall, each bearing a jewelled saddle, to be added to Beowulf's trophies.

XVI. Hrothgar gives gifts to all of Beowulf's men and offers to pay gold for the man whom Grendel had killed. The gleeman sings of a feud between the Frisians and the Danes (mentioned also in "The Fight at Finnesburg") in the course of which the Danish Hnaef (mentioned in "Widsith") is killed. Finn, the Frisian king, loses the battle to the Danish Hengest and concludes a truce. A funeral pyre for Hnaef is prepared on which Hildeburh, Danish wife of Finn, places her own sons with great lamentation.

XVII. The Danish warriors return to their homes while Hengest remains all winter with Finn. When spring returns, aided by some of his men (who had either remained with him or had returned—the whole passage is very obscure) Hengest breaks the truce, kills Finn, and carries Hildeburh and much treasure back to the Danes.

The gleeman concludes his song, the celebration continues, and Wealtheow takes the cup to Beowulf sitting between her sons Hrethric and Hrothmund.

XVIII. She presents Beowulf with gifts of corselet, rings, and a magnificent collar, subsequently given to Hygelac the Goth who wore it on his raid against the Frisians in which he was slain. She asks him to instruct her sons and wishes him joy, prosperity, and long life. At nightfall Hrothgar retires to his chambers while his thanes sleep in the hall, their armor by their sides, as they did before the ravages of Grendel.

XIX. While they are sleeping, Grendel's mother, seeking to avenge the death of her son, enters the hall. The warriors are roused and she departs, taking an old friend and counsellor of Hrothgar, named Aeschhere, as well as the talon of her son with her. At dawn Beowulf, who had slept elsewhere, is summoned to attend Hrothgar.

XX. Hrothgar laments the death of Aeschere and recalls the tale, oft told, of the two monsters, male and female, whose home was a haunted pool in a wild and lonely fen. He promises Beowulf great rewards if he will succeed in finding the monster's abode and destroying Grendel's mother.

XXI. Beowulf nobly accepts the challenge. Hrothgar mounts a horse and, accompanied by Beowulf and a band of men, rides over the moor to a bloody pool where they see Aeschere's severed head. Sea-monsters swim in the pool; one of them is killed and dragged ashore. Beowulf dons his armor and grasps the sword Hrunting, loaned him by Hunferth.

XXII. He makes a parting speech, asking that if he dies the treasures given him be bestowed upon Hygelac and the sword returned to Hunferth. Thereupon he plunges into the water. Nearly a day is required to reach the bottom where Grendel's mother seizes him and drags him to her lair. There, lit by the glow of firelight, he is able to see the monster. With a mighty blow he strikes her head, only to find the sword Hrunting powerless to wound her. Casting the sword aside he grips her shoulder with his hand, but by superior strength she throws him down, kneels upon him, and tries to thrust her dagger into his breast. Saved by his corselet, Beowulf springs to his feet.

XXIII. He espies a giant sword near by, seizes it, and thrusts it into the monster's throat, killing her. Hrothgar and his men waiting above see the pool stained with blood, conclude that Beowulf is slain, and return home, sick at heart. Beowulf's men remain, gazing hopelessly at the pool. Meanwhile, the blade of the giant sword is dissolved by the venomous blood of the monster. Beowulf, clutching the sword-hilt and the monster's severed head, rises to the top of the pool where he is joyously greeted by his companions. All return to Heorot where Beowulf lays the head down in front of the king and queen.

XXIV. Beowulf relates his adventure to Hrothgar and presents him with the hilt of the sword, promising the king that all may now sleep safely in Heorot. The hilt is described as a giant's work, recording in runic letters the origin of the ancient war of the giants before the flood. Hrothgar praises Beowulf and preaches to him a sermon on the evil of pride.

XXV. The sermon against arrogance continues, with Hrothgar pointing out the transitory nature of earthly things. He concludes by inviting Beowulf to sit at the feast, promising him more treasures in the morning. Beowulf joins the feast until, as the night deepens, all retire to rest. Eager to return home Beowulf and his men rise early in the morning. Beowulf returns Hrunting to Hunferth without a word of deprecation of the sword and approaches Hrothgar to bid him farewell.

XXVI. Beowulf praises Hrothgar's hospitality and promises his own and Hygelac's assistance in case of any future need. Hrothgar praises Beowulf's valor and wisdom and prophesies Beowulf's future rise to kingship. Beowulf, he says, has brought peace between their peoples. After more treasures are bestowed upon the hero, he and his thanes depart for their boat.

XXVII. They board the ship, sail home, and carry the

treasures to Hygelac's hall. Here is inserted a short account of Hýgd, the daughter of Haereth and queen of Hygelac, who after her husband's death became the wife of Offa.

XXVIII. Beowulf is greeted by Hygelac and Hygd. Hygelac asks about his adventures, confessing to grave forebodings when Beowulf had departed. With great brevity Beowulf touches upon his achievements and then tells how Wealtheow distributed gifts to the warriors while her daughter Freaware, betrothed to the son of Froda, passed the mead-cup.

XXIX. [This entire canto is missing, along with the last part of Canto XXVIII and the beginning of XXX.]

XXX. After a reference to a feud with the Heathobards which will be ended by the marriage of Froda and Freaware, he resumes in more detail the story of his fight with Grendel, the death of Aeschere, and his conquest of Grendel's mother.

XXXI. He continues to describe the gifts given him by Hrothgar, some of which he gives to Hygelac and Hygd and accepts in return from Hygelac a precious sword that belonged to Hrethel. The story turns suddenly to the succeeding years, mentioning the death of Hygelac and Heardred and the accession of Beowulf to the throne. After fifty years of wise government Beowulf is forced to confront a new danger in the shape of a fire dragon whose concealed treasure had been pilfered.

XXXII. The thief had stolen from dire necessity. The treasure had been hidden there by some nobleman of bygone days. For three hundred years the dragon guarded the hoard until the robber, in trouble with his lord, stole a cup to take to his master to appease him. The dragon discovered the theft and ravaged the dwellings round about with fire.

XXXIII. The dragon vomits embers which consume everything in their path including Beowulf's own mansion. Beowulf orders the fashioning of an iron shield, the aging hero of Heorot not fearing to join combat with another monster. Allusion is made to other feats of Beowulf:

how when Hygelac was killed in Friesland, Beowulf, bearing thirty sets of armor on his back, escaped by swimming. When he was offered the kingdom by Hygd, who had no confidence in the powers of her son Heardred, he refused the honor and acted as advisor to Heardred until he came of age. When the prince was slain in battle by rovers who had overcome the king of the Scylfings, Beowulf ascended the throne.

XXXIV. Further allusion is made to Beowulf's friendship with Eadgils whom he aided. Returning to the immediate problem, the story resumes with an account of Beowulf's going forth with twelve companions to view the dragon, guided by the unfortunate thief who had started the trouble. They sit some distance away from the hoard while Beowulf calls to mind the sad story of the accidental death of Herebeald, the oldest of Hrethel's sons, by an arrow shot from the bow of his brother Haethcyn.

XXXV. Beowulf then turns to a song of the war between the Swedes and the Goths after the death of Hrethel. In this war Haethcyn was killed; Ongentheow was also slain at the hand of Eofer. Beowulf then refers to his battle with Daeghrefn whom he killed. After a brief farewell, he prepares to fight the dragon. Bearing sword and shield he approaches the fiery blasts of the monster. He strikes with his sword but to no avail, nor does his shield offer him as much protection as he had hoped.

XXXVI. A young kinsman, Wiglaf, comes to his aid with armor given him by Onela, heirlooms of Eanmund whom Wiglaf's father Weohstan had killed in battle. Wiglaf calls up the others to give assistance and dashes recklessly into the flames. Reinvigorated, Beowulf swings his great sword Naegling at the dragon's head. The sword breaks and the dragon fastens its fangs in Beowulf's neck.

XXXVII. As Beowulf bleeds, Wiglaf strikes lower at the dragon. The fire lessens and Beowulf draws his knife and cuts the dragon in the middle: the two blows kill the dragon. Beowulf is aware that his death is near, caused by the venom. He sits down while Wiglaf loosens his helmet and brings water to refresh him. Beowulf makes a parting speech and asks Wiglaf to let him see the hoarded treasure so that he may die more tranquilly.

XXXVIII. Wiglaf views the jewels, gold, bowls, helmets, rings, and a golden banner. He returns with some of the spoil to find Beowulf on the point of death. After bathing him with water he listens as Beowulf gives praise to God and directs the building of a funeral barrow on Hrones-naes. Giving Wiglaf his helmet, ring, and byrnie, Beowulf expires.

XXXIX. The men who had retreated to the forest now reappear and are bitterly reproached by Wiglaf.

XL. Wiglaf bids a messenger spread the news of Beowulf's death. The messenger predicts that the news will bring war with the Frisians and Franks, reminding them of a previous war with the Swedes and the killing of Haethcyn.

XLI. He continues with a description of Ongentheow's last battle with Hygelac and bids his hearers to prepare a funeral pyre. They all go to view with amazement the dead king and the slain dragon.

XLII. A homily on the evils of hoarding and the uncertainty of life is followed by Wiglaf's eulogy of Beowulf and directions to bring wood. Choosing seven of the best of the king's thanes, he returns to the dragon's lair where they load a wagon with treasure.

XLIII. A mighty pyre is prepared, hung with armor as Beowulf had commanded. The immense pyre is kindled amidst universal lament. A mound is raised on a cliff to be seen by sailors. Inside the mound is buried the treasure as twelve warriors ride around it singing praises of Beowulf and bemoaning his death.

WIDSITH

Widsith is obviously not intended to be the song of a single gleeman. Rather it summarizes the story of minstrels everywhere, perpetually wandering and glorifying in their songs the deeds of the great men on whose bounty they were dependent for a livelihood. After the long list of famous names, including Attila the Hun, Hrothgar who is prominent in *Beowulf,* and Hagen who figures in *The Niebelungenlied,* the scop concludes his catalogue with praise for the liberality of great rulers.

THE FIGHT AT FINNESBURGH

The fragment known as *The Fight at Finnesburgh* opens with a rousing speech by Finn, the Frisian leader, exhorting his followers to repel a night attack by invaders who have set fire to his hall. There follows a glorification of the five-day battle and the leading warriors. This appears to be the same battle described by the gleeman in Canto XVI of *Beowulf.*

Genealogy of the Scyldings.

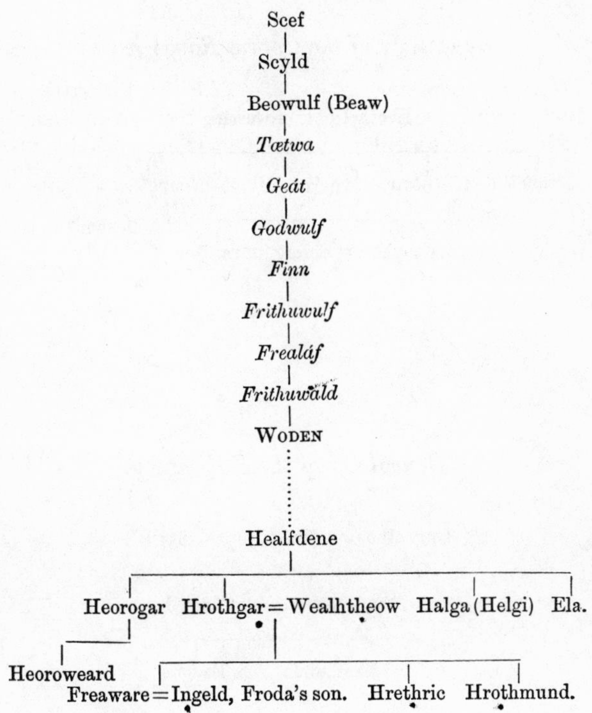

From Tætwa to Woden inclusive, the list is from the Saxon Chronicle, a. 855.

Genealogy of the Gothic Royal Race.

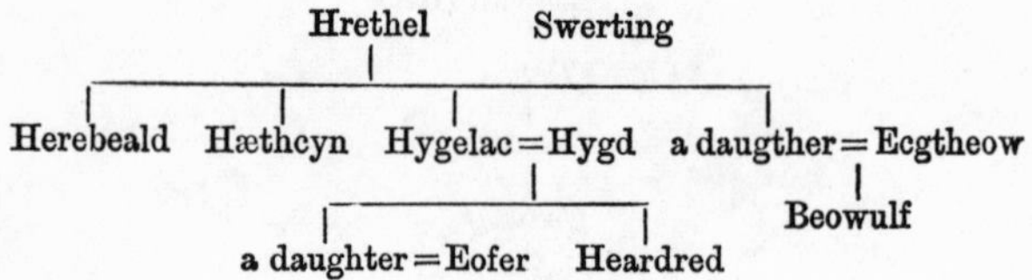

Genealogy of the Scilfings.

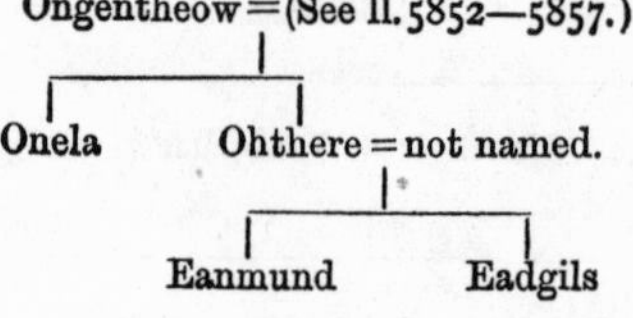

Genealogy of the Kings of Angeln and Mercia of the line of Offa[a].

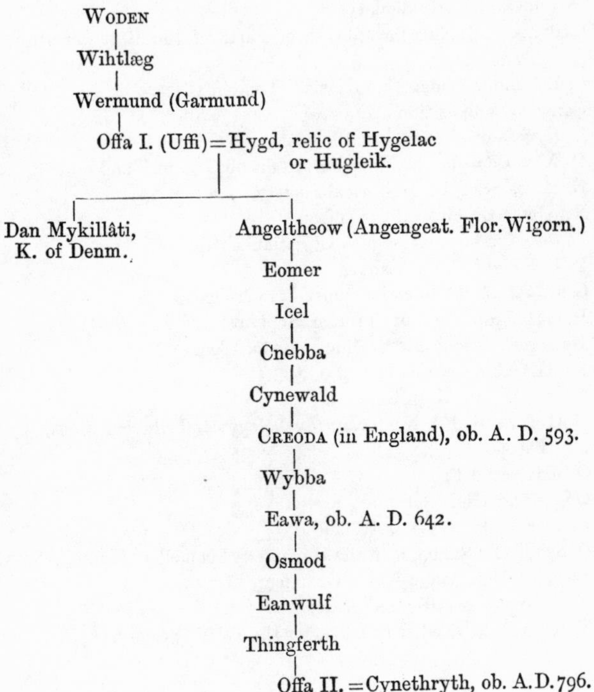

[a] See Lappenberg, "England under the Anglo-Saxon Kings," i. pp. 227, 291.

ABBREVIATIONS EXPLAINED

Aasen = Aasen, Ordbog over det Norske Folkesprog. Christiania 1850.

A. and E. = Andreas und Elene, herausgegeben von Jacob Grimm.

Ælfric Hom. = The Homilies of the Anglo Saxon Church, printed for the Ælfric Society.

Cædm. = Cædmon's Paraphrase of Parts of the Holy Scripture. London 1832.

Cod. Exon. = Codex Exoniensis. London 1842.

Comp. = Composition.

D. G. = Deutsche Grammatik von Jacob Grimm.

D. M. = Deutsche Mythologie von Jacob Grimm. 2nd edit.

E. H. S. = English Historical Society.

Ethelw. = Ethelwerdi Chronicon.

Faye = Norske Folkesagn. Christiania 1844.

F. F. = Fight at Finnesburg.

Graff = Graff, Althochdeutscher Sprachschatz.

H. = Hickesii Thesaurus Lingg. Septent.

Hallager = Norsk Ordsamling. Kjöb. 1802.

K. = Kemble's Beowulf, 2nd edit.

Mhg. = Middle High German.

North. Mythol. = Northern Mythology and Superstitions, by Thorpe.

O. Fris. = Old Frisic.

Ohg. = Old High German.

O. Nor. = Old Norse or Icelandic.

O. Sax. = Old Saxon, as in the Heliand by Schmeller. Munich, 1830.

Rask = Rask's Anglo-Saxon Grammar.

S. T. = Scôp or Gleeman's Tale.

Vercelli Poetry, edit. Kemble, for the Ælfric Society.

BEOWULF.

Hwæt we Gâr-Dena,
in gear-dagum,
þeód-cyninga,
þrym gefrunon :
hû ðа æþelingas
ellen fremedon.
Oft Scyld Scêfing
sceaþena þreâtum,
monegum mægþum,
meodo-setla ofteâh :
egsode eorl[as]
syððan ǽrest wearð
feásceaft funden :
he þæs frôfre gebâd,
weox under wolcnum,
weorþmyntum þâh,
oðþæt him æghwylc
þâra ymb-sittendra
ofer hrôn-râde
hýran scolde,
gomban gyldan :
þæt wæs gôd cyning.
Dǽm eafera wæs

Ay, we *the* Gar-Danes',
in days of yore,
the great kings',
renown have heard of :
how those princes
valour display'd.
Oft Scyld Scef's son
from bands of robbers,
from many tribes,
their mead-benches drag'd away :
inspired earls with fear,
after *he* first was
found destitute :
he thence look'd for comfort,
flourished under *the* clouds,
in dignities throve,
until him every one
of those sitting around
over *the* whale-road
must obey,
tribute pay :
that was *a* good king !
To him *a* son was

11. Suppl. [as] K.

æfter cenned,
geong in geardum,
þone God sende
folce tó frófre:
eyren-þearfe ongeat
eþ híe ǽr drugon
aldor-[le]áse,
lange hwíle.
Him þæs Líf-freá,
Wuldres Waldend,
worold-áre forgeaf.
Beowulf wæs breme,
blæd wíde sprang
Scyldes eaferan
Scede-landum in:
swá sceal [guð-fru]ma
góde gewyrcean,
fromum feoh-giftum,
on fæder-[bea]rme,
fæt hine on ylde
let gewunigen
þil-gesiþas;
þonne wíg cume,
leóde gelǽsten:
lóf-dædum sceal,
in mægþa gehwære,
wan geþeón.
Him ðá Scyld gewát

afterwards born,
a young *one* in *his* courts,
whom God sent
for comfort to *the* people:
he the dire need felt
that they ere had suffered
while princeless,
for *a* long while.
To him therefore *the* Lord of life,
Prince of glory,
gave worldly honour.
Beowulf was renown'd,
the glory widely sprang
of Scyld's offspring
in *the* Scanian lands:
So shall *a* warlike chief
work with good,
with bounteous money-gifts,
in *his* paternal home,
that it in *his* age
again inhabit
his welcome comrades;
and when war comes,
for *the* people act:
by praiseworthy deeds shall,
in every tribe,
a man flourish.
Scyld then departed

29. MS. þæt. 37. MS. eafera. 39. [guð-fru] K.

42. [bea]rme. This word is very doubtful. Mr. Kemble reads [feor]me, but to which I object, 1. because it affords no very apparent sense, and 2. because of the double alliteration, which rarely occurs in the second line of an alliterative couplet. I regret to add that my own reading is far from satisfactory.

sæ gesceap-hwîle,
fela-hror feran
on Freân wǽre.
Hî hyne þâ ætbǽron
tô brimes faroþe,
swæse gesîþas,
twâ he selfa bæd,
þenden wordum weold
wine Scyldinga;
leóf land-fruma
longe âhte.
Þær æt hýðe stód
hringed-stefna
îsig and ût-fûs,
ô elinges fær.
Aledon þâ
leófne þeóden,
beága bryttan,
on bearm scipes,
mǽrne be mæste:
þær was maðma fela,
of feor-wêgum,
frætwa gelǽded.
Ne hýrde ic cymlicor
ceól gegyrwan
hilde wæpnum,
and heaðo-wǽdum,
billum and byrnum.
Him on bearme læg
madma mænigo,
þa him mid scoldon
on flôdes æht,
feor gewîtan.

at *his* fated time,
the much strenuous, to go
into *the* Lord's keeping.
They him then bore away
to *the* sea-shore,
his dear companions,
as he had himself enjoin'd
while with words had sway
the Scyldings' friend;
the beloved land's chief
had long possessed *it*.
There at *the* hithe stood
the ring-prow'd *ship*
icy and eager to depart,
the prince's vehicle.
They laid then
the beloved chief,
the dispenser of rings,
in *the* ship's bosom,
the great *one* by *the* mast:
there were treasures many
from far ways,
ornaments brought.
I have not heard of *a* comelier
keel adorn'd
with war-weapons
and martial weeds,
with glaves and byrnies.
On his bosom lay
treasures many,
which were with him *to* go
into *the* flood's possession,
far depart.

52. MS. gescæp.

Nalæs hí hine læssan	They him not with less
lácum teódan,	gifts provided,
þeód-gestreónum,	lordly treasures,
þonne þa dydon,	than they did,
þe hine æt frumsceafte	who him at *the* beginning
forð onsendon	sent forth
ǽnne ofer ýðe	alone o'er *the* wave,
umbor wesende.	being *a* child.
þá-gyt híe him asetton	They moreover set
segen [gyl]denne	*a* golden ensign
heáh ofer heáfod;	high o'er *his* head;
leton holm beran,	let *the* sea bear *him*,
geafon on gársecg.	gave *him* to ocean.
Him wæs geomor sefa,	Their mind was sad,
murnende mód:	mourning *their* mood:
men ne cunnon	men cannot
secgan tó sóðe,	say for sooth,
séle-rædende,	counsellors in hall,
hæleð under heofenum,	heroes under heaven,
hwá þǽm hlæste onfeng.	who that lading received.

85. The poet, or his prototype, here assigns to Scyld the legend that properly belongs to Scef. The following passages from the chronicles are illustrative of the legend. Ethelw. III. 3: "Ipse Scef cum uno dromone advectus est in insula oceani quæ dicitur Scani, armis circundatus, eratque valde recens puer, et ab incolis illius terræ ignotus; attamen ab eis suscipitur . . . . . . et post in regem eligunt." W. Malmesb. p. 173, edit. E. H. S.: "Iste (Sceaf), ut ferunt, in quandam insulam Germaniæ, Scandzam (de qua Jordanes, historiographus Gothorum, loquitur), appulsus, navi sine remige, puerulus, posito ad caput frumenti manipulo, dormiens, ideoque Sceaf nuncupatus, ab hominibus regionis illius pro miraculo exceptus, et sedulo nutritus, adulta ætate regnavit in oppido quod tunc Slaswic, nunc vero Haithebi appellatur." Simeon of Durham gives similar testimony.

88. MS. þon, no doubt for þoñ.

102. MS. rædenne. K. no doubt correctly. See hereafter.

I.

Ðá wæs on burgum	Then was in *the* towns
Beowulf Scyldinga	Beowulf, *the* Scyldings'
leóf leód-cyning	beloved sovereign
longe þrage	for *a* long time,
folcum gefrǽge :	fam'd among nations :
fæder ellor hwearf,	(*his* father had passed away,
aldor of earde,	*the* prince from *his* dwelling),
oðþæt him eft onwóc	until from him in turn sprang forth
heâh Healfdene ;	*the* lofty Healfdene ;
heóld þenden lîfde,	*he* ruled while *he* liv'd,
gamol and gûð-reouw,	old and war-fierce,
glæde Scyldingas.	*the* glad Scyldings.
Ðǽm feower bearn	From him four children
forð-gerîmed	numbered forth
in worold wócon,	sprang in *the* world,
weoroda ræswan	heads of hosts,
Heorogâr and Hróþgâr	Heorogar and Hrothgar
and Halga til	and Halga *the* good
* * *	* * *
Hŷrde ic þæt Elan cwên,	I have heard that Ela's queen,
Heaðo-Scylfinges	*the* martial Scylfing's
heals-gebedda.	bed-partaker.
* * *	* * *
Þá wæs Hróðgâre	Then was to Hrothgar
here-spêd gyfen,	martial prowess given,
wîges weorðmynd,	warlike glory,

119. MS. wocun. 120. MS. ræswa.

124. Ela I take to be the name of a Scylfing married to a daughter of Healfdene, being the fourth of his children, three of whom are named.

125. MS. Scylfingas.

þæt him his wine-magas
georne hýrdon,
oðþæt seó geogoþ geweox,
mago-driht micel.
Him on mód be-arn
þæt [he] heal-reced
hátan wolde,
medo-ærn micel,
men gewyrcean,
þone yldo-bearn
æfre gefrunon;
and þær on-innan
eall gedǽlan.
geongum and ealdum,
swylc him God sealde,
buton folc-scare
and feorum gumena.
Ðá ic wide gefrægn
weorc gebannan
manigre mægþe
geond þisne middangeard,
folc-stede frætwian.
Him on fyrste gelomp,
ædre mid yldum,
þæt hit wearð eal gearo,
heal-ærna mæst.
Scóp him Heort naman,
se þe his wordes geweald
wide hæfde.

so that him his dear kinsmen
willingly obey'd,
until the youth grew up,
a great kindred train.
It ran through his mind
that [he] *a* hall-house
would command,
a great mead-house,
men to make,
which *the* sons of men
should ever hear of;
and there within
all distribute
to young and old,
as to him God had given,
except *the* people's share,
and *the* lives of men.
Then I heard *that* widely
the work *was* proclaim'd
to many *a* tribe
through this mid-earth,
that *a* public place was building.
Him *it* in time befel,
soon among men,
that it was all ready,
of hall-houses greatest.
Gave it *the* name of Heort,
he who power of his word
widely had.

136. he not in MS.

151. middangeard. So called from its position between Asgard, the abode of the gods, and Utgard, the abode of the giants. See Thorpe, Northern Mythology, vol. i.

152. MS. frætwan.

He beôt ne aleâh	He belied not *his* promise,
beâgas dǽlde,	bracelets distributed,
sinc æt symle.	treasure at *the* feast.
sele hlifade;	*The* hall rose
heâh and horn-geâp;	high and horn-curv'd;
heaðo-wylma bâd	heat intense awaited *it*
lâðan liges.	of hostile flame.
Ne wæs hit lenge þâ-gen,	Nor was it yet long,
þæt se secg hête	when the warrior promis'd
âþum swerian,	with oaths to swear,
æfter wæl-nîðe	*that* after from deadly enmity
wǽcnan scolde.	*he* would cease.
Þâ se ellen-gæst	Then the potent guest
earfoþlîce	with difficulty
þrage geþolode,	for *a* time endur'd,
se þe in þystrum bâd,	(he who in darkness dwelt,)
þæt he dogora gehwâm	that he each day
dreâm gehŷrde	heard merriment
hlûdne in healle.	loud in *the* hall.
Þær wæs hearpan swêg,	There was sound of harp,
swûtol sang scôpes:	loud *the* gleeman's song
sægde se þe cûþe	he said, who could
frumsceaft fira	*the* origin of men
feorran reccan,	from far *back* relate,
cwæþ þæt se Ælmihtiga	told that the Almighty
eorþan w[orhte],	wrought *the* earth,
wlîte beorhtne wang,	*the* plain in beauty bright,
swâ wæter bebûgeð;	which water embraces;
gesette sîge-hreþig	set, in victory exulting,
sunnan and monan,	sun and moon,
leôman to leôhte,	beams for light
land-bûendum,	to *the* dwellers on land,
and gefrætwade	and adorn'd

160. MS. aleh.

foldan sceatas	earth's regions
leomum and leáfum :	with boughs and leaves :
líf eác gesceóp	life eke created
cynna gehwylcum,	for every kind
þára þe cwice hwyrfað.	of those that quick go to and fro.
Swá þa driht-guman	Thus the retainers
dreámum lífdon	lived in delights
eádiglíce ;	happily,
oðþæt án ongan	till that one began
fyrene frem[m]an,	crime to perpetrate,
feónd on helle.	*a* fiend in hell.
Wæs se grimma gæst	The grim guest was
Grendel háten,	Grendel hight,
mǽre mearc-stapa,	*the* great traverser of *the* mark,
se þe móras heold,	that held *the* moors,
fen and fæsten ;	*the* fen and fastness ;
fifel-cynnes eard	*the* Fifel-race's dwelling
wonsǽlig wer,	*the* unbless'd man
weardode hwíle,	inhabited *a* while,
siþðan him Scyppend	after *the* Creator him
forscrifen hæfde.	had proscribed.
In Caines cynne	On Cain's race
þone cwealm gewræc	that death avenged
éce Drihten,	*the* eternal Lord,
þæs þe he Abel slóg.	for that he Abel slew,
Ne gefeáh he þǽre fǽhðe,	He joy'd not in that enmity,
ac he hine feor forwræc,	for he him far banish'd,
Metod for þý máne	*the* Creator for that crime
man-cynne fram.	from mankind.
Þanon untydras	Thence monstrous births
ealle onwócon,	all sprang forth,
eótenas and ylfe,	eotens, and elves,

210. MS. wonsæli.

220—227. This is no doubt of rabbinical origin.

and orcneas,	and orkens,
swẏlce gigantas,	so likewise *the* giants,
þa wið Gode wunnon	who against God war'd
lange þrage :	for *a* long space :
He him þæs leân forgeald.	He for that gave them *their* reward.

II.

Gewât þá neósian,	*He* departed then to visit,
syþðan niht becom,	after night had come,
heân hûses,	*the* lofty house,
hû hit Hring-Dene,	how it *the* Ring-Danes,
æfter beór-þege,	after *their* beer potation,
gebûn hæfdon.	had occupied.
Fand þá þær-inne	*He* then found therein
æþelinga gedriht	*a* company of nobles
swefan æfter symble ;	sleeping after *their* feast ;
sorge ne cuðon,	sorrow *they* knew not,
wonsceaft wera,	misery of men,
wiht unhǽlo.	aught of unhappiness.
Grim and grǽdig	Grim and greedy,
gearo sona wæs,	*he* was soon ready,
reóc and repe	rugged and fierce,
and on reste genam	and in *their* rest took
þritig þegna :	thirty thanes :
þanon eft gewât,	thence again departed,
hûþe hrêmig,	in *his* prey exulting,
tó hâm faran,	to *his* home to go,
mid þære wæl-fylle,	with the slaughter'd corpses,
wíca neósan.	*his* quarters to visit.
Ðá wæs on uhtan,	Then in *the* morning was,
mid ǽr-dæge,	at early day,
Grendles gûðcræft	Grendel's war-craft

gumum undyrne.	to men manifest.
Þá wæs æfter wiste	Then was after *the* repast
wóp up-ahafen,	*a* whoop up-rais'd,
micel morgen-swég.	*a* great morning sound.
Mǽre þeóden,	*The* great prince,
æþeling ǽr-god,	*the* noble excellent,
unblíðe sæt,	unblithe sat,
þolode ðryð-swyð ;	suffered *the* strong in hosts,
þegn sorge dreáh,	*the* thane endur'd sorrow,
syðþan híe pæs láðan	when they the foe's
last sceáwedon	traces beheld,
wergan gástes :	*the* accursed sprite's :
wæs þæt gewin tó strang,	that strife was too strong,
láð and longsum.	loathsome and tedious.
Næs hit lengra fyrst,	*It* was no longer space,
ac ymb áne niht	but after one night
eft gefremede	*he* again perpetrated
morð-beala máre,	greater mortal harms,
and nó mearn fore	and regretted not for
fǽhðe and fyrene ;	*his* enmity and crime ;
wæs tó fæst on þám.	he was too firm in them.
Þá wæs eáð-fynde	Then was easily found
þe him elleshwær	who elsewhere
gerúmlicor reste.	more commodiously would rest.
* *	* * *
* *	* * *
* *	* * *
bed æfter búrum	beds along *the* bowers,
þá him gebeácnod wæs.	when *it* was indicated to him.
Gesǽgde sóðlíce,	Said truly,
sweotolan tácne,	by *a* manifest token,

278. MS. ræste.

282—289. Very unintelligible ; some lines manifestly lost.

284. MS. gesægd.

heal-þegnes hete	*the* hall thane's hate:
heold hyne syðþan	held himself afterwards
fyr and fæstor,	farther and faster,
se þǽm feônde ætwand.	he who from the fiend escap'd.
Swâ rîxode,	So *Grendel* rul'd,
and wið rihte wan,	and against right war'd,
âna wið eallum,	alone against all,
oðþæt îdel stôd	until empty stood
hûsa sêlest.	of houses best.
Wæs seô hwîl micel,	Great was the while,
twelf wintra tîd	twelve winters' tide
torn geþolode	*his* rage endur'd
wine Scyldinga,	*the* Scyldings' friend,
weâna gehwylcne	every woe,
sîdra sorga;	ample sorrows;
forþam [syððan] wearð	for it [after] became
ylda bearnum	to *the* children of men
undyrne cuð,	openly known,
gyddum geomore,	sadly in songs,
þætte Grendel wan	that Grendel war'd
hwîle wið Hrôðgâr,	awhile 'gainst Hrothgar,
hete-nîðas wæg,	waged hateful enmities,
fyrene and fǽhðe,	crime and hostility,
fela missera,	for many years,
singale sæce;	incessant strife;
sibbe ne wolde	peace would not *have*
wið manna hwone	with any man
mægenes Deniga,	of *the* Danes' power,
feorh-bealo feorran	*or* mortal bale withdraw
feô þingian;	with money compromise;

298. MS. Scyldenda. 299. MS. gehwelcne.

301. syððan, not in MS., but necesssry to the sense, the rhythm, and the alliteration.

315. MS. fea.

ne þær nǽnig wihta	nor there any wight
wénan þorfte	might hope for
beorhtre bóte	*a* lighter penalty
tó banan folmum.	at *the* murderer's hands.
[Atol] æglǽca	*The* fell wretch
ehtende wæs,	was persecuting,
deorc deáþ-scua,	*the* dark death shade,
duguþe and geogoþe,	noble and youthful,
seómode and syrede.	oppress'd and snar'd *them.*
Sinnihte heold	In perpetual night *he* held
mistige móras.	*the* misty moors.
Men ne cunnon	Men know not
hwyder hel-rúnan	whither hell-sorcerers
hwyrftum scríþað.	at times wander.
Swá fela fyrena	Thus many crimes
feónd man-cynnes,	*the* foe of mankind,
atol ángengea,	*the* fell solitary,
oft gefremede.	oft perpetrated,
heardra hynða.	cruel injuries.
Heorot eardode,	Heorot *he* occupied,
sinc-fáge seld	*the* seat richly variegated,
sweartum nihtum :	in *the* dark nights :
nó he þone gif-stól	not the gift-seat he
grétan móste,	might touch,
maþðum for Metode,	*that* treasure, for *the* Lord's *protection*,
ne his myne wisse :	nor his design knew :
þæt wæs wrǽt micel.	that was *a* great marvel !
Wine Scyldinga,	*The* Scylding's friend,
módes brecða	in spirit broken,

316. MS. witena. 319. MS. banum.
320. Atol, wanting in MS., supplied from conjecture.
324. MS. seomade. 336. MS. sel.
342. MS. wræc. The allusion is to the gift-seat or throne.

monig-oft gesæt	many *a* time sat,
rīce tō rūne,	*the* powerful *one* in deliberation,
rǣd eahtedon,	counsel they devis'd,
hwæt swīð-ferhðum	what for *the* strong-soul'd
sēlest wǣre,	*it* were best,
wið fær-grȳrum,	against *the* perilous horrors,
tō gefremmanne.	to accomplish.
Hwīlum hīe gehēton	Sometimes they promis'd,
æt hearg-trafum,	at *the* temples,
wīg-weorþunga;	idolatrous honours;
wordum bǣdon,	in words prayed,
þæt him gāst-bona	that them *the* spirit-slayer
geōce gefremede	would aid afford
wið þeōd-þreāum.	against *the* great afflictions.
Swylc wæs þeāw hyra,	Such was their custom,
hǣþenra hyht;	*the* heathens' hope;
helle gemundon	hell *they* remember'd
in mōd-sefan,	in *their* mind,
Metod hīe ne cuþon,	*the* Creator they knew not,
dæda Dēmend,	*the* Judge of deeds,
ne wiston hīe Drihten God,	they knew not *the* Lord God,
ne hīe huru heofena Helm	nor, indeed, *the* heavens' Protector
herian ne cuþon,	knew they *how* to praise,
Wuldres Waldend.	Glory's Ruler.
Wā bið þǣm þe sceal,	Woe shall be to him who shall
þurh sliðne nīð,	through cruel malice,
sawle bescūfan	thrust *a* soul
in fȳres fæþm;	into *the* fire's embrace;
frōfre ne wene	of comfort let *him* not expect
wihte geweorðan.	aught to betide *him*.

353. MS. hrærg trafum.
356. gast-bona, the devil, the soul-slayer.
373. MS. wenan. 374. MS. gewendan.

Wel bið þǽm þe mót,	Well shall *it* be to him who may,
æfter deáð-dæge,	after *his* death-day,
Drihten sécean,	seek *the* Lord,
and tó Fæder fæðmum	and in *his* Father's bosom
freoðo wilnian.	desire peace.

III.

Swá ðá mǽl ceare	So then *a* time of care
maga Healfdenes	Healfdene's son
singala seáð ;	constantly seeth'd ;
ne mihte snotor hæleð,	*the* sagacious hero could not
weán onwendan :	*the* calamity avert :
wæs þæt gewin tó swyð,	the strife was too strong,
láð and longsum,	loathsome and tedious,
þe on þa leóde becom,	that had come on the people ;
nýd-wracu níþ-grim,	force-misery with malice grim,
niht-bealwa mæst.	of night-evils greatest.
Þá fram hám gefrægn	When from home had heard
Higeláces þegn,	Hygelac's thane,
gód mid Geátum,	(*a* good *man* among *the* Goths,)
Grendles dǽda :	of Grendel's deeds ;
se wæs mon-cynnes	who of mankind was
mægenes strengest	in power strongest
on þǽm dæge	in that day
þysses lífes,	of this life,
æþele and eácen,	noble and vigorous,
hét him ýð-lidan	*he* bade for him *a* wave-traverser
gódne gegyrwan ;	good be prepar'd ;
cwǽð he gúð-cyning	said *that* he *the* war-king
ofer swan-ráde	over *the* swan-road
sécean wolde,	would seek,
mǽrne þeóden,	*the* renowned prince,

390. MS. þæt.

þâ him wæs manna þearf.	as he had need of men.
Þone siðfæt him	That voyage to him
snotere ceorlas	prudent men
lythwon logon,	somewhat blam'd,
þeâh he him leóf wǽre :	though he was dear to them ;
* * *	* * *
* * *	* * *
* * *	* * *
hwetton hige-rôfne,	*they* whetted *the* renowned *chief*,
hǽl sceâwedon ;	observed *the* omen ;
hæfde se gôda	the good *chief* had
Geâta leóda	of *the* Goths' people
cempan gecorene,	chosen champions,
þâra þe he cênoste	of those whom he *the* bravest
findan mihte ;	could find ;
fiftena sum	with some fifteen
sund-wudu sôhte :	*the* floating wood *he* sought.
secg wísade	*A* warrior pointed out,
lagu-cræftig mon	*a* water-crafty man,
land-gemyrcu.	*the* land-boundaries.
Fyrst forð-gewât,	*A* time passed on,
flôta wæs on ýðum,	*the* floater was on *the* waves,
bât under beorge ;	*the* boat under *the* mountain ;
beornas gearwe	*the* ready warriors
on stefn stigon ;	on *the* prow stept ;
streâmas wundon	*the* streams roll'd
sund wið sande ;	*the* sea against *the* sand ;
secgas bǽron,	*the* warriors bare,
on bearm nacan,	into *the* bark's bosom,
beorhte frætwa,	bright arms,

409. Many lines seem here to be wanting.

413. Thorkelin hige-forne, the order of the first three letters in rofne being inverted in the printing.

417. MS. gecorone. 434. MS. frætwe.

gûð-searo geatolíc :	*a* sumptuous war-equipment :
guman ût-scufon,	*the* men shov'd out,
weras on wil-sið,	*the* people, on *the* welcome voy-age,
wudu bundenne	*the* bound wood.
Gewât þá ofer wǽg-holm,	Departed then o'er *the* wavy sea,
winde gefýsed,	by *the* wind impell'd,
flóta fámig-heals,	*the* floater foamy-neck'd,
fugle gelícost,	to *a* bird most like,
oðþæt ymb ân tid	till that about an hour
oþres dogores	of *the* second day
wunden-stefna	*the* twisted prow
gewaden hæfde,	had sail'd,
þæt þa líðende	*so* that the voyagers
land gesawon,	saw land,
brim-clifu blican,	*the* ocean-shores shine,
beorgas steápe,	mountains steep,
sîde sǽ-næssas.	spacious sea-nesses.
Þá wæs sund-lida	Then was *the* sea-sailer
ea-lâde æt ende.	at *the* end of *its* watery way.
Þanon up hraðe	Thence up quickly
Wedera leóde	*the* Weders' people
on wang stigon ;	stept on *the* plain ;
sǽ-wudu sǽldon,	*the* sea-wood tied,
syrcan hrysedon,	*their mail*-shirts shook,
gûð-gewædo ;	*their* martial weeds ;
Gode þancedon,	*they* thanked God,
þæs þe him ýþ-lâda	for that to them the wave-paths
eáðe wurdon.	had been easy.
Þá of wealle geseah	When from *the* wall saw
weard Scyldinga,	*the* Scyldings' warder,

441. MS. fami. 452. MS. liden.
453. MS. eoletes; qu. ýð-lâde ? eoletes is no A.S. word.
461. MS. lade.

se þe holm-clifu	who *the* sea-shores
healdan scolde,	had to keep,
beran ofer bolcan	borne o'er *the ship's* bulwark
beorhte randas,	bright shields,
fyrd-searo fúslícu,	*a* war-equipment ready,
hine frywyt bræc	him curiosity brake
mód-gehygdum,	in *his* mind's thoughts,
hwæt þa men wǽron.	*as to* what those men were.
Gewát him þá tó waroðe,	Went then to the shore,
wicge rídan,	on *his* horse riding,
þegn Hróðgáres,	Hrothgar's thane,
þrymmum cwehte	violently quak'd
mægen-wudu mundum,	the mighty wood in *his* hands
meþel-wordum frægn :	in formal words *he* ask'd :
Hwæt syndon ge	" What are ye
searo-hæbbendra,	of arm-bearing *men*,
byrnum werede,	with byrnies protected,
þe þus brontne ceól	who thus *a* surgy keel
ofer lagu-strǽte	over *the* water-street
lǽdan cwomon,	come leading,
hider ofer holmas ?	hither o'er *the* seas ?
* * *	* * *
Ic þæs ende-sæta	I for this, placed at the extremity,
eg-wearde heold,	sea-ward have held,
þæt on land Dena	that on *the* Danes' land
láðra nǽnig	no enemies
mid scip-herge	with *a* ship army
sceðþan ne meahte.	might do injury.
No her cuðlícor	Not here more openly
cuman ongunnon	to come have attempted

478. meþel-wordum, i.e., in set terms, such as were used at the meþel, or public assembly.

485. The alliterating line with this is wanting.

487. MS. wæs. 488. MS. æg, 489. MS. þe.

lind-hæbbende	shield-bearers,
ne geleáfnes-word	nor *who the* credence word
gûð-fremmendra	of warriors
gearwe ne wisson,	ready knew not,
maga gemetu.	*the* observances of kinsmen.
Næfre ic mâran geseah	Never have I seen *a* greater
eorl ofer eorþan	earl on earth
þonne is eower sum	than is one of you,
secg on searwum :	*a* warrior in arms :
nis þæt seld guma	that is no man seldom
wæpnum geweorðad,	honour'd in arms,
næfne him his wlîte leóge,	unless his countenance belie him,
ǽnlîc ansŷn.	*his* distinguished aspect.
Nû ic eower sceal	Now I must your
frum-cyn witan,	origin know,
ǽr ge fyr heonan,	ere ye farther hence,
leáse sceáweras,	*as* false spies,
on land Dena	into *the* Danes' land
furþur feran.	further proceed.
Nû ge feor-bûend,	Now ye far-dwellers,
mere-liðende,	sea-farers,
mînne gehŷrað	hear my
ânfealdne geþoht :	simple thought :
ôfost is sêlest	haste is best
tô gecyðanne	to make known
hwanon eower cyme sŷ.	whence your coming is."

IV.

Him se yldesta	Him the chiefest
andswarode,	answered,

499. MS. gemedu. 501. MS. eorla. 506. MS. næfre.
511. MS. leas. 516. MS. mine.
520. MS. hwanan eówre cyme syndon.

werodes wísa
word-hord onleác :
We synt gum-cynnes
Geáta leóde,
and Higeláces
heorð-geneátas :
wæs mín fæder
folcum gecyþed,
æþele ord-fruma,
Ecgþeów hâten :
gebâd wintra worn,
ǽr he on weg hwurfe,
gamol of geardum :
hine gearwe geman
witena wel hwylc,
wíde geond eorþan.
We þurh holdne hige
hlâford þínne,
sunu Healfdenes,
sécean cwomon,
leód gebyrgean.
Wes þú us lárena gód.
Habbað we tó þǽm mǽran
micel ærende,
Deniga freân.
Ne sceal þær dyrne sum
wesan þæs ic wêne :
þú wâst gif hit is
swâ we soþlíce
secgan hýrdon ;
þæt mid Scyldingum
sceaða ic nât hwylc,
deogol dǽd-hata,

the band's director
his word-hoard unlock'd :
"We are of race
of *the* Goths' nation,
and Hygelac's
hearth-enjoyers :
my father was
known to nations,
a noble chieftain,
Ecgtheow hight :
he abode winters many,
ere he on *his* way departed,
old from *his* courts :
him well remembers
almost every sage,
widely throughout *the* earth.
We through kind feeling
thy lord,
Healfdene's son,
have come to seek,
thy prince to defend.
Be thou our kind informant.
We have to the illustrious
lord of *the* Danes
a great errand.
There shall naught secret
be, from what I ween :
thou knowest if it is
as we soothly
have heard say ;
that with *the* Scyldings
a wretch, I know not who,
a secret deed-hater,

543. gebeorgan ? 544. MS. wæs.

deorcum nihtum	in *the* dark nights,
eáweð þurh egsan	displays through terror
uncuðne níð,	unheard of malice,
hynðu and hrá-fyl.	injury and slaughter.
Ic þæs Hróðgár mæg,	I for this to Hrothgar may,
þurh rúmne sefan,	through *my* capacious mind,
rǽd gelǽran,	counsel teach,
hú he fród and gód	how he, wise and good,
feónd oferswyðeþ,	*the* foe shall overcome
gyf him edwendan	if to him return
æfre scolde ;	*he* ever should ;
bealuwa bisigum	*how* for *these* works of bale
bót eft-cuman,	reparation *may* follow,
and þa cear-wylmas	and those care-boilings
cólran wurðaþ ;	become cooler ;
oððe á syþðan	or he ever after *will*
earfoð-þrage	*a* time of tribulation,
þreá-nýd þólað,	oppression suffer,
þenden þær wunað,	while shall there continue
on heáh-stede	in *its* high place
húsa sélest.	of houses best."
Weard maþelode,	*The* warder spake,
þær on wicge sæt,	where on *his* horse he sat,
ombeht unforht :	*a* fearless officer :
Æghwæþres sceal	"Of both should
scearp scyld-wíga	*a* sharp shield-warrior
gescád witan,	*the* difference know,
worda and worca,	of words and works
ʒo ðe wel þenceþ.	who well thinks.
Ic þæt gehýre,	I hear,
þæt þis is hold weorod	that is *a* frendly band
freán Scyldinga :	to *the* Scyldings' lord :
gew tað forð-beran	depart bearing forth

567 MS. bisigu, no doubt for bisigū.

wæpen and gewǽdu,	weapons and weeds,
ic eow wísige:	I will direct you:
swylce ic magu-þegnas	in like manner I my
míne hâte,	fellow-officers will bid,
wið feónda gehwone	against every foe
flôtan eowerne,	your ship,
niw-tyrwydne,	new-tarred,
nacan on sande,	*your* bark on *the* sand,
ârum healdan,	honourably to hold,
oþðæt eft byreð,	until back shall bear,
ofer lagu-streâmas,	over *the* water-streams,
leófne mannan	*the* beloved man
wudu wunden-heals	*the* wood twisted neck'd
tô Weder-mearce,	to *the* Weder-march,
gôd-fremmendra	of *the* good-doers
swylcum gifeðe bið	to such as *it* shall be given
þæt þone hilde ræs	that the rush of war
hâl gedígeð.	*he* escape from whole."
Gewiton him þâ feran,	*They* departed then to go,
flôta stille bâd;	*the* vessel still abode,
seomode on sole	lay heavy in *the* mud
sid-fæðmed scip,	*the* wide-bosom'd ship,
on ancre fæst.	at anchor fast.
Eofor-líc scion	*A* boar's likeness sheen
on-ofer hleor bǽron,	over *their* cheeks *they* bore,
gehroden golde;	adorn'd with gold;
fâh and fýr-heard,	variegated and fire-harden'd,
ferh wearde heold.	*it* held life in ward.
Gûð-môde grummon;	*the* warlike of mood were fierce;
guman onetton,	*the* men hasten'd,
sigon ætsomne,	descended together,
oþþæt hý æl-timbred,	until they all-built,
geatolíc and gold-ıáh,	elegant and with gold variegated,

613. MS. beran. 617. MS. mod.

ongytan mihton	might perceive
þæt wæs fore-mǽrost,	what was *the* grandest,
fold-bûendum,	to earth's inhabitants,
receda under roderum,	of houses under *the* firmament,
on þǽm se rīca bâd :	in which the powerful *king* abode :
lixte se leóma	*its* light shone
ofer landa fela.	o'er many lands.
Him þá hilde deór	*To* them then *the* beast of war
hof módigra	*the* proud ones' court
torht getæhte,	clearly show'd,
þæt hīe him tó mihton	that they might
gegnum gangan.	towards it go.
Gûð-beorna sum	Of *the* warriors one
wicg gewende,	turn'd *his* steed,
word æfter cwæþ :	then spake *these* words :
Mǽl is me tó feran ;	" Time 'tis for me to go ;
Fæder alwalda	*may the* all-ruling Father
mid ár-stafum	with honour
eowic gehealde,	hold you,
siðа gesunde :	safe in *your* fortunes :
ic tó sǽ wille,	I will to *the* sea *return*,
wið wrâð werod	'gainst *any* hostile band
wearde healdan.	to hold ward."

V.

Strǽt wæs stân-fâh,	*The* street was stone-varied,
stīg wīsode	*it* directed *the* path
gumum ætgædere ;	to *the* men together ;
gûð-byrne scân,	*the* martial byrnie shone,
heard hond-locen ;	hard, hand-lock'd ;
hring-īren scīr	*the* ring'd iron bright
song in searwum,	sang in *their* gear,

622. MS. ongyton. 630. MS. of.

þá hie tó sele furðum,	even as to *the* hall they,
in hyra grýre-geatwum	in their terrific arms,
gangan cwomon.	came walking.
Setton sǽ-méþe	*The* sea-weary set
síde scyldas,	*their* ample shields,
rondas regn-hearde,	*their* disks intensely hard,
wið þæs recedes weal.	against *the* mansion's wall.
Bugon þá tó bence,	Stoop'd then to *a* bench,
byrnan hringdon,	*their* byrnies placed in a ring,
gúð-searo gumena ;	*the* war-gear of men ;
gáras stódon,	*the* javelins stood,
sǽ-manna searo,	*the* seamen's arms,
samod ætgædere,	all together,
æsc-holt ufan græg :	*the* ash-wood grey above :
wæs se íren þreát	the iron band was
wæpnum gewurþad.	with weapons furnish'd.
Þá þær wlonc hæleþ	Then there *a* haughty chief
oret-mecgas	*the* sons of conflict
æfter hæleþum frægn:	concerning *the* heroes ask'd :
Hwanon ferigeað ge	"Whence bear ye
fætte scyldas,	*your* stout shields,
græge syrcan,	grey sarks,
and grim-helmas,	and visor-helms,
here-sceafta heáp ?	*a* heap of war-shafts ?
Ic eom Hróðgáres	I am Hrothgar's
ár and ombiht.	messenger and servant.
Ne seah ic elþeódige	Never saw I stranger
þus manige men	men thus many
módiglícran.	prouder.
Wen' ic þæt ge for wlenco,	I ween that ye for pride,
nalles for wræc-siðum,	not for exile,
ac for hige-þrymmum,	but for soul-greatness,
Hróðgár sóhton.	have Hrothgar sought."

681. MS. wen.

Him þá ellen-róf
andswarode,
wlanc Wedera leód
word æfter spræc,
heard under helme :
We synt Higeláces
beód-geneátas :
Beowulf is mín nama :
wille ic asecgan
suna Healfdenes,
mǽrum þeódne,
mín ǽrende,
aldre þínum ;
gif he us geunnan wile
þæt we hine swá gódne
grétan móton.
Wulfgár maþelode,
þæt wæs Wendla leód ;
wæs his mód-sefa
manegum gecyðed,
wíg and wísdóm :
Ic þæs wine Deniga,
freán Scyldinga,
frínan wille,
beága bryttan,
swá þú béna eart,
þeóden mǽrne,
ymb þínne sið and þe
þa andsware
ædre gecyðan,
þe me se góda
agifan þenceð.

Him then *the* valour-fam'd
answer'd,
the Weders' proud lord
these words after spake,
the bold under *his* helmet :
" We are Hygelac's
table enjoyers :
Beowulf is my name :
I will relate
to Healfdene's son,
the great lord,
my errand,
to thy prince ;
if he to us will grant
that we him so good
may greet."
Wulfgar spake,
he was *the* Wendels' lord :
his mind was
known to many,
his valour and wisdom :
" I therefore *the* Danes' friend,
the Scyldings' lord,
will ask,
the distributor of rings,
as thou requestest,
the great lord,
concerning thy voyage, and to thee
the answer
quickly make known
that me the good *prince*
shall think *fit* to give.

694. MS. sunu.

Hwearf þá hrædlice
þær Hróðgár sæt,
eald and unhár,
mid his eorla gedriht.
Eóde ellen-róf,
þæt he for eaxlum gestód
Deniga freán:
cuþe he duguðe þeáw.
Wulfgár maþelode
to his wine-drihtne:
Her syndon geferede,
feorran cumene
ofer geofenes begang,
Geáta leóde;
þone yldestan
oret-mecgas,
Beowulf nemnað.
Hý bénan synt
þæt hie þeóden mín,
wið þe móton
wordum wrixlan:
nó þú him wearne geteóh.
Þínra gegn-cwida
glædman Hróðgár hý
on wig-getawum
wyrðe þinceað,
eorla geæhtlan:
huru se aldor þeáh,
se þǽm heaðo-rincum
hider wisade.

He then turn'd hastily
to where Hrothgar sat,
old and hairless,
with his assemblage of earls.
The valour-fam'd *chief* went
so that he before *the* shoulders stood
of *the* Danes' lord:
he knew *the* usage of *a* court.
Wulfgar spake
to his friendly lord:
"Hither are borne,
come from afar,
over ocean's course,
people of *the* Goths;
the chief
these sons of conflict
name Beowulf.
They are petitioners
that they, my lord,
with thee may
in words converse:
do not decree them *a* denial.
Of thy reciprocal words
of *the* pleasure, Hrothgar they,
in *their* war-equipments,
appear worthy,
of *the* estimation of earls:
at least the chief certainly,
who *the* warriors
has led hither.

739. MS. cwiða.

VI.

Hrōðgār maþelode,	Hrothgar spake,
helm Scyldinga:	*the* Scyldings' helm:
Ic hine cuðe,	"I knew him,
cniht wesende:	being *a* boy:
wæs his eald-fæder	his old father was
Ecgþeōw hāten,	Ecgtheow named,
þǽm tō hām forgeaf	to whom at home gave
Hreþel Geāta	Hrethel *lord* of *the* Goths.
āngan dohtor:	*his* only daughter:
is his eafora nū,	is *his* offspring now,
heard her cumen,	bold, hither come,
sōhte holdne wine.	sought *a* kind friend?
Ðonne sǽgdon þæt	For that said
sǽ-liþende,	*the* sea-voyagers,
þa ðe gif-sceattas	who *the* gift treasures
Geātum feredon	for *the* Goths bore
þyder to þance,	thither gratuitously,
þæt he xxx tiges	that he of thirty
manna mægen-cræft,	men *the* mighty power,
on his mund-grīpe	in his hand-gripe,
heaþo-rōf hæbbe.	*the* war-fam'd, has.
Hine hālig God,	Him holy God,
for ār-stafum,	in *his* mercies,
us onsende,	to us hath sent,
tō West-Denum:	to *the* West Danes:
þæs ic wēn hæbbe	therefore have I hope

750. Strictly wesendne, accus. masc., but the omission of the *n* in this case is sanctioned by usage.

752. MS. Ecgþeo. 756. MS. eaforan.

762. MS. Geata fyredon. The gifts (l. 761) were sent to appease a feud with the Wylfings. See ll. 922-949. The whole account of the quarrel is very obscure.

wið Grendles grýre.	against Grendel's horror
Ic þǽm gódan sceal,	I to the good *chief* shall
for his mód-þræce,	for his valorous daring,
madmas beódan	treasures offer.
Beó þú on ófeste,	Be thou speedy,
hát in-gán,	bid *them* come in,
seón sibbe-gedriht	see *their* kindred band
samod ætgædere	assembled together.
Gesaga him eác wordum,	Say to them eke in words
þæt híe synt wil-cuman	that they are welcome guests
Deniga leódum.	to the Danes' people.
* * *	* * *
* * *	* * *
word inne abeád:	*the* words announced:
Eow hét secgan	"To you bids *me* say
sige-drihten mín,	my victor-lord,
aldor Eást-Dena,	prince of *the* East Danes,
þæt he eower æþelu can,	that your nobility he knows;
and ge him syndon,	and *that* ye are to him,
ofer sǽ-wylmas	over *the* sea-billows
heard-hicgende,	boldly striving
hider wil-cuman.	hither, welcome guests.
Nú ge móton gangan,	Now ye may go,
in eowrum gúþ-geatawum,	in your war-accoutrements,
under here-griman,	under *the* martial helm,
Hróðgár geseón.	Hrothgar to see.
Lǽtað hilde-bord	Let *your* war-boards
her onbídan,	here await,
wudu wæl-sceaftas,	*your* spears *and* deadly shafts,
worda geþinges.	*the* council of words."

783. Here the text is evidently defective; two lines at least are wanting.

789. At l. 771 they are called West Danes; elsewhere South D. and North D.

Arâs þâ se rîca,
ymb hine rinc manig,
þryðlîc þegna heâp;
sume þær bidon,
heaþo-reâf heoldon,
swâ him se hearda bebeâd.
Snyredon ætsomne,
þ[ær]secg wîsode.
under Heorotes hrôf,
heard under helme,
þæt he on heoðe gestôd.
Beowulf maðelode,
on him byrne scân,
searo-net seôwed
smiþes orþancum:
Wes þû Hrôðgâr hâl.
Ic eom Higelâces
mǽg and mago-þegn:
hæbbe ic mǽrða fela
ongunnen on geogoþe.
Me wearð Grendles þing,
on mînre éþel-tyrf,
undyrne cuð:
secgað sǽ lîðend
þæt þes sele stande,
receda sêlest,
rinca gehwylcum
îdel and unnýt,
siððan æfen-leôht
under heofenes hâdor
beholen weorþeð

Arose then the mighty *chief*,
around him many *a* warrior,
a valiant band of thanes;
some there remain'd,
held *the* war-weeds,
as them the bold *one* bade.
They hasten'd together,
to where *the* warrior directed.
under Heorot's roof,
the bold one under helm,
till that on *the* dais he stood.
Beowulf spake,
on him *his* byrnie shone,
his war-net sewed
by *the* smith's devices.
"Be thou, Hrothgar, hail!
I am Hygelac's
kinsman and fellow-warrior:
I have great deeds many
undertaken in *my* youth.
To me became Grendel's affair:
on my native turf,
manifestly known:
sea-farers say
that this hall stands,
this house most excellent,
for every warrior
void and useless,
after *the* evening light
under heaven's serenity
is conceal'd.

818. MS. wæs.

826. Those that conveyed the presents. See l. 760.

827. MS. þæs.

828. MS. reced selesta.

Þâ me þæt gelǽrdon	Then me counsel'd
leóde mîne,	my people,
þa sêlestan	the most excellent
snotere ceorlas,	sagacious men,
þeóden Hrôðgâr,	prince Hrothgar !
þæt ic þe sôhte ;	that I thee should seek ;
forþan hie mægenes cræft	because they of my strength
mîne cuþon.	*the* power knew.
Selfe ofersawon,	Themselves beheld,
þâ ic of searwum cwom,	when from *their* snares I came,
fâh from feóndum,	blood-stain'd from *the* foes,
þær ic fîfe geband ;	where five I bound ;
ýðde eótena cyn,	(*the* eoten race boil'd *with* rage)
and on ýðum slôg	and on *the* billows slew
niceras nihtes ;	nickers by night ;
nearo-þearfe dreâh :	pinching want *I* suffer'd :
wræc Wedera nîð ;	*I* aveng'd *the* Weders' quarrel ,
weân ahsodon ;	(*they* sought *their* misery ;)
forgrand grâmum ;	fiercely crush'd *them ;*
and nû wið Grendel sceal,	and *I* now against Grendel shall,
wið þâm aglǽcan,	against that miserable being,
âna gehegan	alone hold
ðing wiþ þyrse.	council with *the* giant.
Ic þe nû-þâ,	I thee now,
brego beorht-Dena,	lord of *the* bright Danes,
biddan wille,	will beseech,
eodor Scyldinga,	protector of *the* Scyldings,
ânre bêne :	one prayer :
þæt ðû me ne forwyrne,	that thou deny me not,
wîgendra hleó,	patron of warriors,
freâ-wine folca,	friend of people,
nû ic þus feorran com,	now I am thus come from far,
þæt ic môte âna	that I alone may,

864. MS. freo.

[mid] minra eorla gedryht,	*with* the company of my earls,
and þes hearda heâp,	and this bold band,
Heorot fǽlsian.	Heorot purify.
Hæbbe ic eâc geâhsod	I have also heard
þæt se æglǽca,	that the miserable being,
for his wonhydum,	in his heedlessness,
wæpna ne receð ;	of weapons recks not ;
ic þæt þonne forhicge,	I then will disdain
swâ me Higelâc sie,	(so to me may Hygelac be,
mîn mon-drihten,	my liege lord,
môdes blîðe,	blithe of mood)
þæt ic sweord bere	to bear *a* sword
oþðe sîdne scyld,	or ample shield,
geolo-rand tô gûþe ;	*a* yellow disk, to battle ;
ac ic mid grâpe sceal	but with grasp I shall
fôn wið feônde,	grapple with *the* enemy,
and ymb feorh sacan,	and for life contend,
lâð wið lâðum :	foe against foe :
ðær gelŷfan sceal	there shall trust
Dryhtnes dôme,	in *the* Lord's doom,
se þe hine deâð nimeð.	he whom death shall take.
Wên' ic þæt he wille,	I ween that he will,
gif he wealdan môt,	if he may prevail,
in þǽm gûð-sele,	in the martial hall,
Geôtena leôde	*the* Goths' people
etan unforhte,	eat fearlessly,
swâ he oft dyde	as he oft has done
mægen Hreðmanna.	*the* Hrethmen's strength.
Nô þû minne þearft	Thou wilt not need my
hafelan hŷdan,	head to hide ;

867. mid supplied as necessary to the construction. See l. 720.

872. Rather wonhygdum.

896. MS. hafalan. Thou wilt not need, etc., i.e., in the earth, or thou wilt have no occasion to bury me, as my body will be devoured by Grendel.

ac he me habban wile	for he will have me
dreóre fáhne,	stain'd with gore,
gif mec deáð nimeð ;	if me death shall take ;
byreð blódig wæl,	will bear off *my* bloody corse,
byrgean þenceð ;	will resolve to feast on *it ;*
eteð ángenga	*the* lonely *wretch* will eat it
unmurnlíce ;	without compunction ;
mearcað mór-hópu.	*he my* moor-mound will mark out.
Nó þú ymb mínes ne þearft	Thou needest not about *the*
líces feorme	feeding on my carcase
leng sorgian.	longer care.
Onsend Higeláce,	Send to Hygelac,
gif mec hild nime,	if *the* conflict take me *off*,
beadu-scrúda betst,	*the* best of battle-shrouds,
þæt míne breóst wereð,	that defends my breast,
hrægla sélest ;	of vests most excellent ;
þæt is Hrædlan láf,	it is Hrædla's legacy,
Welandes geweorc :	Weland's work :
gæð á wyrd swá hió sceal.	fate goes ever as it must."

VII.

Hróðgár maþelode,	Hrothgar spake,
helm Scyldinga :	*the* Scyldings' helm :
Fore fyhtum þú,	" For battles thou,
freónd mín Beowulf,	my friend Beowulf,
and for ár-stafum,	and for honour,
usic sóhtest.	us hast sought.
Geslóh þín fæder	Thy father quell'd in fight
fæhðe mæste :	*the* greatest feud :

898. MS. deore.
904. The mound over the urn or vessel containing his bones.
915. MS. scel. 918. fere.
919. MS. wine, with no alliteration.

wearð he Heaðoláfe
tó hand-bonan
mid Wylfingum,
ðá hine gára cyn,
for here-brógan,
habban ne mihte.
Þanon he gesóhte
Súð-Dena folc
ofer ýða gewealc,
âr Scyldingum,
þá ic furþum weold
folce Deniga,
and on geogoðe heold
ginne ríce,
hord-burh hæleþa.
Þá wæs Heregâr deâd,
min yldra mǽg
unlifigende,
bearn Healfdenes;
se wæs betera þonne ic:
siððan þa fǽhðe
feó þingode;

he was of Heatholaf
the slayer,
with *the* Wylfings,
when him *the* Waras' race,
for martial dread,
might not have.
Thence he sought
the South Danes' folk
over *the* rolling of *the* waves,
a messenger to *the* Scyldings,
when I first rul'd
the Danes' people,
and in youth held
spacious realms,
the treasure-city of men.
Then was Heregar dead,
my elder brother
not living,
the son of Healfdene;
he was better than I:
afterwards that quarrel
I with money settled;

926, 927. Between these lines there is no alliteration. I will not venture on an emendation in the dark, though I have little doubt that for gara we should read Wara. But who were the Waras? Possibly the people of Wärnsland, or Wärendshärad, a district of Smaland. Or is Waracyn (like Hæðcyn) a person's name? The whole passage about Heatholaf is extremely obscure. Ecgtheow appears to have fought on the side of the Wylfings.

933. MS. . . . . dinga, but Thorkelin has Scyldinga, and no doubt the word in his time was perfect; though it seems certain that we should read Scyldingum: for how could Ecgtheow the Goth be an envoy *of* the Scyldings? See l. 762 for a similar error.

935. MS. Deninga.

937. MS. gimme rice. See Cædmon, 15. 8.

945. See l. 315.

sende ic Wylfingum,	I sent to *the* Wylfings,
ofer wæteres hrycg	over *the* water's back,
ealde madmas :	old treasures :
he me áðas swór.	he to me swore oaths.
Sorh is me tó secganne,	Sorrow is to me to say,
on sefan mínum,	in my mind,
gumena ǽngum,	to any man,
hwæt me Grendel hafað	what for me Grendel has
hynðo on Heorote,	disgrace in Heorot,
mid his hete-þancum,	with his hostile devices,
fær-níða gefremed.	*what* sudden mischiefs perpetrated.
Is mín flet-werod,	My court-retainers are,
wíg-heâp, gewanod ;	my martial band, diminished :
híe wyrd forsweóp	them fate has swept away
on Grendles grýre.	in horror of Grendel.
God eáðe mæg	God easily may
þone dol-sceaðan	the doltish spoiler
dǽda getwǽfan.	from *his* deeds sever.
Ful oft gebeótedon,	Full oft have promis'd,
beóre druncne,	with beer drunken,
ofer ealo-wǽge,	over *the* ale-cup,
oret-mecgas,	sons of conflict,
þæt híe in beór-sele	that they in *the* beer-hall
bídan woldon	would await
Grendles gúþe	Grendel's warfare
mid grýrum ecga :	with terrors of edges :
þonne wæs þeós medo-heal,	then was this mead-hall,
on morgen-tíd,	at morning-tide,
driht-sele dreór-fâh ;	*this* princely court, stain'd with gore ;
þonne dæg lixte,	when *the* day dawn'd,
eal benc-þelu	all *the* bench-floor
blóde bestýmed,	with blood besteam'd,

heall heoru-dreôre :	*the* hall, with horrid gore :
âhte ic holdra þŷ læs,	of faithful *followers* I own'd the less,
deorre duguðe,	of dear nobles,
þe þâ deâð fornam.	whom then death destroyed.
Site nû tô symle,	Sit now to *the* feast,
and onsæ̂l meodo,	and unbind with mead,
sige-hreðer secgum,	*thy* valiant breast with *my* warriors,
swâ þîn sefa hwette.	as thy mind may excite."
Þâ wæs Geât-mæcgum	Then was for *the* sons of *the* Goths
geador-ætsomne	altogether
on beôr-sele	in *the* beer-hall
benc gerŷmed :	*a* bench clear'd :
þær swîð-ferhþe	there *the* strong of soul
sittan eôdon	went to sit
þryðum dealle :	tumultuously rejoicing :
þegn nŷtte beheold,	*the* thane observed *his* duty,
se þe on handa bær	who in *his* hand bare
hroden ealo-wæ̂ge,	*the* ornamented ale-cup,
scencte scîr-wered ;	*he* pour'd *the* bright, sweet *liquor;*
scôp hwîlum sang	*the* gleeman sang at times
hâdor on Heorote :	serene in Heorot :
þær wæs hæleða dreâm,	there was joy of warriors,
duguð unlytel,	no few nobles,
Dena and Wedera.	of Danes and Weders.

VIII.

Hunferð maþelode,	Hunferth spake,
Ecglâfes bearn,	Ecglaf's son
þe æt fôtum sæt	who at *the* feet sat
freân Scyldinga ;	of *the* Scylding's lord ;

983. MS. meoto. 984. MS. hreð.

onband beadu-rûne.
Wæs him Beowulfes sið,
môdges mere-faran,
micel æfþunca;
forþon þe he ne uþe
þæt ǽnig oþer man
æfre mǽrða mâ
middangeardes
gehedde under heofenum
þonne he sylfa:
Eart þû se Beowulf
se þe wið Brecan wunne
on sîdne sǽ,
ymb sund-flîte,
þær git for wlence
wada cunnedon,
and for dol-gilpe
on deóp wæter
aldrum nêþdon?
Ne inc ǽnig mon,
ne leóf ne lâð,
beleân mihte
sorhfulne sið,
þâ git on sund reón
þær git eagor-streâm,
earmum þêhton,
mǽton mere-strǽta,
mundum brugdon,
glidon ofer gârsecg;
geofon ýþum weol,
wintres wylme:
git on wæteres æht

unbound *a* hostile speech
To him was *the* voyage of Beowulf,
the bold sea-farer,
a great displeasure;
because he grudged
that any other man
ever more glories
of mid-earth
held under heaven
than himself;
"Art thou the Beowulf
who with Breca strove
on *the* wide sea,
in *a* swimming strife,
where ye from pride
tempted *the* fords,
and for foolish vaunt
in *the* deep water
ventured *your* lives?
Nor you any man,
nor friend nor foe,
might blame
for your sorrowful voyage,
when on *the* sea ye row'd,
when ye *the* ocean-stream;
with *your* arms deck'd,
measur'd *the* sea-ways,
with *your* hands vibrated *them*,
glided o'er *the* main;
ocean boil'd with waves,
with winter's fury:
ye on *the* water's domain,

1012. MS. þon ma.

1036. MS. wintrys wylm.

seofon-niht swuncon.	*for* seven nights toil'd.
He þe æt sunde oferflât,	He thee in swimming overcame,
hæfde mâre mægen,	*he* had more strength,
þâ hine on morgen-tîd,	when him at morning tide,
on Heaþo-ræmis	on to Heatho-ræmes
holm up-ætbær ;	*the* sea bore up ;
þonon he gesôhte	whence he sought
swǽsne ·ᛟ·.	*his* dear country,
leóf his leóum,	*the* beloved of his people,
lond Brondinga,	*the* Brondings' land,
freoðo-burh fægere,	*his* fair, peaceful burgh,
þær he folc âhte,	where he *a* people own'd,
burh and beágas.	*a* burgh and rings.
Beót eal wið þe	All *his* promise to thee
sunu Beanstânes	Beanstan's son
sôðe gelǽste.	truly fulfil'd.
Ðonne wêne ic tô þe	Now I expect from thee
wyrsan þinga,	worse things,
þeáh þû heaþo-ræsa	though thou in martial onslaughts
gehwǽr dohte,	hast everywhere excel'd,
grimre gûðe,	in grim war,
gif þû Grendles dearst	if thou to Grendel durst
niht-longne fyrst	*a* night-long space
neán bîdan.	near abide."
Beowulf maþelode,	Beowulf spake,
bearn Ecgþeówes :	Ecgtheow's son :
Hwæt þû worn fela,	"Well ! thou *a* great deal,
wine mîn Hunferð,	my friend Hunferth,
beóre druncen,	drunken with beer,
ymb Brecan spræce,	hast about Breca spoken,

1045. This is the rune denoting the word éðel : swæs may be rendered *own*.

1055. þingea.

sægdest from his siðe ;	hast said of his course.
sôð ic talige,	*The* sooth I tell,
þæt ic mere-strengo	that I strength at sea
mâran âhte,	greater possess'd,
earfeðo on ýþum,	endurance on *the* waves,
þonne ǽnig oþer man.	than any other man.
Wit þæt gecwǽdon,	We agreed,
cniht wesende,	being striplings,
and gebeôtedon,	and promised,
wǽron begen þá-git	(*we* were both yet
on geogoð-feore,	in youthful life,)
þæt wit on gârsecg ût	that we on *the* ocean out
aldrum nêðdon,	*our* lives would venture,
and þæt geæfndon swâ.	and that *we* thus accomplish'd.
Hæfdon swurd nacod,	*We* had *a* naked sword,
þâ wit on sund reôn,	when on *the* deep we row'd,
heard on handa :	hard in hand :
wit unc wið hrôn-fixas	as we us against *the* whale-fishes
wêrian þôhton.	meant to defend.
Nô he wiht fram me	He not aught from me
flôd-ýþum feor	far on *the* flood-waves
fleôtan meahte,	could float,
hraþor on holme ;	not in *the* sea more swiftly ;
nô ic fram him wolde.	nor would I *go* from him.
Þâ wit ætsomne	Then we together
on sǽ wǽron	were in *the* sea
fîf nihta fyrst,	*a* five-nights' space,
oþþæt unc flôd todrâf ;	till that *the* flood drove us asunder ;
wado weallende	*the* boiling fords
wedera cealdost,	*the* coldest of tempests,
nipende niht,	cloudy night,
and norþan wind,	and *the* north wind,
heaðo-grim andhwearf :	deadly grim threw up

hreó wǽron ýþa,	rough were *the* billows,
wæs mere-fixa	of *the* sea-fishes was
mód onhréred :	*the* rage excited :
þær me wiǒ láǒum	there me against *the* foes
líc-syrce mín,	my body-sark,
heard hond-locen,	hard, hand-lock'd,
helpe gefremede ;	afforded help ;
beado-hrægl broden	*my* braided war-rail
on breóstum læg	on *my* breast lay
golde gegyrwed.	with gold adorn'd.
Me tó grunde teáh	Me to *the* ground drew
fáh feónd-scaǒa,	*a* many-colour'd foe,
fæste hæfde	fast had *me*
grim on grápe ;	*a* grim *one* in *his* grasp ;
hwæþre me gyfeþe wearǒ,	yet was *it* granted me,
þæt ic aglǽcan	that I *the* miserable being
orde geræhte,	reach'd with *my* point,
hilde bille.	with *my* war-falchion.
Heaþo-ræs fornam	*A* deadly blow destroy'd
mihtig mere-deór	*the* mighty sea-beast
þurh míne hand.	through my hand.

IX.

Swá mec gelóme	Thus me frequently
láǒ-geteónan	*my* hated foes
þreatedon þearle :	threaten'd violently :
ic him þénode	I serv'd them
deóran sweorde,	with *my* dear sword,
swá hit gedéfe wæs.	as it was fitting.
Nǽs híe ǒǽre fylle	Not they of that glut
gefeán hæfdon,	had joy,
mán-fordǽdlan,	*the* foul destroyers,
þæt híe me þegon,	in eating me,

symbel ymbsǽton	in sitting round *the* feast
sǽ-grunde neâh:	near to *the* sea-ground:
ac on mergenne,	but in *the* morning,
mecum wunde,	with falchions wounded,
be ýð-lâfe	along *the* waves' leaving,
uppe-lǽgon,	up *they* lay,
sweotum aswefede;	put to sleep in shoals;
þæt syðþan nâ	*so* that not afterwards
ymb brontne ford	about *the* surgy ford
brim-lîðende	to ocean sailers
lâde ne letton.	have *they the* way hinder'd.
Leoht eâstan com,	Light came from *the* east,
beorht beâcen Godes,	God's bright beacon,
brimu sweþrodon,	*the* seas grew calm,
þæt ic sǽ-næssas	*so* that *the* sea-nesses I
geseôn mihte,	might see,
windige weallas.	windy walls.
Wyrd oft nereð	Fate often saves
unfǽgne eorl,	*an* undoom'd man,
onne his ellen deâh.	when his valour avails.
Hwæþere me gesǽlde	Yet 'twas my lot
þæt ic mid sweorde ofslôh	that with *my* sword I slew
niceras nigene.	nickers nine.
Nô ic on niht gefrægn,	I have not heard of by night,
under heôfenes hwealf,	under heaven's vault,
heardran feohtan,	*a* harder fight,
ne on êg-streâmum	nor in *the* ocean-streams
earmran mannan;	*a* man more miserable;
hwæþere ic fara feng,	yet from *the* grasp of dangers I
feore gedîgde,	with life escap'd
sîþes wêrig.	of *my* journey weary.
Þâ mec sǽ oþbær,	Then *the* sea bore me away,
flôd æfter faroðe,	*the* flood along *the* shore,

1145. MS. swaþredon. 1159. MS. mannon.

on Finna land,
wadu weallende.
Nó ic wiht fram þe
swylcra searu-níða
secgan hýrde,
billa brógan.
Breca næfre git,
æt heaþo-láce,
ne gehwæþer incer
swá deórlíce
dǽde gefremede
fágum sweordum.
Nó ic þæs gylpe,
þeáh ðú þínum broðrum
tó banan wurde,
heáfod-mægum;
þæs þú in helle scealt
werhðo dreógan,
þeáh þín wit duge.
Secge ic þe tó sóðe,
sunu Ecgláfes,
þæt næfre Grendel swá fela
grýra gefremede,
atol ǽglǽca,
ealdre þínum,
hynðo on Heorote,
gif þín hige wǽre,
sefa swá searo-grim,
swá þú self talast.
Ac he hafað onfunden,
þæt he þa fǽhðe ne þearf,
atole ecg-þræce

on *the* Fins' land,
the boiling fords.
I never aught of thee
of such hostile snares
have heard say,
such falchions' terrors.
Breca never yet,
at *the* game of war.
nor either of you,
so dearly
deed perform'd
with hostile swords.
(Of this I boast not),
although thou of thy brothers
wast *the* murderer,
thy chief kinsmen;
for which in hell thou shalt
damnation suffer,
although thy wit be good.
I say to thee in sooth,
son of Ecglaf,
that never Grendel so many
horrors had perpetrated,
the fell wretch,
against thy prince,
harm in Heorot,
if thy spirit were,
thy mind so war-fierce,
as thou thyself supposest.
But he has found,
that he the hostility needs not,
the fell sword-strength

1166. MS. wudu weallendu. 1175. MS. dǽd.

eower leôde,	of your people,
swiðe onsittan,	greatly care for,
sige-Scyldinga ;	of the victor-Scyldings ;
nymeð nŷd-bâde,	*he* takes *a* forced pledge,
nǽnegum ârað	on none has mercy,
leôde Deniga ;	of *the* Danes' people ;
ac he lust-wigeð,	but he wars at pleasure,
swefeð ond scendeð,	slays and shends *you*,
sæcce ne wêneþ	nor strife expects
tô Gâr-Denum ;	from *the* Gar-Danes ;
ac him Geâta sceal	but *a* Goth shall him
eafoð and ellen,	toil and valour,
ungeara nû	now unexpectedly,
gûþe gebeôdan.	battle, offer.
Gǽð eft se þe môt	Shall go afterwards he who may,
to medo môdig,	elate to *the* mead,
siððan morgen-leôht,	after *the* morning light,
ofer ylda bearn,	over *the* children of men,
oþres dôgores,	of *the* second day,
sunne swegel-weard	*the* sun, heaven's guardian,
sûþan scineð.	from *the* south shines."
Þâ wæs on salum	Then was rejoiced
sinces brytta,	*the* distributor of treasure,
gamol-feax and gûð-rôf,	hoary-lock'd and war-fam'd,
geôce gelŷfde	trusted in succour
brego beorht-Dena :	*the* bright Danes' lord :
gehŷrde on Beowulfe	in Beowulf heard
folces hyrde	*the* people's shepherd
fæstrædne geþôht.	steadfast resolve.
Þær wæs hæleþa hleahtor,	There was laughter of men,
hlyn swynsode,	*the* din resounded,

1204. MS. sendeð.

1216. MS. wered. In Judith, 144. 4, the Almighty is designated swegles weard.

word wǽron wynsume ;	words were winsome ;
eóde Wealhþeów forð,	Wealhtheow went forth,
cwén Hróðgáres ;	Hrothgar's queen ;
cynna gemyndig,	mindful of *their* races,
grétte gold-hroden	*the* gold-adorn'd *one* greeted
guman on healle,	*the* men in hall,
and þá freólíc wíf	and then *the* joyous woman
ful gesealde	gave *the* cup
ǽrest East-Dena	first to *the* East-Danes'
éþel-wearde ;	country's guardian ;
bæd hine blíðne [beón]	bade him [be] blithe
æt þǽre beór-þege,	at the beer-drinking,
leódum leófne.	*the* dear to his people.
He on lust[e] geþáh	He joyfully partook of
symbel and sele-ful,	*the* feast and hall-cup,
sige-róf kyning.	*the* king renown'd for victory.
Ymb-eóde þá	Went round then
ides Helminga	*the* Helmings' dame
duguþe and geogoþe	of old and young
dǽl æghwylcne,	every part,
sinc-fato sealde,	treasure vessels gave,
oþþæt sǽl alamp,	until occasion offer'd,
þæt hió Beowulfe,	that she to Beowulf,
beág-hroden cwén,	*the* ring-adorned queen,
móde geþungen,	of mind exalted,
medo-ful ætbær :	*the* mead-cup bore :
grétte Geáta leód,	greeted *the* Goths' lord,
Gode þancode	thank'd God
wísfæst wordum,	sagacious in words,
þæs þe hire se willa gelamp,	that *the* will had befall'n her,
þæt heó on ǽnigne	that she in any
eorl gelýfde,	warrior should trust,
fyrena frófre.	for comfort against crimes.

1238. beón is added from conjecture. 1241. MS. geþeah.

He þæt ful geþâh	He of *the* cup partook,
wæl-reow wîga,	*the* fierce warrior,
æt Wealhþeówe,	from Wealhtheow,
and þâ gyddode,	and then said,
gûþe gefŷsed :	for battle eager :
Beowulf maþelode,	Beowulf spake,
bearn Ecgþeówes :	Ecgtheow's son :
Ic þæt hogode,	" I resolv'd,
þâ ic on holm gestâh,	when on *the* main I went,
sǽ-bât gesæt,	*the* sea-boat occupied,
mid mînra secga gedriht,	with my warrior band,
þæt ic ânunga	that I alone
eowra leóda	your people's
willan geworhte,	will would work,
oþðe on wæl crunge,	or bow in death,
feónd-grâpum fæst.	fast in hostile grasps.
Ic gefremman sceal	I shall perform
eorlîc ellen,	*deeds of* noble valour,
oþðe ende-dæg,	or my last day,
on þisse meodu-healle,	in this mead hall,
mînne gebîdan.	await."
Þâm wîfe þa word	The woman those words
wel lîcodon,	well lik'd,
gilp-cwide Geâtes ;	*the* Goths' proud speech ;
eóde gold-hroden,	adorn'd with gold went
freólîcu folc-cwên,	*the* joyful people's queen,
to hire freân sittan.	by her lord to sit.
Þâ wæs eft swâ ǽr,	Then was again as ere,
inne on healle,	within *the* hall,
þryð-word sprecen,	*the* bold word spoken,
ðeód on sǽlum,	*the* people joyous,
sige-folca swêg,	*the* victor nations' cry,
oþþæt semninga	until suddenly

1261. MS. geþeah. 1263. MS. Wealhþeon.

sunu Healfdenes	Healfdene's son
sēcean wolde	would seek
æfen-reste :	*his* evening rest :
wiste þǣm ahlǣcan	*he* knew for the miserable
tō þǣm heāh-sele	in the high hall
hilde geþinged,	conflict was destin'd,
siððan hie sunnan leōht	after *the* sun's light they
geseōn [ne] meahton,	might [not] see,
oþðe nipende	or murky
niht ofer ealle,	night over all
scadu-helm gesceapa,	(*the* shadow-covering of creatures)
scrīðan cwome,	came advancing,
wan under wolcnum.	dusky under *the* clouds.
Werod eall arās ;	*The* company all arose ;
grētte þā	greeted then
guma oþerne,	*one* man another,
Hrōðgār Beowulf,	Hrothgar Beowulf,
and him hǣl abeād,	and bade him hail,
wīn-ærnes geweald,	*gave him* command of *the* wine-hall,
and þæt word acwæð :	and the word said :
Næfre ic ǣnegum men	" Never have I to any man
ǣr alȳfde,	before entrusted,
siþðan ic hond and rond	since I hand and shield
hebban mihte,	could raise,
ðryþ-ærn Dena,	*the* Danes' festive hall,
buton þe nū-þā.	save now to thee.
Hafa nū and geheald	Have now and hold
hūsa sēlest ;	*the* best of houses ;
gemyne mǣrþo,	be of glory mindful,

1296. MS. ræste. 1301. ne inserted from conjecture.
1304. MS. scadu helma gesceapu.
1305. MS. cwoman.

mægen-ellen cyð,	show *thy* mighty valour,
waca wið wrâþum :	keep watch against *the* foes ;
ne bið þe wilna gâd,	no lack of things desirable shall be for thee,
gif þû þæt ellen-weorc	if thou that work of valour
aldre gedígest.	with life escapest from."

X.

Þâ him Hrôðgâr gewat	Hrothgar then departed
mid his hæleþa gedryht,	with his band of warriors,
eôdur Scyldinga	*the* Scyldings' protector.
ût of healle :	out of *the* hall :
wolde wíg-fruma	*the* martial leader would
Wealhþeôw sêcan,	Wealhtheow seek,
cwên tô gebeddan.	*the* queen, as bed-companion.
Hæfde kyninga wuldor	*The* glory of kings had
Grendle tô-geanes,	against Grendel,
swâ guman gefrugnon,	as men have heard tell,
sele-weard aseted :	*a* hall-ward set :
sunder-nýtte beheold	*he* held a separate office
ymb aldor Dena,	about *the* prince of *the* Danes,
eôten weard abeâd.	*the* ward announced *the* eoten.
Huru Geâta leôd	But *the* Goths' chief
georne trûwode	well trusted in
môdgan mægnes,	*his* haughty might,
Metodes hyldo.	*his* Creator's favour.
Ðâ he hím ofdyde	Then he doff'd from him
ísern-byrnan,	*his* iron byrnie,

1325. i.e., of things to be desired, *desiderabilia*.

1333. MS. Wealhþeo. 1335. MS. kyning.

1337. MS. gefrungon.

1341. MS. eoton. It was his office to announce the monster's approach.

helm of hafelan,	*the* helmet from *his* head,
sealde his hyrsted sweord,	gave his ornate sword,
îrena cyst,	choicest of irons,
ombiht-þegne,	to *an* attendant,
and gehealdan hêt	and bade *him* hold
hilde geâtwe.	*the* gear of war.
Gespræc þâ se gôda	Spake the good *chief* then
gylp-worda sum,	some words of pride,
Beowulf Geâta,	Beowulf *the* Goth,
ǽr he on bed stîge :	ere on *his* bed he stept :
Nô ic me an here-wæstmum	"I myself *do not* in martial vigour
hnâgran talige,	feebler account,
gûð-geweorca,	of warlike works,
þonne Grendel hine ;	than Grendel *does* himself ;
forþan ic hine sweorde	therefore I him with sword
swebban nelle,	will not lull to rest,
aldre beneôtan,	of life deprive,
þeâh ic eâðe mæge.	although I easily may.
Nât he þǽre gûðe,	He knows not of that warfare,
þæt he me ongean sleâ,	that he strike against me,
rand geheâwe,	hew *my* shield,
þeâh ðe he rôf sîe	fam'd though he be
nîþ-geweorca :	for hostile works :
ac wit on niht sculon,	but we two shall to-night
sæcce ofersittan,	apply *ourselves* to strife,
gif he gesêcean dear	if he dare seek
wîg ofer wæpen ;	war without weapon ;
and siþðan wîtig God,	and afterwards *the* wise God,
on swâ-hwæþere hond,	on whichsoever hand,
hâlig Dryhten,	*the* holy Lord,
mǽrðo dême,	shall glory doom,

1358. MS. wæsmun.
1365. MS. eal.
1366. MS. þara goda.
1372. MS. secge.
1373. MS. het.

swâ him gemet þince.	as to him meet shall seem."
Hylde hine þâ heaþo-deôr,	Inclin'd him then *the* martial beast,
hleor bolster onfeng,	*the* bolster received *his* cheek,
eorles andwlîtan;	*the* warrior's face;
and hine ymb monig	and around him many *a*
snellic sǽ-rinc	keen seaman
sele-reste gebeâh.	bow'd to *his* hall-couch.
Nǽnig heora þôhte	Not one of them thought
þæt he þanon scolde	that he should thence
eft eard-lufan	*his* lov'd home again
æfre gesêcean,	ever seek,
folc oþðe freô-burh,	*his* people or free city,
þær he afêded wæs;	where he was nurtur'd;
ac hîe hæfdon gefrunen þæt hîe	for they had heard tell that of them
ǽr tô fela micles,	before by much too many,
in þǽm wîn-sele,	in that wine-hall,
wæl-deâð fornam,	*a* bloody death had taken,
Deniga leôde.	of *the* Danes' people.
Ac him Dryhten forgeaf	But to them *the* Lord gave
wîg-spêda gewiôfu;	*the* webs of battle-speed;
Wedera leôdum,	to *the* Weders' people,
frôfor and fultum,	comfort and succour,
þæt hîe feônd heora,	*so* that they their foe,
ðurh ânes cræft,	by might of one,
ealle ofercomon,	all overcame,
selfes mihtum.	by *his* single powers.
Sôð is gecyþed,	Truly is *it* shown,
þæt mihtig God	that mighty God
manna cynnes weold.	rules *the* race of men.
Wîde-ferhð com,	From afar came,
on wanre niht,	in *the* murky night,

1388. MS. earð. 1392. hyra?

scriðan sceadu-genga;	*the* shadow-walker stalking;
sceōtend swǣfon,	*the* warriors slept,
þa þæt horn-reced	who that pinnacled mansion
healdan scoldon,	should defend,
ealle buton ānum.	all save one.
Þæt wæs yldum cuð,	It to men was known,
þæt hie ne mōste,	that them might not
þa Metod nolde,	(since the Lord will'd it not)
se syn-scaþa	*the* sinful spoiler
under sceadu bregdan;	under *the* shade drag off.
ac he wæccende	But he watching
wrāþum on andan,	in hate *the* foe,
bād bolgen-mōd	in angry mood awaited
beadwe geþinges.	*the* battle-meeting.

XI.

Þā com of mōre,	Then came from *the* moor,
under mist-hleōþum,	under *the* misty hills,
Grendel gongan;	Grendel stalking;
Godes yrre bær:	*he* God's anger bare:
mynte se mān-scaða	expected the wicked spoiler
manna cynnes	of *the* race of men
sumne besyrwan	one to ensnare
in sele ām heān.	in the lofty hall.
Wōd under wolcnum,	*He* strode under *the* clouds,
tō þæs þe he wīn-reced,	until he *the* wine-house,
gold-sele gumena,	*the* golden hall of men,
gearwost wisse,	most readily perceiv'd,
fættum fāhne.	richly variegated.
Ne wæs þæt forma sið	Nor was that time *the* first
þæt he Hrōþgāres	that he Hrothgar's

1414. ánum, i.e., Beowulf. 1420. he, i.e., Beowulf.
1423. MS. beadwa.

hâm gesôhte.	home had sought.
Næfre he on aldor-dagum,	Never in *his* life-days he,
ǽr ne siþðan,	ere nor since,
heardran hǽle,	*a* bolder man,
heal-þegnas fand.	*or* hall-thanes found.
Com þâ to recede	Came then to *the* mansion
rinc siðian,	*the* man journeying,
dreâmum bedǽled;	of joys depriv'd;
duru sôna on-arn	forthwith on *the* door he rush'd,
fŷr-bendum fæst,	fast with fire-*hard* bands,
syþðan he hire folmum [hrân];	then he with *his* hands it [touch'd];
onbræd þâ bealo-hydig,	undrew then *the* baleful minded
þâ he abolgen wæs,	(as he was angry)
recedes mûþan:	*the* mansion's mouth:
raþe æfter þon	soon after that
on fâgne flôr	on *the* variegated floor
feônd treddode;	*the* fiend trod;
eôde yrre-môd;	went wroth of mood;
him of eâgum stôd,	from his eyes stood,
lige gelîcost,	to flame most like,
leôht unfæger.	*a* horrid light.
Geseah he in recede	He in *the* mansion saw
rinca manige	warriors many
swefan sibbe-gedriht	sleeping, *a* kindred band,
samod-ætgædere,	all together,
mago-rinca heâp;	*a* company of fellow-warriors;
þâ his môd ahlôg:	then his mood laugh'd:
mynte þæt he gedǽlde,	*he* expected that he would separate,
ǽrþon dæg cwome,	ere *the* day came,

1449. hrán is supplied to complete the sense. Rask conjectured ærthrán; but the æt is needless.

1458. MS. ligge.

atol aglǽca,	*the* fell wretch,
ânra gehwylces	of every one
lîf wið lîce ;	life from body ;
þâ him alumpen wæs	then had arisen in him
wist-fylle wên :	hope of *a* dainty glut :
ne wæs wyrd þâ-gen,	yet 'twas not *his* fate,
þæt he mâ môste	that he might more
manna cynnes	of *the* race of men
ðicgean ofer þa niht.	eat after that night.
Þryð-swyð beheold	Beheld *the* strenuous
mǽg Higelâces	kinsman of Hygelac
hû se mân-scaða,	how the wicked spoiler,
under fǽr-gripum,	during *his* sudden grasps,
gefaran wolde.	would proceed.
Ne þæt se aglǽca	Nor did that the miserable wight
yldan þôhte ;	mean to delay ;
ac he gefeng hraðe,	for he quickly seiz'd,
forman siðe,	at *the* first time,
slǽpendne rinc,	*a* sleeping warrior,
slât unwearnum,	tore *him* unawares,
bât bân-locan,	bit *his* bone-casings,
blôd edrum dranc,	*the* blood drank from *his* veins,
syn-snǽdum swealh ;	in endless morsels swallow'd *him;*
sôna hæfde	soon had *he*
unlîfigendes	of *the* lifeless
eal gefeormod,	all devour'd,
fêt and folma :	feet and hands :
forð neâr ætstôp,	nearer forth *he* stept,
nam þâ mid handa	took then with *his* hand
hige-þihtigne	*the* doughty-minded
rinc on reste.	warrior on *his* couch.
Ræhte ongean	*He* reach'd towards
feônd mid folme ;	*the* foe with *his* hand ;

1498. MS. ræste.

he onfeng hraþe
inwit-þancum,
and wið earm gesæt.
Sōna þæt onfunde
fyrena hyrde,
þæt he ne mētte
middangeardes,
eorþan sceatta,
on elran men,
mund-grīpe māran,
he on mōde wearð
forht on ferhðe;
no þȳ ǽr fram meahte;
hyge wæs him hinfūs,
wolde on heolster fleōn,
sēcan deofla gedræg;
ne wæs his drohtoð þær
swylce he on ealder-dagum
ǽr gemētte.
Gemunde þā se gōda
mæg Higelāces
æfen-spræce;
uplang astōd,
and him fæste wið-feng;
fingras burston,
eōten wæs ūtweard;
eorl furþur stōp;
mynte se mǽra
hwæþer he meahte swā
wīdre gewindan,
and on-wēg þanon
fleōn on fen-hópu;

he instantly perceiv'd
the guileful thoughts,
and on *his* arm rested.
Soon as discover'd
the criminal,
that he had not found
of mid-earth,
of *the* world's regions,
in *a* stranger man,
a stronger hand-gripe,
he in mind became
fearful in soul;
not for that the sooner could he escape;
his mind was bent on flight,
he would into *his* cavern flee,
the pack of devils seek;
his condition there was not
such as he in *his* life-days
before had found.
Remember'd then the good
kinsman of Hygelac
his evening speech;
upright *he* stood,
and at him firmly grasp'd;
his fir.gers yielded,
the eoten was outward;
the earl stept further;
the renown'd *champion* thought,
whether he might *not* so
more widely wheel *about*,
and away thence
flee to *his* fen-mound;

1501. he, i. e. Beowulf.

1529. MS. hwær. he, i. e. Grendel.

wiste his fingra geweald,	*he* knew his fingers' power,
on grâmes grápum,	in *his* grasps of *the* fierce *one*,
þæt he wæs geócor.	that he *the* stronger was.
Siðþæt se hearm-scaða	After the pernicious spoiler
tó Heorute ateáh,	to Heorot came,
dryht-sele dynede,	*the* princely hall thunder'd,
Denum eallum wearð,	was for all *the* Danes,
ceaster-bûendum,	*the* city-dwellers,
cênra gehwylcum,	every valiant one,
eorlum ealu scerwen.	*the* earls, *the* ale spilt.
Yrre wǽron begen,	Angry were both,
reðe rên-weardas,	fierce, *the* powerful warders,
reced hlynsode ;	*the* mansion resounded ;
þâ wæs wundor micel,	then great wonder was *it*,
þæt se wîn-sele	that *the* wine-hall
wið-hæfde heaþo-deórum,	withstood *the* warlike beasts,
þæt he on hrûsan ne feol,	*so* that it fell not on *the* ground,
fæger fold-bold ;	*the* fair earthly dwelling ;
ac he þæs fæste wæs,	but it was thus fast,
innan and ûtan,	within and without,
îren-bendum,	with iron bands,
searo-þoncum besmiþod.	cunningly forged.
Þær fram sylle abeág	There from *its* sill inclin'd
medu-benc monig,	many *a* mead-bench,
mîne gefrǽge,	as I have heard tell,
golde geregnad,	with gold adorn'd,
þær þa grâman wunnon :	where the fierce *ones* fought :
þæs ne wêndon ǽr	therefore before ween'd not
wîtan Scyldinga,	*the* Scyldings' sages,
þæt hit á mid gemête	that it ever in any wise
manna ǽnig,	any man,
hetlîc and bân-fâg,	malicious and murder-stain'd,
tobrecan meahte,	could in pieces break,
listum tolûcan,	*or* craftily lay open,

nymþe liges fæðm	*naught* save *the* flame's embrace
swulge on swaloðe.	should with *its* heat devour *it.*
Swêg up-astâg,	*A* noise arose,
niwe geneâhhe;	newly, abundantly;
Norð-Denum stôd	over *the* North Danes stood
atelîc egesa,	dire terror,
ânra gehwylcum,	on every one,
þâra þe of wealle	of those who from *the* wall
wôp gehŷrdon,	heard *the* whoop,
grŷre-leoð galan	*the* horrid lay sung
Gôdes andsacan,	of God's denier,
sigeleasne sang,	*the* triumphless song,
sâr wanigean,	*his* pain bewailing,
helle-hæftan:	of *the* thrall of hell:
heold hine [tô] fæste,	held him [too] fast,
se þe manna wæs	he who of men was
mægene strengest,	strongest of might,
on þǽm dæge	in that day
þysses lîfes.	of this life.

XII.

Nolde eorla hleô	Would not *the* refuge of earls
ǽnige þinga,	for any thing
þone cwealm-cuman	the deadly guest
cwicne forlætan,	leave living,
ne his lîf-dagas	nor his life-days
leôda ǽnigum	to any people
nytte tealde.	accounted useful.
Þær genehost brægd	Then forthwith drew
eorl Beowulfes	*a* warrior of Beowulf's
ealde lâfe;	*an* ancient relic;
wolde freâ-drihtnes	*he* would *his* lord's

1568. MS. swaþule. 1580. MS. hæfton. 1596. MS. fréah.

feorh ealgian,	life defend,
mǽres þeódnes,	*the* great prince's,
þær híe meahton swâ.	if they might so *do.*
Híe þæt ne wiston,	They knew it not,
þâ híe gewin drugon,	when they endur'd *the* strife,
heard-hicgende	*the* bold eager
hilde mecgas,	sons of battle,
and on healfa gehwone	and on every side
heáwan þóhton,	thought to hew,
sawle sêcan,	*his* soul to seek,
þone syn-scaðan	*that* the wicked scather
ǽnig ofer eorþan	on earth not any
írenna cyst,	choicest of irons
gûð-billa nân	no battle falchion,
grêtan nolde :	would touch :
ac'he sige-wæpnum	but he martial weapons
forsworen hæfde,	had forsworn,
ecga gehwylcre.	every hedge whatever.
Scolde his aldor-gedâl,	His life-divorce was,
on ðǽm dæge	on that day
þysses lífes,	of this life
earmlic wurðan,	to be miserable,
and se ellor-gast	and the departing ghost
on feónda geweald	into *the* power of fiends
feor siðian.	far to travel,
Ðá þæt onfunde,	Then that found,
se e fela ǽror,	he who before many,
môdes myrðe,	in mirth of mood,
manna cynne,	against *the* race of men,
fyrena gefremede,	crimes had perpetrated,
he [wæs]fág wið God,	(he was *the* foe of God,)
þæt him se líchoma	that him his body

1612. he, i.e. Beowulf. 1615. his, i. e. Grendel's.

1626. MS. fryne.

lǽstan nolde;	would not avail;
ac hine se môdega	for him the proud
mǽg Higelâces	kinsman of Hygelac
hæfde be honda;	had in hand;
wæs gehwæþer oðrum	was each to other
lifigende lâð;	hateful living;
lîc-sâr gebâd	body pain endur'd
atol æglǽca;	*the* fell wretch;
him on eaxle wearð	on his shoulder was
syn-dolh sweotol,	*a* deadly wound manifest,
seonowa onsprungon	*the* sinews sprang asunder,
burston bân-locan;	*the* bone-casings burst;
Beowulfe wearð	to Beowulf was
gûð-hreð gyfeþe;	warlike fierceness given;
scolde Grendel þonan	Grendel must thence
feorh-seóc fleón	death-sick flee
under fen-hleóðu,	under *his* fen-shelters
sêcean wynleás wîc:	seek *a* joyless dwelling;
wiste þe geornor	*he* the better knew
þæt his aldres wæs	that was his life's
ende gegongen,	end pass'd,
dôgora dæg-rîm.	*his* day's number.
Denum eallum wearð,	For all *the* Danes was,
æfter þâm wæl-ræse,	after that mortal conflict
willa gelumpen.	*their* will accomplish'd.
Hæfde þâ gefǽlsod,	Had then purified
se þe ǽr feorran com,	he who had before come from afar,
snotor and swyð-ferhð,	wise and strong of soul,
sele Hrôðgâres,	Hrothgar's hall,
genered wið niðe	sav'd *it* from malice.
Niht-weorce gêfêh,	In *his* night-work *he* rejoiced
ellen-mǽrþum;	*his* valour glories;

1639. MS. seonowe.

hæfde Eást-Denum
Geât-mecga leód
gilp gelǽsted,
swylce on cýþðe
ealle gebētte
inwid-sorge,
þe hie ǽr drugon,
and for þreâ-nýdum
þolian scoldon,
torn unlytel.
Þæt wæs tâcen sweotol,
syþðan hilde deór
hond alegde,
earm and eaxle :
þær wæs eal-geador
Grendles grâpe
under geâpne hrôf.

had to *the* East-Danes
the Goths' chieftain
his boast fulfilled,
as also in *the* country
he had heal'd
the preying sorrow,
that they before had suffer'd,
and for hard necessity
had to endure,
affliction not *a* little,
It was *a* token manifest
when *the* beast of war
laid down *the* hand.
the arm and shoulder :
there was altogether
Grendel's grasp
under *the* vaulted roof.

XIII.

Þâ wæs on morgen,
míne gefrǽge,
ymb þa gif-healle
gûð-rinc monig :
ferdon folc-togan,
feorran and neân
geond wíd-wegas,
wunder sceawian,

Then was in *the* morning,
as I have heard tell,
around the gift-hall
many *a* warrior :
the nation's chieftains came,
from far and near
o'er distant ways,
the wonder to behold,

1676. After this line there seems to be a want of connection with what follows, though there is no lacuna in the MS. Perhaps for grápe we should read gràp or grípe, meaning Grendel's entire limb, or *his means of grasping*.

1677. For hróf Thorkelin has hrægl, which must be an error, 1st, because it is void of sense, and 2dly, because it is a neuter. There seems no doubt of the accuracy of hrōf, which is also adopted by K.

lâþes lastas:
nô his lîf-gedâl
sârlîc þûhte
secga ǽnigum,
þâra þe tirleâses
trôde sceawode;
hû he wêrig-môd
on-weg þanon,
nîða ofercumen,
on nicera mere,
fǽge and geflýmed,
feorh-lastas bær.
Ðær wæs on blôde
brim weallende,
atol ýða geswing
eal gemenged;
hât on heolfre
heoro-dreôre weol,
deâð-fǽge deog,
siððan dreâma-leâs,
in fen-freôðo
feorh-alegde,
hǽþene sawle:
þær him hel onfeng.
Þanon eft gewiton
eald-gesiðas,
swylce geong manig,
of gomen-waþe,
fram mere môdge,
mearum rîdan,
beornas on blancum.
Þær wæs Beowulfes
mǽrðo mǽned;
monig oft gecwæð,

the traces of *the* foe:
his life-divorce did not
seem painful
to any warrior,
who *the* inglorious's
track beheld;
how he in spirit weary
away thence,
in hostilities overcome,
to *the* nickers' mere,
death-doom'd and put to flight,
death-traces bare.
There was with blood
the surge boiling,
the dire swing of waves
all mingled;
hot with clotted blood
it well'd, with fatal gore,
the death-doom'd had dyed *it*,
after *he* joyless,
in *his* fen-asylum,
laid down *his* life,
his heathen soul:
there him hell receiv'd.
Thence again departed
the old comrades,
as also many *a* young *one*,
from *the* joyous way,
proud from *the* mere,
to ride on horses,
the warriors on steeds.
There was Beowulf's
glory celebrated;
many oft said,

þætte sûð ne norð,	that *nor* south nor north,
be sǽm tweonum,	between *the* seas
ofer eormen-grund,	over *the* spacious earth
oþer nǽnig,	not any other,
under swegles begong,	under heaven's course,
sêlra nǽre	better were
rond-hæbbendra,	of shield-bearers,
rîces wyrðra.	worthier of power.
Ne hîe huru wine-drihten	Nor yet did they *their* belov'd lord
wiht ne logon	*in* aught reprehend,
glædne Hrôðgâr,	*the* joyful Hrothgar,
ac wæs þæt gôd cyning.	for that was *a* good king.
Hwîlum heaþo-rôfe	At times *the* fam'd in war
hleâpan leton,	let run,
on geflit faran,	in contest go,
fealwe mearas,	*their* fallow steeds,
þær him fold-wegas	where to them *the* earth-ways
fǽgere þûhton,	fair appear'd,
cystum cuþe.	*the* fam'd for virtues.
Hwîlum cyninges þegn,	At times *a* king's thane,
guma gilp-hlæden,	*a* vaunt-laden man,
gidda gemyndig,	mindful of songs,
se ðe eal-fela	who full many
eald-gesegena	old legends,
worn gemunde,	*a* great number, remember'd,
word oþer fand	found another theme
sôðe gebunden.	with truth combin'd.
Secg eft ongan	Then *the* man began
sið Beowulfes	Beowulf's enterprize
snyttrum styrian,	discreetly to celebrate,
and on spêd wrecan,	and diligently to relate,
spel gerâde	*the* tale with skill
wordum wrixlan.	in words impart.

Wel hwylc gecwæð	Well *he* each thing told
þæt he fram Sigemunde	that he of Sigemund
secgan hýrde,	had heard related,
ellen-dǽdum,	of valorous deeds,
uncuþes fela,	much unknown,
Wælsinges gewin,	*the* Wælsing's battles,
wîde siðas,	wide journeyings,
þâra þe gumena bearn	of which *the* children of men
gearwe ne wiston,	well knew not,
fǽhðe and fyrena,	*his* warfare and *his* crimes,
buton Fitela mid hine.	save Fitela *who was* with him.
Þonne he swylces hwæt	Then he something such-like
secgan wolde,	would tell,
eâm his nefan,	*of the* uncle *and* his nephew,
swâ hîe â wæron,	how they ever were,
æt nîða gehwâm,	at every strife,
nýd-gesteallan.	needful associates.
Hæfdon eal-fela	*They* had full many
Eótena cynnes	of *the* Jutes' race
sweordum gesæged.	with *their* swords laid low.
Sigemunde gesprong,	To Sigemund sprang,
æfter deâð-dæge,	after *his* death-day,
dóm unlytel,	no little glory,
syþðan wîges heard	after *the* bold in battle
wyrm acwealde,	*the* worm had slain,
hordes hyrde.	*the* guardian of *the* hoard.
He under hârne stân,	He under *a* hoar stone,
æþelinges bearn,	*the* prince's child,
âna geneðde	alone ventur'd on
frecne dǽde :	*the* daring deed :
ne wæs him Fitela mid ;	Fitela was not with *him ;*

1764. MS. swulces : he refers to the narrator.

1766. be eame and his nefan? Sigemund was Fitela's father as well as uncle. See Glossary of Persons.

hwæþre him gesǽlde,	yet 'twas his fortune,
þæt þæt swurd þurh-wód	that his sword pierced through
wrætlícne wyrm,	*the* wondrous worm,
þæt hit on wealle ætstód	*so* that in *the* wall stood *fast*
drihtlíc íren :	*the* noble iron :
draca morðre swealt.	*the* dragon by death perish'd.
Hæfde aglǽca	*The* miserable being had
elne gegongen,	by daring gain'd,
þæt he beáh-hordes	that he *the* ring-hoard
brúcan móste	might enjoy
selfes dóme.	at *his* own pleasure.
Sǽ-bát gehlód,	*The* sea-boat loaded,
bær on bearm scipes	bore into *the* ship's bosom
beorhte frætwa	*the* bright ornaments
Wælses eafera.	Wælse's offspring.
Wyrm hát gemealt.	Heat *the* worm consum'd.
Se wæs wreccena	He of wanderers was
wíde mǽrost	by far *the* greatest
ofer wer-þeóde,	throughout *the* human race,
wígendra hleó,	*the* warriors' refuge,
ellen-dǽdum :	by valiant deeds :
he þæs ǽr onþáh :	therefore at first *he* throve :
siððan Heremódes	*but* after Heremod's
hild sweðrode,	war had ceas'd,
earfoð and ellen :	*his* toil and energy :
he mid Eótenum wearð,	he among *the* Jutes was,
on feónda geweald	into *the* foes' power
forð forlácen,	forthwith betray'd,
snúde forsended ;	quickly exil'd ;
hine sorh-wylmas	him sorrow's boilings
lemedon to lange ;	had too long afflicted ;

1791. By the murder of his father. 1795. MS. gehleod.
1800. He, i. e. Sigemund. 1809. He, i. e. Sigemund.
1814. MS. lemede.

he his leódum wearð,
eallum æðelingum,
to aldor-ceare.
Swylce oft bemearn,
ǽrran mǽlum,
swið-ferhðes sið
snotor ceorl monig,
se ðe him bealwa
tó bóte gelýfde;
þæt þæt ðeódnes bearn
geþeón scolde,
fæder æþelum onfón,
folc gehealdan,
hord and hleó-burh,
hæleþa ríce,
•ᛟ• Scyldinga.
He þær eallum wearð,
mæg Higeláces,
manna cynne,
freóndum gefægra;
hine fyren onwód.
Hwílum flítende,
fealwe strǽte
mearum mǽton.
Ðá wæs morgen-leóht
scofen and scynded,
eóde scealc monig
swið-hicgende
tó sele þám heán,

to his people he became,
to all *his* nobles,
a life-long care.
In such guise oft bewail'd,
in former times,
the bold-heart's lot
many *a* sagacious man,
who had to him of bales
for reparation trusted;
and that *the* prince's child
should thrive,
succeed to *his* father's honours,
defend *his* people,
his treasure and refuge-city,
the realm of heroes,
the country of *the* Scyldings.
There to all was he,
Hygelac's kinsman,
to *the* race of men,
to *his* friends, more grateful;
him crime had enter'd.
Sometimes contending,
the fallow street
they with *their* horses measur'd.
When *the* morning light was
sent forth and hasten'd,
went many *a* warrior
of strong purpose
to the high hall,

1819. "In former times," i. e. in their days of calamity, when Hrothgar and his people were suffering from the atrocities of Grendel.

1830. The rune denoting éðel, as at l. 1045.

1831. He, i. e. Beowulf.

1835. hine, i. e. Sigemund.

searo-wundor seôn.
Swylce self cyning
of brŷd-bûre,
beâh-horda weard,
treddode tirfæst,
getrume micle,
cystum gecyþed,
and his cwên mid him,
medo-stîg gemæt
mǽgþa hose.

to see *the* curious wonder.
So also *the* king himself
from *his* nuptial bower,
the guardian of ring-treasures,
stept glorious,
with *a* large company,
for virtues fam'd,
and his queen with him,
the meadow-path measur'd
with *a* company of maidens.

XIV.

Hrôðgâr maþelode:
he tô healle gong,
stôd on stapole,
geseah steâpne hrôf
golde fâhne,
and Grendles hond:
Ðisse ansŷne
Alwealdan þanc
lungre gelimpe.
Fela ic lâþes gebâd,
grynna æt Grendle:
â mæg God wyrcan
wundor æfter wundre,
wuldres Hyrde.
Ðæt wæs ungeara,
þæt ic ǽnigra me
weâna ne wênde,
tô wîdan feore,
bôte gebîdan,
þonne blôde fâh

Hrothgar spake:
(he to *the* hall went,
stood in *the* fore-court,
saw *the* steep roof
with gold variegated,
and Grendel's hand:)
"For this sight
to *the* Almighty thanks
forthwith take place!
Much of malice I have endur'd,
snares from Grendel:
ever can God work
wonder after wonder,
glory's Guardian.
It was not long since,
that I of any
woes ween'd not,
for all time,
compensation to await me,
when with blood stain'd

1848. MS. tryddode. 1855. MS. geong. 1866. MS. wunder.

hûsa sêlest	*the* best of houses
heoro-dreórig stôd ;	all gory stood ;
weá wîd-scofen,	misery *was* wide-spread
wîtena gehwylcum,	*o'er* each of *my* counsellors,
ðâra þe ne wêndon	who weened not
þæt hîe wîde-ferhð	that they evermore
leóda land-geweorc	*the* people's land-work
lâþum beweredon,	could from foes defend,
scuccum and scinnum.	devils and phantoms
Nû scealc hafað,	Now *this* warrior has,
þurh Drihtnes miht,	through *the* Lord's might,
dǽde gefremede,	*a* deed perform'd,
ðe we ealle	which we all
ǽr ne meahton	ere could not
snyttrum besyrwan.	with cunning machinate.
Hwæt þæt secgan mæg,	Yes ! that may say,
efne swâ hwylc mægþâ	lo ! whatever matron,
swâ þone magan cende	who this son brought forth,
æfter gum-cynnum,	after human kind,
gyf heó gyt lyfað,	if she yet lives,
þæt hyre eald Metod	that to her *the* great Creator
este wǽre	was gracious
bearn-gebyrdo.	in *her* child-bearing.
Nû ic Beowulf,	Now I, Beowulf,
þec secg betsta,	thee, best of warriors,
me for sunu wylle	as *a* son will
freógan on ferhþe :	love in *my* heart :
heald forð tela	hold henceforth well
niwe sibbe :	*our* new kinship :
ne bið þe ǽnigra gâd	*there* shall not be to thee any lack
worolde wilna,	of worldly things desirable,
þe ic geweald hæbbe.	that I have power over.

1877. MS. gehwylcne. K. proposes gehwylcum no doubt, rightly.
1885. M.. dæd. 1903. MS. ænigre. See l. 1325.

Ful oft ic for læssan
leân teôhhode,
hord-weorþunge,
hnâhran rince,
sǣmran æt sæcce.
Þû þe self hafast
dǣdum gefremed,
þæt þîn [dôm] lyfað
âwa tô aldre.
Alwalda þec
gôde forgylde,
swâ he nû gyt dyde.
Beowulf maþelode,
bearn Ecgþeowes:
We þæt ellen-weorc
estum miclum,
feohtan fremedon,
frecne geneðdon
eafoð uncuþes:
uþe ic swiþor,
þæt þû hine selfne
geseôn môste,
feônd on frætewum,
fyl-wêrigne.
Ic hine hrædlice,
heardan clammum,
on wæl-bedde,
wrîþan þôhte,
þæt he for mund-gripe
mînum scolde
licgean lîf-bysig,

Full oft I for less
have *a* reward decreed,
treasure-honour
to *a* feebler warrior,
worse in conflict.
Thou for thyself hast
so by deeds achiev'd,
that thy glory lives
through every age.
May the Omnipotent thee
with good reward,
as he yet as done."
Beowulf spake,
Ecgtheow's son:
"We that arduous work
with great good will,
that fight have achiev'd,
boldly ventur'd on
the monster's warfare:
rather would I have given,
that thou himself
mightest have seen,
the foe in *his* trappings,
slaughter-weary.
I him quickly,
with hard bonds,
on *his* death-bed,
thought to bind,
so that through my hand-gripe
he should
lie for life struggling,

1913. dôm is not in the MS., but rightly supplied by K.
1929. See ll. 1484—1494. 1930. MS. him.
1934. MS. hand-gripe.

butan his lic-swíce.	without his carcase's escape.
Ic hine ne mihte,	I could not him
þá Metod nolde,	(as *the* Creator will'd it not)
ganges getwǽman,	from *his* course cut off;
nó ic him þæs georne at-fealh	I did not him therefore easily assail,
feorh-geniðlan;	*the* deadly enemy;
wæs tó fore-mihtig	was too greatly powerful
feónd on feþe;	*the* foe on foot;
hwæþere he his folme forlet,	ye he his hand has left,
tó lif-wraþe,	as *a* life-support,
last weardian,	to guard *his* track,
earm and eaxle:	*his* arm and shoulder:
nó þær ǽnige swa-þeáh	yet not any there
feásceaft guma	*the* wretched man
frófre gebóhte;	comfort bought,
nó þý leng leofað	nor will the longer live
láð-geteóna,	*the* hateful criminal,
synnum geswenced;	with sins oppress'd;
ac hyne sâr hafað	for pain has him
in níð-grípe	in hostile gripe
nearwe befongen,	straitly clasp'd,
balw on bendum:	harm, in *its* bonds:
þær abídan sceal	there shall await
maga mâne fâh	*the* wretch stain'd with crime
miclan dómes,	*the* great doom,
hú him scír Metod	how to him *the* bright Creator
scrífan wille,	will prescribe."
Ðá wæs swigra secg,	Then was *the* warrior more silent,
sunu Ecgláfes,	Ecglaf's son,
on gylp-spræce	in vaunting speech
gúð-geweorca,	of works of war,

1956. MS. mid gripe.
1965. MS. Eclafes. See ll. 1002, 1003.

siððan æþelingas,	after *the* nobles,
eorles cræfte,	through *the* hero's might,
ofer heánne hrôf	over *the* high roof
hand sceâwedon,	had beheld *the* hand,
feóndes fingras :	*the* foe's fingers :
foran æghwylc wæs,	each was before,
stede nægla [gehwylc],	instead of nails, [each]
stŷle gelícost,	to steel most like,
hǽþenes hand-sporu,	*the* heathen's hand-spurs,
hilde rinces	*the* warrior's,
eglan heoru.	*the* terrific *one's* sword.
Æghwylc gecwæð þæt him	Every one said that it,
heardra nân	(of *the* bold ones) none
hrínan wolde ;	would touch ;
íren ǽr-gôd,	*no* iron of prime goodness,
þæt ðæs ahlǽcan	that the miserable being's
blôdge beadu-folme	bloody battle-hand
onberian wolde.	would taste of.

XV.

Þá wæs hâten hrâþe,	Then was quickly order'd
Heort innanweard	Heort inward
folmum gefrætwod :	*to be* with hands adorn'd :
fela þǽra wæs,	many were of those,
wera and wífa	men and women,

1974. MS. steda. gehwylc I believe should be expunged.

1976. I suspect that hand-sporu is a blunder of the scribe for hand-sceó. See hereafter.

1978. MS. eglun. My translation of the line is purely conjectural. The whole text, to the end of the canto, is hardly intelligible, and evidently corrupt. K. reads egl un-heoru, and translates, *the rude terror.*

1985. MS. onberan. 1986. MS. hreþe.

þe þæt wîn-reced,
gest-sele gyredon ;
gold-fâg scinon,
web æfter wagum,
wundor-siôna fela
secga gehwylcum,
þâra þe on swylc stârað.
Wæs þæt beorhte bold
tôbrocen swiðe,
eal inneweard
îren-bendum fæst ;
heorras tôhlidene ;
hrôf âna genæs,
ealles ansund,
þâ se aglǽca,
fyren-dǽdum fâg,
on fleâm gewand,
aldres orwêna.
Nô þæt ýðe byð
tô befleônne,
fremme se þe wille ;
ac gesêcan sceal
sawl-berendra,
nýde genydde,
niþða bearna,
grund-bûendra,
gearwe stôwe,
þær his lîchoma,
leger-bedde fæst,
swefeð æfter symle.

who the wine-house,
the guest-hall prepar'd ;
gold-varied shone
the webs along *the* walls,
wondrous sights many
to every human being,
of those who gaze on such.
That bright dwelling was
much shatter'd,
all within
with bands of iron fast ;
the hinges *were* rent asunder ;
the roof alone was sav'd,
wholly sound,
when the miserable being,
stain'd with criminal deeds,
turn'd to flight,
hopeless of life.
That is not easy
to flee from,
accomplish *it* who will ;
but *he* shall seek
for soul-bearers,
by need compel'd,
for *the* children of men,
for earth's inhabitants
the place prepar'd,
where his body,
fast in *its* bed of death.
after *the* feast shall sleep.

2005. MS. þe.

2009—2020. These lines are extremely obsure : þæt (l. 2009), no doubt means *death*, implied in aldres orwéna.

2012. MS. gesacan.

Þá wæs sǽl and mǽl,
þæt to healle gang
Healfdenes sunu ;
wolde self cyning
symbel þicgan.
Ne gefrægn ic þa mægþe
mâran werode
ymb hyra sinc-gyfan
sêl gebæran.
Bugon þá tó bence
blǽd-âgende,
fylle gefǽgon,
fægene geþegon
medo-ful manig
magas pâra
swið-hicgendra
on sele þâm heân,
Hróðgár and Hróðulf.
Heorot innan wæs
freóndum afylled ;
nalles fácn-stafas
Þeód-Scyldingas
penden fremedon.
Forgeaf þá Beowulfe,
bearn Healfdenes,
segen gyldenne,
sigores tó leáne,
hroden-hilte cumbor,
helm and byrnan ;
mǽre maðþum sweord
manige gesawon
beforan beorn beran.

Then was *the* time and moment,
that to *the* hall should go
Healfdene's son ;
the king himself would
of *the* feast partake.
Never have I heard of the tribe
in *a* greater body
about their treasure-giver
better bearing themselves.
Bow'd then to *the* bench
the prosperous *warriors*,
in *the* plenty *they* rejoiced,
joyful partook of
many *a* mead cup
the kinsmen of those
stout-daring *warriors*,
in the high hall,
Hrothgar and Hrothulf.
Heorot within was
fill'd with friends ;
no treacheries
the noble Scyldings
the while perpetrated.
Gave then to Beowulf,
the son of Healfdene,
a golden banner,
in reward of victory,
an ensign with hilt adorn'd,
a helm and byrnie ;
a sword, *a* great treasure,
many saw
before *the* hero borne.

2033. MS. fægere geþægon. 2036. MS. hicgende.
2045. MS. brand.

Beowulf geþâh
ful on flette;
nô he þǽre feoh-gyfte,
fore sceôtendum
scamigan þorfte.
Ne gefrægn ic freôndlîcor
feôwer madmas
golde gegyrede
gum-manna fela,
in ealo-bence
oðrum gesellan.
Ymb þæs helmes hrôf,
heafod-beorg,
wîrum bewunden,
wæl on-ûtan heold,
þæt him fealo lâf
frecne ne meahte,
scûr-heard sceþþan,
þonne scyld-freca
ongean grâmum
gangan scolde.
Hêht ðâ eorla hleô
eahta mearas,
fæted-hleore,
on flet teôn,
in under eoderas;

Beowulf partook of
the cup in *the* court;
not of that precious gift he,
before *the* warriors,
needed feel shame.
Never have I heard more friendly
four precious things,
with gold adorn'd,
many men,
on *the* ale-bench,
to others give.
Around the helmet's roof,
the head-guard,
with wires bound round,
held slaughter without,
so that him *the* fallow sword
might not dangerously,
scour-harden'd, injure,
when *the* bold shielded warrior
against *his* foes
should go.
Bade then *the* shelter of warriors
eight steeds,
with cheek adorn'd,
into *the* court be led,
in under *the* enclosures;

2056. MS. for scotenum.

2065. MS. beorge. The heafod-beorg seems to be an additional guard on the crown of the helmet, analogous with heals-beorh, *hauberk*. Ohg. halsperga.

2067. MS. walan utan.

2068. MS. fela laf, perfectly devoid of sense. The sword was, no doubt, of bronze or copper; fealo-brun, as in brún-ecg. See note hereafter.

2069. MS. meahton.

þára ánum stód
sadol searwum fáh,
since gewurþad :
þæt wæs hilde setl
heáh-cyninges,
þonne sweorda gelác
sunu Healfdenes
efnan wolde ;
næfre on ore læg
wíd-cuþes wíg,
þonne walu feollon,
and þá Beowulfe
béga gehwæþres
eodor Ingwina
onweald geteáh,
wicga and wæpna :
hét hine wel brúcan.
Swá manlíce
mǽre þeóden,
hord-weard hæleþa,
heaþo-ræsas geald,
mearum and madmum.
Swá hý næfre man lyhð,
se þe secgan wile
sóð æfter rihte.

on one of them stood
a saddle cunningly variegated,
with treasure ornamented :
that was *the* war-seat
of *the* high king,
when *the* game of swords
the son of Healfdene
would perform :
(never in warfare flag'd
the wide-fam'd's martial ardour,
when *the* slaughter'd fell),
and then to Beowulf
of both one and other
the Ingwinas' protector
possession gave,
of horses and weapons :
bade him *them* well enjoy.
Thus manfully
the great prince,
the treasure-ward of heroes,
warlike onslaughts requited,
with steeds and treasures.
So them never man will blame.
who will say
the sooth rightly.

XVI.

Ðá gyt æghwylcum
eorla drihten,
þára þe mid Beowulfe
brim-láde teáh,
on þǽre medu-bence

Then besides to each,
the lord of warriors,
of those who with Beowulf
the sea-way came,
on the mead-bench,

2087. on orlege alæg ?

2107. MS. leade.

maþðum gesealde,
yrfe lâfe;
and þone ǽnne hêht
golde forgyldan,
þone ðe Grendel ǽr
mâne acwealde,
swâ he hyra mâ wolde,
nefne him witig God
wyrd forstôde,
and þæs mannes môd.
Metod eallum weold
gumena cynnes,
swâ he nû git dêð;
forþan bið andgit
æghwær sêlest,
ferhðes foreþanc:
fela sceal gebîdan
leôfes and lâþes,
se þe longe her
on ðyssum win-dagum
worulde brûceð.
Þær wæs sang and swêg
samod-ætgædere
for Healfdenes
hilde-wîsan,
gomen-wudu grêted,
gid oft wrecen,
þonne heal-gamen
Hrôðgâres scôp,
æfter medo-bence,
mǽnan scolde
[be] Finnes eaferum,
þâ hie se fǽr begeat;

a present gave
an hereditary relic;
and bade the one
with gold be paid for,
whom Grendel ere
wickedly had slain,
as he would more of them,
had not him *the* wise God,
fate, prevented,
and the man's courage.
The Creator rul'd all
the race of men,
as he now yet does;
therefore is understanding
everywhere best,
forethought of spirit:
much shall abide
of lov'd and loath'd,
who long here
in these days of strife
in *the* world participates.
There were song and sound
at once together
before Healfdene's
martial leaders,
the glee-wood *was* touch'd,
the lay oft recited,
when *the* joy of hall
Hrothgar's gleeman,
after *the* mead-bench,
should recount
[of] Fin's offspring,
when them peril o'erwhelm'd;'

2118 Beowulf's. 2140. be supplied from conjecture.

hæleþ Healfdenes
Hnæf Scyldinga,
in Fres-wæle
feallan scolde.
Ne huru Hildeburh
herian þorfte
Eótena treówe:
unsynnum wearð
beloren leófum
æt þâm lind-plegan,
bearnum and brôðrum;
hie on gebyrd hruron,
gâre wunde;
þæt wæs geomuru ides.
Nalles hôlinga
Hoces dôhtor,
metodsceaft bemearn,
syþðan morgen com,
þâ heó under swegle
gaseón meahte
morþor-bealo maga,
þær heó ǽr mæste heold
worolde wynne.
Wig ealle fornam
Finnes þegnas,
nemne feáum ânum,
þæt he ne meahte
on þǽm meðel-stede
wið Hengeste
wiht gefeohtan,
nê þa weá-lâfe

when Healfdene's hero,
the Scyldings' Hnæf,
in Friesland
was doom'd to fall.
Not Hildeburh at least
had need to praise
the faith of *the* Jutes:
sinless she was
of *her* belov'd *ones* depriv'd
at the linden play,
her children and brothers;
they in succession fell,
by *the* dart wounded;
that was *a* mournful woman.
Not without cause
Hoce's daughter,
the Lord's decree bemourn'd,
after morning came,
when she under heaven
might see
the slaughter of *her* kinsmen,
where she ere had most possess'd
of *the* world's joy.
War had destroy'd all
Fin's thanes,
save *a* few only,
so that he might not
on the battle-place
against Hengest
aught gain in fight,
nor the sad remnant

2142. MS. Healfdena. 2149. unsinnig? 2151. MS. hild.
2163. MS. he. 2168. MS. mehte. 2170. MS. wig.

wige forþringan	by war protect
þeódnes þegne ;	from *the* king's thane ;
ac híg him geþingo budon,	but they offer'd him conditions,
þæt híe him oðer flet	that they to him another dwelling
eal gerýmdon,	would wholly yield,
healle and heâh-setl,	*a* hall and throne,
þæt híe healfne geweald	that they half power
wið Eótena bearn	with *the* sons of *the* Jutes
âgan móston,	might possess,
and æt feoh-gyftum,	and at *the* money-gifts,
Folcwaldan sunu,	Folcwalda's son,
dógra gehwylce,	every day,
Dene weorþode,	*the* Danes should honour,
Hengestes heâp·	Hengest's band
hringum þênede,	with rings should serve,
efne swâ swiðe	even as much
sinc-gestreónum	with precious treasures
fættan goldes,	of rich gold,
swâ he Fresena cyn	as he *the* Frisian race
on beór-sele	in *the* beer-hall
byldan wolde.	would decorate.
Ðá híe getrûwedon	Then they confirm'd
on twâ healfa	on *the* two sides
fæste frioðu-wǽre ;	*a* fast peaceful compact ;
Fin Hengeste,	Fin to Hengest,
elne unflitme,	earnestly without dispute,
âðum benemde,	with oaths declar'd,
þæt he þa weâ-lâfe,	that he the sad remnant,
weotena dóme	by *his* 'witan's' doom
ârum heolde,	piously would maintain,
þæt ðær ǽnig mon,	*so* that there *not* any man,
wordum ne worcum,	by words or works,

2174. i.e. Hengest. 2179. MS. healfre.
2187. MS. wenede.

wǽre ne bræce,
ne þurh inwit-searo
æfre gemǽndon,
þéah híe hira béag-gyfan
banan folgedon,
þeódenleáse,
þá him swá geþearfod wæs:
gyf þonne Frysna hwylc,
frecnan spræce
ðæs morþor-hetes
myndgiend wǽre,
þonne hit sweordes ecg
sweðrian scolde.
Að wæs geæfned,
and icge gold
ahæfen of horde.
Here-Scyldinga
betst beado-rinca
wæs on bǽl gearu:
æt þǽm áde wæs
eþ-gesýne
swát-fáh syrce,
swýn eal-gylden,
eofer íren-heard,
æþeling manig
wundum awyrded,
sume on wæl crungon.
Hét ðá Hildeburh,
æt Hnæfes áde,
hire selfre suna,
sweoloðe befæstan,

should break *the* compact,
nor through guileful craft
should *they* ever lament,
though they their ring-giver's
slayer follow'd,
now lordless,
as *it* was thus needful to them:
but if of *the* Frisians any,
by audacious speech,
this deadly feud
should call to mind,
then it *the* edge of sword
should appease.
The oath was taken,
and moreover gold
rais'd from *the* hoard.
Of *the* martial Scyldings
the best of warriors
on *the* pile was ready:
at the heap was
easy to be seen
the blood-stain'd sark,
the swine all golden,
the boar iron-hard,
many *a* noble
with wounds injur'd,
(some had in *the* slaughter fall'n).
Bade then Hildeburh,
at Hnæf's pile,
her own sons
be to *the* fire committed,

2207. MS. gemænden.

2210. lordless: their lord, Hnæf, being slain.

2213. MS. frecnen. 2217. MS. syððan. 2234. MS. sunu.

bán-fatu bærnan,	*their* carcases be burnt,
and on bǽl dón	and on *the* pile be done
earme on axe.	*the* luckless *ones* to ashes.
Ides gnornode,	*The* lady mourn'd,
geomrode giddum;	bewail'd in songs;
gúð-rinc astáh,	*the* warrior ascended,
wand to wolcnum;	eddied to *the* clouds;
wæl-fyra mæst	*the* greatest of death-fires
hlynode for hlǽwe,	roar'd before *the* mound,
hafelan multon,	*their* heads were consum'd,
ben-geato burston,	*their* wound-gates burst,
ðonne blód ætsprang,	then *the* blood sprang out
láð-bite líces:	from *the* corpse's hostile bite:
lig ealle forswealg,	flame swallow'd all
gǽsta gifrost,	(greediest of guests)
þára þe þær gúð fornam:	those whom there war had destroy'd:
béga folces wæs	of both nations was
hira blǽd scacen.	their prosperity departed.

XVII.

Gewiton him þá wígend	*The* warriors then departed
wíca neósian,	*the* dwellings to visit,
freóndum befeallen,	of *their* friends bereft,
Frysland geseón,	Friesland to see,

2238. MS. eaxle.

2241. i.e. Hnæf ascended (in flame and smoke), like the Ger. (in Feuer und Rauch) aufgehen. So also in Homily (Ælfric's Homilies, v. ii. p. 68. þæt ceaf he forbærnð . . . . forþan ðe þǽra mánfulra smíc astihð on écnysse.

2244. MS. hlawe. 2247. MS. ætspranc.

2254. After the suspension of hostilities, it appears that Hengest's Jutes dispersed themselves over Friesland, for the purpose of seeing it, and, no doubt, of quartering themselves for the winter.

hâmas and heâh-burh.	*the* homes and chief city.
Hengest ðâ-gyt	Hengest still
wæl-fâgne winter	*the* death-hued winter
wunode mid Finne	dwelt with Fin
unflitme;	without dissension;
eard gemunde,	*his* home remember'd,
þeâh þe he meahte	though he might
on mere drífan	on *the* sea drive
hringed-stefnan.	*the* ringed prow.
Holm storme weol,	*The* deep boil'd with storm,
won wið winde,	war'd 'gainst *the* wind,
winter ýþe beleâc	winter lock'd up *the* wave
ís-gebinde,	with icy bond,
oþðæt oþer com	until *there* came *a* second
gear in geardas;	year into *the* courts;
swâ nû gyt dôð	so now yet do
þa ðe syngales	those who constantly
sǽle bewitiað,	watch *a* happy moment,
wuldor-torhtan weder.	gloriously bright weather.
Ðâ wæs winter scacen,	Then was winter departed,
fæger foldan bearm,	earth's bosom fair,
fundode wrecca,	*the* stranger hasten'd,
gist of geardum;	*the* guest from *the* dwellings:
he tô gyrn-wræce	he on wily vengeance
swiðor þôhte	was more intent
þonne tô sǽ-lâde,	than on *a* sea-voyage,
gif he torn-gemôt	if he *a* hostile meeting
þurhteôn mihte;	could bring to pass;
þæs he Eôtena bearn	because he *the* sons of *the* Jutes

2261. MS. Finnel. 2262. MS. unhlitme. See l. 2198.
2273. MS. deð. 2275. MS. sele.

2286. MS. þæt. Eotena bearn, in allusion apparently to the Jutes that had fallen in the conflict with the Frisians. Or bearn may here

inn-gemunde:
swâ he ne forwyrnde
worold-rǽdenne,
þonne him Hunláfing,
hilde leóman,
billa sêlest,
on bearm dyde;
þæs wæron mid Eótenum
ecge cuðe,
swylce ferhð-frecan.
Fin eft begeat
sweord-bealo sliðen,
æt his selfes hâm.
Siþðan grimne grîpe
Gûðláf and Osláf,
æfter sǽ-siðe,
sorge mǽndon:
ætwiton weâna dǽl,
ne meahte wæfre-môd
forhabban in hreþre.
Ðá wæs heal hroden
feónda feorum,

inwardly remember'd:
so he refus'd not
worldly converse,
when he Hunlafing,
the flame of war,
the best of falchions,
in his bosom placed;
for with *the* Jutes there were
men for *the* sword renown'd,
also of spirit bold.
Fin afterwards o'erwhelm'd
hard misery from *the* sword,
at his own home.
When *him* fierce of gripe
Guthlaf and Oslaf,
after *their* sea voyage,
had grievously upbraided,
reproach'd for part of *their* woes,
he might not *his* wavering courage.
in *his* breast retain.
Then was *his* hall beset
with hostile men,

be in the singular number, and allude to Hnæf, the Jutish leader, with Hengest, whose fall is related at ll. 2143, sqq.

2290. Hunláfing I take to be the name of Hengest's sword, as Hrunting, Nageling, etc. The meaning is not that he stabbed himself, but that he merely placed the weapon in or on his bosom, in allusion probably to the mode of wearing it in front, examples of which may be seen in old illuminations. (An exactly similar passage occurs hereafter, where there is no question of stabbing.) In other words, that he girded or prepared himself for a renewal of the contest. The whole passage, indeed the whole episode, is extremely obscure.

2301. The Ordláf of the "Fight at Finnesburg;" which seems the more correct orthography.

swilce Fin slægen,	Fin also slain,
cyning on corþre,	*the* king amid *his* train,
and seó cwên numen.	and the queen taken.
Sceótend Scyldinga	*The* Scyldings' warriors
tô scypum feredon	to *their* ships convey'd
eal in-gesteald	all *the* house chattels
eorð-cyninges,	of *the* land's king,
swylce hie æt Finnes-hâm	such as they at Finnesham
findan meahton,	might find,
sigla searo-gimma.	of jewels and curious gems.
Hie on sǽ-lâde	They on *the* sea-way
drihtlice wif	*the* princely woman
tô Denum feredon,	to *the* Danes convey'd,
læddon tô leódum.	to *their* people led.
Leóð wæs asungen,	*The* lay was sung,
gleómannes gyd,	*the* gleeman's song,
gamen eft astâh,	pastime rose again,
beorhtode benc-swêg,	*the* bench-noise was loud,
byrelas sealdon	*the* cupbearers gave
win of wunder-fatum.	wine from curious vessels.
Þá cwom Wealhþeów forð,	Then came Wealtheow forth,
gân under gyldnum beáge,	walking under *a* golden diadem,
þær þa gôdan twêgen	*to* where the two good
sæton suhter-gefæderan;	cousins sat;
þá-gyt wæs hiera sib ætgædere,	as yet was their peace together,
æghwylc oðrum trŷwe:	each to other true;

2313. MS. scipon.

2316. Finnes-hám is no doubt meant as the proper name of Fin's town, and identical with Finnes-burh, the name given it in the fragment entitled "the Fight at Finnesburg."

2329. MS. Wealhþeo.

2332. Hrothgar and Hrothulf. For this long species of verse see Rask's Anglo-Saxon Grammar, p. 158.

swylce þær Hunferþ þyle	there also Hunferth *the* orator
æt fôtum sæt freân Scyldinga:	sat at *the* feet of *the* Scyldings' lord;
gehwylc hiora his ferhðe treôwde,	every *one* of them was confident in his mind,
þæt he hæfde môd micel,	that he had great courage,
þeâh þe he his magum nǽre	although he to his kinsman had not been
ârfæst æt ecga gelâcum.	true in *the* plays of swords.
Spræc ðâ ides Scyldinga:	Spake then *the* Scyldings' dame:
Onfôh þissum fulle,	"Accept this cup,
freô-drihten mîn,	my beloved lord,
sinces brytta;	dispenser of treasure;
þû on sǽlum wes,	be thou happy,
gold-wine gumena:	gold-friend of men:
and to Geâtum spræc	and to *the* Goths speak
mildum wordum,	with kind words,
swâ sceal man dôn:	as one should do:
beô wið Geâtas glæd,	be cheerful towards *the* Goths,
geofena gemyndig,	mindful of gifts,
neân and feorran:	near and far:
þû nû hafast,	thou hast now [promis'd,]
me man sægde,	I have been told,
þæt þû for sunu wolde	that thou for *a* son wouldst
here-rinc habban.	*the* warrior have.
Heorot is gefǽlsod,	Heorot is purified,
beâh-sele beorhta:	*the* bright hall of rings:
brûc þenden þû môte	enjoy while thou mayest
manigra medo,	*the* mead of *the* many,
and þinum magum læf	and to thy sons leave

2339. See ll. 1178, sqq. 2351. Correctly geofa (gifa).

2353. After hafast a word is wanting, probably gehâten, *promised.* 2356. MS. here ric.

2360. i.e. the mead of which the others (the many) were partaking.

folc and rice,	folk and realm,
þonne ðû forð scyle	when thou forth must *go*
metodsceaft seôn.	to see *the* Godhead.
Ic mînne can	I know my
glædne Hrôðulf,	festive Hrothulf,
þæt he þa geogoðe wile	that he the youthful will
ârum healdan;	piously maintain;
gyf þû ǽr þonne he,	if thou earlier than he,
wine Scyldinga,	O friend of Scyldings,
worold oflætest:	leavest *the* world:
wêne ic þæt he mid gôde	I ween that he with good
gyldan wille	will repay
uncran eaferan;	our offspring;
gif he þæt eal gemon	if he that all remembers
hwæt wit tô willan	what we two for *his* pleasure
and tô worðmyndum,	and honours,
umbor wesendum ǽr	erst when *a* child,
ârna gefremedon.	of benefits perform'd."
Hwearf þâ bi bence,	Turn'd then by *the* bench,
þær hyre byre wǽron,	where her sons were,
Hrêðric and Hrôðmund,	Hrethric and Hrothmund,
and hæleþa bearn,	and *the* children of warriors,
giogoð ætgædere;	*the* youth together,
þær se gôda sæt,	where sat the good
Beowulf Geâta,	Beowulf *the* Goth,
be þǽm gebrôðrum twǽm.	by the two brethren.

XVIII.

Him wæs ful boren,	To him *the* cup was borne,
and freônd-laþu	and friendly invitation
wordum bewǽgned,	in words offer'd,
and wunden-gold	and twisted gold
êstum geeâwed,	kindly shown,

earm-reâf twâ,	sleeves two,
hrægl and hringas,	*a* mantle and rings,
heals-beâga mæst	of collars *the* largest
þâra þe ic on foldan	of those that I on earth
gefrægen hæbbe :	have heard tell of :
nǽnigne ic under swegle	not any under heaven I
sêlran hŷrde	more excellent have heard of
hord-madmum hæleþa,	treasure-hoard of men,
syþðan Hama ætwæg	since Hama bore off
to here-byrhtan byrig	to *the* noble bright city
Brósinga mene,	*the* Brosings' necklace,
sigle and sinc-fæt :	*the* jewel and *its* casket :
searo-nîðas fealh	*he* into *the* guileful enmity fell
Eormenrîces ;	of Eormenric ;
geceâs êcne rǽd.	*and* choose th' eternal council.
Þone hring hæfde	That ring had
Higelâc Geâta,	Hygelac *the* Goth,
nefa Swertinges,	Swerting's nephew,
nyhstan sîðe,	*the* last time,
siðþan he under segne	when he under *his* banner
sinc ealgode,	*his* treasure defended,
wæl-reâf werede :	guarded *the* spoil of *the* slain :
hine wyrd fornam,	him fate took off,
siþðan he for wlenco	after he for pride
weân ahsode,	sought *his own* woe,
fǽhðe tô Frysum :	*a* war with *the* Frisians :
he þa frætwe wæg,	he the ornament convey'd,
eorcnan-stânas,	*the* precious stones,

2393. MS. reade, which affords no sense. If it is meant for the adjective *red*, with what does it agree ? and with what does the neuter or fem. twâ agree ? not with the masc. hringas. By earm-reáf we are probably to understand long pendant sleeves, no doubt of some costly material.

2405. feol ? 2407. i. e. death. 2420. MS. eorclan-stánas.

ofer ýða ful,	over *the* cup of waves,
rice þeóden;	*the* powerful king;
he under rande gecranc:	he fell beneath *his* shield:
gehwearf þá in Francna fæðm	departed then into *the* grasp of *the* Franks
feorh cyninges,	*the* king's life,
breóst-gewǽdu,	*his* breast-weeds,
and se beáh somod:	and the collar also:
wyrsan wig-frecan	worse warriors
wæl reafedon,	plunder'd *the* fall'n,
æfter gúð-sceare;	after *the* lot of war;
Geáta leóde	*the* Goths' people
hreá-wíc heoldon.	held *the* mansion of *the* dead.
Heal swége onfeng:	*The* hall receiv'd *the* sound:
Wealhþeów maþelode,	Wealhtheow spake,
heó fore þǽm werede spræc:	before the company she said:
Brúc ðisses beáges,	"Use this collar,
Beowulf leófa,	dear Beowulf,
hyse mid hǽle,	O youth, with prosperity,
and þisses hrægles neót,	and this mantle enjoy,
þeód-gestreóna,	*these* lordly treasures,
and geþeóh tela:	and thrive well:
cén þec mid cræfte,	animate thyself with vigour,
and þyssum cnyhtum wes	and to these boys be
lára liðe;	in counsels gentle;
ic þe þæs leán geman.	I will therefore be mindful to reward thee.
Hafast þú gefered,	Thou hast *that* achiev'd,
þæt ðe feor and neáh,	that thee far and near,
ealne wíde-ferhð,	throughout all time,
weras ehtigað,	men will esteem,
efne swá síde	even as widely
swá sǽ bebúgeð	as *the* sea encircles

2429. MS. reafeden. 2440. MS. þeo.

windge eard-weallas,	*the* windy land-walls.
Wes þenden þû lifige,	Be while thou livest
æþeling eádig :	*a* prosperous noble :
ic þe an tela	I will well grant thee
sinc-gestreóna :	precious treasures :
beó þû sunum mînum	be thou to my sons
dǽdum gedéfe,	gentle in deeds,
dreám-healdende.	holding *them* in joy.
Her is æghwylc eorl	Here is every man
oþrum getrýwe,	to other true,
módes milde,	mild of mood,
man-drihtne hold ;	to *his* liege lord faithful ;
þegnas syndon geþwǽre,	*the* thanes are united,
þeód eal gearo,	*the* people all ready,
druncne dryht-guman	*the* drunken vassals
dóð swá ic bidde.	do as I bid."
Eóde þá tó setle :	*She* went then to *her* seat :
þær wæs symbla cyst,	there was of feasts *the* choicest,
druncon wîn weras	*the* men drank wine,
wyrd ne cuþon,	fate *they* knew not,
geósceaft grimne,	grim calamity,
swá hit agangen wearð	how it had befallen
eorla manegum.	many *a* man.
Syþðan æfen cwom,	After evening came,
and him Hróðgár gewât	and Hrothgar had departed
tó hófe sînum,	to his court,
rîce to reste,	*the* powerful *one* to rest,
reced weardode	guarded *the* mansion
unrîm eorla,	countless warriors,
swá hie oft ǽr dydon ;	as they oft ere had done ;

2452. MS. wind geard weallas.
2457. MS. suna, originally perhaps sunū.
2463. MS. heol, the *e* with a stroke through it.
2472. geocsceaft ?

benc-þelu bêredon :	*they* bared *the* bench-floor :
hit geond-brǽded wearð	it was overspread
beddum and bolstrum.	with beds and bolsters.
Beór-scealca sum,	Of *the* beer-skinkers one,
fús and fǽge,	ready and fated,
flet-reste gebeág :	bow'd to *his* domestic couch :
setton him tó heáfdum	they set at *their* heads
hilde randas,	*their* disks of war,
bord-wudu beorhtan,	*their* shield-wood bright ;
þær on bence wæs,	there on *the* bench was,
ofer æþelinge,	over *the* noble,
ýþ-gesýne	easy to be seen
heaþo-steápa helm,	*his* high martial helm,
hringed byrne,	*his* ringed byrnie,
þræc-wudu þrymlíc.	*and* war-wood stout.
Wæs þeáw hyra,	*It* was their custom,
þæt híe oft wǽron	that they oft were
an wíg gearwe,	for war prepar'd,
ge æt hám ge on herge,	both at home and in *the* host,
ge gehwæþer þára ;	or both of them ;
efne swylce mǽla	just at such times
swylce hira man-dryhtne	as to their liege lord
þearf gesǽlde	need befel
wæs seó þeód tilu.	was the people ready.

XIX.

Sigon þá tó slǽpe :	*They* sank then to sleep :
sum sáre ongeald	one sorely paid for
æfen-reste,	*his* evening rest,

2486. Why the beór-scealc was fús and fǽge does not appear, as no further mention of him occurs : probably some lines are wanting.

2488. MS. heafdon. 2493. MS. gesene.

2496. MS. þrec. 2507. MS. angeald.

swâ him ful oft gelamp,	as to them full oft had happen'd,
siþðan gold-sele	since *the* gold-hall
Grendel warode,	Grendel occupied,
unriht æfnde,	unrighteousness perpetrated,
oþþæt ende becwom,	until *an* end came,
swylt æfter synnum.	death after sins.
Þæt gesŷne wearð,	That was seen,
wîd-cuþ werum,	wide-known to men,
þætte wrecend þâ-gyt	that *an* avenger yet
lîfde æfter lâþum,	liv'd after *the* foe,
lange þrage,	for *a* long space,
æfter gûð-ceare,	after *the* battle-care,
Grendles môdor;	Grendle's mother;
ides aglǽc wîf	*the* woman, wretched crone,
yrmðe gemunde,	was of *her* misery mindful,
seô þe wæter-egesan	she who *the* watery horrors
wunian scolde,	must inhabit,
cealde streâmas,	*the* cold streams,
siþðan Cain gewearð	after Cain became
to ecg-banan	*the* murderer
ângan brêþer,	of his *only* brother,
fæderen-mæge.	*his* father's son.
He þâ fâg gewât	He then blood-stain'd departed
morþre gemearcod,	by murder mark'd,
man-dreâm fleôn,	fleeing *the* joy of man,
westen warode;	dwelt in *the* waste;
þanon wôc fela	thence arose many
geosceaft-gâsta,	wretched sprites,
wæs þǽra Grendel sum,	of those was Grendel one,
heoro-wearh hetelic;	*the* hateful fell wolf;
se æt Heorote fand	who had at Heorot found
wæccendne wer	*a* watching man

2524. MS. se þe.

2527. MS. camp wearð.

2536. geocsceaft?

wîges bîdan,	*the* conflict awaiting,
þær him [se] aglǽca	where for him the miserable being
æt-grǽdig wearð;	food-greedy was;
hwæþre he gemunde	yet he remember'd
mægenes strenge,	*the* strength of *his* might,
ginfæste gife,	*the* abundant gift,
ðe him God sealde,	that God had given him,
and him to ânwaldan	and in him as sole Ruler
âre gelyfde,	piously trusted,
frôfre and fultum;	*his* comfort and support;
ðý he þone feônd ofercwom,	therefore he overcame the foe,
gehnægde helle gâst;	subdued *the* sprite of hell;
þá he heân gewât,	then he humble departed,
dreáme bedǽled,	of joy depriv'd,
deâþ-wîc seôn,	*the* mansion of death to see,
man-cynnes feônd;	*the* foe of mankind;
ac his môdor þá-gyt,	but his mother yet,
gifre and galg-môd,	greedy and gallows-minded,
gegân wolde	would go
sorhfulne sið,	*a* sorrowful journey,
sunu þeôd-wrecan.	direfully to avenge *her* son.
Com þá tô Heorote,	*She* came then to Heorot,
ðær Hring-Dene	where *the* Ring-Danes
geond þæt sæld swǽfon.	throughout the hall were sleeping.
Ðá þær sôna wearð	Then forthwith there was
edhwyrft eorlum.	*a* relapse to *the* warriors.
Siþðan inne fealh	When in rush'd
Grendles môdor,	Grendle's mother,

2542. se is not in the MS. 2543. MS. græpe.
2544. he, i.e. Beowulf.
2546. MS. gimfæste. See Boet. p. 179. edit. Rawl.
2555. sécan? 2557. MS. and. 2564. MS. swæfun.
2566. That is of the miseries caused by Grendel.

wæs se grŷre læssa,
efne swâ micle
swâ bið mægþa cræft,
wîg-grŷre wîfes,
bewæpned-men,
þonne heoru-bunden,
hamere geþuren,
sweord swâte fâh,
swîn ofer helme,
ecgum þyhtig,
andweard scîreð.
Þâ wæs on healle
heard-ecg togen,
sweord ofer setlum,
sîd-rand manig
hafen handa-fæst,
helm ne gemunde,
byrnan sîde,
þâ hine se brôga angeât.
Heô wæs on ôfste,
wolde ût þanon
feore beorgan,
þâ heô onfunden wæs.
Hraðe heô æðelinga
ânne hæfde
fæste befangen,
þâ heô to fenne gang;
se wæs Hrôðgâre
hæleþa leôfost,
on gesiðes hâd,
be sǽm tweônum,

was the terror less,
by just as much
as is *the* power of maidens,
the hostile dread from women,
to *that* from *an* arm'd man,
when strongly bound,
with hammer beaten,
the sword stain'd with gore,
the swine above *the* helm,
doughty of edges,
present shears,
Then was in *the* hall
the hard edge drawn,
the sword over *the* seats,
many *a* broad disk
rais'd fast in hand,
helm *the warrior* remember'd not,
nor ample byrnie,
when terror was on him shed.
She was in haste,
would out from thence
save *her* life,
as she was discover'd.
Of *the* nobles quickly she
had one
fast seiz'd,
as to *the* fen she went;
he was to Hrothgar
of heroes dearest,
in *a* comrades' character,
between *the* seas,

2578. Thorkelin has dyhttig. In the MS. the word is destroyed.

rîce rand-wîga,	*a* powerful shield-warrior,
þone þe heô on reste abreat	whom she on *his* couch destroy'd,
blǽd-fæstne beorn.	*a* prosperous hero.
Næs Beowulf ðær,	Beowulf was not there,
ac wæs oþer in	for another dwelling had been
ǽr geteohhod,	before assign'd,
æfter maþðum-gife,	after *the* costly gift,
mǽrum Geâte.	to *the* renown'd Goth.
Hreâm wearð in Heorote;	There was *a* cry in Heorot;
heô under heolfre genam	she amid clotted gore took
cuþe folme:	*the well* known hand;
cearu wæs geniwod	grief had renew'd
geworden in wicum.	become in the dwellings.
Ne wæs þæt gewrixle til,	That was no good exchange,
þæt hie on bâ healfa	that they on both sides
bicgan scoldon	must buy
freônda feorum.	with *the* lives of friends.
Þâ wæs frôd cyning,	Then was *the* wise king,
hâr hilde-rinc,	*the* hoary man of war,
on hreôn môde,	in angry mood,
syðþan he aldor-þegn	when he *his* senior thane
unlyfigendne,	lifeless,
þone deôrestan,	the dearest,
deâdne wisse.	knew *to be* dead.
Hraþe wæs tô bûre	Quickly to *his* bower was
Beowulf fetod,	Beowulf fetch'd,
sigor-eâdig secg.	*the* victorious warrior.
Samod ǽr dæge	Together ere day
eôde eorla sum,	went with some of *his* earls
æþele cempa,	*the* noble champion,
self mid gesiðum,	himself with *his* comrades,
þær se snotera bâd,	to where the wise *prince* awaited,
hwæþre him Alwalda	whether him *the* All-powerful

2612. MS. wicun.

2632. MS. alfwalda.

æfre wille,
æfter weâ-spelle
wyrde gefremman.
Gang ðâ æfter flôre
fyrd-wyrðe man
mid his hand-scole,
heal-wudu dynede,
þæt he þone wisan
wordum hnægde,
freân Ingwina;
frægn gif him wǽre,
æfter neôd-lâðu,
niht getǽse.

ever would,
after *the* sad intelligence,
his fortune prosper,
Went then along *the* floor
the warlike man
with his suite,
(*the* hall-wood resounded)
till that he the wise *prince*
by *his* words sooth'd,
the Ingwinas' lord;
ask'd if he had had,
after *the* urgent summons,
an easy night.

XX.

Hrôðgâr maþelode,
helm Scyldinga:
Ne frin þû æfter sǽlum;
sorh is geniwod
Denigea leôdum;
deâd is Æschere,
Yrmenlâfes
yldra brôþor,
mîn rûn-wita,
and mîn rǽd-bora,
eaxl-gestealla,
þonne we on orlege
hafelan wêredon,
þonne hniton feþan

Hrothgar spake,
the Scylding's protector:
"Ask thou not after happiness;
sorrow is renew'd
to *the* Danes' people;
Æschere is dead,
Yrmenlaf's
elder brother,
my confident,
and my counsellor,
my near attendant,
when we in war
our heads defended,
when hosts against *each other*
rush'd

2635. MS. wyrpe. 2638. MS. scale.
2644. i.e. after having sent so urgent a summons to Beowulf.

eoferas cnysedon :	*and* boar-crests crash'd :
swylc scolde eorl wesan	such should *a* man be,
ǽr-gód * *	preeminently good * *
swylc Æschere wæs.	such as Æschere was.
Wearð him on Heorote	To him in Heorot there has been
tő hand-banan	for murderer
wæl-gæst wæfre.	*a* deadly wandering guest.
Ic ne wât hwæþer	I know not whether
atol æse-wlanc	*the* fell glorier in carrion
eft siðas teâh,	*her* steps back has traced,
fylle gefrefrod.	with slaughter comforted.
Heő þa fǽhðe wræc,	She has avenged the quarrel,
þe þû gystran niht	for that thou yesternight
Grendel cwealdest,	didst Grendel slay,
þurh hǽstne hâd,	through *thy* vehement nature,
heardum clammum ;	with hard grasps ;
forþan he tő lange	for that he too long
leőde mîne	my people
wanode and wyrde :	diminish'd and destroy'd :
he æt wîge gecrang,	he in battle succumb'd,
ealdres scyldig,	*his* life forfeiting,
and nû oþer cwom	and now is come another
mihtig mân-scaða,	mighty fell destroyer,
wolde hyre mæg wrecan ;	*who* would her son avenge,
gefeor hafað	*she* far off has
fǽhðe gestǽled ;	warfare establish'd,
þæs þe þincean mæg,	as *it* may seem,
þegne monegum,	for many *a* thane,
se þe æfter sinc-gyfan	who after *his* treasure-giver
on sefan greőteþ,	in spirit weeps,
hreþer-bealo hearde.	in hard heart-affliction.
Nû seő hand ligeð,	Now the hand lies *low*,
se þe eow wel hwylcra	which you for every

2660. MS. cnysedan. 2670. MS. gefrægnod.

wilna dohte.	desire avail'd.
Ic þæt lond-bûend,	I it *the* land's inhabitants,
leóde mîne,	my people,
sele-rǽdende,	*my* hall-counsellors,
secgan hýrde,	have heard say,
þæt hîe gesawon	that they have seen
swylce twêgen	two such
micle mearc-stapan	huge march-stalkers
môras healdan,	inhabiting *the* moors,
ellor-gæstas,	stranger guests,
ðǽra oðer wæs,	of which one was,
þæs þe hîe gewîslîcost	from what they most certainly
gewîtan meahton,	could know,
idese onlîcnes,	*a* woman's likeness,
oþer earm-sceapen,	*the* other wretched wight,
on weres wæstmum	in *a* man's figure,
wræc-lastas træd,	trod *a* wanderer's footsteps,
næfne he wæs mâra þon	save that he greater was than
ǽnig man oþer,	any other man,
þone on gear-dagum	whom in days of yore
Grendel nemdon	Grendel nam'd
fold-bûende :	earth's inhabitants :
nó hîe fæder cunnon,	they *a* father know not,
hwæþer him ǽnig wæs	whether any to them was
ǽr acenned	before born
dyrnra gâsta.	of *the* dark ghosts.
Hîe dygel lond	They *that* secret land
warigeað wulf-hleóðu,	inhabit, *the* wolf's retreats,
windige næssas,	windy nesses,
frecne fen-gelâd,	*the* dangerous fen-path,
ðær fyrgen-streâm,	where *the* mountain-stream,
under næssa genipu,	under *the* nesses' mists.
niþer gewîteð,	downward flows,

2706. MS. onlicnæs.

flôd under foldan.	*the* flood under *the* earth.
Nis þæt feor heonon,	*It* is not far thence,
mil gemearces,	*a* mile's distance,
þæt se mere standeð,	that *the* mere stands.
ofer þǽm hongiað	over which hang
hrinde-bearwas;	barky groves;
wudu wyrtum fæst	*a* wood fast by *its* roots
wæter oferhelmað:	*the* water overshadows:
þær mæg nihta gehwǽm	there every night may
nîð-wundor seón,	*a* dire miracle be seen,
fŷr on flôde.	fire in *the* flood.
Nô þæs frôd leofað	No one so wise lives
gumena bearna	of *the* children of men,
þæt þone grund wite.	who the bottom knows.
Þeâh þe hǽð-stapa	Although *the* heath-stalker,
hundum geswenced,	by *the* hounds wearied,
heorot hornum trum,	*the* hart firm of horns,
holt-wudu sêce,	seek *that* holt-wood,
feorran geflymed,	driven from afar,
ǽr he feorh seleð,	ere will he life resign,
aldor on ofre,	*his* breath upon *the* bank,
ǽr he in wille	ere he will in *it*
hafelan [hŷdan]:	[hide] *his* head:
nis þæt heoru stôw;	that is no holy place;
þonon ŷð-geblond	thence *the* wave-blending
up-astîgeð	rises up
won to wolcnum,	dark to *the* clouds,
þonne wind styreð	when *the* wind stirs
lâð-gewidru,	hateful tempests,
oðþæt lyft dryrmað,	until *the* air grows gloomy,
roderas reôtað.	*the* heavens shed tears.
Nû is se rǽd gelang	Now is counsel long
eft æt þe ânum;	again of thee alone;

2748. hydan added from conjecture. 2755. MS. drysmað.

eard git ne const,
frecne stówe,
þær þû findan miht
fela-sinnigne secg.
Séç gif þû dyrre;
ic þe þa fǽhðe
feó leánige,
eald-gestreónum,
swâ ic ǽr dyde,
wunden-golde,
gyf þû onweg cymest.

the spot *thou* yet knowest not,
the perilous place,
where thou mayest find
this much sinful man.
Seek *it* if thou durst;
I will thee for the strife
with money recompense,
with old treasures,
as I before did,
with twisted gold,
if away thou comest."

XXI.

Beowulf maþelode,
bearn Ecgþeówes:
Ne sorga snotor guma,
sêlre bið æghwǽm
þæt he his freónd wrece,
þonne he fela murne.
Ure æghwylc sceal
ende gebidan
worolde lífes:
wyrce se þe môte
dômas ǽr deáðe;
þæt bið driht-guman
unlífgendum
æfter sêlest.
Arís ríces weard,
uton hraþe feran
Grendles magan
gang sceawigan:
ic hit þe gehâte,

Beowulf spake,
Ecgtheow's son:
"Sorrow not, sage man,
better 'tis for every one
that he his friend avenge,
than that he greatly mourn.
Each of us must
an end await
of *this* world's life:
let him who can, work
high deeds ere death;
to *the* warrior that will be,
when lifeless,
afterwards best.
Arise, guardian of *the* realm,
let us quickly go
of Grendel's parent
the course to see:
I promise it thee,

2768. MS. wundum.

2780. MS. dome

nó heó on holm losað,	not into *the* sea shall she escape,
ne on foldan fæþm,	nor into earth's bosom,
ne on fyrgen-holt,	nor into *the* mountain-wood,
ne on geofones grund,	nor in ocean's ground,
gá þær heó wille.	go whither she will.
Þys dógor þú	This day *do* thou
geþyld hafa	have patience
weána gehwylces,	for every woe,
swâ ic þe wêne tó.	as I expect from thee."
Ahleóp ðá se gomela,	Leapt up then the aged *man*,
Gode þancode,	thank'd God,
mihtigan Drihtne,	*the* mighty Lord,
þæs se man gespræc.	for what the man had said.
Þá wæs Hróðgâre	Then was for Hrothgar
hors gebǽted,	*a* horse bitted,
wicg wunden-feax.	*a* steed with curled mane.
Wísa fengel	*The* wise prince
geatolíc gengde ;	stately went ;
gum-feþa stóp	*a* troop of men proceeded,
lind-hæbbendra.	shield-bearing.
Lastas wæron	Traces were
æfter wald-scaþan	after *the* forest-spoiler
wíde gesýne,	widely seen,
gang ofer grundas	*her* course o'er *the* grounds
gegnum-for,	before them,
ofer myrcan mór :	over *the* murky moor :
mago-þegna bær	of *their* fellow thanes *she* bore
þone sêlestan	the best
sawolleásne,	soulless,
þâra þe mid Hróðgâre	of those who with Hrothgar
hâm eahtode.	*their* home defended.

2789. MS. he, and helm.
2792. MS. gyfenes.
2793. MS. he.
2806. MS. gende.
2810. swaþum.
2819. ealgode ?

Ofer-eóde þá
æþelinga bearn
steáp stán-hliðo,
stíge nearwe,
enge ánpaðas,
uncuð, gelád,
neowle nǽssas,
nicor-húsa fela.
He feara sum
beforan gengde
wísra monna,
wong sceáwian,
oþþæt he fǽringa
fyrgen-beámas
ofer hárne stán
hleónian funde,
wynleásne wudu;
wæter under stód
dreórig and gedréfed;
Denum eallum wæs,
winum Scyldinga,
weorce on móde
tó geþolianne,
ðegne monegum,
oncyð eorla gehwǽm,
syðþan Æscheres,
on þám holm-clife,
hafelan métton.
Flód blóde weol,
folc tósægon
hátan heolfre;
horn stundum song
fúslíc furþon leóð.

Went over then
these sons of nobles
deep rocky gorges,
a narrow road,
strait lonely paths,
an unknown way,
precipitous headlands,
nicker-houses many.
He with *a* few
went before,
wise men,
the plain to view,
until he suddenly
mountain-trees,
o'er *the* hoar rock
found leaning,
a joyless wood;
water stood beneath
gory and troubled;
To all *the* Danes *it* was,
the Scyldings' friends,
grievous in mind
to suffer,
to many *a* thane,
portentous to every warrior,
when of Æschere,
on the sea-shore,
the head *they* found.
The flood boil'd with blood,
the people look'd on
the hot gore;
the horn at times sang
also *a* death song.

2852. Thork. fughton. The word has perished from the MS.

Feþa eal gesæt ;	*The* band all sat ;
gesawon þâ æfter wætere	*they* saw along *the* water
wyrm-cynnes fela,	of *the* worm-kind many,
sêllîce sǽ-dracan,	strange sea dragons,
sund cunnian ;	tempting *the* deep ;
swylce on nǽs-hleoþum	also in *the* headland-clefts
nicras licgean,	nickers lying,
ða on undern mǽl	which at morning time
oft bewitigað	oft keep
sorhfulne sið	*their* sorrowful course
on segl-râde,	on *the* sail-road,
wyrmas and wildeôr :	worms and wild beasts :
hîe onweg hruron,	they sped away,
bitere and gebolgne,	bitter and angry,
bearhtm ongeâton,	*the* instant they heard
gûð-horn galan :	*the* war-horn sing :
sumne Geâta leôd,	one *the* Goths' lord,
of flân-bogan,	from *his* arrow-bow,
feores getwǽfde,	from life separated,
ŷð-gewinnes,	*from his* wave-strife,
þæt him on aldre stôd	*so* that in his vitals stood
here-stræl hearda :	*the* hard war-shaft :
he on holme wæs	he in *the* sea was
sundes þe sænra,	in swimming the slower,
þâ hyne swylt fornam.	when him death took off.
Hraþe wearð on ŷðum,	Quickly on *the* waves was *he*
mid eofer-spreôtum,	with boar-spears
heoro-hôcihtum,	sharply hook'd,
hearde genearwod,	hardly press'd,
nîða genæged,	humbled of *his* mischiefs,
and on nǽs togen,	and on *the* headland drawn,
wundorlic wǽg-bora :	*the* wondrous wave-bearer :

2877. MS. þe. 2880. MS. hoc yhtum.
2884. i.e. the monster that Beowulf had shot, l. 2869 sqq.

weras sceâwedon	*the* men gaz'd on
grŷrelîcne gist.	*the* grisly guest.
Gyrede hine Beowulf	Clad himself Beowulf
eorl-gewæ̂dum :	in warlike weeds :
nalles for ealdre mearn ;	for life *he* car'd not ;
scolde here-byrne,	*his* martial byrnie must,
hondum gebroden,	with hands twisted,
sîd and searo-fâh,	ample and curiously variegated.
sund cunnian,	tempt *the* deep,
seô ðe bân-cofan	which *his* body
beorgan cuþe,	could *well* secure,
þæt him hilde grâp	*so* that hostile gripe his
hreþre ne mihte,	breast might not,
eorres inwit-feng,	*the* wrothful's wily grasp,
aldre gesceþðan :	*his* life injure :
ac se hwîta helm	but the bright helm
hafelan wêrede,	guarded *that* head,
se þe mere-grundas	(which *the* sea-grounds
mengan scolde.	should disturb,
sêcan sund-gebland,	seek *the* mingle of *the* deep,)
since geweorþad,	with treasure ornamented,
befongen freâ-wrasnum,	with noble chains encircled,
swâ hine fyrn-dagum	as it in days of yore
worhte wæpna smið,	*the* armourer wrought,
wundrum teôde,	wondrously fram'd,
besette swîn-lîcum,	beset with forms of swine,
þæt hine syððan nô	*so* that it afterwards no
brond ne beado-mecas	brand nor battle-falchions
bîtan nê meahton.	might bite.
Næs þæt þonne mæ̂tost	Nor then was that *the* least
mægen-fultuma,	of powerful aids,
þæt him on ðearfe lâh	which at need him lent

2891. "Helm nor hauberk's twisted mail."—Gray.

þyle Hrôðgâres.
Wæs þǽm hæft-mece
Hrunting nama;
þæt wæs án foran
eald-gestreóna;
ecg wæs íren
ater-tânum fáh,
ahyrded heaþo-swâte;
næfre hit æt hilde ne swâc
manna ǽngum,
þâra þe hit mit mundum bewand,
se ðe grýre siðas
gegân dorste,
folc-stede fara.
Næs þæt forma sið,
þæt hit ellen-weorc
æfnan scolde:
huru ne gemunde
mago Ecglâfes,
eafoþes cræftig,
þæt he ǽr gespræc,
wíne druncen,
þâ he þæs wæpnes onlâh
sêlran sweord-frecan.
Selfa ne dorste
under ýða gewin
aldre genêþan,
drihtscype dreógan;
þær he dôm forleás
ellen-mǽrþum;

Hrothgar's orator.
Was of that hafted falchion
Hrunting *the* name;
that had before been one
of *the* old treasures;
its edge was iron
tainted with poisonous twigs,
harden'd with warrior-blood;
never in battle had it deceiv'd
any man,
of those who brandish'd it with hands,
who ways of terror
durst go,
the trysting place of perils.
That time was not *the* first,
that it *a* work of valour
should achieve:
at all events remember'd not
Ecglaf's son,
crafty in trouble,
what he ere had said,
with wine drunken,
when he the weapon lent
to *a* better sworded warrior.
Himself durst not
amid *the* strife of waves
venture *his* life,
a noble deed perform;
there he *his* credit lost
for valorous deeds;

2917. Hunferth. See l. 1002.
2922. See note on l. 3070.
2935. See l. 1003.
2945. MS. dome.

ne wæs þǽm oðrum swá,	not so was *it* with *the* other,
syðþan he hine to gúðe	when himself for battle he
gegyred hæfde.	had prepared.

XXII.

Beowulf maðelode,	Beowulf spake,
bearn Ecgþeówes :	Ecgtheow's son :
Geþenc nú se mǽra	"Let now bear in mind the great
maga Healfdenes,	son of Healfdene,
snottra fengel,	*the* sagacious prince,
nú ic eom siðes fús,	now I am ready for *my* journey,
gold-wine gumena,	gold-friend of men,
hwæt wit geó spræcon :	what we have before spoken :
Gif ic æt þearfe	If I for thy
þínre scolde	need should
aldre linnan,	lose my life,
þæt þú me á wǽre	that thou wouldst ever be to me,
forð-gewítenum	*when* hence departed,
on fæder stæle.	in *a* father's stead.
Wes þú mundbora	Be thou *a* guardian
mínum mago-þegnum,	to my fellow thanes,
hond-gesellum,	*my* near comrades,
gif mec hild nime ;	if war take me *off ;*
swylce þú ða madmas,	also *do* thou the treasures,
þe þú me sealdest,	which thou hast given me,
Hróðgár leófa,	dear Hrothgar,
Higeláce onsend :	send to Hygelac :
mæg þonne on þǽm golde ongitan	then by that gold may know
Geáta dryhten,	*the* Goth's lord,
geseón sunu Hreðles,	the *son* of Hrethel see,
þonne he on þæt sinc stárað,	when he on that treasure gazes,

2974. MS. Hrædles.

þæt ic gum-cystum	that I for *his* bounties
gôdne funde,	found *a* good
beâga bryttan :	distributor of rings :
breâc þonne môste.	*I* enjoyed *them* when *I* might.
And þû Hunferð læt	And do thou let Hunferth
ealde lâfe,	*the* ancient relic,
wrætlic wig-sweord,	*the* curious war-sword,
wid-cuðne man,	*the* far-fam'd man,
heard-ecg habban :	*the* hard-edged, have :
ic me mid Hruntinge	I will with Hrunting me
dôm gewyrce,	work renown,
oþðe mec deâð nimeð.	or me death shall take."
Æfter þǽm wordum	After those words
Weder-Geâta leôd	*the* Weder-Goths' lord
êfste mid elne,	with ardour hasten'd,
nalas andsware	nor answer
bidan wolde :	would await :
brim-wylm onfeng	*the* ocean-surge receiv'd
hilde rince.	*the* warlike man.
Ðâ wæs hwîl dæges	Then was *a* day's space
ǽr he þone grund-wong	ere he the ground-plain
ongytan mihte.	could perceive.
Sona þæt onfunde	Forthwith discover'd
seô ðe flôda begong	*she* who *the* floods' course
heoro-gifre beheold	bloodthirsty had held
hund missera,	*a* hundred years,
grim and grǽdig,	fierce and greedy,
þæt þær gumena sum	that there *a* man
ælwihta eard	*the* country of strange creatures
ufan cunnode ;	was from above exploring ;
grâp þâ tô-geanes,	then grasp'd towards *him*,
gûð-rinc gefeng	*the* warrior seiz'd

2982. MS. wæg sweord, wig-sweord = gúð-sweord.
2997. MS. mehte. 2999. MS. se þe.

atolan clommum :	in *her* horrid clutches :
no þý ǽr in-gestód	*yet* not the sooner did *she* penetrate
hálan lice,	*the* sound body,
hring útan-ymb beárh,	*for the* ring-*mail* protected *him* without,
þæt heó þone fýrd-hom	*so* that she that war-case
þurh-fón ne mihte,	might not pierce through,
locene leóðo-syrcan,	*the* lock'd limb-sark,
láþan fingrum.	with *her* hostile fingers.
Bær þá seó brim-wylf,	Bore then the sea-wolf,
þá heó to botme com,	when she to *the* bottom came,
hringa þengel	*the* prince of rings
to hófe sinum,	to her dwelling,
swá he ne mihte nó,	so *that* he might not
he þǽm módig wæs,	(resolute as he was)
wæpna gewealdan ;	his weapons command ;
ac hine wundra þæs fela	but him therefore many wondrous beings
swencte on sunde,	oppress'd in *the* deep,
sǽ-deór monig	many *a* sea-beast
hilde tuxum	with *its* battle-tusks
here-syrcan bræc,	*the* martial sark brake,
ehton aglǽcan.	*the* miserable beings pursued *him*.
Þá se eorl ongeat	Then the warrior found
þæt he [in] níð-sele	that he in *a* hostile hall,
nát hwylcum wæs,	*he* knew not what, was,
þær him nǽnig wæter	where him no water
wihte ne sceþede,	*in* aught could scathe,
ne him for hróf-sele	nor him for *the* roofed-hall
hrinan ne mihte	could touch

3009. MS. gescod.
3014. MS. leodo.
3016. MS. wyl. See l. 3202.
3024. MS. swecte.
3030. in is inserted as necessary to the sense.
3035. MS. mehte

fǽr-grîpe flôdes ;	*the* flood's sudden gripe ;
fýr-leóht geseah,	*he* saw *a* fire-light,
blâcne leóman,	*a* pale beam,
beorhte scînan :	brightly shine :
ongeat þâ se gôda	then the good *warrior* perceiv'd
grund-wyrgenne,	*the* ground-wolf,
mere-wîf mihtig ;	*the* mighty mere-wife ;
mægen-ræs forgeaf	*he* made *a* powerful onslaught
hilde bille ;	with *his* war-falchion ;
heoro-sweng nê ofteâh,	*the* sword-blow withheld not,
þæt hire on hafelan	*so* that on her head
hring-mǽl agôl	*the* ringed brand sang
grýrelîc gûð-leoð.	*a* horrid war-song.
Þâ se gist onfand	Then the guest found
þæt se beado-leôma	that the war-beam
bîtan nolde,	would not bite,
aldre sceþðan,	life injure,
ac seô ecg geswâc	but *that* the edge fail'd
þeôdne æt þearfe ;	*its* lord at need ;
þolode ǽr fela	erst *it* had endur'd many
hond-gemôta,	hand-encounters,
helm oft gescær,	*the* helmet often slash'd,
fǽges fyrd-hrægl ;	*the* fated's war-garb ;
þâ wæs forma sîð	then was *the* first time
deôrum madme,	for *the* precious treasure,
þæt his dôm alæg.	that its power fail'd.
Eft wæs ânrǽd,	Again was resolute,
nalas elnes læt,	slacken'd not *his* ardour,
mǽrða gemyndig,	of *his* great deeds mindful,
mæg Hygelâces ;	Hygelâc's kinsman ;
wearp ðâ wunden-mǽl,	cast then *the* twisted brand,
wrættum gebunden,	curiously bound,

3045. MS. hord swenge.
3048. MS. grædig.
3065. MS. Hylaces.
3066. MS. wundel.

yrre oretta,
þæt hit on eorðan læg
stið and stýl-ecg,
strenge getrûwode,
mund-grípe mægenes;
swâ sceal man dôn,
þonne he æt gûðe
gegân þenceð
longsumne lôf,
nâ ymb his líf cearað.
Gefeng ðâ be eaxle,
nalas for fǽhðe mearn,
gûð-Geâta leód
Grendles môdor:
brægd þâ beadwe heard,
þâ he gebolgen wæs,
feorh-geniðlan,
þæt heô on flet gebeâh.
Heô him eft hraþe
hand-leân forgeald
grimman grâpum,
and him tô-geanes feng:
ofer-wearp þâ wérig-
môd
wígena strengest,
feþe-cempa,
þæt he on fylle wearð.
Ofsæt þâ þone sele-gyst,

the angry champion,
so that on *the* earth it lay
stiff and steel-edged,
in *his* strength he trusted,
in *his* hand-gripe of power;
so must *a* man do,
when in battle he
thinks of gaining
lasting praise,
nor about his life cares,
Seiz'd then by *the* shoulder,
(*he* reck'd not of *her* malice)
the war-Goths' lord,
Grendel's mother:
then *the* fierce warrior drag'd
(as he was incens'd,)
the mortal foe,
so that on *the* place she bow'd.
She him again quickly
paid *a* hand-reward
with *her* fierce grasps,
and at him caught:
overthrew then *the* weary of
mood,
of warriors strongest,
the active champion,
so that he was about to perish.
She then press'd down the hall-
guest,

3070. This is to be understood literally; the weapon, whether sword or axe, being, like those of Homer's heroes, of bronze or copper, and having an edge of iron or steel fastened on it by means of rivets. Specimens of this kind are preserved in the Museum of Northern Antiquities at Copenhagen.

and hyre seaxe geteâh,
brâd brûn-ecg;
wolde hire bearn wrecan,
ângan eaferan.
Him on eaxle læg
breóst-net broden,
þæt gebeârh feore,
wið ord and wið ecge
ingang forstód.
Hæfde ðâ forðsiðod
sunu Ecgþeówes
under ginne grund,
Geâta cempa,
nemne him heaðo-byrne
helpe gefremede,
here-net hearde,
and hâlig God
geweold wíg-sigor;
wítig Drihten,
rodera Rǽdend,
hit on ryht gescód
yðelíce,
syþðan he eft astód.

and her poniard drew,
broad, brown-edged;
she would avenge her son,
her only offspring.
On his shoulder lay
the braided breast-net,
which *his* life protected,
against point and against edge
entrance withstood.
Had then perish'd
Ecgtheow's son
under *the* spacious ground,
the Goths' champion,
had not him *his* martial byrnie
help afforded,
his war-net hard,
and holy God
in war triumphant, rul'd;
the wise Lord,
Ruler of *the* skies,
decided it with justice
easily,
when he again stood up.

XXIII.

Geseah þâ on searwum
sige-eâdig bil,
eald sweord eótenisc
ecgum þyhtig,
wígena weorðmynd;

Then saw *he* among *the* arms
a victorious falchion,
an old eotenish sword
of edges doughty,
the pride of warriors;

3104. MS. forsiðod.
3106. MS. gynne.
3115. MS gesced.
3117. he, i.e. Beowulf.

þæt [wæs] wæpna cyst,	that [was] of weapons choicest,
buton hit wæs máre þonne	save it was greater than
ǽnig mon oðer	any other man
tő beadu-láce	to *the* game of war
ætberan meahte,	might bear forth,
gőd and geatolíc,	good and elegant,
giganta geweorc.	*the* work of giants.
He gefeng þâ fetel-hilt,	Then seiz'd he *the* knotted hilt,
freca Scyldinga;	*the* Scyldings' warrior;
hreőh and heoro-grim,	fierce and deadly grim,
hring-mǽl gebrægd,	*the* ringed brand *he* drew,
aldres orwêna	of life hopeless
yrringa slôh,	angrily struck,
þæt hire wið halse	*so* that against her neck
heard grâpode,	*it* grip'd *her* hard,
bân-hringas bræc,	*her* bone-rings brake,
bil eal ðurh-wód,	*the* falchion pass'd through all
fǽgne flæsc-homan:	*her* fated carcase:
heő on flet gecrong.	on *the* ground she sank.
Sweord wæs swâtig,	*The* sword was gory,
secg weorce gefêh;	*the* warrior in *his* work rejoiced;
lixte se leőma,	the beam shone,
leőht inne stőd;	light stood within,
efne swâ of heofene	even as from heaven
hâdre scîneð	serenely shines
rodores candel.	*the* candle of *the* firmament.
He æfter recede wlât;	He through *the* dwelling look'd;
hwearf þâ be wealle,	then by *the* wall turn'd,
wæpen hafenade,	*his* weapon rais'd
heard be hiltum,	hard by *the* hilt,
Higeláces ðegn,	Hygelac's thane,
yrre and ânræd;	angry and resolv'd;

3123. wæs is not in the MS., but inserted as necessary to the sense.
3146. MS. hefene. 3154. MS. unræd.

næs seó ecg fracod	(nor was the edge useless
hilde rince;	to *the* warrior;)
ac he hraþe wolde	for he would forthwith
Grendle forgyldan	Grendel requite for
gûð-ræsa fela,	*the* many onslaughts
þâra þe he geworhte	that he had made
tó West-Denum,	on *the* West-Danes,
oftor micle	oftener by much
þonne on ǽnne sið,	than on one occasion,
þonne he Hróðgâres	when he Hrothgar's
heorð-geneâtas	hearth-enjoyers
slóh on sweofote,	slew in *their* rest,
slǽpende frǽt	sleeping devour'd
folces Denigea	of *the* Danes' folk
fýftyne men,	fifteen men,
and oðer swylc	and as many others
ût of-ferede	convey'd away,
lâðlicu lâc.	hateful offerings.
He him þæs leân forgeald,	He had for that paid him *his* reward,
reþe cempa,	*the* fierce champion,
tó ðæs þe he on reste geseah,	so well that on *his* couch he saw,
gûð-wérigne,	of contest weary,
Grendel licgan	Grendel lying
aldorleâsne,	lifeless,
swâ him ǽr gescód	as had for him before decided
hild æt Heorote.	*the* conflict at Heorot.
Hrâ wíde sprong,	(*The* corpse sprang far away,
syþðan he æfter deâðe	when after death he
drepe þrowade,	*the* stroke suffer'd,
heoro-sweng heardne,	*the* hard sword-blow,)

3175. MS. ræste.

and hine þá heáfde be-cearf.	and him then sever'd from *his* head.
Sona þæt gesawon	Saw it forthwith
snottre ceorlas,	*the* sagacious men,
þa ðe mid Hróðgáre	those who with Hrothgar,
on holm wliton,	were on *the* water looking,
þæt wæs ýð-geblond	that *the* wave-blending was
eal gemenged,	all mingled,
brim blóde fáh;	*the* deep stain'd with blood;
blonden-feaxe	*the* grizzly hair'd,
gomele ymb góđne	*the* old, about *the* good *warrior*
on-geador sprǽcon,	together spake,
þæt hig þæs æðelinges	that of the noble they
eft ne wéndon,	expected not again,
þæt he sige-hreðig	that he in victory exulting,
sécean come	would come to seek
mǽrne þeóden;	*their* great prince;
þá ðæs monige gewearð,	as of this *it* was *a* notice,
þæt hine seó brim-wylf	that him the seawolf
abróten hæfde.	had destroy'd.
Þá com nón dæges,	Then came *the* noon of day,
nǽs ofgeafon	left *the* headland
hwâte Scyldingas;	*the* bold Scyldings;
gewât him hám þonon	departed home thence
gold-wine gumena,	*the* gold-friend of men,
gistas sécan,	*his* guests to seek,
módes seóce,	sick of mood,
and on mere stâredon,	and on *the* mere *they* gaz'd,
wiscton and ne wéndon þæt híe	wish'd and ween'd not that they
heora wine-drihten	their dear lord
selfne gesawon.	himself should see.

3203. MS. abreoten.
3212. MS. wiston. K., no doubt rightly, reads wiscton.

Đá þæt sweord ongan
æfter heaþo-swâte
hilde gicelum,
wíg-bil wanian,
þæt wæs wundra sum,
þæt hit eal gemealt
íse gelícost,
þonne forstes bend
Fæder onlæteð,
onwindeð wǽg-râpas,
se geweald hafað,
sǽla and mǽla;
þæt is sóð Metod.
Ne nom he in þǽm wícum
Weder-Geáta leód,
maðm-æhta má,
þéh he þær monige geseah,
buton þone hafelan,
and þa hilt somod,
since fâge;
sweord ǽr gemealt,
forbarn broden mǽl;
wæs þæt blód tó þæs hât,
ættren ellor-gæst,
se þær-inne swealt.
Sona wæs on sunde
se þe ǽr æt sæcce gebâd
wíg-hrýre wrâðra;
wæter up þurh-deáf,
wǽron ýð-gebland,
eal gefǽlsod,
eácne eardas,

Then that sword began
after *with* battle-gore
in icicles of blood,
that war-falchion, to fade away;
(that was a miracle!)
so that it all melted
to ice most like,
when *the* frost's band
the Father relaxes,
unwinds *the* wave-ropes,
who has power
of times and seasons;
that is *the* true Creator.
He took not in those dwellings,
the Weder-Goths' lord,
more treasures,
(though he there many saw,)
except *the* head,
and *the* hilt also,
with treasure variegated;
the sword had already melted,
the drawn brand was burnt;
so hot was the blood,
so venomous *the* stranger guest,
who therein had perish'd.
Forthwith was afloat
he who before at strife awaited
the battle-fall of foes;
he div'd up through *the* water,
the wave-blendings were
all clear'd,
the vast dwellings,

3217. Lit. in icicles of war.

3224. MS. wæl, for which K., no doubt rightly, reads wǽg.

þá se ellor gast	when the stranger guest
oflet líf-dagas,	left *her* life-days,
and þas lǽnan gesceaft.	and this miserable creation.
Com þá tó lande	Came then to land
lídmanna helm,	*the* sailors' refuge,
swiðmód swymman,	stoutly swimming,
sǽ-láce gefeáh,	in *his* sea-offerings rejoiced,
mægen-byrþenne,	*his* mighty burthen,
þára þe he him mid hæfde.	of the *spoils* that he had with him.
Eódon him þá tó-geánes,	Went then towards him,
Gode þancodon,	thank'd God,
ðryðlic þegna heáp,	*the* stout band of thanes,
þeódnes gefegon,	in *their* lord rejoiced,
þæs þe hí hyne gesundne	for that they him sound
geseón móston.	might see.
Đá wæs of þǽm hróran	Then was from the vigorous *chief*
helm and byrne	helm and byrnie
lungre alýsed,	quickly loosed,
lagu drúsade,	*the* stream trickled down,
wæter under wolcnum,	water under *the* clouds,
wæl-dreóre fág.	stain'd with deadly gore.
Ferdon forð þonon,	*They* went forth thence,
feþe-lastum	with *their* foot-steps,
ferhþum fægne,	(in *their* souls rejoicing,)
fold-wég mǽton,	*the* high-way measur'd,
cuþe strǽte ;	*the* well-known road ;
cyning-balde men,	*the* nobly bold men,
from þǽm holm-clife,	from the sea-shore,
hafelan bæron,	bore *the* heads,
earfoðlíce	with difficulty
heora æghwæþrum,	to each of them,

3253. Offerings, i.e. to Hrothgar, the heads of his deadly foes.

3255. Spoils, i.e. the heads of Grendel and his mother and the ponderous sword-hilt.

fela-mődigra :	of *those* much-daring *ones* :
feower scoldon,	four must,
on þǽm wæl-stenge,	on the deadly stake,
weorcum geferian	laboriously convey
to pǽm gold-sele	to *the* gold-hall
Grendles heáfod ;	Grendel's head ;
opðæt semninga	until at once
tő sele comon	to *the* hall came
frome fyrd-hwấte	stout active in warfare
feowertyne	fourteen
Geáta gongan,	Goths marching,
gum dryhten mid :	with *their* lord :
mődig on gemonge	proud in *the* throng
meodo-wongas træd.	*he* trod *the* meadow-plains.
Þá com in-gân	Then came entering
ealdor ðegna,	*the* prince of thanes,
dǽd-cêne mon,	*the* deed-bold man,
dőme gewurþad,	with glory honour'd,
hæle-hilde-deőr,	*the* human war-beast,
Hrőðgâr grêtan.	Hrothgar to greet.
Þá wæs be feaxe	Then by *the* locks was
on flet boren	into *the* court borne
Grendles heáfod,	Grendel's head,
þær guman druncon,	where men were drinking,
egeslic for eorlum,	terrific before *the* warriors,
and þǽre idese mid ;	and the woman's also ;
wlîte seőn wrætlic	*an* aspect wonderful to see
weras onsawon.	men look'd on.

XXIV.

Beowulf maþelode,	Beowulf spake,
bearn Ecgþeőwes :	Ecgtheow's son :
Hwæt we þe þas sǽ-lác,	"Behold, we thee these sea-offerings,

sunu Healfdenes,	son of Healfdene,
leód Scyldinga,	lord of Scyldings,
lustum brohton,	joyfully have brought,
tires tő tácne,	in token of glory,
þe þú her tő-locast.	which thou here lookest on.
Ic þæt unsofte	I it hardly
ealdre gedigde,	with life escap'd from,
wigge under wætere,	*the* conflict under water,
weorce genéþde;	with pain ventur'd on *it;*
earfoðlice	with difficulty
æt rihte wæs	according to right had been
gúð getwǽfed,	*the* contest parted,
nymðe mec God scylde.	had not God shielded me.
Ne meahte ic æt hilde	I might not in *the* conflict
mid Hruntinge	with Hrunting
wiht gewyrcan,	aught accomplish,
þeáh þæt wæpen duge;	though that weapon be good;
ac me geuðe	but me granted
ylda Waldend,	*the* Ruler of men,
þæt ic on wage geseah	that on *the* wall I saw
wlitig hangian	hang beautiful
eald sweord eácen,	*an* old powerful sword,
oftost wisode	(full oft has *He* directed
wineleásum	*the* friendless,)
þæt ic þý wæpne gebræd.	*and* that I the weapon drew.
Ofslóh þá æt þǽre sæcce,	*I* slew then in that conflict
þá me sǽl ageald	(as me *the* opportunity requited)
húses hyrdas;	*the* house's keepers;
þá þæt hilde bil	then that battle-falchion,
forbarn brogden mǽl,	that drawn brand, was burnt up,
swá þæt blód gesprang,	as the blood sprang,
hátost heaþo-swáta:	hottest of hostile gores:

3332. wingea, Thork.; but the *w* has perish'd from the MS. What remains appears like nigea.

ic þæt hilt þanon
feóndum ætferede,
fyren-dǽda wræc,
deáð-cwealm Denigea,
swá hit gedéfe wæs.
Ic hit þe þonne geháte,
þæt þú on Heorote móst
sorhleás swefan
mid þínra secga gedryht,
and þegna gehwylc
þínra leóda,
dugoðe and iogoþe;
þæt þú him ondrædan ne
  þearft,
þeóden Scyldinga,
on þá healfe,
aldor-bealu eorlum,
swá þú ǽr dydest.
Ðá wæs gylden hilt
gamelum rince,
hárum hild-fruman,
on hand gyfen,
enta ǽr-geweorc:
hit on æht gehwearf,
æfter deófla hrýre,
Denigea freán,
wundor-smiþa geweorc;
and þá þas worold ofgeaf
grom-heort guma,
Godes andsaca,
morðres scyldig,
and his módor eác,
on geweald gehwearf
worold-cyninga

I the hilt thence
from *the* foes bore away,
avenged *the* crimes,
the Dane's deadly plague,
as it was fitting.
I now promise it thee,
that thou in Heorot may'st
sleep secure
with *the* company of thy warriors,
and every thane
of thy people,
noble and youthful;
so that for them thou needest
  not to fear,
O prince of Scyldings,
on that side,
the life's bane of *thy* warriors,
as thou erst didst."
Then was *the* golden hilt
to *the* aged warrior,
the hoar war-leader,
in hand given,
the giants work of old:
it pass'd into *the* possession,
after *those* devils' fall,
of *the* Danes' lord,
the work of wondrous smiths;
and when this world resign'd
the fierce hearted man,
God's denier,
of murder guilty,
and his mother eke,
it pass'd into *the* power
of worldly kings

ðǽm sêlestan	the best
be sǽm tweónum,	between *the* seas,
þâra þe on Sceden-igge	of those who in Scania
sceattas dǽlde.	treasures dealt.
Hróðgâr maðelode,	Hrothgar spake,
hylt sceáwode,	gaz'd on *the* hilt,
ealde láfe,	*the* old relic,
on ðǽm wæs ór writen	on which *the* origin was written
fyrn-gewinnes,	of *the* ancient war,
syðþan flód ofslôh,	after *the* flood had slain,
geofon geótende,	*the* flowing ocean,
giganta cyn;	*the* giants' race;
frecne geferdon.	insolently *they* bore them.
Þæt wæs fremde þeód	that was *a* people strange
écean Dryhtne;	to *the* eternal Lord;
him þæs ende-leân,	to them, therefore, *a* final reward,
þurh wæteres wylm,	through *the* water's rage,
Waldend sealde.	*the* Almighty gave.
Swâ wæs on ðǽm scennum	So was on the mounting
scíran goldes,	of bright gold,
þurh rûn-stafas,	in runic letters,
rihte gemearcod,	rightly mark'd,
geseted and gesæd,	set and said,
hwâm þæt sweord geworht,	for whom that sword,
írena cyst,	of irons choicest,
ǽrest wǽre,	first was wrought,
wreoþen-hilt and wyrm-fâh.	with hilt bound round and serpentine.
Ða se wísa spræc	Then spake the wise

3384. MS. gifen.

3400. That is, adorned with figures of snakes interlaced, a favourite and universal ornament among the Scandinavian nations, innumerable specimens of which still exist in works of metal, wood and stone, as capitals of pillars, etc.

sunu Healfdenes :	son of Healfdene :
swígedon ealle :	(all were silent)
þæt lá mæg secgan,	" Lo, that may say,
se þe sóð and riht	he who truth and right
fremeð on folce,	practises among people,
feor eal gemon,	far back all remembers,
eald ·ᛟ·-weard,	*an* old country's guardian,
þæt ðes eorl wǽre	that this earl should have been
geboren betera.	born better.
Blæd is arǽred	Thy glory is exalted
geond wíd-wégas,	through wide ways,
wine mín Beowulf,	my friend Beowulf,
þín ofer þeóda gehwylce.	over every nation.
Eal þû hit geþyldum healdest,	Thou supportest it all patiently,
mǽgen mid módes snyttrum.	*thy* might, with prudence of mind.
Ic þe sceal míne gelǽstan	I shall evince to thee my
freode swâ wit furðum spræcon :	love, even as we two have said :
ðû scealt tó frófre weorþan,	thou shalt for *a* comfort be,
eal lang-tídig,	*a* very long time,
leódum þínum,	to thy people,
hæleðum to helpe.	for *a* help to warriors.
Ne wearð Heremód swâ,	Not so was Heremod
eaforum Ecgwelan,	to Ecgwela's children,
âr Scyldingum ;	*a* blessing to *the* Scyldings ;
ne geweox he him tó willan,	he wax'd not for their benefit,
ac to wæl-fylle,	but for *their* slaughter,
and to deáð-cwalum	and for *a* deadly plague
Deniga leódum ;	to *the* Danes' people ;
breât bolgen-mód	*he* in angry mood destroy'd

3410. That is of higher degree; that he should have been a king.
3420. MS. twidig. 3427. MS. fealle.

beód-geneátas,	*his* table sharers,
eaxl-gesteallan,	*his* nearest friends,
oþþæt he âna hwearf,	until he lonely departed,
mǽre þeóden,	*the* great prince,
mon-dreámum from;	from *the* joys of men;
ðeáh þe hine mihtig God	although him mighty God
mægenes wynnum,	with *the* delights of power,
eafeþum stépte,	with energies had exalted,
ofer ealle men	above all men
forð gefremede;	advanced *him*;
hwæþere him on ferhðe greow	yet in his soul *there* grew
breóst-hord blód-reów;	*a* sanguinary heart;
nallas beágas geaf	*he* gave no rings
Denum æfter dóme:	to *the* Danes according to desert:
dreámleas gebâd,	joyless *he* continued,
þæt he þæs gewinnes	*so* that of war he
weorc þrówade,	*the* misery suffer'd,
leód-bealo longsum.	*a* longsome public bale.
Þû þe lǽr be þon,	Teach thou thyself by this *man*,
gum-cyste ongit.	understand munificence.
Ic þis gid be þe	This strain of thee I
awræc wintrum fród.	in winters wise have recited.
Wundor is tó secganne	Wonderful 'tis to say
hû mihtig God	how mighty God,
manna cynne,	to *the* race of men,
þurh sídne sefan,	through *his* ample mind,
snyttru bryttað,	dispenses wisdom,
eard and eorlscipe:	land and valour:
He áh ealra geweald;	He possesses power of all;
hwílum He on lufan	sometimes He as it likes
læteð hworfan	lets wander
monnes mód-geþonc,	*the* mind's thought of man.

3442. Lit. breast-hoard.

mǽran cynnes,	of *the* great race,
seleð him on ēþle	gives him in *his* country
eorþan wynne	joy of earth
tō healdanne,	to possess,
hleō-burh wera ;	*a* shelter-city of men ;
gedēð him swâ gewealdene	thus makes to him subject
worolde dǽlas,	*the* portions of *the* world,
sīde rīce,	ample realms,
þæt he his selfa ne mæg,	*so* that he himself may not,
for his unsnyttrum	through his lack of wisdom,
ende geþencean :	think of *his* end :
wunaþ he on wiste,	he continues in feasting,
ne hine wiht drefeð	nor him *in* aught afflicts,
âdl ne yldo,	disease or age,
ne him inwit-sorh	nor for him guileful care
on sefan sweorceð,	in *his* mind darkens,
ne gesacu ohwær	nor strife anywhere
ecg-hete eōweð ;	shows hostile hate ;
ac him eal worold	but for him all *the* world
wendeð on willan ;	turns at *his* will ;
he þæt wyrse ne con,	he *the* worse knows not,

XXV.

Oþþæt him on-innan	Until within him
ofer-hygda dǽl	*a* deal of arrogance
weaxeð and wridað,	grows and buds,
þonne se weard swefeð,	when the guardian sleeps,
sawele hyrde ;	*the* soul's keeper ;
bið se slǽp tō fæst	too fast is the sleep
bisgum gebunden,	bound by cares,
bona swiðe neáh,	*the* slayer very near,
se þe of flân-bogan	who from *his* arrow-bow,

3470. Correctly rīcu. 3475. MS. dweleð.

fyrenum sceōteð ;	wickedly shoots ;
þonne bið on hreþre,	then will *he* be in *the* breast,
under helm drepen,	beneath *the* helm stricken,
biteran strǣle ;	with *the* bitter shaft ;
him bebeorgan ne con	*he* cannot guard himself
wom-wundor-bebodum	from *the* wicked wondrous commands
wergan gāstes ;	of *the* cursed spirit ;
þinceð him tō lytel	seems to him too little
þæt he tō lange heold,	what he too long had held,
gytsað grom-hydig,	fierce-minded *he* covets,
nallas on gylp seleð	gives not in *his* pride
fætte beāgas,	rich rings,
and he þa forð-gesceaft	and he the future state
forgyteð and forgȳmeð,	forgets and neglects,
þæs þe him ǣr God sealde,	because God to him before has given,
wuldres Waldend,	Ruler of glory,
weorðmynda dǣl.	*a* deal of dignities.
Hit on ende-stæf	It in *the* final close
eft gelimpeð,	afterwards befals,
þæt se-licrhoma	that the body
lǣne gedreōseð,	miserably sinks,
fǣge gefealleð ;	fated falls ;
fehð oþer tō,	another succeeds,
se þe unmurnlice	who without reluctance
madmas dǣleð,	treasures dispenses,
eorles ǣr-gestreōn,	*the* warrior's former gains,
egesan ne gȳmeð.	terror heeds not.
Bebeorh þe þone bealo-nīð,	Keep from thee that baleful evil,
Beowulf leōfa,	dear Beowulf,
secg betsta,	best of warriors,

3504. MS. fædde. 3513. MS. læge.

and þe þæt sêlre geceôs,
êce rǽdas;
ofer-hyda ne gŷm,
mǽre cempa:
nû is þînes mægnes blǽd
âne hwîle;
eft-sona bið þæt þec
ǽdl oððe ecg
eafoþes getwǽfeð,
oððe fŷres feng,
oððe flôdes wylm,
oððe grîpe meces,
oððe gâres fliht,
oððe atol yldo,
oððe eâgena bearhtm,
forsiteð and forsworceð:
semninga bið,
þæt þec dryht-guma
deâð oferswyðeð.
Swâ ic Hring-Dena
hund missera
weold under wolcnum,
and hîg wîgge be leâc
manegum mægþa
geond þysne middangeard,
æscum and ecgum;
þæt ic me ǽnigne
under swegles begong
gesacan ne tealde.
Hwæt me þæs on êþle
edwendan cwom
gnyrn æfter gomene,

and choose for thee the better,
eternal counsels;
heed not arrogance,
renown'd champion!
now is *the* flower of thy might
for a while;
eftsoons *'t* will be that thee
disease or sword
from *thy* energy separates,
or fire's clutch,
or rage of flood,
or falchion's gripe,
or arrow's flight,
or dire age,
or twinkling of eyes,
oppresses and darkens:
suddenly *it* will be:
that thee, warrior,
death overpowers.
Thus I *the* Ring-Danes
for half *a* hundred years
had rul'd under *the* clouds,
and them from war secur'd
from many tribes
throughout this mid-earth,
with spears and swords,
so that I me any,
under heaven's course,
adversary counted not.
Lo, to me of this in *my* country
a reverse came,
sadness after merriment,

3537. This alludes to the evil eye, for which see Grimm, D.M. p. 1053.

3554. MS. gyrn.

seoþðan Grendel wearð,	since Grendel became,
eald gewinna,	*my* old adversary,
in-genga mín:	my invader:
ic þǽre sócne	I for that visitation
singales wæg	constantly have borne
mód-ceare micle;	great mental care;
þæs síg Metode þanc,	therefore be to *the* Creator thanks,
ēcean Drihtne,	to *the* eternal Lord,
þæs ðe ic on aldre gebâd,	for that I have remain'd in life,
þæt ic on þone hafelan,	that I on that head,
heoro-dreórigne,	clotted with gore,
ofer eald gewin,	after *our* old contention,
eágum stárige.	with *my* eyes may gaze.
Gá nú to setle,	Go now to *thy* seat,
symbel-wynne dreóh,	enjoy *the* pleasure of *the* feast,
wíg-geweorþad;	for battle honour'd:
unc sceal worn fela	for us two shall *a* great many
maþma gemǽnra,	common treasures *be*,
siþðan morgen bið.	when *it* shall be morning."
Geát wæs glǽd-mód,	*The* Goth was glad of mood,
gong sona tó	went straightways to
setles neósan,	occupy *his* seat,
swá se snottra hêht.	as the sage commanded.
Þá wæs eft swá ǽr,	Then were again as before,
ellen-rófum,	*the* valour-fam'd
flet-sittendum,	court-residents,
fægere gereorded	fairly feasted,
niówan stefne.	with new spirit.
Niht-helm geswearc,	*The* helm of night grew murky
deorc ofer dryht-gumum;	dark o'er *the* vassals,
duguð eal arás;	*the* courtiers all arose;

3573. After this line I suspect that two lines are wanting.

3575. MS. geong.

wolde blonden-feax	*the* grizzly hair'd *prince* would
beddes neósan,	*his* bed visit,
gamela Scylding;	*the* aged Scylding;
Geát ungemetes wel	*the* Goth immeasurably well
rófne rand-wigan	*the* renown'd shield-warrior
restan lyste.	wished *to* rest.
Sona him sele-þegn,	Forthwith *the* hall-thane him,
siðes wergum,	from *his* journey weary,
feorran-cumenum,	*the* comer from afar,
forð wísade,	guided forth,
se for andrysnum	who from reverence
ealle beweotede	had all *things* provided
þegnes þearfe,	for *the* thane's need,
swylce þý dógore	such as in that day
heaþo-líðende	navigators of *the* main
habban scoldon.	should have.
Reste hine þá rúm-heort,	Rested him then *the* ample-hearted;
reced hlifade,	*the* mansion tower'd,
geáp and gold-fáh:	vaulted and golden-hued:
gæst inne swæf,	*the* guest slept therein,
oþþæt hrefn blaca	until *the* black raven
heofenes wynne	heaven's delight
blíð-heort bódode	blithe of heart announced
cuman beorhte [sunnan]	*the* bright [sun] coming,
scacan scaþan,	robbers fleeing away.
[Scealcas] onetton,	[*The* warriors] hasten'd,
wǽron æþelingas	*the* nobles were
eft to leódum	again to *their* people

3594. MS. feorran cundum. 3597. MS. beweotene.
3603. MS. hliuade.
3609. Thork. coman. The word has perished from the MS. MS. beorht Sunnan is supplied from conjecture.
3611. Scealcas is added from conjecture.

fûse tô farenne;
wolde feor þanon
cuma collen-ferhð
ceôles neôsan.
Hêht þâ se hearda
Hrunting beran,
sunu Ecglâfes
hêht his sweord niman,
leôflic íren;
sǽgde him þæs leânes þanc,
cwæð he þone gûð-wine
gôdne tealde,
wíg-cræftigne;
nales wordum lôg
meces ecge:
þæt wæs môdig secg.
And þâ síð-frome,
searwum gearwe
wígend wǽron,
eôde West-Denum
æþeling tô-yrnan,
þær se oþer wæs,
hæle-hilde-deôr:
Hrôðgâr grêtte.

anxious to go;
would far from thence
the high-soul'd guest
his vessel visit.
Bade then the bold *chief*
Hrunting be borne,
the son of Ecglaf
bade take *back* his sword,
the precious iron;
gave him for the loan thanks,
said *that* he the war-friend
accounted good,
in battle powerful;
nor with words blam'd *he*
the falchion's edge:
that was *a* high-soul'd warrior,
And when eager for departure,
with arms all ready
the warriors were,
went to *the* West-Danes
the noble running, to
where the other was,
the human war-beast:
he Hrothgar greeted.

XXVI.

Beowulf maþelode,
bearn Ecgþeôwes:

Beowulf spake,
Ecgtheow's son:

3614. MS. farene.

3615. The MS. has ne before wolde, apparently a repetition of that immediately preceding.

3624. gûð-wine, i.e. the sword.

3633. MS. weorð

3634. MS. to yppan.

3636. MS. helle.

Nû þe sǽ-lîðend	"Now to thee *we* sea-farers
secgan wyllað,	desire to say,
feorran cumene,	*we* comers from afar,
þæt we fundiað	that we are most desirous
Higelâc sécan;	Hygelac to seek;
wǽron her tela	we have here been kindly,
willum beþenede,	cordially, serv'd,
þû us wel dohtest.	thou hast well treated us.
Gif ic þonne on eorþan	If I now on earth
owihte mæg,	in aught can,
þînre môd-lufan,	for thy mind's love,
mâran tilian,	execute more,
gumena dryhten,	O lord of men,
ðonne ic gyt dyde,	than I yet have done,
gûð-geweorca,	of warlike works,
ic beó gearo sona;	I shall be straightways ready;
gif ic þæt gefricge,	if I learn,
ofer flôda begang,	over *the* floods' course,
þæt þec ymb-sittend	that thee *those* dwelling around
egesan þywað,	with terror urge,
swâ þec hetende	as *those* hating thee
hwîlum dydon,	at times have done,
ic þe þusenda	I to thee thousands
þegna bringe,	of warriors will bring,
hæleþa to helpe.	of heroes, to *thy* help.
Ic on Higelâce wât,	I know of Hygelac,
Geâta dryhten,	lord of Goths,
þeâh ðe he geong sŷ	although he be *a* young
folces hyrde,	shepherd of *his* folk,
þæt he mec fremman wile,	that he will enable me,
wordum and weorcum,	by words and works,
þæt ic þe wel werige,	that I may well defend thee,

3646. MS. bewenede. 3670. MS. weordum and worcum.
3671. MS. herige.

and þe tô geôce	and to thee for succour
gâr-holt bere,	*the* javelin-shaft bear,
mægenes fultum,	*a* support to *thy* power,
þær ðe bið manna þearf.	if thou have need of men.
Gif him þonne Hreþríc	If then Hrethric
tô hôfum Geâta	at *the* Goths' courts,
geþingað þeôdnes bearn,	*the* king's son, craves *it*,
he mæg þær fela	he may there many
freônda findan :	friends find :
feor-cŷþða beôð	far countries are,
sêlran gesôhte,	better *when* sought,
þæ̂m þe him selfa deâh.	to him who on himself relies."
Hrôðgâr maþelode,	Hrothgar spake
him on andsware :	to him in answer :
Þe þa word-cwydas	"To thee those words
wittig Drihten	*the* wise Lord
on sefan sende :	into *thy* mind has sent ;
ne hŷrde ic snotorlicor,	never have I heard more prudently,
on swâ geongum feore,	in so young *a* life,
guman þingian.	*a* man discourse.
Þû eart mægenes strang,	Thou art strong of might,
and on môde frôd,	and in mind sage,
wîs word-cwida :	wise of verbal utterances :
wên' ic tâlige,	I think *there is* expectation,
gif þæt gegangeð,	if it happen,
þæt se gâr nimeð,	that the dart take,
hild heoru-grim,	war fiercely grim,
Hreþles eaferan,	Hrethel's offspring,
âdl oþðe îren,	disease or iron,
ealdor ðinne,	thy prince,

3676. MS. Hreðrinc : Hrothgar's son. See l. 2382.
3678. MS. geþinged, 3681. MS. cyþðe.
3687. MS. wigtig. 3697. MS. þe. 3698. MS. grimme.

folces hyrde,	*his* people's shepherd,
and þō þīn feorth hafast,	and thou thy life hast,
þæt þā Sǣ-Geātas	that the Sea-Goths
sēlran næbben	will not have *a* better
tō geceōsenne,	to choose,
cyning ǣnigng,	not any king,
hord-weard hæleþa;	*or* treasure-ward of heroes:
gif þū healdan wylt	if thou wilt hold
maga rīce.	*thy* kinsmen's realm.
Me þīn mōd-sefa	Me thy mind
līcað leng swā wel,	pleases *the* longer *the* better,
leōfa Beowulf:	dear Beowulf:
hafast þū gefered	thou hast borne *thyself*
þæt þām folcum sceal,	*so* that for the nations shall
Geāta leōdum	(*the* Goths' people
and Gār-Denum,	and *the* Gar-Danes)
sib gemǣnum	peace *be* to both,
and sacu restan,	and contention rest,
inwit-nīþas,	*the* guileful enmities,
þe hīe ǣr drugon,	which they erst have borne,
wesan þenden ic wealde	*shall* be while I rule
wīdan rīces,	*the* ample realm,
maþmas gemǣne:	treasures common;
manig oþerne	many *a one* another
gōdum gegrētan;	greet with benefits;
ofer ganotes bǣð	over *the* gannet's bath
sceal hring-naca,	*the* ring-*prow'd* bark shall,
ofer heāþu bringan	o'er *the* main, bring
lāc and luf-tācen.	gifts and love-tokens.
Ic þa leōde wāt	I the nations know
ge wið feōnd ge wið freond	both towards foe and towards friend
fæste geworhte,	fast constituted,

3704. MS. þe.

3726. MS. gegrettan.

æghwæs untǽle,	blameless in everything,
ealde wísan.	in *the* old wise."
Ðá git him eorla hleó	To him besides *the* warriors protector
inne gesealde,	gave to possess,
mago Healfdenes,	*the* son of Healfdene,
maþmas xii;	treasures twelve;
hét hine mid þǽm lácum	bade him with the gifts
leóde swǽse	*his* own people
sécean on gesyntum;	seek in safety;
snúde eft cuman.	quickly come again.
Gecyste þá	Kiss'd then
cyning æþelum gód,	*the* king nobly good,
þeóden Scyldinga,	*the* Scyldings' prince,
ðegn betstan,	*the* best of thanes,
and be healse genam;	and round *the* neck *him* took;
hrúron him teáras,	tears fell from him,
blonden feaxum;	*the* grizzly hair'd *prince;*
him wæs béga wén,	he had hope of both,
ealdum infródum,	*the* old sage,
oþres swiðor,	*but* of *the* second stronger,
þæt hí seoððan	that *they* themselves afterwards
geseón móston,	might see,
módige on meþle.	*the* lofty *ones,* in conference.
Wæs him se man to þon leóf,	To him was *the* man so dear,
þæt he þone breóst-wylm	that he the fervour of his breast
forberan ne mihte;	might not restrain;
ac him on hreþre,	but in his bosom,
hyge-bendum fæst,	fast in bonds of thought,
æfter deórum men,	after *the* dear man,

3740. MS. inne.

3751. Hope of both, i.e. of his safe arrival at home, and of his speedy return to Denmark, referring to ll. 3740-3743.

3759. MS. mehte.

dyrne langað	longing secretly
born wið blôde.	burn'd against blood.
Him Beowulf þanon,	Beowulf thence,
gûð-rinc gold-wlanc,	*the* warrior proud with gold,
græs-moldan træd,	trod *the* grassy mould,
since hrêmig.	in treasure exulting.
Sǽ-genga bâd	*The* sea-ganger awaited
âgend-freân,	*its* owning lord,
se þe on ancre râd.	which at anchor rode.
Þâ wæs on gange	Then was on *the* way
gifu Hrôðgâres	*the* gift of Hrothgar
oft geæhted.	often prized.
Þæt wæs ân cyning	That was a king
æghwæs ôrleahtre,	in everything faultless,
oþþæt hine yldo benam	until age him took
mægenes wynnum,	from *the* delights of vigour,
se þe oft manegum scôd.	which oft had overpower'd many.

XXVII.

Cwom þâ tô flôde	Came then to *the* flood
fela môdigra	many proud
hægstealdra ;	bachelors ;
hring-net bǽron,	ring-nets *they* bore,
locene leóðo-syrcan.	clos'd limb-sarks.
Land-weard onfand	*The* land-warden perceiv'd
eft-sîð eorla,	*the* warriors' return,
swâ he ǽr dyde :	as he before had done :

3764. MS. beorn. The words 'wið blôde' are very questionable. The only interpretation of which the line seems susceptible is, that he (Hrothgar) entertained a stronger affection for Beowulf than for his own blood, that is, his own children. I consider the case an incurable one.

3765. MS. þanan. 3770. MS. aged. 3785. See ll. 473, seq.

nô he mid hearme,	not with insult he,
of hliðes nosan,	from *the* hill's point,
gæst ne grêtte,	greeted *the* guest,
ac him tô-geanes râd ;	but towards him rode ;
cwæð þá wilcuman	bade welcome then
Wedera leódum.	to *the* Weders' people.
Scacan scír-hâme	Departing, *the* bright-clad *warriors*
tô scipe fôron.	went to *the* ship,
Ðá wæs on sande	Then was on *the* sand
sǽ-geâp naca	*the* sea-curv'd bark
hladen here-wǽdum,	laden with martial weeds,
hringed-stefna,	*the* ringed prow,
mearum and maðmum;	with steeds and treasures ;
mæst hlifade	*the* mast tower'd
ofer Hrôðgâres	over Hrothgar's
hord-gestreônum.	hoard-treasures.
He þǽm bât-wearde,	He to the boat-guard,
bunden golde,	bound with gold,
swurd gesealde,	gave *a* sword,
þæt he syðþan wæs,	*so* that he was afterwards,
on meodo-bence,	on *the* mead-bench,
madme þý weorþra,	the worthier for *the* treasure,
yrfe-lâfe.	*the* heritable relic.
Gewât him on nacan,	*He* departed in *the* bark,
drefan deóp wæter,	agitating *the* deep water,
Dena land ofgeaf.	*the* Danes' land left.
Þá wæs be mæste	Then was by *the* mast
mere-hrægla sum,	a sea-mantle,
segl sale fæst :	*a* sail, by *a* cord fast :

3792. MS. þæt. 3794. MS. scawan.

3804. He, i.e. Beowulf. 3809. MS. madma þy weorþre.

3810. No alliteration with the following line ; for nacan we should probably read ýþum.

sund-wudu þunede ;
no þær wǽg-flotan
wind ofer ýðum
síðes getwǽfde ;
sǽ-genga fór,
fleât fâmig-heals
forð ofer ýðe,
bunden-stefna
ofer brim-streâmas,
þæt híe Geâta clifu
ongitan meahton,
cuþe næssas.
Ceól up-geþrang,
lyft-geswenced
on lande stód.
Hrâþe wæs æt holme
hýð-weard geara,
se þe ǽr lange tíd
leófra manna,
fús æt faroðe.
fór wlâtode :
sǽlde to sande
síd-fæðmed scip
oncer-bendum fæst,
þý læs hit ýþa ðrym,
wudu wynsuman,
forwrecan meahte.
Hét þâ úp beran
æþelinga gestreón,
frætwa and fæt gold :
næs him feor þanon.

the sea-wood rattled ;
not there *the* wave-floater
the wind above *the* billows
from *its* course parted :
the sea-ganger went,
floated *the* foamy neck'd
forth o'er *the* wave,
the bounden prow
over ocean's streams,
so that they *the* Goths' shores
might perceive,
the known headlands.
The vessel press'd up,
weather-beaten
on land *it* stood.
Quickly at *the* sea was
the hithe-guard ready,
who, *a* long time before,
the dear men's
(prompt at *the* shore)
course had beheld :
he bound to *the* sand
the broad-bosom'd ship
with anchor-bonds fast,
lest it *the* billows' force,
the gallant wood,
might wreck.
He then bade be borne up
the nobles' treasures,
ornaments and rich gold :
he had not far thence

3818. MS. weg. 3837. MS. feor. 3839. MS. fæðme.
3840. MS. on cear bendum. The rectification is Grundtvig's.
3841. MS. hym. 3846. MS. frætwe.

tṓ gesḗcanne	to seek
sinces bryttan,	*the* dispenser of treasure,
Higelā́c Hreþling,	Hygelac, Hrethel's son,
þær æt hā́m wunode	where at home dwelt,
selfa mid gesiðum,	himself with *his* companions,
sǣ́-wealle neā́h.	near *the* sea-wall.
Bold wæs bētlic,	*The* mansion was excellent,
brego rṓf cyning,	*a* chief renown'd *the* king,
heā́ healle;	high *the* hall;
Hygd swiðe geong,	Hygd very young,
wīs wel-þungen,	wise, well-nurtur'd,
þeā́h ðe wintra lyt	though winters few
under burh-locan	amid *the* burgh-encloser
gebiden hæfde	had abided
Hǣ́reþes dohtor:	Hæreth's daughter:
næs hiṓ hnā́h swā́-þeā́h,	although she was not mean,
nḗ tṓ gneð gifa	nor of gifts too sparing
Geā́ta leṓdum,	to *the* Goths' people,
maþm-gestreṓna,	of treasure-acquisitions,
mṓd-þryðo wæg	*yet* violence of mood mov'd
fremu folces cwēn,	*the* folk's bold queen,
firen ondrysne.	crime appalling.
Nǣ́nig þæt dorste	No one durst that
deṓr genegan,	beast address,
swǣ́sra gesīða,	of *the* dear companions,
nefne sin-freā́,	save *her* wedded lord,
þe hire ā́n-dæges	who on her daily
eā́gum stā́rede;	with eyes gaz'd;
ac him wæl-bende	but to him *a* death band
weotode tealde,	decreed, calculated,

3851. MS. wunað. 3861. MS. hæbbe. 3864. MS. gneað.

3868. Fremu seems here without sense. Perhaps we should read frome, *bold, strenuous.*

3871. MS. geneþan.

hand-gewriþene,
hraðe seoþðan wæs,
æfter mund-grîpe
mece geþinged;
þæt hit sceaðen mǽl
scyran móste,
cwealm-bealu cyðan:
ne bið swylc cwênlíc þeâw
idese to efnanne,
þeâh ðe hió ǽnlicu sý,
þætte freoðu-webbe
feores onsæce,
æfter lig-torne,
leófne mannan;
huru þæt onhohsnode
Heminges mǽg,
ealo-drincende;
oðre sǽdon,
þæt hió leód-bealewa
læs gefremede,
inwit-níða,
syððan ǽrest wearð
gyfen gold-hroden
geongum cempan,
æðelum dióre,
syððan hió Offan flet,

hand-bound,
was quickly after,
after *the* hand-grasp,
with *the* sword resolv'd;
so that it *the* pernicious brand
must decide,
the deadly bale make known:
such is no feminine usage
for *a* woman to practise,
although she be beautiful,
that *a* peace-weaver
machinate *to deprive* of life,
after burning anger,
a dear man;
at least with that reproach'd *her*
Hemming's son,
while drinking ale;
others said,
that she dire evils
less perpetrated,
guileful iniquities,
after *she* was first
given gold-adorn'd
to *the* young warrior,
the noble beast,
after she Offa's court,

3880. The grasp of affected reconciliation.

3882. MS. sceaden.

3884. From this line the MS. is written in another and worse hand.

3888. A periphrasis for a woman. See also "The Scôp or Gleeman's Tale," l. 11.

3890. MS. lige. 3892. MS. onhohsnod. (qu. on hosp dyde ?)

3893. MS. Hemninges. Hemming's son is Eomer. See l. 3925.

3895. MS. oðer sæden.

ofer fealone flôd,
be fæder lâre,
siðe gesôhte,
þær hió syððan wel
in gum-stôle,
gôde mǽre
lîf-gesceafta
lifigende breâc,
heold heâh-lufan
wið hæleþa brego,
ealles mon-cynnes,
mîne gefrǽge,
þone sêlestan
bi sǽm tweônum,
eormen-cynnes;
forþam Offa wæs,
geofum and gûþum,
gâr-cêne man,
wîde geweorþod;
wîsdôme heold
êðel sinne;
þonon Eomer wôc
hæleðum to helpe,
Heminges mæg,
nefa Gârmundes,
nîða cræftig.

over *the* fallow flood,
through *her* father's counsel,
by journey sought,
where she afterwards well
on *the* throne,
the good *and* great
life's creations
living enjoy'd,
high love entertain'd
towards *the* prince of heroes,
of all mankind,
as I have heard,
the best
between *the* seas,
of *the* human race;
for Offa was,
for gifts and wars,
(*a* bold man in arms)
widely honour'd;
he in wisdom held
his country;
from him Eomer sprang
for help to heroes,
Heming's son,
Garmund's grandson,
mighty in conflicts.

3916. MS. þæs. 3925. MS. geomor.

3928. It would seem from this line that nefa signified not only *nephew* and *grandson*, but also *great-grandson*, unless it be an error for gen. nefan, as I suspect it to be, and in opposition to Heminges, meaning that Heming was the grandson of Garmund.

3929. The preceding digression about Hygd and Offa is barely intelligible.

XXVIII.

Gewât him þâ se hearda
mid his hond-scôle,
sylf æfter sande,
sǽ-wong tredan,
wîde waroðas.
Woruld-candel scân,
sigel sûðan fûs:
hî sið drugon,
elne geeódon,
tô þæs þe eorla hleó,
bonan Ongenþeówes,
burgum in innan,
geongne gûð-cyning
gôdne gefrunon
hringas dǽlan.
Higeláce wæs
sið Beowulfes
snûde gecyðed,
þæt þær on worðig,
wîgendra hleó,
lind-gestealla,
lîfigende cwom,
heaðo-láces hâl
tô hôfe gongan.
Hraðe wæs gerŷmed,
swâ se rîca bebeád,
feðe-gestum
flet innanweard.
Gesæt þâ wið sylfne
se ðe sæcce genæs,

Departed then the bold *warrior*
with his chosen band,
himself along *the* sand,
the sea-plain treading,
the wide shores.
The world's candle shone,
the sun from *the* south hastening:
they dragg'd on *their* way,
resolutely went,
until *the* protector of men,
the slayer of Ongentheow,
within *his* burghs,
the young martial king,
the good, they had heard,
was rings dispensing.
To Hygelac was
Beowulf's voyage
speedily made known,
that there into *the* place
the protector of warriors,
his shield-companion,
was come alive,
whole from *the* game of war
proceeding to *his* mansion.
Quickly was clear'd,
as the chief commanded,
for *the* pedestrian guests
the hall within.
Sat then facing himself
he who had come safely from *the* conflict,

3940. MS. Ongenþeoes.

3959. MS. se ða.

mæg wið mæge.	kinsman facing kinsman.
Syððan man-dryhten,	After *his* liege lord,
þurh hleóðor-cwyde,	in sonorous speech,
holdne gegrétte,	*his* faithful *friend* had greeted,
meaglum wordum,	in powerful words,
meodo-scencum hwearf,	with mead-libations went,
geond þæt heal-reced,	through the hall,
Hǽreðes dohtor :	Hæreth's daughter :
lufode ða leóde,	*she* lov'd the people,
lið-wǽge bær	*the* wine-cup bare
heánum tó handa	to *the* high *chief's* hand.
Higelác ongan	Hygelac began
sínne geseldan	his guest
in sele þám heán	in the high hall
fægre fricgean :	kindly to question :
hyne fyrwet bræc,	curiosity was bursting him,
hwylce Sǽ-Geáta	*as to* what *the* Sea-Goths'
siðas wǽron.	courses had been.
Hú lomp eow on láde,	" How befel *it* you on *the* way,
leófa Beowulf,	dear Beowulf,
þá ðú fǽringa	when thou suddenly
feorr gehógodest	didst resolve afar.
sæcce sécean	conflict to seek
ofer sealt wæter,	over *the* salt water,
hilde to Heorote,	contest at Heorot,
þæt ðú Hróðgáre	that thou to Hrothgar
wíd-cuðne weán	*his* wide-known calamity
wihte gebétte,	mightest somewhat compensate,
mǽrum þeódne.	*the* great prince ?
Ic pæs mód-ceare	I on this account *my* mind's care
sorh-wylmum seáð ;	have in sorrow-boilings seeth'd ;

3966. MS. side reced. The alliteration requires heal.

3970. MS. hænum.

3985. MS. ac.

3986. MS. wið.

3987. MS. gebettest.

siðe ne trûwode	*I* trusted not in *the* voyage
leófes mannes;	of *the* dear man;
ic þe lange bæd,	I pray'd thee long,
þæt ðû þone wæl-gæst	that thou the deadly guest
wihte ne grêtte,	shouldest in no wise greet,
lete Sûð-Dene	*but* let *the* South Danes
sylfe geweorðan	themselves decide
gûðe wið Grendel.	*the* contest with Grendel.
Gode ic þanc secge,	To God I say thanks,
þæs ðe ic ðe gesundne	for that I thee sound
geseón móste.	might see."
Beowulf maðelode,	Beowulf spake,
bearn Ecgþeówes:	Ecgtheow's son:
Þæt is undyrne,	"It is not secret,
dryhten Higelác,	*my* lord Hygelac,
[uncer] gemeting	[our] meeting
monegum fýra,	to many men,
hwylce [orleg]-hwîl	what while [of conflict]
uncer Grendles	of myself and Grendel
wearð on þâm wange,	was on the place,
þær he worna fela	where he *a* great abundance,
Sige-Scyldingum	to *the* victorious Scyldings,
sorge gefremede,	had of sorrow caus'd,
yrmðe tó aldre.	misery everlasting.
Ic þæt eall gewræc,	I have avenged all that,
swâ ne gylpan þearf	so *that* need not boast

4006. uncer is supplied from conjecture.

4008. orleg is supplied from conjecture.

4009. This is an O. Norse construction. The rule is, that where in other tongues a personal pronoun is joined with a proper name by the conjunction *and* (ok), the ok is in O. Nor. omitted, and the pronoun put in the dual or plural number, and the same case as the proper name. Rask, Anvisn. till Isländskan. Stockh. 1823, p. 228. See Cædmon, p. 296, 6; and Cod. Exon. pp. 324, 31; 467, 7—for other instances.

Grendles maga	of Grendel's kinsmen
[ǽnig] ofer eorðan	any on earth
uht-hlem þone,	of that twilight tumult,
se þe lengest leofað	who shall longest live
láðan cynnes.	of *the* hateful race.
Fǽr-bifongen,	With perils encompass'd,
ic þær furðum cwom,	I had but just come there,
tó ðâm hring-sele,	to the ring-hall,
Hróðgâr grêtan	Hrothgar to greet:
sona me se mǽra	*when* forthwith to me the great
mago Healfdenes,	son of Healfdene,
syððan he mód-sefan	after he my
minne cuðe,	mind's purpose knew,
wið his sylfes sunu	opposite his own son
setl getæhte.	*a* seat assign'd.
Weorod wæs on wynne;	*The* company was joyous;
ne seah ic wídan-feorh,	not in *my* life have I seen
under heofones hwealf,	under heaven's vault,
heal-sittendra	of hall-sitters
medu-dreám máran;	*a* mead-joy greater;
hwílum mǽru cwên,	at times *the* great queen,
friðu-sibb folca,	*the* peaceful tie of nations,
flet eall geond-hwearf,	*the* hall all travers'd,
bædde byras geonge;	*her* young sons address'd;
oft hió beáh-wriðan	oft she *a* ringed wreath
secge [sealde],	to *the* warrior gave,
ǽr híe to setle gong.	ere to *her* seat she went.
Hwílum for duguðe	At times before *the* nobles
dóhtor Hróðgâres	Hrothgar's daughter
eorlum on ende,	to *the* earls in order
ealu-wǽge bær,	*the* ale-cup bore,
þa ic Freáwaie	whom I Freaware

4042. sealde is supplied from conjecture.
4043. MS. geong.

flet-sittende	*the* court residents
nemnan hŷrde,	heard name,
þær hiô gled-sinc	where she bright treasure
hæleþum sealde:	to *the* warriors gave:
siô gehâten [wæs],	she was promis'd,
geong gold-hroden,	young, gold-adorn'd,
gladum suna Frôdan;	to *the* glad son of Froda;
[ha] fað þæs geworden	therefore is *he* become
wine Scyldinga,	*the* Scylding's friend,
rîces hyrde;	*the* kingdom's shepherd;
and þæt rǽd talað,	and that report tells,
þæt he mid ðŷ wîfe	that with the wife he
wæl-fǽhða dǽl,	*a* deal of deadly feuds
sæcca gesette;	*and* strifes has allay'd;
oft seldan hwær,	though seldom anywhere,
æfter leôd-hrŷre,	after *a* people's fall.
lytle hwîle	*even* for *a* little while
bôn-gâr bûgeð,	*the* fatal dart ceases,
þeâh seô brŷd duge	although the bride be good.

XXX.

* * * * * *

* * * * * *

Mæg þæs þonne ofþyncan	This then may ill endure
þeôdne Heaðo-beardna 4071	*the* Heathobeards' prince

4053. wæs is supplied from conjecture.

4063. Oft seldan present a very incompatible juxta-position. For oft I suspect we should read þeáh. But ignorance of the events alluded to and the defective state of the MS. render every attempt at interpretation little else than guess-work.

4070. Here a part of the MS. is wanting, consisting of the remainder of Canto XXVIII., the whole of XXIX., and the beginning of XXX.

4071. MS. þeoden.

and þegna gehwâm	and every thane
þâra leóda,	of those peoples,
þonne he mid fæmnan	when with *the* woman he
on flet gæð,	walks in *the* court,
dryht-bearn Dęna,	*the* Dane's princely child,
duguðe beþênede,	by *the* noble served
on him gyrdeð	on him girds
gomelra lâfe,	*the* relic of *the* old,
heard and hring-mǽl,	hard and ring-mail'd,
Heaðo-beardna gestreón,	*the* treasure of the Heathobeards,
þenden hîe þâm wæpnum	while they those weapons
wealdan môston,	might command,
oððæt hîe forlæddon	until they misled
tô ðâm lind-plegan	to the shield-play
swǽse gesiðas	*their* dear associates
ond hyra sylfra feorh.	and their own lives.
Þonne cwið æt beore	Then at *the* beer will say
se þe beáh gesyhð,	he who *the* ring shall see,
eald æsc-wîga,	*an* old spear-warrior,
se þe eall geman	who remembers all
gâr-cwealm gumena,	*the* slaughter of *the* men,
him bið grim [se] fa,	(fierce will be his spirit,)
onginneð geomor-môd	sad of mood will *he* begin
geong[ne] cempan,	of *the* young warrior,
þurh hreðra gehygd,	through *his* bosom's thought,
higes cunnian,	*the* mind to prove,
wîg-bealu weccean,	war-bale waken,
and þæt word acwyð :	and that word will say :
Meaht ðû mîn wine	"Thou, my friend, mightest
mece gecnâwan,	*the* falchion know,
þone þin fæder	which thy father
tô gefeohte bær	bore to *the* fight

4077. MS. duguða bewenede. 4078. MS. gladiað.
4081. Heaða-bearna. 4084. MS. forlæddan.

under here-grîman,	under *the* martial helm,
hindeman siðe,	for *the* last time,
dýre îren,	*the* dear iron,
þær hine Dene slôgon,	where *the* Danes him slew,
weoldon wæl-stôwe,	were masters of *the* slaughter place,
syððan Wiðergyld læg,	when Withergyld had perish'd,
æfter hæleþa hrýre,	after *the* fall of heroes,
hwâte Scyldingas.	*the* bold Scyldings.
Nû her þâra banena	Now here of those murderers
byre nât hwylces	*the* son, I know not whose
frætwum hrêmig	in arms exulting
on flet gæð,	walks in the court,
morþres gylpeð,	of *the* slaughter boasts,
and þone maðþum byreð	and the treasure bears,
þone þe ðû mid rihte	which thou with right
rǽdan sceoldest.	shouldst command."
Manað swâ and myndgað,	Thus prompts *he* and reminds,
mǽla gehwylce,	on every occasion,
sârum wordum,	with painful words,
oððæt sǽl cymeð,	until *the* time comes,
þæt se fægs þegn,	when *the* fated thane,
fore fæder dǽdum,	for *his* father's deeds,
æfter billes bîte,	after *the* falchion's bite,
blôd-fâg swefeð	blood-stain'd sleeps,
ealdres scyldig.	to death condemn'd.
Him se oþer þonan	Thence the other
losað wigende,	warrior escapes,
con him land geare.	*he the* land well knows.
Þonne bióð brocene,	Then will be broken,
on bâ healfa,	on both sides,
âð-sweord eorla,	*the* oath-swearing of warriors.
[Syð]þan Ingelde	Afterwards in Ingeld

4124. MS. fæmnan. 4133. MS. healfe.

weallað wæl-níðas,	deadly hates will boil,
and him wíf-lufan,	and his woman's love,
æfter cear-wælmum,	after *the* heats of care,
cólran weorðað.	will become cooler.
Þý ic Heaþo-beardna	Therefore I *the* Heathobeards'
hyldo ne talige,	affection esteem not,
dryht-sibbe dǽl	*nor* part of lordly kinship
Denum unfǽcnc,	to *the* Danes guileless,
freóndscipe fæstne.	*their* friendship fast.
Ic sceal forð sprecan	I shall *now* speak on
gen ymbe Grendel,	again about Grendel.
þæt ðú geare cunne,	that thou well mayst know,
sinces brytta,	O dispenser of treasure,
tú hwân syððan wearð	how afterwards fell out
hond-ræs hǽleþa.	*the* hand conflict of warriors.
Syððan heofenes gim	After heaven's gem
glâd ofer grundas,	had glided o'er *the* earth,
gæst yrre cwom,	*the* guest came angry,
eatol ǽfen-grom,	*the* giant fierce at eve,
úser neósan,	to visit us,
þær we gesunde	where we sound
sele weardodon:	guarded *the* hall:
þær wæs hond-sció	there was *his* glove
hilde onsæge,	in *the* war not idle,
feorh-bealu fǽgum:	*a* life-bale to *the* fated:
se þe fyrmest læg,	who foremost lay,

4140. MS. Heaþo-bearna. 4141. MS. telge.

4154. Giants are no doubt said to be fierce at eve, because, shunning the light of day, it was only after nightfall that they issued forth bent on deeds of violence. If surprised by the light of the sun, they became transformed to stone. See Glossary, v. eatol. Eatol may, however, be an error for atol.

4157. MS. sæl.

4161. se þe. Thorkelin has he, but in the MS. all that remains is e. K., rightly I think, supplies the defect with se þe.

gyrded cempa.	*a* girded champion,
him Grendel wearð,	to him was Grendel,
mǽrum magu-þegne,	to *my* great fellow-thane,
tő műð-bonon ;	*a* mouth-murderer ;
leőfes mannes	*the* belov'd man's
lîc eall forswealg ;	body *he* all swallow'd ;
nő ðý ǽr ût þâ-gen,	nor yet for that the earlier out,
îdel-hende,	empty-handed,
bona blődig-tőð,	*the* bloody-tooth'd murderer,
bealewa gemyndig,	of evils mindful,
of ðâm gold-sele	from that gold-hall
gongan wolde ;	would go ;
ac he mægnes rőf	but he, proud of *his* might,
mîn costode,	trial made of me,
grâpode gearo-folm,	grasp'd ready-handed,
glőf [hangode]	*his* glove hung
sîd and syllîc,	wide and wondrous,
searo-bendum fæst,	with curions bindings fast ;
sió wæs őrðoncum	it was cunningly
eall gegyrwed	all prepared
diófles cræftum	with *a* devil's crafts
and dracan fellum :	and dragon's skins :
he mec þær on-innan	he me there within
unsynnigne	unsinning,
diőr-dǽd-fruma,	*the* brutal perpetrator,
gedőn wolde	would make
manigra sumne :	one of many :

4165. i.e. because he devoured his victims.

4177. This about Grendel's glove (hond-sció, l. 4158) is not very intelligible. I imagine it to be identical with what at l. 1976 is called his hand-sporu. I once thought with Grundtvig that hand-sció was the name of the warrior slain by Grendel (as Handschuh does exist as a proper name), but both the context and this mention of his glove are adverse to this interpretation.

hyt ne mihte swá,	it might not so *be*,
syððan ic on yrre	when in anger I
upp-riht astód	upright stood.
Tó lang ys tó reccenne	Too long is *it* to recount
hú [ic] þám leód-scaðan,	how [I] to the miscreant,
yfla gehwylces,	for every evil,
hond-leán forgeald;	paid *a* manual reward;
þær ic, þeóden mín,	there I, my prince,
þin leóde	thy people
weorðode weorcum.	honour'd by *my* works.
He onwég losade;	He escap'd away;
lytle hwíle	for *a* little while
líf-wynna breác;	life's pleasures enjoy'd:
hwæþre him sió swiðre	yet his right hand
swaðe weardade	guarded on *his* track
hand on Hiorte,	in Heorot,
and he heán ðonan,	and he humble thence,
módes geomor,	sad of mood,
mere-grund gefeoll.	*to the* lake-ground fell.
Me þone wæl-ræs	Me for that deadly onslaught
wine Scyldinga	*the* Scyldings' friend
fættan golde	with rich gold
fela leánode,	abundantly rewarded,
manegum maðmum,	with many treasures,
syððan mergen com,	after morning came,
and we tó symble	and we to *the* feast
geseten hæfdon.	had sat.
Þær wæs gidd and gleó,	There was song and glee,
gomela Scylding,	*the* aged Scylding,
fela fricgende,	much inquiring,
feorran rehte;	related *things* from *times* remote,
hwílum hilde deór	at whiles *the* beast of war
hearpan wynne,	*the* joy of harp
gomen-wudu grétte;	greeted, the wood of mirth,

hwîlum gyd awræc	sometimes *the* lay recited
sôð and sârlîc;	sooth and sorrowful;
hwîlum syllîc spell	sometimes *a* wondrous tale
rehte æfter rihte	told in order due
rûm-ḣeort cyning:	the liberal-hearted king;
hwîlum eft ongan,	sometimes again began,
eldo-gebunden,	by age restrain'd,
gomel gûð-wîga	*the* old warrior
geoguðe cwiðan,	with *the* youth to speak,
hilde strengo;	*the* strength of war;
hreðer inne weoll,	*his* breast within *him* boil'd,
þonne he wintrum frôd	when he in winters wise
worn gemunde.	many things call'd to mind.
Swâ we þær-inne	So we therein
andlangne dæg	*the* livelong day
nióṭe namon,	in enjoyment pass'd,
oððæt niht becwom	until night came
oþer to yldum.	*the* second to men.
Þá wæs eft hraðe	Then was in turn quickly
gearo gyrn-wræce	ready with wily vengeance
Grendel's môdor;	Grendel's mother;
siðode sorhfull:	*she* journey'd sorrowful;
sunu deáþ fornâm,	*her* son death had taken,
wîg-hete Wedera:	*the* Weders' hostile hate:
wîf unhŷre	*the* monster woman
hyre bearn gewræc,	her child avenged,
beorn acwealde	*a* warrior slew
ellenlîce.	daringly.
Þær wæs Æschere,	There was from Æschere,
frôdan fyrn-witan,	*the* sage ancient councillor,
feorh ûðgenge;	life departed;
nô ðær hŷ hine ne môston,	nor there might they him,
syððan mergen cwom,	when morning came,

4238. MS. niode naman.

deâð-wêrigne,	*the* death-weary *one*,
Deniga leôde	*the* Dane's people
bronde forbærnan,	with fire consume,
ne on bǽl hladan	nor on *the* pile raise
leôfne mannan :	*the* dear man :
hiô þæt lic ætbær,	she the corpse bore away,
feôndes fædrunga,	*the* fiend's parent,
þær under firgen-streâm.	there under *the* mountain stream.
Þæt wæs Hrôðgâre	That was to Hrothgar
hreôwa tornost,	of sorrows saddest,
þâra þe leôd-fruman	of those which *the* nation's chief
lange begeâte :	had long o'erwhelmed :
Þâ se ðeôden mec,	Then the prince me,
[be] þîne life,	by thy life,
healsode hreôh-môd,	besought, fierce of mood,
þæt ic on holma geþring	that in *the* throng of waters I
eorlscipe efnde,	would *a* valorous deed perform,
ealdre genêðde,	*my* life would venture,
mǽrðo fremede :	great glory achieve :
he we mêde gehêt.	he me *a* meed promis'd.
Ic ðâ ðæs wælmes,	I then of the boiling *deep*,
þe is wîde cûð,	which is widely known,
grimne grŷrelîcne	*the* grim, horrific
grund-hyrde fond ;	ground-keeper found ;
þær unc hwîle wæs	there we had *a* while
hand-gemǽne ;	*a* hand-conflict ;
holm-heolfre weoll,	*the* water bubbled with blood,
and ic heafde becearf,	and from *her* head I cut,
in ðâm [gûð]-sele,	in that battle-hall,

4257. MS. Denia.

4269. be is supplied from conjecture.

4278. MS. grimme.

4284. gúð is not in the MS., but supplied as necessary to the rhythm and alliteration.

Grendles módor
eácnum ecgum;
unsofte þonan
feorh oðferede:
nǽs ic fǽge þá-gyt:
ac me eorla hleó
eft gesealde
maðma menigeo,
maga Healfdenes.

Grendel's mother
with powerful edge;
with difficulty thence
I my life bore away:
I was not yet doom'd
but me *the* protector of warriors
again gave
many treasures,
Healfdene's son.

XXXI.

Swâ se ðeód-cyning
þeáwum lyfde;
nealles ic ðâm leánum
forloren hæfde,
mægnes mêde:
ac he me [maðmas] geaf,
sunu Healfdenes,
on [mînne] sylfes dôm,
ðâ ic ðe, beorn-cyning,
bringan wylle,
êstum gegyrwan;
gen is eall æt ðe
lissa gelong:
ic lyt hafo
heáfod-maga,
nefne Hygelác þec.
Hêt ðâ in-beran
eofor-heáfod-segn,
heaðo-steápne helm,

So the great king
becomingly liv'd;
not the rewards
had I lost,
the meed of might;
for he me [treasures] gave,
Healfdene's son,
in [my] own power,
which I to thee, warrior-king,
will bring,
with gladness make ready;
moreover of thee are all
my pleasures long:
I have few
near kinsmen,
save thee, Hygelac."
Bade then in be borne
the boar-head banner,
the warlike towering helm,

4285. MS. Grendeles.

4299. maðmas is supplied from conjecture; it has perished from the MS. So likewise K.

4311. MS. eafor.

[here]-byrnan,	*the* [martial] byrnie,
gûð-sweord geâtolîc ;	*the* splendid battle-sword ;
gyd æfter wræc :	*this* speech afterward recited :
Me ðis hilde-sceorp	" To me this war-gear
Hrôðgâr sealde ;	Hrothgar gave ;
snotra fengel	*the* sagacious prince
sume worde hêt,	some *things* by word commanded,
þæt ic his ǽrend þe	that I to thee his errand
eft gesægde :	again should say :
cwæð þæt hyt hæfde	said that it had had
Hiorogâr cyning,	king Hiorogar,
leôd Scyldinga,	*the* Scyldings' lord
lange hwîle :	for *a* long while :
nô ðý ǽr suna sînum	*yet* not the sooner to his son
syllan wolde,	would he give,
hwatum Heorowearde,	to *the* bold Heoroweard,
þeâh he him hold wǽre,	though he to him was kind,
breôst-gewǽdu :	*these* breast-weeds :
brûc ealles well.	enjoy *it* all well !"
Hýrde ic þæt þâm frætwum	I heard that of *these* appointments
feôwer mearas,	four steeds,
lungre gelîce,	swift alike,
last weardode,	follow'd *the* track,
æppel-fealuwe.	apple-fallow.
He him êst geteâh	He gave to him *a* present
meara and maðma.	of steeds and treasures.
Swâ sceal mǽg dôn,	So should *a* kinsman do,
nealles inwit-net	not *a* net of treachery
oðrum bregdan	for another braid

4313. here is supplied from conjecture.

4320. MS. ærest, for which Conybeare justly substitutes ærend.

4341. M.S. bregdon.

dyrnum cræfte,	with secret craft,
deáð re * *	death * *
hond-gesteallan.	for *an* associate.
Hygeláce wæs,	Was to Hygelac,
níþa heardum,	*the* bold in conflicts,
nefa swyðe hold,	*his* nephew very affectionate,
and gehwæþer oðrum	and each to other
hroþra gemyndig.	mindful of benefits.
Hýrde ic þæt he þone heals-beáh	I heard that he the neck-ring
Hygde gesealde,	to Hygd gave,
wrætlícne wundor-maþðum,	*the* curious, wondrous treasure,
þone ðe him Wealhþeów geaf,	which to him Wealhtheow had given,
ðeódnes dohtor,	*a* prince's daughter,
þrio wicg somod,	together with three horses,
swarte and sadol-beorhte :	black and with saddles bright :
hyre syððan wæs,	was then,
æfter beáh-ðege,	after *the* presentation of rings,
breost geweorðod.	*her* breast honour'd.
Swá bealdode	Thus flourish'd
bearn Ecgðeówes,	Ecgtheow's son,
guma gúðum cuð,	*the* man known in wars,
gódum dǽdum ;	for good deeds ;
dreáh æfter dóme ;	*he* acted after judgment ;
nealles druncne slóg	nor struck *he the* drunken
heorð-geneátas ;	enjoyers of *his* hearth ;

4353. MS. Wælþeo.

4356. MS. swancor and sadol-beorht, both sing., though the noun wicg is plur.

4358. Not improbably an error for beor-þege, as at l. 234; though the reading of the text receives support from hring-þege, Cod. Exon. 308. 24.

4359. MS. brost. Her breast was honoured or adorned with the collar.

næ̂s him hreô sefa,	his was no rugged soul,
ac he man-cynnes	but he of mankind
mæste cræfte,	*the* greatest strength,
ginfæstan gife,	*the* ample gift,
þe him God sealde,	that God had given him,
heold hilde deôr.	possess'd, *the* beast of war.
Heân wæs lange,	Long was *the* shame,
swâ hine Geâta bearn	when him *the* sons of *the* Goths
gôdne ne tealdon,	not good accounted,
ne hyne on medo-bence	nor him on *the* mead-bench
micles wyrðne	of much worthy
Drihten wereda	*the* Lord of hosts
gedôn wolde ;	would make ;
swyðe [oft sæg] don	very [oft *they* said]
þæt he sleâc wæ̂re,	that he was slack,
æðeling unfrom :	*a* sluggish prince :
edwendan cwom	*a* reverse came
tir-eâdigum men	to *the* glorious man
torna gehwylces.	of every grievance.
Hét ðâ eorla hleô	Bade then *the* protector of warriors
in gefetian,	fetch in,
heaðo-rôf cyning,	*the* war-fam'd king,
Hreðles lâfe,	Hrathel's relic,
golde gegyrede ;	with gold adorn'd ;
næ̂s mid Geâtum ðâ	*there* was then not among *the* Goths
sinc-maðþum sêlra	*a* better treasure
on sweordes hâd ;	of *a* sword's kind ;
þæt he on Beowulfes	which he on Beowulf's
bearm alegde,	bosom laid,

4380. [oft sæg] is supplied from conjecture.

4383. MS. edwenden.

4395. See ll. 2290-2293 for a similar expression.

and him gesealde	and to him gave
seofon þusendo,	seven thousand,
bold and brego-stôl.	*a* habitation and *a* princely seat.
Him wæs bâm samod	To them both together was
on ðâm leódscipe	in the community
lond gecynde,	*the* land natural,
eard-êðel-riht	*the* patrimonial right
oðrum swiðor,	in *the* one stronger,
sîde rîce	*the* ample realm
þâm ðær sêlra wæs.	his, who there was *the* better.
Eft þæt geeóde	Afterwards that pass'd away.
uferan dógrum,	in later days,
hilde hlemmum,	in war's tumults,
syððan Hygelác læg,	when Hygelac had fall'n,
and Heardrede	and to Heardred
hilde mecas,	battle-falchions,
under bord-hreóðan,	under *the* shield,
tó bonan wurdon,	became *the* bane,
þá hyne gesóhton,	when him sought
on sige-þeóde,	among *the* victor-people.
hearde hilde-frecan,	bold-daring warriors,
heaðo-Scylfingas	*the* martial Scylfings
nîða genægdon	quell'd in wars
nefan Hererîces.	Hereric's nephew.
Syððan Beowulfe	Afterwards of Beowulf
brâde rîce	*the* broad realm
on hand gehwearf:	into *the* hand devolv'd:

4397. This expression has undergone many attempts at explanation, but none of them satisfactory.

4405. i.e. the better (higher) born, namely Hygelac.

4406. MS. Æft þæt geiode.

4407. MS. ufaran.

4408. MS. hlammum.

4410. MS. Hearede.

4411. MS. meceas.

4414. MS. gesohtan.

4418. MS. gehnægdan.

4421. MS. bræde.

he geheold tela	he held *it* well
fiftig wintru ;	fifty winters ;
wæs þæt frôd cyning,	that was *a* wise king,
eald êþel-weard,	*an* old land-guardian,
oððæt ân ongan,	until one began,
deorcum nihtum,	in *the* dark nights,
draca rícsian,	*a* dragon, to hold sway,
se ðe on heâpe	which in *a* heap
hord beweotede ;	*his* hoard watch'd over ;
stân-beorh steâpne	*a* steep stone mount
stíg under læg,	*the* path lay beneath,
eldum uncuð.	to men unknown.
Þær on-innan gong	There within went
niða nât *hwylc*	of men I know not who
* * *	* * *
hæ̂ðnum horde	to *the* heathen hoard
hond * * hwylc	* * *
since fâh	* * *
he þæt syððan	he that after
* * *	* * *
slæ̂pende be fire,	sleeping by *the* fire,
fyrena hyrde	*the* guardian of crimes
þeôfes cræfte,	by *a* thief's craft,
þæt sie * *	that * *
* * folc-biorn	* * *
þæt he gebolge wæs.	that he was angry.

XXXII.

Nealles [mid] geweoldum,	Not spontaneously,
wyrm-horda cræft,	*the* worm-hoards' craft,
sylfes willum,	of his own will,

4425. MS. þa. 4427. MS. on. 4432. MS. stearne.
4435. MS. giong.

se ðe him * * gesceōd,
ac for þreā-nedlan
* * nāt hwylces,
hæleða bearna,
hete-swengeas
* * þea
and þær-inne weall
secg syn * sig
sona in-wlatode,
þæt * * ðām gyste
bræg * * stōd
Hwæ * * sceapen
* * *
* * *
* se fæs begeāt
* * *

Þær wæs swylcra fela,
in ðām eorð-[scræfe],
ǣr-gestreōna,
swā he on gear-dagum,
gumena nāt hwylc,
eormen-lāfe
æþelan cynnes,
þanc-hycgende,
þær gehydde,
deōre maðmas.
Ealle hīe deāð fornam,
ǣrran mǣlum,
and se ān ðā-gen
leōda duguðe,
se ðær lengest hwearf,
wearð wine geomor;

he who * * *
but from dire need
* * I know not of what,
sons of men,
hateful strokes
* * *
and therein *
* * *
forthwith look'd in
* * *
* * *
* * *
* * *
* * *
* * *
* * *

There of such were many,
in that earth-cave,
ancient treasures,
as he in days of yore,
what man I know not,
the great legacy
of *a* noble race,
thoughtful,
there had hidden,
precious treasures.
Death had taken them all,
in former times,
and the one at length
of peoples' nobles,
who there longest wander'd,
was *a* sad man;

4454. MS. in watide. 4467. MS. si. 4469. MS. ðer.
4470. MS. weard.

wiscte þæs yldan,	*he* wish'd for *a* delay,
þæt he lytel fæc	that he *a* little space
leng gestreóna	longer *the* treasures
brúcan móste.	might enjoy.
Beorh eal gearo	*The* mound all ready
wunode on wonge,	stood on the plain,
wæter-ýðum neáh	near to *the* water-waves,
niwel be næsse,	down by *the* headland,
nearo-cræftum fæst :	fast by arts stringent :
þær on-innan bær	there within bore
eorl gestreóna,	*the* earl *his* treasures,
hringa hyrde,	*the* guardian of rings,
heáp-fundne dǽl	*the* heap-found portion
fættan goldes ;	of rich gold ;
feá worda cwæð :	*a* few words said :
Hold ðú nú hrúse,	"Hold thou now, earth !
nú hæleð ne móston,	(now men must not)
eorla æhte ;	*the* possession of nobles ;
hwær hit ǽr on ðe	where it erst on thee
góde begeaton ;	good *men* acquir'd ;
gúð-deáð fornam,	war-death has taken,
feorh-bealo frecne,	*a* cruel life-bale,
fyra gehwylcne	every man
leóda mínra ;	of my people ;
þára ðe þis [líf] ofgeaf :	of those who this life resign'd :
gesawon sele-dreám	*they* had seen joy of hall
* hwá sweord-wege,	* brandishing of swords,
oððe fe * *	or * *
fæted wǽge,	*the* rich cup,
drync-fæt deóre,	*the* precious drink-vessel,

4471. MS. rihde. 4473. MS. long. 4478. MS. niwe.
4483. MS. hard fyrdne. 4485. MS. fec. 4487. MS. mæstan.
4489. MS. hwæt. 4493. MS. fyrena.
4495. MS. þa na. líf is supplied from conjecture.

dug[uðe] ellen-seóc :	nobles valour sick :
sceal se hearda helm,	*the* hard helm shall,
[hyr]sted golde,	adorn'd with gold,
fægum befeallan ;	from *the* fated fall ;
feorh-wund swefað	mortally wounded sleep
þa ðe beado grîmman	those who war to rage
bymian sceoldon :	by trumpet should announce,
geswylce seó here-pâd,	in like manner the war-shirt,
seó æt hilde gebâd,	which in battle stood,
ofer borda gebræc,	over *the* crash of shields,
bîte îrena,	*the* bite of swords,
brosnað æfter beorne ;	shall moulder after *the* warrior ;
ne mæg byrnan hring	*the* byrnie's ring may not
æfter wîg-fruman	after *the* martial leader
wîde feran	go far
hæleðum be healfe ;	on *the* side of heroes ;
nis hearpan wyn,	*there* is no joy of harp,
gomen gleó-beâmes,	*no* glee-wood's mirth,
ne gôd hafoc	no good hawk
geond sǽl swingeð,	swings through *the* hall,
ne se swifta mearh	nor the swift steed
burh-stede beâteð,	tramps *the* city-place,
bealo-cwealm hafað	baleful death has
fela feorh-cynna	many living kinds
[forð] onsended.	sent [forth]."
Swâ giomor-môd	So, sad of mood,
giohðo mǽnde	*his* afflictions bewail'd
ân æfter eallum	one after all,
unblîðe hwæ * *	unblithe * *
dæges and nihtes,	by day and night,

4501. MS. ellor.
4504. MS. fætum befeallen.
4505. MS. feor mynd.
4507. MS. bywan.
4517. MS. næs.
4520. sele ?
4525. forð is supplied from conjecture.

oððæt deâðes folm
hrân æt heortan.
Hord-wynne fond
eald uht-sceaða
opene standan
se ðe byrnende
biorgas sêceð ;
nacod nîð-draca
nihtes fleôgeð
fŷre be fangen ;
hynd fold-buend
* * he ge *
* * sceall
bearn * *
* * hrûsan,
þær he hǽðen gold
warað wintrum frôd ;
ne byð him wihte
* * *
* * *
* * *

Swâ se þeôd-sceaða
þreô hund wintra
heold on hrûsan
hord-ærna sum
eâcen-cræftig,
oððæt hyne ân abealh
mon on môde :
man-dryhtne bær
fæted wǽge,
frioðo-wǽre bæd
hlâford sinne.
Þâ wæs hord rasod,

until death's hand
touch'd *him* at heart.
The hoard-delight found
the old twilight scather
standing open,
who burning
seeks *out* mounts ;
the naked, spiteful dragon
flies by night
in fire envelop'd ;
him *the* land-dwellers
* * *
* * *
* * *
* * *

where he heathen gold
defends, with winters wise ;
he has not aught
* * *
* * *
* * *

So the great scather
three hundred winters
held in *the* earth
a hoard-house
exceeding strong,
until him enraged one
man in mood :
to *his* liege lord *he* bore
a rich cup,
pray'd *a* covenant of security
of his lord.
Then was *the* hoard explor'd,

4531. MS. wylm. 4547. hrusam. 4556. reáfod ?

oðboren beága hord,
bēn getiðad
feasceaftum men.
Freá sceawode
fyra fyrn-geweorc
forman siðe.
Þá se wyrm onwóc
wroht wæs geniwad;
stonc ðá æfter stáne,
stearc-heort onfand
feóndes fót-last;
he tó forð gestóp,
dyrnan cræfte,
dracan heáfde neáh.
Swá mæg unfǽgė
eáðe gedígan
weán and wræc-sið,
se ðe Waldendes
hyldo gehealdeð.
Hord-weard sóhte
georne æfter grunde,
wolde guman findan,
þone þe him on sweofote
sáre geteóde:
hát and hreóh-mod
hlǽw oft ymbe-hwearf,
ealne útanweardne;
ne ðær ǽnig mon
on þám westene

the hoard of rings borne off,
the prayer granted
to *the* poor man.
The lord beheld
the ancient work of men
for *the* first time.
When the worm awoke
the crime had been renew'd;
he then smelt along *the* stone,
the stout of heart found
the foe's foot-trace;
he had stept forth,
by secret craft,
near to *the* dragon's head:
Thus may *an* undoom'd man
easily escape from
calamity and exile,
who *the* Almighty's
favour holds.
The hoard-ward sought
diligently along *the* ground,
he the man would find,
him who to him in sleep
had caused pain:
hot and savage of mood
the mound *he* oft wander'd round,
all outward;
not there any man
in that desert,

4557. MS. onboren. emend. K.
4558. MS. bene.
4568. he, i.e. the foe.
4582. MS. hlæwú.
4585. Thork. þære. MS. westenne. The sense seems to be that the dragon went prowling about, but found no one inclined

hwæðere hilde geféh,	however, in conflict rejoiced,
beâ[do]-weorces ;	in *the* work of war ;
hwílum on beorh æt-hwearf,	sometimes he return'd to *the* mount,
sinc-fæt sôhte ;	*his* treasure vessel sought ;
he þæt sona onfand,	he forthwith found,
þæt hæfde gumena sum	that some man had
goldes gefandod,	meddled with *the* gold,
heâh-gestreôna.	*the* chief treasures.
Hord-weard onbâd	*The* hoard-ward awaited
earfoðlíce	with difficulty
oððæt æfen cwom ;	until evening came ;
wæs ðâ gebolgen	then was angry
beorges hyrde,	*the* mount's guardian,
wolde fela ðâ	would much then
fýre forgyldan	with fire requite
drync-fæt dýre.	dearly for *his* drink-vessel.
Þâ wæs dæg sceacen,	Then was day departed,
wyrme on willan ;	after *the* worm's wishes ;
nô on wealle leng	not within *his* mound longer
bídan wolde ;	would he abide ;
ac mid bǽle fór,	but with burning went,
fýre gefýsed.	with fire hastening.
Wæs se fruma egeslíc	The beginning was dreadful
leôdum on lande,	to *the* people in *the* land,
swâ hit lungre wearð,	as it quickly was,
on hyra sinc-gífan,	in their treasure giver,
sâre geendod.	painfully ended.

to contend with him. The whole story, owing to the bad state of a very bad MS., is very unintelligible.

4600. MS. lige, with no alliteration.

4604. MS. læg.

XXXIII.

Þá se gæst ongan	Then the guest began
glédum spíwan,	with gleeds to vomit,
beorht-hofu bærnan ;	*the* bright dwellings to burn ;
byrne-leóma stód	*the* fire-beam stood
eldum on andan ;	in hate to men ;
nó ðær áht cwices	nothing living there
láð lyft-floga	*the* hostile air-flier
lǽfan wolde.	would leave.
Wæs þæa wyrmes wig	That worm's war was
wíde gesýne,	widely seen,
nearo-fáges níð,	*the* torturing foe's malice,
neáh and feorran,	near and far,
hú se guð-sceaða	how the hostile scather
Geáta leóde	*the* Goths' people
hatode and hýnde ;	hated and oppress'd ;
hord eft gesceát,	*then* darted back to *his* hoard,
dryht-sele dyrnne,	*his* secret hall,
ǽr dæges hwíle.	ere day-time.
Hæfde landwara	*He* had *the* land-inhabitants
lige befangen,	in flame envelop'd,
bǽle and bronde ;	with fire and burning ;
beorges getrúwode,	in *his* mount he trusted,
wíges and wealles :	*his* war and mound :
him seó wén geleáh.	him that hope deceiv'd.
Þá wæs Beowulfe	Then was to Beowulf
bróga gecyðed	*the* terror made known
snúde tó sóðe,	speedily in sooth,
þæt his sylfes hám,	that his own home,
bolda sélest,	of mansions best,
bryne-wylmum mealt,	was by fire-heats consum'd,
gif-stól Geáta.	*the* Goths' gift-chair.

4640. MS. him.

Þæt ðâm gôdan wæs	That to the good *prince* was
hreôw on hreðre,	grievous in mind,
hyge-sorga-mæst:	of mental sorrows greatest:
wênde se wîsa	*the* wise *chief* ween'd
þæt he Wealdende,	that he with *the* Almighty,
ofer ealle riht,	against all right,
êcean Dryhtne,	with *the* eternal Lord,
bitre gebulge:	should be bitterly incens'd:
breôst innan weoll	*his* breast boil'd within
þeostrum geþoncum,	with dark thoughts,
swâ him geþwære ne wæs.	as *it* was not befitting him.
Hæfde lig-draca	*The* fire-drake had
leôda fæsten,	*the* people's fastness,
ealond ûtan,	*an* island without,
eorð-weard ðone,	the country's safeguard,
glêdum forgrunden.	with gleeds destroyed.
Him þæs gûð-cyning,	For this *the* warlike king,
Wedera þeôden,	*the* Weders' prince,
wræce leornode:	vengeance learn'd;
hêht him þâ gewyrcean	bade for him then be wrought
wîgendra hleô,	*the* protector of warriors,
eall îrenne,	all of iron,
eorla dryhten,	*the* lord of earls,
wîg-bord wrætlîc:	*a* wondrous war-board:
wisse he gearwe	he well knew
þæt him holt-wudu	that him *the* forest-wood
helpan ne meahte,	might not help,
lind wið lige.	linden against fire.
Sceolde lǽn-daga	Of *these* miserable days must
æþeling ǽr-gôd	*the* good prince

4649. MS. ealde. 4654. MS. geþywe. 4658. eard?
4660. Him here seems redundant.
4672. MS. þend, without either sense or alliteration. I adopt with K. lǽn.

ende gebîdan	*an* end abide,
worulde lîfes,	of *this* world's life,
and se wyrm somod ;	and the worm with *him ;*
þeâh ðe hord-welan	although *the* hoard-wealth
heolde lange.	*he* long had held.
Oferhogode ðâ	Disdain'd then
hringa fengel	*the* prince of rings
þæt he þone wîd-flogan	that he *the* wide-flier
weorode gesôhte,	wth *a* host should seek,
sîdan herge ;	*a* numerous band ;
nô he him þa sæcce ondred,	he dreaded not the conflict,
ne him þæs wyrmeś wîg	nor the worm's warfare
for wiht dyde,	for aught accounted,
eafoð and ellen ;	*his* energy and valour ;
forþon he ǽr fela,	because he erst many,
nearo-nêðende,	rashly daring,
nîða gedîgde,	strifes had escap'd from,
hilde-hlemma,	tumults of war,
syððan he Hrôðgâres,	since he Hrothgar's
sigor-eâdig secg,	(victorious warrior)
sele fǽlsode,	hall had purified,
and æt gûðe forgrâp	and in conflict grasp'd
Grendles magan,	Grendel's relation,
lâðan cynnes.	of loathsome race.
Nô þæt lǽsest wæs	Nor was that least
hond-gemôta,	of hand-meetings,
þær mon Hygelâc slôh,	where Hygelac was slain,
syððan Geâta cyning,	when *the* Goths' king,
gûðe-ræsum,	in war-onslaughts,
freâ-wine folca,	*the* lordly friend of nations,
Freslondum on,	in *the* Frieslands,
Hreðles eafora,	Hrethel's offspring,

4684. MS. þá. 4696. MS. Grendeles mægum.

heoro-druncen swealt,	sword-drunken perish'd,
bille gebeâten.	by *the* falchion beaten.
Þonan Beowulf com	Thence Beowulf came
sylfes cræfte,	by his own power,
sund-nŷde dreâh ;	*the* need of swimming suffer'd;
hæfde him on earme	*he* had on his arm
* * xxx.	* * thirty
hilde geâtwa,	war-equipments
þâ he to holme [st]âg.	when he to *the* sea went down.
Nealles Hetware	Not *the* Hetwaras
hreâm geþorfton,	had need of exultation,
feðe-wîges,	*in that* host of war,
þe him foran ongean	who in front against him
linde bǽron :	bore *the* linden ;
lyt eft becwom	few again came
fram þâm hild-frecan,	from that warlike darer,
hâmes niôsan :	*their* home to visit :
ofer-swam þâ sioleða bigong	swam over then *the* seals' course
sunu Ecgðeôwes,	Ecgtheow's son,
earm ánhaga,	*a* poor solitary,
eft to leôdum,	again to *his* people,
þær him Hygd gebeâd	where him Hygd offer'd
hord and rîce,	treasure and realm,
beâgas and brego-stôl :	rings and princely throne :
bearne ne trûwode,	in *her* child *she* trusted not,
þæt he wið ælfylcum	that he against foreign folks
êþel-stôlas	*his* paternal seats
healdan cuðe.	could hold.

4706. MS. hioro dryncum. 4710. MS. nytte.

4723. I suspect that the word éðel is lurking in this sioleða, and that bigong is merely a gloss dragged into the text by the copyist, to the destruction of both sense and rhythm, and that we should read,

ofer-swam þâ siol-éðel
sunu Ecgðeôwes, etc.

Ðá wæs Hygelâc deâd,	Then was Hygelac dead,
nó þý ǽr feásceafte	*yet* not for that sooner *the* poor *people*
findan meahton	could prevail
æt ðâm æðelinge,	with the prince,
ǽnige þinga	on any account,
þæt he Heardrede	that he to Heardred
hlâford wǽre,	would be lord,
oððe þone cynedóm	or the kingdom
ciósan wolde;	would choose:
hwæðre he hine on folce	yet he him among *his* people
freónd-lârum heold,	with friendly instructions maintain'd,
éstum mid âre;	kindly with honour;
oððæt he yldra wearð,	until he became older,
Weder-Geâtum weald.	*and* rul'd *the* Weder-Goths.
Hyne wræc-mecgas	Him rovers
ofer sǽ sôhton;	over *the* sea sought;
sunu Ohtheres	*the* son of Ohthere
hæfdon hý forhealden,	they had subdued,
helm Scylfinga,	*the* Scylfings' helm,
þone sélestan	the best
sǽ-cyninga,	of sea-kings,
þâra ðe in Swio-rice	of those who in Sweden
sinc brytnade,	treasure dispens'd,
mǽrne þeóden;	*a* great prince;
him þæt to mearge wearð:	that to his marrow went:
he þær orfeorme	he there fruitlessly

4737. i.e. Beowulf, 4743. MS. him. 4748. MS. mæcgas.
4749. MS. sohtan. 4750. MS. suna Ohteres; but see l. 4764.
4752. Eadgils.
4758. MS. mearce. Es geht einem durch Mark und Bein. Him refers to Heardred, as also he in the line following.
4759. he, i.e. Heardred.

feorh-wunde hleât,
sweordes swengum,
sunu Hygeláces;
and him eft gewât
Ohtheres bearn,
hâmes niósan,
syððan Heardred læg;
let ðone brego-stol
Beowulf healdan,
Geâtum wealdan:
þæt wæs gûd cyning.

sank with *a* mortal wound,
with strokes of *the* sword,
the son of Hygelac;
and again departed
Ohthere's son.
his home to visit,
after Heardred had fall'n;
he the royal seat left
Beowulf to hold,
over *the* Goths to rule:
that was *a* good king.

XXXIV.

Se ðæs leód-hrýres
leân gemunde
uferan dógrum;
Eadgilse wearð
feasceaftum freónd;
folce gestêpte
ofer sǽ sîde
sunu Ohtheres,
wîgum and wæpnum:
he gewræc syððan
* * *
* * *
cealdum cear-siðum,
cyning ealdre bineât.

He for *the* people's fall
retribution remember'd
in after days;
he became to Eadgils
when in distress *a* friend;
with people *he* supported,
over *the* wide sea,
Ohthere's son,
with warriors and weapons:
he afterwards avenged
* * *
* * *
with cold sad fortunes,
their king of life depriv'd.

4764. MS. Ongenðiowes. 4767. let refers to Heardred.

4778. MS. Ohteres.

4780. Here some couplets are evidently wanting, containing an account of Beowulf's, or Eadgils's proceedings against the "Wræc-mecgas" (l. 4748), who had slain Heardred, and driven Eadgils to seek aid of Beowulf. The king mentioned at l. 4782 is, no doubt, the king of those rovers.

Swâ he nîðа gehwane
genesen hæfde,
slîðra geslyhta,
sunu Ecgðiôwes,
ellen-weorca,
oð ðone ânne dæg,
þe he wið þâm wyrme
gewegan sceolde.
Gewât þâ xiia sum,
torne gebolgen,
dryhten Geâta,
dracan sceâwian;
hæfde þâ gefrunen
hwanan sio fǽhð âras,
bealo-nîð beorna;
him tô banan cwom
maðþum-fæt mǽre,
þurh þæs meldan hond,
se wæs on ðâm ðreâte
þreotteoða secg,
se ðæs orleges
ôr onstealde;
hæfde hyge giômor,
sceolde heân ðanon
wong wîsian:
he ofer willan gong,
tô ðæs ðe he eorð-sele
âna wisse,
hlǽw under hrûsan,
holm-wylme neâh,
ŷð-gewinne,

Thus he every enmity
had outliv'd,
every fierce conflict,
Ecgtheow's son,
every valorous work,
until that one day,
when he against *the* worm
must proceed.
Went then with xii. others,
with anger swollen,
the Goths' lord,
the dragon to behold;
he had then learn'd
whence the hostility arose,
baleful enmity of warriors;
for *his* bane to him had come
the fam'd precious vessel,
through tbe discoverer's hand,
who in that band was
the thirteenth man,
who of that strife
the beginning caus'd;
he had *a* sad mind,
he must humble thence
the plain point out:
against *his* will he went,
because that he *the* earth-hall
alone knew,
the mound under *the* earth,
to *the* sea-raging near,
the strife of waves,

4797. MS. hæft.
4800. MS. bearme.
4802. MS. mældan.
4808. MS. þonon.
4810. MS. giong.
4812. MS. anne.
4814. MS. neh.

se wæs innan full	it was full within
wrætta and wíra ;	of ornaments and wires ;
weard unhióre,	*a* monstrous guardian,
gearo gûð-freca,	*a* ready bold warrior,
gold-maðmas heold,	held *the* golden treasures,
eald under eorðan :	old, under *the* earth :
næs þæt yðe ceâp	that was no easy bargain
tó gegangenne	to obtain
gumena ǽnigum.	for any man.
Gesæt ðá on næsse	Sat then on *the* ness
níð-heard cyning,	*the* bold warrior king,
þenden hǽlo abeád	while *he* bade farewell
heorð-geneátum,	to *his* hearth-enjoyers,
gold-wine Geáta :	*the* Goths' gold-friend :
him wæs geómor sefa,	his mind was sad,
wæfre and wæl-fús,	wandering and death-bound,
wyrd ungemete neâh,	*the* fate close at hand,
se þone gomelan	which the aged *man*
grêtan sceolde,	must greet,
sêcean sáwle hord,	must seek *his* soul-treasure,
sundur-gedǽlan	asunder part
líf wið lice :	life from body :
nó þon lange wæs	not then long was
feorh æþelinges	the prince's life
flǽsce bewunden.	wrapt in flesh.
Beowulf maþelode,	Beowulf spake,
bearn Ecgðeówes :	Ecgtheow's son :
Fela ic on giogoðe	" I in youth many
gûð-ræsa genæs,	war-onslaughts have outliv'd,
orleg-hwíla ;	hours of warfare ;
ic þæt eall gemon :	I all that remember :
ic wæs syfan wintre,	I was seven winters *old*,
ðá mec sinca baldor,	when me *the* lord of treasures,

4841. MS. maþelade.

freá-wine folca,
æt mínum fæder genam,
heold mec and hæfde
Hreðel cyning;
geaf me sinc and symbel,
sibbe gemunde;
næs ic him tó life
láðra owihte,
beorn in burgum,
þonne his bearna hwylc,
Herebeald and Hǽðcyn,
oððe Hygelác mín.
Wæs þám yldestan
ungedéfelíce,
mǽges dǽdum,
morþor-bed stred,
syððan hyne Hǽðcyn
of horn-bogan,
his freá-wine
fláne geswencte;
miste mercelses,
and his mǽg ofscét,
bróðor oðerne,
blódigan gáre:
þæt wæs feohleás gefeoht,
fyrenum gesyngad,
hreðre hyge-méðe:
sceolde hwæðre swá-þeáh
æþeling unwrecen
ealdres linnan;
swá bið geómorlic,

the noble friend of nations,
from my father took,
held and had me
Hrethel *the* king;
gave me treasure and feasting,
of *our* kinship was mindful;
I was not to him in life
in aught more unwelcome,
a warrior in his burghs,
than any of his children,
Herebeald and Hæthcyn,
or my Hygelac.
For the eldest was
unbecomingly,
by his brother's deed,
the death-bed strew'd,
when Hæthcyn him
from *his* horn'd bow,
his lord *and* friend,
with *a* shaft laid low;
he miss'd *his* mark,
and his kinsman shot,
one brother another,
with *a* bloody arrow:
that was *a* priceless fight,
criminally perpetrated,
heart-wearying to *the* soul:
yet nathless must
the prince unavenged
lose *his* life;
so sad it is,

4873. i.e., inexpiable with money. The Swedish seems at variance with what we know of the old German law, by which every crime had its price.

gomelum eorle	for *an* aged man
tṓ gebīdanne	to await
þæt his byre rīde	that his child hang
giong on galgan :	young on *the* gallows :
þonne he gyd wrece,	then may he *a* lay recite,
sârigne sang,	*a* sorrowful song,
þonne his sunu hangað	when his son hangs
hrefne to hroðre,	for solace to *the* raven,
and he him helpe ne mæg,	and he him help may not,
eald and infrṓd,	old and feeble,
ǣnige gefremman :	any afford :
symble bið gemyndgad,	ever will *he* be reminded,
morna gehwylce,	every morning,
eaforan ellor-sið ;	of *his* offspring's death ;
oðres ne gȳmeð	another *he* cares not
tṓ gebīdanne	to await
burgum on-innan	within *his* burghs,
yrfe-weardes,	*another* heir,
þonne se ân hafað,	when the one has,
þurh deā́ðes nȳd,	through death's necessity,
dǣda gefondad.	*his* deeds expiated.
Gesyhð sorh-cearig,	*He* sees sorrow-anxious
on his suna bûre	in his son's bower
wīn-sele westne,	*the* wine-hall desert,
wind-geræste,	wind-rush'd,
rṓte berṓfene :	of *the* rote bereft :
rīdend swefað	hanging sleeps
hæleð in hoðman ;	*the* warrior in darkness ;
nis þær hearpan swēg,	there is no sound of harp,
gomen in geardum,	*no* mirth in *the* courts,
swylce þær iū wæron.	as there were of old.

4880. MS. ceorle. 4888. MS. helpan.
4896. MS. in innan. 4897. MS. weardas.
4900. gefǣlsod ? 4904. MS. gereste. 4905. MS. reote.

XXXV.

Gewíteð þonne on sealman,	Then passes he to songs,
sorh-leóð gǽleð,	*a* sad lay sings,
án æfter ánum :	one after one :
þuhte him eall to rúm,	all seem'd to him too spacious,
wongas and wíc-stede.	*the* plains and habitation.
Swá Wedera helm,	Thus *the* Weders' helm,
æfter Herebealde,	after Herebealde,
heortan sorge	heart's sorrow
weallende wæg ;	boiling bore ;
wihte ne meahte,	*he* in no wise might,
on ðám feorh-bonan	on the murderer
fǽhðe gebétan ;	*the* feud avenge ;
nó ðý ǽrhe þone heaðo-rinc	nor the sooner he the warrior
hatian ne meahte	could hate
láðum dǽdum,	with hostile deeds,
þeáh him leóf ne wæs.	although *he* was not dear to him.
He ðá mid þǽre sorge,	He then with that sorrow,
þá him sió sár belamp,	when him that pain befel,
gum-dreám ofgeaf,	gave up *the* joy of men,
Godes leoht geceás,	chose God's light,
eaferum lǽfde,	to *his* offspring left
swá déð eádig mon,	(as does *a* prosperous man)
lond and leód-byrig,	land and native city,
þá he of líf gewát.	when he from life departed.
Þá wæs synn and sacu	Then was sin and strife
Sweóna and Geáta,	of Swedes and Goths,
ofer wíd wæter	over *the* wide water

4922. MS. fæghðe. 4927. MS. sorhge.

4937. The wide water is, no doubt, the Mälar sea or lake, which formed the boundary between the Swedes and Goths, or Geats. It extends about 60 miles from the sea into the interior, and in breadth varies from 20 to 40 miles.

wroht gemǽne,	dissension common,
here-níð hearda,	cruel war-hate,
syððan Hreðel swealt,	after Hrethel died,
oððe him Ongenðeówes	or to him Ongentheow's
eaferan wǽron,	sons were
* * *	* * *
* * *	* * *
frome fyrd-hwate,	bold martial leaders,
freóde ne woldon	peace would not
ofer heafo healdan,	over *the* water hold,
ac ymb Hreosna-beorh	but around Hreosna-beorh
atolne inwit-scear	dire artifice
oft gefremedon ;	oft perpetrated ;
þæt mæg-winas	that my kinsmen
mine gewræcon,	avenged,
fǽhðe and fyrene,	*the* enmity and crime,
swâ hit gefrǽge wæs,	as *it* was well known,
þeâh þe oðer [hyra]	although one [of them]
his ealdre gebôhte,	with his life *it* bought,
heardan ceâpe :	*a* hard bargain :
Hǽðcynne wearð,	for Hæthcyn was,
Geâta dryhtne,	*the* Goths' lord,
gûð onsæge.	war not idle.
Þâ ic on morgne gefrægn,	Then on *the* morrow, I have heard,
mǽg oðerne	that *the* other kinsman
billes ecgum	with falchion's edge
on bonan stælan :	stole on *the* slayer :

4942. MS. wæran. I agree with K. that several lines are here wanting, which, no doubt, contained an account of the continuation of the war between the Goths and Swedes.

4949. MS. eatolne. 4951. MS. wine.

4952. MS. gewræcan.

4955. hyra supplied from conjecture.

þær [wæs] Ongenþeów
Eofores níðes sæd,
gúð-helm tóglád;
gomela Scylfing
hreás blác:
hond gemunde
fǽhðe genoge,
feorh-sweng ne ofteáh.
Ic him þa máðmas,
þe he me sealde,
geald æt gúðe,
swá me gifeðe wæs,
leohtan sweorde.
He me lond forgeaf,
eard éðel-wyn;
næs him ǽnig þearf,
þæt he tó Gifðum,
oððe tó Gár-Denum,
oððe in Swio-ríce,
sécean þurfe,
wyrsan wíg-frecan
weorðe gecýþan.
Swylc ic him on feðan
beforan wolde,
ána on orde,
and swá tó aldre sceal
sæcce fremman,
þenden þis sweord þolað,
þæt mec ǽr and sið
oft gelǽste,
syððan ic for dugeðum
Dæghrefne wearð

there [was] Ongentheow
sated with Eofor's enmity,
his war-helm glided off;
the aged Scylfing
fell pale:
yet did *his* hand remember
the feud full well,
nor withdrew *the* fatal stroke.
I him the treasures,
that he had given me,
paid in warfare,
as was granted me,
with *my* bright sword.
He gave me land,
a paternal home's delight;
he had no want,
so that he among Gifthas,
or Gar-Danes,
or in Sweden,
needed seek,
a worse warrior
buy with value.
Thus in *the* host I
would before him *go*,
alone in front,
and so while living shall
conflict engage in,
while this sword endures,
which me early and late
has oft bestead,
since I valorously
of Dæghrefn was

4965. wæs inserted from conjecture. 4966. MS. niosað.
4971. MS. fæhðo. 4973. him, i.e. Hrethel.

tô hand-bonan,	*the* slayer,
Huga cempan,	*the* Hugas' champion ;
nalles he ða frætwe	not the decoration he
Fres-cyninge,	to *the* Frisian king,
breost-weorðunge,	*the* breast-honour,
bringan môste,	might bring,
ac in campe gecrong	but in battle sank
cumbles hyrde,	*the* standard's guardian,
æþeling on elne.	*the* noble valorously.
Ne wæs [ic] ecg-bona,	I slew *him* not with *the* sword,
ac him hilde grâp	but in battle grasp'd his
heortan wylmas,	heart's throbbings,
bân-hûs gebræc.	*the* bone-house brake.
Nû sceal billes ecg,	Now shall *the* falchion's edge,
hond and heard sweord,	*the* hand and hard sword,
ymb hord wîgan.	for *the* hoard do battle."
Beowulf maþelode,	Beowulf spake,
beôt-wordum sprǽc	words of threat utter'd
niehstan siðe :	for *the* last time :
Ic genêþde fela	"I have dar'd many
gûða on geogoðe ;	battles in *my* youth ;
gyt ic wylle,	I will yet,
fród folces weard,	*a* sage guardian of *my* people,
fǽhðe sêcan,	*a* conflict seek,
mǽrðum fremman,	gloriously accomplish,
gif mec se mân-sceaða	if me *the* atrocious spoiler
of eorð-sele	from *his* earth-hall
ût-gesêceð.	will seek out."
Gegrêtte ðá	*He* then greeted
gumena gehwylcne,	each of *the* men,
hwate helm-berend,	*the* bold helm-bearer,

5000. MS. cyning. 5001. breost-weorðunge ; i.e., he gained no spoil from Beowulf to carry home to his king.

5003. MS. cempan. 5006. ic supplied from conjecture.

hindeman siðe,	for *the* last time,
swǽse gesiðas :	*his* dear companions :
Nolde ic sweord beran,	"I would not bear *a* sword,
wæpen tó wyrme,	nor weapon to *the* worm,
gif ic wiste hú	if I knew how
wið ðám aglǽcean	against the miserable being
elles meahte	*I* might else
grípe wið-grípan,	with gripe grasp at *him*,
swá ic gió wið Grendle dyde;	as I of old against Grendel did;
ac ic ðær heaðu-fýres	but I there intense fire,
hâtes wêne,	hot, expect,
reðes and hattres ;	fierce and venomous ;
forðon ic me on hafu	therefore I will have on me
bord and byrnan :	shield and byrnie :
nelle ic [me] beorges weard	I will not [me] *the* guardian of *the* mount
ofer-fleôn [lætan]	[suffer] to fly over
[ne] fôtes trem ;	[not] *a* foot's step ;
ac unc sceal weorðan æt wealle	but to us *it* shall be at *the* mound
swâ unc wyrd geteóð,	as fate shall to us decree,
metod manna gehwæs.	*the* lord of every man.
Ic eom môde from,	I am in mind resolute,
þæt ic wið þone gûð-flogan	*so* that I against the war-fly
gylp ofer-sitte.	lay aside vaunt.
Gebíde ge on beorge	Await ye on *the* mount
byrnum werede,	with byrnies protected,
secgas on searwum,	*ye* men, in arms,
hwæðer sêl mæge,	which may *the* better,
æfter wæl-ræse,	after *the* fatal onslaught,
wunde gedýgan	from wound escape

5035. MS. gylpe. 5039. hattredes (attredes)?

5042, 5043, 5044. The words between brackets are supplied from conjecture.

uncer twēga.	of us two.
Nis þæt eower sið,	*It* is no enterprise of yours,
no gemet-mannes,	nor of *a* common man,
nefne mīn ānes,	(*of none* save me alone)
þæt he wīð aglǽcean	that he against *the* miserable being
eafoðo dǽle,	labours share,
eorlscipe efne.	stoutness prove.
Ic mid elne sceal	I with valour shall
gold gegangan,	obtain *the* gold,
oððe gūð nimeð,	or war shall take,
feorh-bealu frecne,	fierce, deadly bale,
freān eowerne.	your lord."
Arás ðá bi ronde	Arose then by *his* shield
rōf oretta,	*the* renown'd champion,
heard under helme ;	bold beneath *his* helm ;
hioro-sercean bær	*he* bore *his* war-sark
under stān-cleofu,	under *the* stony cliffs,
strengo getrūwode	*he* trusted in *the* strength
ānes mannes :	of *a* single man :
ne bið swylc earges sið.	such is no coward's enterprise.
Geseah þá be wealle,	*He* saw then by *the* mound
se ðe worna fela,	(he who a number,—
gum-cystum gōd,	for *his* bounties good,—
gūða gedigde,	of battles had escap'd from,
hilde hlemma,	tumults of war,
þonne hnitan feðan,	when hosts assail)
stondan stān-bogan,	*a* stone arch stand,
streām ūt þonan	*and a* stream out thence
brecan of beorge ;	break from *the* mount ;
wæs þǽre burnam wælm	*the* boiling of that bourn was

5061. MS. wat. 5062. MS. eofoðo.
5083. MS. stod on, perhaps originally stódan.

heaðo-fyrum hât ;	with intense fires hot ;
ne meahte horde neâh	*he* might not near to *the* hoard
udbyrnende,	unburn'd
ǣnige hwîle	for any while
deop gedŷfan	deep dive,
for dracan lege.	for *the* dragon's flame.
Let ðâ of breostum,	Let then from *his* breast,
ðâ he gebolgen wæs,	as he was incensed,
Weder-Geâta leôd	*the* Weder-Goths' lord
word ût-faran.	words issue forth.
Stearc-heort styrmde ;	*The* stout of heart storm'd ;
stefn in-becom	*the* voice enter'd
heaðo-torht hlynnan,	sounding loudly clear,
under hârne stân.	under *the* hoar stone.
Hete wæs onhrêred,	*His* hate was rous'd,
hord-weard oncneôw	*the* hoard-ward recogniz'd
mannes reorde.	*the* voice of man.
Næs þær mâra fyrst	No more time was there
freôðe to friclan ;	to demand peace ;
from ǣrest cwom	first came forth
oruð aglǣcean	*the* miserable being's breath
ût of stâne,	out of *the* rock,
hât hilde swât :	hot sweat of battle :
hrûse dynede,	*the* earth resounded,
born under beorge ;	burn'd under *the* mount ;
bord-rand onswâf	*his* shield's disc turn'd
wið ðâm grŷre gieste,	against the grisly guest,
Geâta dryhten.	*the* Goths' lord.
Ðâ wæs hring-bogan	Then was *the* ring-bow'd's
heorte gefŷsed	heart excited
sæcce tô sêceanne :	to seek *the* conflict :
sweord ǣs gebræd	*his* sword had before drawn

5091. MS. gedygan. 5105. MS. freode. 5111. MS. **biorn.**

gôd gûð-cyning,	*the* good warlike king,
gomele lâfe,	*an* ancient relic,
ecgum unsleâw :	of edges not dull :
æghwæðrum wæs	to either was
bealo-hycgendra	of *the* bale-intention'd
broga fram oðrum :	fear from *the* other :
stið-môd gestôd	stubborn of mood stood
wið steâpne rond	against *his* towering shield
Wedera bealdor ;	*the* Weders' prince ;
ðâ se wyrm gebeâh	then the worm bent
snûde tôsomne ;	quickly together ;
he on searwum bâd :	(he in arms awaited :)
gewât ðâ byrnende	went then burning
gebôgen scrîðan	bow'd departing,
tô gesceape scyndan.	hastening to *his* fate.
Scyld-weall gebearg	*The* shield-wall secur'd
lîf and lîce	*the* life and body
læssan hwîle	for *a* less while
mǽrum þeôdne	of *the* great prince
þonne his myne sôhte,	than his mind sought,
ðær he þý fyrste	if he the time
forman dôgore,	at early day
wealdan môste ;	might have commanded :
swâ him wyrd ne gescrâf.	so fate ordain'd not for him.
Hreð æt hilde,	Fierce in conflict,
hond ûp-abræd	rais'd his hand
Geâta dryhten,	*the* Goths' lord,
grýre-fâhne slôh	*the* grisly variegated *monster* struck

5121. MS. ungleaw.

5127. MS. winia.

5130. he, i.e. Beowulf.

5133. MS. gescipe. See l. 52.

5134. MS. wel. From this line to l. 5142 the sense is particularly obscure.

Incges lâfe,	with Inge's relic,
þæt siô ecg gewâc,	*so* that *the* edge fail'd,
brûn on bâne	*the* brown *falchion* on *the* bone
bât unswiðor	bit less strongly
þonne his ðiôd-cyning	than its great king
þearfe hæfde,	had need,
bysigum gebǽded.	oppress'd with labours.
Þâ wæs beorges weard,	Then was *the* mount's guardian
æfter heaðu-swenge,	after *the* mighty stroke,
on hreôum môde;	in *a* fierce mood;
wearp-wæl-fŷre,	*he* cast deadly fire,
wîde sprungon	widely sprung
hilde leôman:	*the* rays of conflict:
hreð sîgora ne gealp,	*the* fierce conqueror boasted not,
gold-wine Geâta,	*the* Goths' gold-friend,
gûð-bill geswâc,	his battle-falchion fail'd,
nâ gôd æt nŷde,	(not good at need,)
swâ hit nô sceolde,	as it should not,
îren ǽr-gôd;	*an* iron primely good;
ne wæs þæt eðe sið;	that was no easy enterprize;
þæt se mǽra	that the great
maga Ecgðeôwes	son of Ecgtheow
grund-wong þone	*the* earth-plain
ofgyfan wolde,	would give up,
sceolde willan	*that he* should spontaneously
wîc eardian	*a* dwelling inhabit
elles-hwergen.	elsewhere.
Swâ sceal æghwylc mon	So must every man
alætan lǽn-dagas.	leave *these* transitory days.
Næs ðâ long to ðon,	Nor was *it* then long until,

5147. MS. Incge. My interpretation is quite conjectural, the word Incge being unknown to me. I believe it, however, to be a corruption of some proper name.

5163. MS. nacod æt niðe.

þæt ðа aglǽcean
hŷ eft gemetton;
hyrte hyne hord-weard,
hreðer æðme weoll,
niwan stefne;
nearo þrowade,
fŷre befongen,
se ðe ǽr folce weold:
nealles him on heápe
hand-gesteallan,
æðelinga bearn
ymbe gestódon,
hilde cystum;
ac hŷ on holt bugon,
ealdre burgan:
hiora in ânum weoll
sefa wið sorgum:
sibb æfre ne mæg
wiht onwendan
þâm ðe wel þenceð.

that those fell beings
again each other met;
had recruited himself *the* hoard-ward,
his breast heav'd with breathing,
with new energy;
suffer'd distress,
by fire encompass'd,
he who had ere *a* people rul'd:
not in *a* body him
his hand-companions,
sons of nobles
stood around,
in warlike bands;
but they to *the* wood retir'd,
their life to save:
in one of them boil'd
his mind with sorrows:
kinship can never
aught pervert
in him who rightly thinks.

XXXVI.

Wîglâf wæs hâten
Weoxstânes sunu,
leóflîc lind-wîga,
leód Scylfinga,
mæg Ælfheres:
geseah his mon-dryhten
under here-grîman
hât þrôwian:

Wiglaf was hight
Weoxstan's son,
a belov'd shield-warrior,
a Scylfings' lord,
Ælfhere's kinsman:
he saw his liege lord
under *his* martial helm
heat suffering:

5185. hine? 5186. MS. heand.

gemunde ðâ ða âre	*he* then call'd to mind the possession
þe he him ǽr forgeaf,	that he had formerly given him,
wîc-stede weligne	*the* wealthy dwelling-place
Wǽgmundinga,	of *the* Wægmundings,
folc-rihta gehwylc,	every public right,
swâ his fæder âhte.	as his father had possess'd.
Ne mihte ðâ forhabban,	*He* could not then refrain,
hond-rond gefeng,	*but* grasp'd *his* shield,
geolwe linde,	*the* yellow-linden,
gomel swyrd geteâh,	drew *his* ancient sword,
þæt wæf mid eldum	that among men was
Eanmundes lâf,	*a* relic of Eanmund,
suna Ohtheres	Ohthere's son,
þâm æt sæcce wearð,	of whom in conflict was,
wreccan wineleâsum,	*when a* friendless exile,
Weohstân bana,	Weohstan *the* slayer,
meces ecgum;	with falchion's edges,
and his magum æt-bær	and from his kinsmen bore away,
brǽn fâgne helm,	*the* brown-hued helm,
hringde byrnan,	*the* ringed byrnie,
eald sweord eôtonisc,	*the* old eotenish sword,
þæt him Onela forgeaf,	which him Onela had given,
his gædelinges	his companion's
gûð-gewǽdu,	battle-weeds,
fyrd-searu fûslîc:	ready martial gear:
nô ymbe ða fǽhðe sprǽc,	*he* spake not of the feud,
þeâh ðe he his brôðor bearn	although he his brother's child
abrâdwade.	had exil'd.
He frætwe geheold	He *the* armour held
fela missera,	many years,
bill and byrnan,	*the* falchion and byrnie,

5217. MS. Ohteres. 5219. MS. wræce. 5220. MS. Weohstanes.

oððæt his byre mihte	until his son might
eorlscipe efnan,	*some* valorous deed achieve,
swâ his ǽr-fæder:	as his father erst:
geaf him ðâ mid Geâtum	*he* gave him then among *the* Goths
gûð-gewǽda	of war-weeds
æghwæs unrîm;	every kind numberless;
þâ he of ealdre gewât	then he from life departed
frôd on forð-wêg.	aged on *his* way forth.
Þâ wæs forma sið	Then was *the* first time
geongan cempan,	for *the* young champion,
þæt he gûðe ræs	that he *a* war-onslaught
mid his freâ-dryhtne	with his noble lord
fremman sceolde:	should achieve:
ne gemealt him se môd-sefa,	nor did his courage melt,
ne his mægenes lâf	nor his kinsman's legacy
gewâc æt wîge;	fail in *the* contest;
þæt se wyrm onfand,	that the worm found,
syððan hîe tôgædre	when they together
gegân hæfdon.	had come.
Wîglâf maðelode	Wiglaf spake
word-rihta fela,	many sentences,
sægde gesiðum,	said to *his* comrades.
him wæs sefa geômor:	(his mind was sad:)
Ic ðæt mǽl geman,	"I that time remember,
þâ we medu þegon,	as we were drinking mead,
þonne we gehêton	when we promis'd
ûssum hlâforde	our lord
in biôr-sele,	in *the* beer-hall,
ðe us ðâs beâgas geaf,	who gave us these rings,
þæt we him ða gûð-getawa	that we him the war equipments
gyldan woldon,	would repay,
gif him þyslîcu	if him such-like

5252. MS. þa. 5260. MS. þær.

þearf gelumpe,	need befel,
helmas and hearde sweord,	*the* helms and hard swords,
ðá he usic on herge gecéas	when us in *his* band he chose
tó þyssum siðfæte,	for this expedition,
sylfes willum,	of his own accord,
onmúnde usic mǽrða,	reminded us of glories,
and me þæs maðmas geaf,	and me presents gave,
þe he usic gár-wígend	because he us warriors
góde tealde,	good accounted,
hwâte helm-berend :	bold helm-bearers :
þeáh ðe hláford user	although our lord
þis ellen-weorc	this bold work
âna þohte	thought alone
tó gefremmanne,	to perform,
folces hyrde ;	*the* people's guardian,
forþam he manna mæst	because he of *all* men most
mǽrða gefremede,	glories had achiev'd,
dǽda dollícra.	rash deeds.
Nú is se dæg cumen	Now is the day come
þæt úre man-dryhten	that our liege lord
mægenes behófað,	has need of might,
gódra gúð-rinca :	of good warriors :
wutun gongan tó	let us advance
helpan hild-fruman,	to help *the* warlike leader,
þenden hât sý	while be hot
gled-egesa grim.	*the* fierce fiery terror.
God wât on mec,	God knows in me,
þæt me is micle leófre	that to me *it* is far preferable
þæt mínne líc-haman,	that my body,
mid mínne gold-gyfan,	with my gold-giver,
gled fæþmie :	fire should clasp :

5269. MS. heard. 5270. MS. þe. 5271. MS. siðfate.
5274. MS. þas. 5278. MS. us. 5280. MS. aðohte.
5292. MS. hit : hát conj. K.

ne þynceð me gerýsne	*it* seems to me not fitting
þæt we rondas beron	that we *our* shields bear
eft to earde,	back to *our* home,
nemne we ǽnor mægen	unless we before may
fâne gefyllan,	fell *the* foe,
feorh ealgian	*the* life defend
Wedra ðeódnes.	of *the* Weders' prince.
Ic wât geare	I well know
þæt nǽron eald-gewyrht,	that *his* old deserts were not *such*,
þæt he âna scyle	that he alone should
Geâta duguðe	of *the* flower of the Goths
gnorn þrôwian,	tribulation suffer,
gesîgan æt sæcce :	sink in conflict :
unc sceal sweord and helm,	for us two shall sword and helm,
byrne and beadu-scrûd,	byrnie and martial garb,
bâm gemǽne ;	to both *be* common ;
wôd þâ þurh þone wæl-rêc.	*he* then waded through the deadly reek.
Wiglâf ellen bær	Wiglaf *his* courage bare
freân on fultum ;	to *his* lord's aid ;
feâ worda cwæð :	few words *he* said :
Leófa Beowulf,	"Dear Beowulf,
lǽst eall tela,	perform all well,
swâ þû on geoguð-feore	as thou in youthful life
geara gecwæde,	long since didst say,
þæt ðû ne alæte,	that thou wouldst let not,
be ðe lîfigendum,	while thou didst live,
dôm gedreósan :	*thy* greatness sink :
scealt nû dǽdum rôf	*thou* shalt now, for deeds renown'd,

5312. MS. urum. 5313. MS. byrdu.

5314. Thork. ban. 5315. MS. ræc.

5316. MS. wig hea folan. If we adopt hafelan, the more usual orthography, the validity of the emendation becomes still more evident.

æðeling ânhydig,	*a* resolute prince,
ealle mægene	with all might
feorh ealgian;	*thy* life defend:
ic ðe fullǽstu.	I will support thee."
Æfter ðâm wordum	After those words
wyrm yrre cwom,	*the* worm came angry,
atol inwit-gest,	*the* fell, guileful guest,
oðre siðe,	*a* second time,
fŷr-wylmum fâh,	with fire-boilings colour'd,
fiónda niósan,	*his* foes to visit,
lâðra manna:	*the* hostile men:
lig-ŷðum forborn	with flame-waves was burnt
brâd wîg-rond;	*the* broad war-disk;
byrne ne meahte	*the* byrnie might not
geongum gâr-wîgan	to *the* young warrior
geóce gefremman;	aid afford;
ac se maga geonga	but *the* young man
under his mæges scyld	under his kinsman's shield
elne geeóde,	valorously went,
þâ his âgen [wæs]	when his own was
gledum forgrunden.	by *the* gleeds consum'd.
Þá-gen gûð-cyning	Then again *the* warlike king
[mǽrþa] gemunde,	*his* glories call'd to mind,
mægen-strengo slôh	with main strength struck
hilde bille,	with *his* battle falchion,
þæt hit on heafolan stôd,	*so* that on *the* head it stood
nîðe genŷded;	by hate impell'd;
Nægling forbærst,	Nægling snapt asunder,
geswâc æt sæcce,	fail'd in *the* conflict,
sweord Beowulfes,	Beowulf's sword,

5339. MS. bord wið rond.

5346. wæs supplied from conjecture.

5349. mǽrða supplied from conjecture.

5354. Nægling is the name of Beowulf's sword.

gomol and grǽg-mǽl :	*an* ancient and grey brand :
him þæt gifeðe ne wæs	it was not granted him
þæt him îrenne	that him iron
ecga mihton	edges might
helpan æt hilde :	in battle help :
wæs siố hond tố strong,	the hand was too strong,
seố ðe meca gehwane,	which every falchion,
mîne gefrǽge,	as I have heard,
swenge ofer-swiðde,	by its stroke overpower'd,
þeâh he tố sæcce bær	although he to *the* contest bore
wæpen wundrum heard :	*a* weapon wondrously hard,
næs him wihte ðe sêl.	*yet* 'twas naught for him the better.
Þâ wæs þeốd-sceaða,	Then was *the* great destroyer,
þriddan siðe,	*a* third time,
frecne fŷr-draca,	*the* fell fire-drake,
fǽhða gemyndig ;	mindful of enmities ;
ræsde on ðone rốfan,	*he* rush'd on the renown'd *chief*,
þâ him rûm ageald,	then him amply requited,
hât and heaðo-grim	hot and fiercely grim
heals ealhe ymb-feng	*his* whole neck *he* clasp'd
biteran bânum :	with *his* horrid bones :
he geblốdegod wearð	he ensanguin'd was
sâwul-driốre ;	with life-gore ;
swât ŷðum weoll.	*the* blood in waves bubbled.

XXXVII.

Þâ ic æt þearfe [gefrægn]	Then I have learn'd *that* at need
þeốd-cyninges	of *the* great king

5359. MS. irenna. 5360. MS. ecge. 5363. MS. seðe.
5365. MS. ofersohte. 5366. MS. þonne.
5367. MS. wundum.
5381. gefrægn supplied by conjecture. K.

andlongne eorl	*the* warrior earl
ellen cyðan,	valour manifested,
cræft and cênðu,	craft and courage,
swâ him gecynde wæs :	as to him was natural :
ne hêdde he þæs heafolan,	he heeded not the head,
ac siô hann gebarn	but the hand burn'd
môdiges mannes,	of *the* bold man,
þæt he his mæges healpe ;	that he might his kinsman help;
þâ he þone nîð-gæst	then he the hostile guest
nioðor hwêne slôh,	somewhat lower struck,
secg on searwum,	*the* warrior in arms,
þæt þæt sweord gedeâf	*so* that *the* sword div'd
fâh and fæted ;	blood-stain'd and ornate,
þæt þæt fŷr ongon	*so* that the fire began
sweðrian syððan ;	afterwards to abate ;
þâ-gen sylf cyning	then again *the* king himself
geweold his gewitte,	got command of his senses,
wæl-seaxe gebræd,	drew *his* deadly knife,
biter and beadu-scearp,	bitter and battle-sharp,
þæt he on byrnan wæg :	that he on *his* byrnie bore :
forwrât Webra helm	*the* Weders' protector scor'd
wyrm on middan,	*the* worm in *the* middle,
feônd gefylde,	fell'd *the* foe,
ferh-ellen wræc,	avenged *his* deadly ardour,
and hî hyne þâ bêgen	and they him then both
abroten hæfdon,	had destroy'd,
sib-æðelingas :	*the* kindred princes :
swylc sceolde secg wesan,	such should a warrior be,
þegn æt þearfe.	*a* thane at need.

5383. The word andlongne is very doubtful.

5387. i.e. the head of the dragon.

5390. MS. þær he his mægenes healp.

5391. MS. þæt.

5392. i.e. than the head.

5405. MS. gefyldan.

Þæt ðám þeódne wæs
siðes sige-hwíl,
sylfes dǽdum,
worlde geweorces.
Ðá sió wund ongon,
þe him se eorð-draca
ǽr geworhte
swelan and swellan.
He þæt sona onfand
þæt him on breóstum
bealo-níð weoll,
attor on-innan:
ðá se æðeling gong,
þæt he bi wealle,
wís-hycgende,
gesæt on sesse;
seah on enta geweorc,
hú ða stán-bogan,
stapulum fæste,
êce eorð-reced
innan healde.
Hyne þá mid handa
heoro-dreórigne
þeóden mǽrne,
þegn ungemete till,
wine-dryhten his,
wætere gelafede,
hilde sædne,
and his hǽlo onspeón.
Beowulf maþelode,
he ofer benne spræc,

That to the prince was
a victorious moment of *his* enterprize,
by his own deeds,
of *his* worldly work.
Then the wound began,
that him the earth-drake
erst had wrought,
to burn and swell.
He soon found
that in his breast
baleful harm boil'd,
venom, within:
then *the* prince went,
so that he by *the* mound,
wisely thinking,
sat on *a* seat;
look'd on *the* giants' work,
how the stone arches,
on pillars fast,
the eternal earth-house
held within.
Him then with *his* hand
the battle-gory
great prince,
the thane infinitely good,
his liege lord,
with water lav'd,
him with conflict sated,
and his health allur'd.
Beowulf spake,
of *his* wound he said,

5413. MS. siðas sige hwile. 5424. MS. giong.
5440. MS. helo.

wunde wæl-bleâte;	*his* wound deadly livid;
wisse he gearwe,	*he* knew well,
þæt he dæg-hwîla	that he *his* day-moments
gedrogen hæfde,	had pass'd through,
eorðan wynne;	*his* joy of earth;
ðâ wæs eall sceacen	then was departed all
dógor-gerîmes,	of his days' number,
deâð ungemete neâh:	death immediately nigh:
Ic nû suna mînum	"I to my son now
syllan wolde	would give
gûð-gewǽdu,	*my* war-weeds,
þær me gifeðe swâ	if so granted me
ǽnig yrfe-weard	any heir
æfter wurde,	were after *me*,
lîce gelenge.	belonging to *my* body.
Ic ðas leóde heold	I have this people rul'd
fiftig wintra;	fifty winters;
næs se folc-cyning	*there* has been no nation's king
ymb-sittendra,	of *those* surrounding,
ǽnig ðâra,	*not* any of them,
þe mec gûð-winnum	who me in martial strifes
grêtan dorste,	durst greet,
egesan ðenian.	with terror serve.
Ic on earde bâd	In *my* land I have sustain'd
mǽl-gesceafta;	vicissitudes;
heold mîn tela,	held my *own* well,
ne sôhte searo-nîðas,	sought no treacheries,
ne ne swór fela	nor swore many
âþa on unriht.	oaths unrighteously.
Ic þæs ealles mæg,	I for all this may,

5463. MS. winum.

5465. MS. ðeon, of no meaning here, and the correction is far from certain.

5467. Translation purely conjectural.

5470. MS. ne me.

feorh-bennum seóc,
gefeân habban;
forðâm me wîtan ne ðearf
Waldend fira
morðor-bealo maga,
þonne mîn sceaceð
lîf of lîce.
Nû ðû lungre gong
hord sceâwian
under hârne stân,
Wiglâf leófa;
nû se wyrm ligeð,
swefeð sâre wund,
since bereâfod:
bió nû on ófoste,
þæt ic ǽr-welan,
gold-æht ongite,
gearo sceâwige
sigel searo-gimmas,
þæt ic ðý seft mæge,
æfter maððum-welan,
mín alætan,
lîf and leódscipe,
þone ic longe heold.

sick with mortal wounds,
have joy;
because upbraid me need not
the Ruler of men
with the deadly bale of kinsmen,
when shall depart my
life from *its* body.
Now go thou quickly
the hoard to view
under *the* hoar stone,
Wiglaf dear;
now the worm lies,
sleeps sorely wounded,
of *his* treasure bereft:
be now in haste,
that I *the* ancient wealth,
the gold-treasure, may perceive,
well behold
the jewels, curious gems,
that I the softer may,
after *the* treasure-wealth,
resign my
life and people,
that I long have held."

XXXVIII.

Þâ ic snûde gefrægn
sunu Wihstânes,
æfter word-cwydum,
wundum dryhtne
hýran heaðo-siócum,
hring-net beran,

Then heard I *that* quickly
Wihstan's son,
after *these* verbal sayings,
his wounded lord
obeyed, mortally sick;
bore *his* ringed net,

5480. MS. geong.

5491. MS. swegle.

brogdne beadu-sercean,	*his* twisted war-sark,
under beorges hrốf.	under *the* mount's roof.
Geseah ðá sige-hreðig,	Saw then in victory exulting,
þá he bi sesse gong,	as he went by *the* seat,
mago-þegn mốdig,	*the* bold kindred thane,
maððum-sigla fela,	treasure-jewels many,
gold glitinian,	gold glittering,
grunde getenge,	heavy on *the* ground,
wundur on wealle,	wonders in *the* mound,
and þæs wyrmes denn,	and the worm's den,
ealdes uht-flogan,	*the* old twilight flyer's,
orcas stondan,	dishes standing,
fyrn-manna fatu,	vessels of men of yore,
feormenleáse,	foodless,
hyrstum behrorene :	*their* ornaments fall'n off :
þær wæs helm monig	there was many *a* helm
eald and ốmig,	old and rusty,
earm-beága fela	armlets many
searwum gesǽled :	cunningly fasten'd :
sinc eáðe mæg,	(treasure easily may
gold on grunde,	gold in *the* earth,
gum-cynnes gehwone	every one of human race
oferhigian,	despise,
hýde se ðe wylle :	hide it who will :)
swylce he siốmian geseah	he also saw hang heavily
segn eall gylden	*an* ensign all golden
heáh ofer horde,	high o'er *the* hoard,
hond-wundra mæst,	of hand-wonders greatest,
gelocen leóðo-cræftum,	lock'd by arts of song,
of ðám leóma stốd,	from which *there* stood a ray,

5506. MS. geong. 5508. MS. fealo.

5516. MS. feormendlease.

5522. treasure is here the nominative. The sense is obscure.

5532. MS. leoman.

þæt he þone grund-wong	*so* that he the ground-surface
ongitan meahte,	might perceive,
wræte geond-wlîtan.	*the* wonder over-scan.
Næs ðæs wyrmes þær	Not of the worm was there
onsýn ǽnig,	appearance any,
ac hyne ecg fornam.	for him had *the* edge destroy'd.
Ðâ ic on hlǽwe gefrægn	Then heard I *that* in *the* mound
hord reáfian,	*the* hoard had robb'd,
eald enta geweorc,	*the* old giants' work,
ânne mannan,	one man,
him on bearm hlâdan	in his bosom loaded
bunan and discas,	cups and dishes,
sylfes dôme ;	at his own will ;
segn eác genom,	*an* ensign also took,
beácna beorhtost,	of signs brightest,
bill ǽr-gescod,	*a* falchion brass-shod,
ecg wæs îren ;	*the* edge was iron ;
eald-hlâfordes,	*the* old lord's,
þe ðâra maðma	who of those treasures
mundbora wæs	had been *the* guardian
longe hwîle ;	*a* long while ;
lig-egesan wæg	fire-dread *he* bore
hâtne for horde,	hot before *the* hoard,
hioro-weallendne,	fiercely boiling,
middel-nihtum,	at midnights,
oðþæt he morðre swealt.	until he by murder died.
Ar wæs on ôfoste,	*The* messenger was in haste,
eft-siðes georn,	desirous of return,
frætwum gefyrðred :	by *the* ornaments accelerated :
hyne fyrwet bræc,	him curiosity brake,
hwæðer collen-ferð	whether *the* bold warrior
cwicne gemêtte	*he* should living find

5535. MS. wræce. Qu. wrætta? 5543. MS. hlodon.
5549. See l. 3070. 5551. MS. þā. 5556. MS weallende.

in ðâm wong-stede,	on the field,
Wedra þeóden,	*the* Weders' prince,
ellen-siócne,	valour-sick,
þær he hine ǽr forlet.	where he before had left him.
He ðâ mid ðâm maðmum	He with the treasures then
mǽrne þeóden,	*the* great prince,
dryhten sînne,	his lord,
driórigne fand,	found gory,
ealdres æt ende :	at life's end :
he hine eft ongon	he again began him
wætere weorpan,	with water to sprinkle,
oðþæt wordes ord	until *the* word's point
breóst-hord þurh-bræc.	brake through *the* treasure of *his* breast.
Gomel on giohðe	*The* aged *man* in sorrow
gold sceâwode :	*the* gold beheld :
Ic ðâra frætwa	"I, for those ornaments,
Freân ealles þanc,	thanks to *the* Lord for all,
Wuldur-cyninge,	*the* Glory-king,
wordum secge,	in words say,
êcum Dryhtne,	*the* Lord eternal,
þe ic her on-starie ;	which I here gaze on ;
þæs ðe ic móste,	because I have been able,
mînum leódum,	for my people,
ǽr swylt-dæge,	ere *my* death-day,
swylc gestrŷnan :	such to acquire :
nû ic on maðma ḥord	now I for *the* treasures' hoard
mînne bebôhte	have prudently sold
frôde feorh-leg :	my life-flame :
fremmað ge nû	perform ye now
leóda þearfe :	*the* people's need :
ne mæg ic her leng wesan ;	I may here no longer be

5575. MS. wæteres. 5578. MS. giogoðe.
5592. MS. lege. 5593. MS. na.

hâtað heaðo-mǽre,	command *the* warlike brave
hlǽw gewyrcean	*a* mound to make
beorhtne æfter bǽle,	bright after *the* pile,
æt brimes nosan,	at *the* sea's naze,
se sceal tô gemyndum	which shall for *a* remembrance
mînum leôdum	to my people
heâh hlifian	tower on high
on Hrones-næsse;	on Hrones-næs;
þæt hit sǽ-lîðend	that it sea-farers
syððan hâtan	afterwards may call
Biowulfes biorh,	Beowulf's mount,
ða ðe brentingas	those who *their* foamy barks
ofer flôda genipu	over *the* mists of floods
feorran drîfað.	drive from afar."
Dyde him of healse	Doff'd *then* from his neck
hring gyldenne	*a* golden ring
þiôden þristhydig,	*the* bold-hearted prince,
þegne gesealde,	to *his* thane gave it,
geongum gâr-wîgan,	to *the* young javelin-warrior,
gold-fâhne helm,	*his* gold-hued helm,
beâh and byrnan;	*his* ring and byrnie;
hêt hine brûcan well:	bade him use *them* well:
Þû eart ende-lâf	"Thou art *the* last remnant
usses cynnes,	of our race,
Wægmundinga;	of *the* Wægmundings;
ealle wyrd forsweôp	fate has swept away all
mîne magas	my kinsmen
tô Metodsceafte,	to *the* Godhead,
eorlas on elne:	earls in *their* valour:
ic him æfter sceal.	I shall follow them."
Þæt wæs þâm gomelan	That was *the* aged *chieftain's*
gingeste word,	latest word,

5600. MS. scel. 5621. MS. forsweof. 5627. MS. gingæste.

breóst-gehygdum,	from *his* breast's thoughts,
ǽr he bǽl cure,	ere he chose *the* pile,
hâte heaðo-wylmas :	hot intense flames :
him of hreðre gewât	from his bosom departed
sâwol sécean	*his* soul, to seek
sóðfæstra dóm.	*the* doom of *the* just.

XXXIX.

Þá wæs gegongen	Then *it* befel
gumum unfródum	*the* youthful man
earfoðlíce,	sorely,
þæt he on eorðan geseah	that on *the* earth he saw
þone leófestan	his dearest *friend*
lífes æt ende	at life's end
bleâtne gebǽran ;	livid appearing ;
bona swylce læg,	*his* slayer in like manner lay,
egeslíc eorð-draca,	*the* formidable earth-drake,
ealdre bereâfod,	of life bereft,
bealwe gebǽded ;	by bale compell'd ;
beâh-hordum leng	*his* ring-hoards longer
wyrm wóh-bogen,	*the* crook-bent worm
wealdan ne móste ;	might not command ;
ac him írenne	for from him iron
ecga fornamon,	edges had taken *them* away,
hearde heaðo-scearpe,	hard, war-sharp,
homera láfa ;	*the* hammer's legacies ;
þæt se wíd-floga	*so* that the wide-flyer
wundum stille	with wounds still
hreâs on hrûsan,	had fall'n on *the* earth,
hord-ærne neâh ;	nigh to *the* hoard-house,

5631. MS. hwæðre. 5640. MS. bleate. 5648. MS. irenna.
5650. MS. scearede. 5651. MS. lafe.

nalles æfter lyfte
lâcende hwearf
middel-nihtum;
maðm-æhta wlonc,
ansŷn ŷwde;
ac he eorðan gefeoll
for ðæs hild-fruman
hond-geweorce.
Huru þâm on lande
lyt manna ðâh
mægen âgendra,
mîne gefræge,
þeâh ðe he dǽda gehwæs
dyrstig wǽre,
þæt he wið attor-sceaðan
oreðe geræsde,
oððe hring-sele
hondum styrede,
gif he wæccendne
weard onfunde
bûan on beorge.
Biowulfe wearð
dryht-maðma dǽl
deâðe forgolden;
hæfde æghwæðrum
ende gefered
lǽnan lifes.
Næs ðâ lang tô þon,
þæt ða hild-latan
holt ofgeafon,

not along *the* air
sporting went *he*
at midnights;
of *his* treasures proud,
showed *his* countenance;
but to earth he fell
before the war-chief's
handiwork.
Yet in *the* land
few men have thriven
possessing might,
as I have heard,
although he in every deed
were daring,
if he against *a* venomous destroyer's
breath rush'd,
or *his* ring-hall
with hands disturb'd,
if he waking
found *the* guardian
dwelling in *the* mount.
By Beowulf was
his share of noble treasures
with death paid for;
he had to each
an end brought
of *this* transitory life.
'Twas then not long until,
that the battle-tardy *ones*
left *the* holt,

5664. MS. þæt. 5674. MS. wæccende. 5676. MS. buon. 5680. MS. æghwæðre. he. i.e. death, referring to Beowulf and the dragon. 5685. MS. ofgefan.

tydre treów-logan,	dastardly faith-breakers,
tyne ætsomne,	ten together,
ðа ne dorston ǽr	who durst not before
dareðum lácan,	with javelins play,
on hyraman-dryhtnes	at their liege lord's
miclan þearfe;	great need;
ac hý scamiende	but they ashamed
scyldas bǽron,	bare *their* shields,
gúð-gewǽdu,	*their* war-weeds,
þær se gomela læg,	to where the aged *warrior* lay
wlítan on Wígláf.	looking on Wiglaf.
He gewergad sæt,	He wearied sat,
feðe cempa,	*the* active champion,
freán eaxlum neáh,	near *his* lord's shoulders,
wehte hine wætre;	quicken'd him with water;
him wiht ne speow,	he no whit succeeded,
ne meahte he on eorðan,	he might not on earth,
ðeáh he uðe welan,	though he had given wealth,
on ðám frum-gáre	in *the* chieftain
feorh gehealdan,	life retain,
ne þæs Wealdendes	nor the Almighty's
willan oncirran;	will avert;
wolde dóm Godes	*the* doom of God would
dǽdum rǽdan	in deeds rule
gumena gehwylcum,	over every man,
swá he nú gen déð.	as it now yet does.
Þá wæs æt ðám geongum	Then was from the youth
grim andswaru	*a* fierce answer
éð begete	easily gotten
þám ðe ǽr his elne forleás.	for him who had before his rage lost.
Wígláf maðelode,	Wiglaf spake,

5693. MS. bæran. 5696. MS. Wilaf. 5701. MS. speop. 5703. MS. wel. 5707. MS. wiht.

Weohstânes sunu,	Weohstan's son,
secg sârig-ferð	*the* warrior sorrowful in soul
seah on unleófe :	look'd on *the* odious *cowards :*
Þæt lâ mæg secgan	" Lo, that may say
se ðe wyle sóð sprecan,	who truth will speak,
þæt se mon-dryhten,	that the liege lord,
se eow ða maðmas geaf,	who to you those treasures gave
eored-geatwe,	*the* martial gear,
þe ge þær on-standað ;	in which ye there stand ;
þonne he on ealu-bence	(when he on *the* ale-bench
oft gesealde	often gave
heal-sittendum	to *the* hall-sitters
helm and byrnan,	helm and byrnie,
þeóden his þegnum	*the* prince to his thanes,
swylce he þryðlîcost	such as he most valiant
ohwær feor oððe neâh	anywhere far or near
findan meahte,	might find ;)
þæt he gegnunga	that he totally
gûð-gewǽdu	*those* war-weeds,
wraðe forwurpe,	*his* defence, cast away,
þâ hyne wîg begeat.	when him war should overtake.
Nealles folc-cyning	*The* people's king
fyrd-gesteallum	of *his* comrades in arms
gylpan þorfte ;	needed not to boast ;
hwæðre him God uðe,	yet did God grant him,
sigora Waldend,	*the* Ruler of victories,
þæt he hyne sylfne gewræc	that he himself avenged
âna mid ecge,	alone with edge,
þâ him wæs elnes þearf.	when he had need of valour.
Ic him lîf-wraðe	I to him life-support
lytle meahte	could little
ætgifan æt gûðe,	give in *the* conflict,

5718. MS. sec. 5731. MS. þrydlicost. 5732. MS. ower.
5734. MS. genunga. 5737. MS. beget.

and ongan swâ-þeâh	and yet *I* undertook
ofer mîn gemet	above my means
mǽges helpan :	to help *my* kinsman :
symle wæs þý sǽmra,	ever was *I* the worse,
þonne ic sweorde drep	when with *my* sword I struck
ferhð-genîðlan,	*the* deadly foe,
fýr ran swiðor	*the* fire ran stronger,
weoll of gewitte :	boil'd from *his* entrails :
wergendra to lyt	defenders too few
þrong ymbe þeóden,	throng'd round *their* prince,
þá hyne sió þreag becwom.	when the calamity came on him.
Nú sceal sinc-þego	Now shall *the* partaking of treasure
and sweord-gifu,	and gift of swords,
eall êðel-wyn,	all joy of country,
eowrum cynne	to your beloved
leófum alicgean :	kindred fail :
lond-rihtes mót	of land-right must
þǽre mǽg-burge	of the tribe
monna æghwylc	every man
îdel hweorfan,	wander void,
syððan æðelingas	after nobles
feórran gefricgean	from afar shall hear of
fleám eowerne,	your flight,
dómleásan dǽd.	*your* inglorious deed.
Deáð bið sêlla	Death is better
eorla gehwylcum	for every man
þonne edwit-lîf.	than *a* life of reproach."

XL.

Heht ðá þæt heaðo-weorc	*He* bade then the mighty work
tó hagan biódan,	at *the* enclosure be announced,

5755. MS. fyran. 5757. MS. fergendra. 5759. MS. þrag.
5760. MS. Hu. 5764. MS. lufena licgean.

up ofer eg-clif,
þær þæt eorl-werod,
morgen-longne dæg,
môd-giômor sæt,
bord-hæbbende,
bêga on wênum,
ende dôgores,
and eft-cymes
leôfes monnes.
Lyt swîgode
niwra spella
se ðe næs gerâd ;
ac he sôðlîce
sægde ofer ealle :
Nû is wil-geofa
Wedra leôda,
dryhten Geâta,
deâð-bedde fæst :
wunað wæl-ræste,
wyrmes dǽdum ;
him on efn ligeð
ealdor-gewinna,
seax-bennum seôc :
sweorde ne meahte
on ðâm aglǽcean
ǽnige þinga
wunde gewyrcean.
Wîglâf siteð
ofer Biowulfe,
byre Wihstânes,
eorl ofer oðrum
unlîfigendum ;
healdeð hige mêðum

up on *the* ocean's shore,
where the warrior band,
the livelong day,
sad of mood, sat,
shield-bearers,
of both in expectation,
of *the* day's end,
and of *the* return
of *the* dear man.
Little was he silent
of *the* new intelligence
who to *the* ness rode ;
but he truly
said of all :
"Now is *the* kind giver
of *the* Weders' people,
the Goths' lord,
on *his* death-bed fast :
he rests on *his* fatal couch,
through *the* worm's deeds ;
by him lies
his deadly adversary,
with knife-wounds sick :
with *his* sword *he* could not
on the fell being
by any means
cause *a* wound.
Wiglaf sits
over Beowulf,
Wihstan's son,
one warrior over another
lifeless *one* ;
holds with weary spirit

5778. MS. ecg. 5800. MS. siex. 5810. MS. mæðum.

heáfod-wearde	chief ward
leófes and láðes.	over friend and foe.
Nú is leódum wên	Now to *the* people is expectation
orleg-hwíle,	of *a* time of war,
syððan under [bêgen]	after among [both]
Froncum and Frysum	Franks and Frisians
fyll cyninges	*the* king's fall
wíde weorðeð.	becomes widely *known.*
Wæs sió wroht sceapen	The quarrel was form'd
heard wið Hugas,	fierce against *the* Hugas,
syððan Hygelác cwom	after Hygelac came
faran flót-herge	faring with *a* naval force
on Fresna land,	to Friesland,
þær hyne Hetware	where him *the* Hetwaras
hilde gehnǽgdon,	in war vanquish'd,
elne geeódon	boldly went
mid ofer-mægene,	with over-might,
þæt se byrn-wíga	*so* that *the* mail'd warrior
búgan sceolde;	must bow;
feoll on feðan:	*he* fell in *his* host,
nalles frætwe geaf	no martial gear gave
ealdor duguðe.	*the* prince to *his* warriors.
Us wæs á syððan	To us has been ever since
Mere-Wioinga	*the* Mere-Wioings'
milts ungyfeðe.	mercy denied.
Ne ic tó Sweó-ðeóde	Nor *do* I with *the* Swedish people
sibbe oððe treówe	*of* peace or faith
wihte ne wêne;	aught expect;
ac wæs wíde cuð	for *it* was widely known
þætte Ongenðeów	that Ongentheow
ealdre besnýðede	had of life depriv'd

5815. bégen added from conjecture, the line being defective.
5819. MS. scepen. 5834. MS. Wioingas. 5836. MS te.
5840. MS. Ongenþio.

Hǽðcyn Hreþling,	Hæthcyn, Hrethel's son,
wið Hrefna-wudu,	by Hrefna-wood,
þá for onmedlan,	when in *their* pride
ǽrest gesóhton	first sought
Geáta leóde	*the* Goths' people
gúð-Scylfingas.	*the* warlike Scylfings.
Sona him se fróda	Forthwith him the venerable
fæder Ohtheres	father of Ohthere,
eald and egesfull,	old and terrific,
hond-slyht ageaf;	*a* hand-blow gave ;
abreót brim-wísan	*the* sea-leader bore away
brýda heorde,	from *the* bridal hearth,
gomela io meowlan	*the* old *warrior*, long since, *the* maid
golde berofene,	with gold adorn'd,
Onelan modor,	Onela's mother,
and Ohtheres ;	and Ohthere's ;
and ðá folgode	and then pursued
feorh-geníðlan,	*his* deadly enemies,
oððæt hí oð-eódon	until they escap'd
earfoðlíce	with difficulty
in Hrefnes-holt,	into Hrefnes-holt,
hláfordleáse.	lordless.
Besæt ðá scip-here	Beset then *the* naval force
sweorda láfe,	*the* sword's leaving,

5842. MS. Hæðcen. 5849. i.e. Ongenþeów.

5850, 5851. Here the alliteration is defective; but see ll. 5898, 5899. 5852. abræd brim-wísa ?

5853. brýd-heorðe ? The text of this and the preceding line is, I fear, hopelessly corrupt. My version is founded on the conjectural readings. The meaning seems to be, that many years had passed since the old sea-leader (Ongentheow) bore away his bride from Hæthcyn, the maiden, who became his queen, and was the mother of his sons, Onela and O hthere.

5855. gehrodene ? 5864. MS. sin herge.

wundum werge:	with wounds weary:
weân oft gehêt	woe *he* oft promis'd
earmre teóhhe,	to *the* miserable progeny,
andlonge niht:	*the* livelong night;
cwæð he on mergenne,	said *that* he *them* at morn,
mêces ecgum	with falchion's edges
grêtan wolde,	would greet,
sume on galg-treôwu,	some *hang* on gallows-trees,
[fulgum] to gamene.	[to *the* birds] for sport.
Frôfor eft gelamp	Comfort afterwards came to
sárig-môdum,	*the* sad of mood,
somod ǽr dæge,	together ere day,
syððan hîe Hygelâces	when they Hygelac's
horn and býman	horns and trumpets
gelan ongeaton,	sounding perceiv'd,
þá se góda com,	when the good *king* came,
leóda duguðe,	with *the* flower of *his* people,
on last faran.	marching on *their* track.

XLI.

Wæs sió swât-swaðu	Was the bloody trace
Sweóna and Geáta,	of Swedes and Goths,
wæl-ræs wera,	*the* deadly rush of men,
wíde gesýne;	widely seen;
hû ða folc mid him	how the people with them
fǽhðe tó-wehton.	enmity excited,
Gewât him ðá se góda	Departed then the good *king*
mid his gædelingum,	with his associates,

5869. MS. ondlonge. 5872. MS. getan. 5873. MS. sum.
5874. fuglum inserted from conjecture. "fuglum to frófre." Judith (Anal. A. S. p. 150).
5880. MS. gealdor. 5885. MS. Swona.
5886. MS. weora. 5890. i.e. Hygelac.

frôd fela-geômor,
fæsten sêcean.
Eorl Ongenþeów
ufor oncirde;
hæfde Higelâces
hilde gefrunen,
wlonces wîg-cræft;
wiðres ne trûwode
þæt he sǽ-mannum
onsacan mihte,
heâðo-lîðendum
hord forstandan,
bearn and brŷde.
Beáh eft þonan
eald under eorð-weall

Ðâ wæs æht boden
Sweóna leódum,
segn Higelâces,
freoðo-wong þone.
Ford ofer-eódon,
syððan Hreðlingas

sage *and* much sad,
the fastness to seek.
The warrior Ongentheow
had proceeded higher;
he of Hygelac's
warfare had heard,
the proud *chief's* war-craft;
yet believ'd not
that he *the* seamen
could repel,
from the traversers of *the* deep
his hoard defend,
his children and bride.
Withdrew again thence
the aged *chief* under *the* earth wall.

Then was wealth announced
to *the* Swedes' people,
the banner of Hygelac,
the peaceful plain.
The ford *they* went over,
after *the* Hrethlings

5893. In Hrefnes-holt, where it would seem the remnant of the Goths had entrenched themselves.

5894. MS. Ongenþio.

5899. wiðres. This I take to be an error, possibly for hwæpre, *yet.* I have so rendered it; as instances are not wanting of an aspirated syllable alliterating with one unaspirated. See ll. 5850 and 5851, also 5936, 5937.

5900. he, i.e. Higelac.

5906. eorð-weall, i.e. the entrenchment above mentioned, where Ongentheow was attacked and slain by the Hrethlings (Goths) under Eofor and Wulf.

5909. MS. Higelace. This was part of the spoil promised by Ongentheow to his Swedes.

tō hagan þrungon.	had to *the* entrenchment throng'd.
Đær wearð Ongenðeōw,	There was Ongentheow,
ecgum sweorda,	with swords' edges,
blonden-fexa,	*the* grizzly-hair'd,
on beado wrecen,	in *that* conflict punish'd,
þæt se þeōd-cyning	*so* that the great king
ðafian sceolde	must submit to
Eofores ānne dōm.	Eofer's sole doom.
Hyne yrringa	Him angrily
Wulf Wonreding	Wolf, Wonred's son,
wæpne geræhte,	with *his* weapon reach'd,
þæt him for swenge	*so* that, for *the* blow, his
swāt ædrum sprong,	blood sprang from *the* veins,
forð under fexe :	forth under *his* locks :
næs he forht swā-ðēh,	yet was he not afraid,
gomela Scylfing,	*the* aged Scylfing,
ac forgeald hraðe,	but requited quickly,
wyrsan wrixle,	with *a* worse exchange,
wæl-hlem þone,	that deadly onslaught,
syððan ðeōd-cyning	when *the* great king
þyder oncirde ;	turn'd thitherward ;
ne meahte se snella	nor could the swift
sunu Wonredes	son of Wonred
ealdum eorle	to *the* old warrior
hond-slyht gifan,	*a* hand-stroke give :
ac he him on heafde	for he on his head
helm ǣr gescær	*the* helm clave previously,
þæt he blōde fāh	*so* that he blood-stain'd
būgan sceolde ;	must bow :

5914. MS. Ongenðio. 5917. MS. bid.

5920. MS. eafores. He fell by the hand of Eofor. See ll. 5953—5, and 4965, sqq.

5936. MS. ceorle. 5937. MS. giofan. 5939. MS. gescer.

feoll on foldan,	*he* fell on *the* earth,
næs he fǽge þá-gyt ;	yet was he not doom'd ;
ac he hyne gewyrpte,	but he recover'd himself,
þeáh ðe him wund hrīne.	though *the* wound had touch'd him.
Let se hearda	Caus'd *then* the fierce
Higeláces þegn	thane of Hygelac
brádne mece,	*his* broad falchion,
þá his bróðor læg,	as his brother lay,
eald sweord eótonisc,	*his* old eotenish sword,
entiscne helm	*the* giant helm
brecan ofer bord-weal :	to break o'er *the* shield-wall :
ðá gebeáh [se] cyning,	then sank [the] king,
folces hyrde,	*the* people's shepherd,
wæs him feorh drepen.	his life was stricken.
Ðá wǽron monige	Then were many
þe his mæg wriðon.	who his kinsman bound,
ricone arǽrdon,	quickly rais'd,
ðá him gerýmed wearð,	when it was clear'd for them,
þæt hīe wæl-stowe	*so* that they *the* slaughter-place
wealdan móston,	might command,
þenden reáfode	while stript
rinc oðerne.	*one* warrior another.
Namon Ongenðeówe	*They* took from Ongentheow
īren byrnan,	*his* iron byrnie,
heard swyrd hilted,	*his* hilted hard sword,
and his helm somod ;	and his helm also ;
háres hyrste	*the* hoar *warrior's* trapping
Higeláce bǽron,	*they* to Hygelac bore.
[He ðám] frætwum feng,	[He the] war-gear receiv'd,

5947. Eofor. 5948. MS. brade. 5953. se not in MS.
5955. MS. in and dropen. 5957. i.e. his wounds.
5964. MS. Ongenþio. 5969. MS. bær.
5970. He þam has perished from the MS.

and him fægre gehêt
leâna [on] leódum,
and gelǽste swá :
geald þone gûð-ræs
Geâta dryhten,
Hreðles eafora,
þâ he to hâm becom,
Eofere and Wulfe mid :
ofer maðmum sealde
hiora gehwæðrum
hund þusenda
landes and locenra beâga :
ne ðorfte him ða leân oð-
witan
mon on middangearde,
syððan hîe ða mǽrða ge-
slógon ;
and ðâ Eofore forgeaf
ângan dohtor,
hâm-weorðunge,
hyldo tó wedde.
Ðæt ys sió fǽhðo
and se feóndscipe,
wæl-nîð wera ;
ðæs ðe ic [wêne] hafo
þæt us sêceað tó
Sweóna leóde,
syððan hîe gefricgeað

and them promis'd fair
rewards among *the* people,
and so perform'd :
requited *the* martial onslaught
the Goths' lord,
Hrethel's offspring,
when to *his* home he came,
to Eofer and Wulf with *him ;*
he besides treasures gave,
to each of them,
a hundred thousand
of land and closed rings :
nor needed to reproach them
for those rewards
any one on mid-earth,
since they those honours had
in battle won ;
and then *he* to Eofer gave
his only daughter,
an honour to *his* home,
as *a* pledge of favour.
That is the feud
and the enmity,
the deadly hate of men ;
whence I expect
that us will seek
the Swedes' people,
when they shall learn

5972. on has perished from the MS. 5973. MS. gelæsta.
5978. MS. Iofore. The A.S. paraphrast has evidently here, and l. 5986 retained the orthography of his Scandinavian original.
5979. MS. maðmam. 5986. MS. Iofore.
5993. wéne is omitted in the MS.
5994. MS. þe. 5995. MS. leoda.

freân userne	our lord *is*
ealdorleâsne,	lifeless,
þone ðe ǽr geheold,	who had before defended,
wið hettendum,	against enemies,
hord and rîce,	treasure and realm,
æfter hæleða hrŷre	*and*, after *the* fall of heroes,
hwâte Scyldingas ;	*the* bold Scyldings ;
folc-riht fremede,	public right establish'd,
oððe furður gen	or yet further,
eorlscipe efnde.	valorous deeds perform'd.
Nû is ôfost betost,	Now is speed best,
þæt we þeôd-cyning	that we *the* great king
þær sceâwian,	there behold,
and þone gebringan	and bring him
þe us beâgas geaf	who gave us rings
on âd-fære :	on *the* way to *the* pile :
ne sceal ânes hwæt	*there* shall not aught of *any* one
meltan mid þâm môdigan ;	be consum'd with the bold *king* ;
ac þær is maðma hord,	for there is *a* hord of treasures,
gold unrîme,	gold without number,
grimme geceâ[po]d ;	cruelly purchas'd ;
and nû æt siðestan,	and now at last,
sylfes feore,	with *his* own life,
beâgas [boh]te ;	*he* has bought rings ;
þa sceal brond fretan	these shall fire devour,
æled þeccean,	flame cover,
nalles eorl wegan	no warrior *shall* bear
maððum tô gemyndum,	*a* treasure in remembrance,
ne mægð scŷne	nor maiden fair

6003. Hence it would appear that Beowulf, in consequence of the fall of Hrothgar's race, was called to rule also over the Danes (Scyldings).

6004. MS. red. 6007. MS. me. 6013. MS. scel.

6025. Perhaps a glee-maiden is meant, who, having lost her patron, is compelled to wander abroad.

habban on healse
hring-weorðunge ;
ac sceal geômor-môd,
golde bereâfod,
oft nalles ǽne,
el-land tredan ;
nû se here-wîsa
hleahtor alegde,
gamen and gleô-dreâm :
forðon sceal gâr wesan,
monig morgen ceald,
mundum ne wunden,
hæfen on handa ;
nalles hearpan swêg
wîgend weccean ;
ac se wonna hrefn,
fûs ofer fǽgum
fela reordian,
earne secgan
hû him æt ǽte speow,
þenden he wið wulfe
wæl reâfode.
Swâ se secg hwâta
secgende wæs
lâðra spella ;
he ne leâg fela
wyrda ne worda.
Weorod eall arâs,
eôdon unblîðe
under Earna-næs,
weollon teâras,

have on *her* neck
a ring-honour ;
but shall, sad of mood,
of gold bereft,
often not once,
a strange land tread ;
now *the* martial leader
has ceas'd from laughter,
sport and joy of song ;
therefore shall *the* javelin be,
many *a* morning cold,
not by hands brandish'd,
nor rais'd in hand ;
no sound of harp
shall the warrior raise ;
but the dusk raven,
eager o'er *the* fallen,
much shall tell,
shall to *the* eagle say
how *it* with him at *his* food sped.
while with *the* wolf he
spoil'd *the* slain."
Thus the bold warrior
was speaking
unwelcome speeches ;
he falsified not much
of events or words.
The band all arose,
went unblithe
under Earna-næs,
(*their* tears bubbled forth)

6037. MS. be wunden.
6055. The Eagles' ness or promontory.
6056. MS. wollen teare.

wundur sceáwian.	*the* wonder to view.
Fundon ðá on sande	*They* then found on *the* sand
sawulleásne,	soulless,
hlin-bed healdan,	holding *his* couch,
þone þe him hringas geaf	him who had given them rings
ǽrran mǽlum :	in earlier times :
þá wæs ende-dæg	then was *the* end-day
gódum gegongen,	for *the* good *chief* gone,
þæt se gúð-cyning,	*so* that the war king,
Wedra þeóden,	the Weders' prince,
wundor-deáðe swealt :	*a* wondrous death should die
ac hí þær gesegon	but they there saw
syllícran wiht,	*a* stranger thing,
wyrm on wonge,	*the* worm on *the* plain,
wiðerrǽdne þær,	*the* adverse *one* there,
láðne licgean ;	*the* hostile, lying ;
wæs se leg-draca,	the fire-drake was,
grimlíc grýre,	*the* grim horror,
gledum beswǽled ;	with gleeds scorch'd ;
se wæs fiftiges	he was fifty
fót-gemearces	feet of measure
lang on legere :	long on *his* bed :
lyft-wynne heold	*he the* delight of air enjoy'd
nihtes hwílum,	in *the* night's hours,
nyðer eft gewát	again came down
dennes niósian ;	*his* den to visit :
wæs ðá deáðe fæst ;	*he* was then fast in death ;
hæfde eorð-scrafa	*he* had of *his* earth-dens
ende genyttod ;	*the* end enjoy'd ;
him big-stódon	by him stood
bunan and orcas ;	cups and bowls ;

6060. MS. hlim ; rightly corrected by Grimm, D. G. ii. 484.
6068. MS. ær . . . . gesegan. 6071. MS. wiðer ræhtes.
6086. MS. stodan.

discas lagon	dishes lay *there*,
and dŷre swyrd	and costly swords
ômige þurh-etene,	rusty, eaten through,
swâ hie wið eorðan fæðm	as if they in *the* lap of earth
þusend wintra	*a* thousand winters
þær eardodon :	had there continued :
þonne wæs þæt yrfe	for that heritage was
eâcen cræftig,	exceedingly strong,
iû-monna gold,	*the* gold of men of old,
galdre bewunden,	encircled by enchantment,
þæt ðâm hring-sele	*so* that that ring-hall
hrînan ne môste	might not touch
gumena ǽnig,	any man,
nefne God sylfa,	unless God himself,
sîgora sôð Kyning,	true King of victories,
sealde þâm ðe he wolde,	should give *it* to whom he would
He is manna gehyld,	(He is *the* well-willer of men)
hord openian,	*the* hoard to open,
efne swâ-hwylcum manna	just to whatever man
swâ him gemet ðûhte.	as might to him seem meet.

XLII.

Þâ wæs gesŷne	Then was seen
þæt se sið ne þâh	that fortune favour'd not
þâm ðe unrihte	him who unrighteously
inne gehydde	within had hidden
wræte under wealle.	treasure, under *the* mound.
Weard ǽr ofslôh	*The* guardian had before slain
feara sume,	some of a few,
þâ siô fǽhð gewearð	then was the quarrel
gewrecen wrâðlîce.	wrothfully avenged.
Wundur hwæt þonne	What wonder when

6090. MS. etone. 6112. MS. wræce. 6117. MS. hwar

eorl ellen-rôf	*a* brave renown'd warrior
ende gefere	to *the* end journey
lîf-gesceafta,	of living creatures,
þonne long ne mæg	when long may not
mon mid his magum	*a* man with his kinsmen
medu-seld bûan.	*the* mead-bench occupy?
Swâ wæs Biowulfe;	So 'twas to Beowulf;
þâ he biorges weard	when he *the* mount's guardian
sôhte searo-nîðas,	sought, his guileful hate,
seolfa ne cuðe	himself knew not
þurh hwæt his worulde gedâl	through what his parting from *the* world
weorðan sceolde,	should be,
swâ hit oð dômes dæg	*or* how it till doomsday
diôpe benemndon	solemnly declar'd
þeôdnas mǽre,	*those* great princes,
þa þæt ðær dydon	who there that *treasure* put,
þæt se secg wǽre	that the man should be
synnum scyldig,	with sins guilty,
hergum geheaðerod,	with harryings hemm'd in,
hell-bendum fæst,	in hell-bonds fast,
wommum gewitnad,	by terrors punish'd,
se þone wong strâde.	who should that plain despoil.
Næs he gold-hwæte:	He was not covetous of gold:
gearwor hæfde	more readily had *he*
âgendes est	*the* owner's favour
ǽr geceâpod.	previously purchas'd.
Wiglâf maðelode,	Wiglaf spake,
Wihstânes sunu:	Wihstan's son:
Oft sceal eorl monig,	"Oft must *a* man many,

6121. MS. leng.

6134. This is the usual malediction laid on whoever should carry off a hidden treasure.

6140. he, i.e. Beowulf.

6143. MS. gesceawod.

ânes willan,	for *the* sake of one,
wræca dreógan,	hardships suffer,
swâ us geworden is.	as has befallen us.
Ne meahton we gelǽran	We could not inculcate on
leófne þeóden,	*our* dear prince,
rîces hyrde,	*the* realm's guardian,
rǽd ǽnigne,	any counsel,
þæt he ne grêtte	that he should not assail
gold-weard þone ;	that gold-ward ;
lete hyne licgean	*but* let him lie
þær he longe wæs,	where he long had been,
wîcum wunian	in *his* habitation continue,
oð woruld-ende,	till *the* world's end,
healdan heâh gesceap.	hold *the* high appointment.
Hord ys gesceâwod,	*The* hoard has been seen,
grimme gegongen.	cruelly acquir'd.
Wæs þæt gifeðe tô swið,	Too powerful was that grant,
þe ðone þyder ontyhte.	which impell'd him thither.
Ic wæs þær-inne,	I was therein,
and þæt eall geond-seah,	and it all look'd over,
recedes geatwa,	*the* house's furniture,
þâ me gerŷmed wæs ;	when *it* was clear'd for me ;
nealles swǽslîce	not pleasantly
sið alŷfed	*the* way permitted
inn under eorð-weall ;	in under *the* earth-mound ;
ic on ôfoste gefeng	I in haste seiz'd
micle mid mundum	with *my* hands *a* great
mægen-byrðenne	mighty burthen
hord-gestreóna,	of hoard-acquisitions,
hider ût ætbær	bare *them* out hither
cyninge mînum ;	to my king ;
cwico wæs þâ-gêna,	*he* was yet living,

6148. MS. dreogeð. 6160. MS. heoldon.
6164. ðone (him), i.e. Beowulf.

wís and gewittig;
worn eall gespræc
gomol on gehðo,
and eowic grétan hêt
bæd þæt ge geworhton,
æfter wincs dǽdum,
in bǽl-stede,
beorh þone heân,
micelne and mǽrne,
swâ he manna wæs
wígend weorðfullost
wíde geond eorðan,
þenden he burh-welan
brûcan móste.
Uton nû efstan,
oðre * *
seón and sêcean
searo-geþræc,
wundur under wealle:
ic eow wísige,
þæt ge genoge
ne onsceâwiað
beágas and brâd gold.
Síe sió bǽr gearo,
ædre geæfned,
þonne we ût cymen,
and þonne geferian
freân userne,
leófne mannan,
þær he longe sceal
on ðæs Waldendes
wǽre geþolian.
Hét ðâ gebeódan
byre Wihstânes,

wise and sensible;
very many *things* said
the aged prince in sadness.
and bade me greet you,
pray'd that ye would make,
befitting *our* friend's deeds,
in *the* pile's stead,
a lofty mount,
great and glorious,
as he of *all* men was
the worthiest warrior
widely throughout *the* earth,
while he *the* wealth of cities
might enjoy.
Let us now hasten,
other * *
to see and seek
the curious mass,
the wonders beneath the mound.
I will guide you,
so that enough ye
will not gaze on
rings and broad gold.
Let the bier be ready,
quickly made,
when we come out,
and then bear
our lord,
the dear man
to where he long shall
in the All-powerful's
care endure."
Bade then command
Wihstan's son,

hæle-hilde-deór,	*the* human war-beast,
hæleða monegum	many men,
bold-âgendra,	house-owning,
þæt hie bǽl-wudu	that they pile-wood
feorran feredon,	from afar should convey,
folc âgende	folk-owning,
gódum tó-geânes :	towards *the* good *prince :*
Nû sceal glêd fretan,	"Now shall *the* gleed devour,
wyrdan wonna leg,	*the* dusky flame destroy,
wígena strengel,	*the* prince of warriors,
þone ðe oft gebâd	him who oft awaited
isern scûres ;	*the* iron shower ;
þonne strǽla storm,	*who* when *the* storm of shafts,
strengum gebǽded,	from strings impell'd,
scóc ofer scyld-weall,	pass'd o'er *the* shield-wall,
sceaft-nytte heold,	*the* shaft-notch held,
feðer-gearwum fûs,	*when*, prompt with *its* feather-gear,
flâna fyll eóde.	*the* fall of arrows went."
Huru se snotra	Forthwith the prudent
sunu Wihstânes	son of Wihstan
acígde of corðre	call'd from *the* band
cyninges þegnas	king's thanes
syfone [to-som]ne	seven together
þa sêlestan,	the choicest,
eóde eahta sum	went himself *the* eighth
under inwit-hróf ;	under *the* treacherous roof :
hilde rinc sum	*a* warrior
on handa bær	in *his* hand bare
æled-leóman,	a fire-brand,
se ðe on orde gong.	who went at *the* head.

6219. MS. togenes. 6221. MS. weaxan. 6222. þengel ?
6224. MS. scure. 6229. MS. fæder. gárum ?
6230. MS. flane full. 6231. Sona ? 6242. MS. geong.

Næs ðá onhlytme
hwá þæt hord strude,
syððan or-wearde
ǽnigne dǽl
secgas gesegon
on sele wunian,
lǽne licgan;
lyt ǽnig mearn,
þæt hie ófostlíce
út geferedon
dýre maðmas;
dracan eác scufon,
wyrm ofer weall-clif,
leton wǽg niman,
flód fæðmian,
frætwa hyrde:
þær wæs wunden gold
on wǽn hladen,
æghwǽs unrím;
æþeling geboren,
hár hilde-[rinc]
tó Hrónes-næsse.

It was not then without lot
who should the hoard despoil,
when without *a* guard
some deal
the men saw
in *the* hall remaining,
thinly scatter'd lying;
little regretted any,
that with all speed they
might convey out
the precious treasures;
the dragon eke they shov'd,
the worm, o'er *the* wall-cliff,
let *the* wave take,
the flood embrace,
the treasure's guardian:
there was twisted gold
on *the* wain laden,
of every kind numberless;
and the prince borne,
the hoar warrior,
to Hrones-næs.

XLIII.

Him ðá gegiredon
Geáta leóde
ád on eorðan
unwáclícne,
helm-behongen,
hilde-bordum,

For him then prepar'd
the Goths' people
a pile on *the* earth,
a mighty *one*,
with helmets hung,
war-boards,

6254. MS. ec scufun. 6259. MS. þæt.
6262. MS. æðelinge boren. conj. K.
6263. rinc supplied from conjecture.

beorhtum byrnum,	bright byrnies,
swâ he bêna wæs.	as he had requested.
Alegdon ðá tó-middes	Laid then in the midst
mǽrne þeóden	*the* great prince
hæleð hiófende,	*the* warriors lamenting,
hláford leófne :	*their* beloved lord :
ongunnon þá on beorge	began then on *the* mount,
bǽl-fýra mæst	of bale-fires *the* greatest
wígend weccan :	*the* warriors to kindle :
wudu-réc astâh	*the* wood-reek ascended
sweart of Swío-ðole,	swart from *the* Swedish pine,
swógende leg,	*the* roaring flame,
wópe bewunden,	with weeping mingled,
wind-blond gelæg,	(*the* wind-blonding ceas'd)
oðþæt he þæt bán-hús	until it the bone-house
gebrocen hæfde,	had broken,
hât on hreðre.	hot on *the* breast.
Higum unróte	Sad in spirits
mód-ceare mǽndon	*they* with mind-care bewail'd
mon-dryhtnes cwealm;	*their* liege lord's death;
swylce geómor-gyd	as if *a* mournful lay
* * under	* * *
heorde * *	* * *
sorg-cearig sǽlde	sorrowing bound
* * neâh,	* * *
þæt hió hyre *	* * *
* * gas hearde	* * *
* ode wa * ylla won	* * *
* * *	* * *
* egesan	* * *
* * *	* * *
heofon réce swealg.	heaven swell'd with smoke.

6281. MS. swic.
6282. MS. let.
6285. MS. þa.
6292. MS. sealg.

Geworhton ðá
Wedra leóde
hlǽw on hliðe ;
se wæs heáh and brád,
wǽg-líðendum
wíde tó-sýne ;
and betimbredon
on tyn dagum
beadu-rófes beácn
bronda be *
wealle beworhton,
swá hit weorðlícost
fore-snotre men
findan mihton.
Hí on beorg dydon
beágas and siglu,
eall swylce hyrsta,
swylce on horde ǽr
níð-hydige men
genumen hæfdon.
Forleton eorla gestreón
eorðan healdan,
gold on greóte,
þær hit nú gen lífað
[yldum] swá unnyt
swá hit [ǽr] wæs.
Þá ymbe hlǽw ridon
hilde deór * *
æðeling * *
ealra twelfa
woldon * * cwiðan
cyning mǽnan,

Wrought then
the Weders' people
a mound on *the* hill ;
it was high and broad,
by wave-farers
widely to be seen ;
and constructed
in ten days
the renown'd warrior's beacon,
* * *
with *a* wall surrounding *it*,
as it most honourable
highly sagacious men
might find.
In *the* mound they placed
rings and jewels,
also ornaments,
such as before in *the* hoard
hostile men
had taken.
They left *the* treasure of earls
to *the* earth to hold,
gold in *the* dust,
where it now yet remains
[to men] as useless
as it [ere] was.
Then round *the* mound rode
war-beasts * *
nobles * *
of all *the* twelve
would * * speak
their king bewail,

6295. MS. lide. 6297. MS. et líðendum. 6308. MS. beg.
6319. MS. riodan. 6320. MS. deore.

word-gyd wrecan,	*a* verbal lay recite,
and worn sprecan;	and many things say;
eahtodon eorlscipe,	esteem'd *his* bravery,
and his ellen-weorc	and his valiant works
* * *	* * *
duguðum dêmdon,	nobly judged,
swâ hit ge[defe] bið,	as it is fitting,
þæt mon his wine-dryhten	that *a* man his liege lord
wordum herge,	with *his* words praise,
ferhðum freoge,	in *his* soul love,
þonne he forð scyle	when he shall *go* forth
of lîc-haman,	from *the* body,
* * weorþan.	* * become.
Swâ begnornodon	Thus deplor'd
Geâta leôde	*the* Goths' people
hlâfordes [hrŷre],	*their* lord's fall,
heorð-geneâtas;	*his* hearth-enjoyers;
cwǣdon þæt he wǣre	said that he was
woruld-cyninga,	of world-kings,
manna mildust,	of men, mildest,
[and mon-]þwǣrost,	and kindest,
leôdum lîðost,	to *his* people gentlest,
and lôf-geornost.	and of praise most desirous.

6326. MS. ymb se. 6335. MS. scile.

WIDSITH

AND

THE FIGHT AT FINNESBURG.

WIDSITH

Wídsið maðelode,
word-hord onleác,
se þe mæst mægða
[mette] ofer eorþan,
folca geond-ferde :
oft he flette geþâh
mynelicne maþþum.
Hine from Myrgingum
æþele onwócon ;
he mid Ealhhilde,
fǽlre freóðu-webban,
forman siþe,
Hreð-cyninges
hâm gesôhte,
eástan of Ongle,

Widsith spake,
his word-hoard unlock'd,
he who *a* vast many tribes
had met on earth,
travel'd through many nations :
oft he had in court receiv'd
a memorable present.
From him to *the* Myrgings
nobles sprang ;
he with Ealhhild,
faithful peace-weaver,
at *the* first time,
the Hreth-king's
home had sought,
east of Angeln,

1. Wídsið is the name assigned to the gleeman, in allusion to his erratic calling ; analogous to Gangráðr, assumed by Odin in his character of a wanderer ; Gangleri, Farvìd, etc.

1. MS. maðolade.

3. MS. mærða. K., with great probability, suggests mægða.

4. mette supplied from conjecture. There is no hiatus in the MS.

8. For Hine from I would substitute Him from, the prep. after its case, as I am not aware that onwacan is used actively. At l. 106 the poet speaks of his offspring.

Eormanrîces,	Eormanric's,
* * *	* * *
* * *	* * *
wrâþes wǽrlogan.	hostile faith-breaker.
Ongon þâ worn sprecan:	Began then much to say:
Fela ic monna gefrægn	Of many men I have heard
mægþum wealdan:	ruling over tribes:
sceal þeódna gehwylc	(every prince should
þeáwum lîfgan,	live fittingly,
eorl æfter oþrum	chief after other
êðle rǽdan,	rule *o'er* the country,
se þe his þeóden-stôl	who his princely throne
geþeón wile.	desires should flourish).
Þára wæs Hwala	Of these was Hwala
hwîle sêlest,	*a* while *the* best,
and Alexandreas	and Alexander
ealra rîcost	of all most powerful
monna cynnes;	of mankind;
and he mæst geþâh	and he most prosper'd
þâra þe ic ofer foldan	of those whom I on earth
gefrægen hæbbe.	have heard of.
Ætla weold Hunum,	Attila rul'd *the* Huns
Eormanrîc Gotum,	Eormanric *the* Goths,
Becca Baningum,	Becca *the* Banings
Burgendum Gifica;	*the* Burgundians Gifica;
Câsere weold Creacum,	Cæsar rul'd *the* Greeks
and Cælic Finnum,	and Cælic *the* Fins

16. Here some lines are evidently wanting, although there is no hiatus in the MS., as the words wrâþes wǽrlogan cannot apply to Eormanrîc, the object of the poet's praise (see ll. 175 sqq.). The lost lines would no doubt have informed us who the persons were before whom the tale was recited or sung.

23. H. þeoda. K., with great probability, suggests þeódna, which I adopt.

29. MS. Wala.

30. MS. selast.

Hagena Holmrýcum,
and Henden Glommum;
Witta weold Swǽfum,
Wada Hælsingum,
Meaca Myrgingum,
Mearchealf Hundingum;
Ðeódríc weold Froncum,
Ðyle Rondingum,
Breoca Brondingum,
Billing Wernum;
Oswine weold Eowum,
and Ytum Gefwulf;
Fin Folcwalding
Fresna cynne;
Sígehere lengest
Sǽ-Denum weold;
Hnæf Hocingum,
Helm Wulfingum,
Wald Woingum,
Wód Ðyringum,
Sǽferð Sycgum,
Sweóm Ongendþeów;
Sceafthere Ymbrum,
Sceafa Longbeardum
Hún Hætwerum,
and Holen Wrosnum,
Hringweald wæs haten
Here-farena cyning;
Offa weold Ongle,
Alewih Denum,
se wæs þára manna
módgast ealra,
no hwæþre he ofer Offan
eorlscipe fremede;

Hagena *the* Holmrycs,
and Henden *the* Gloms;
Witta rul'd *the* Swæfs,
Wada *the* Helsings,
Meaca *the* Myrgings,
Mearchealf *the* Hundings;
Theodric rul'd *the* Franks,
Thyle *the* Rondings,
Breoca *the* Brondings,
Billing *the* Werns;
Oswine rul'd *the* Eows,
and *the* Yts Gefwulf;
Fin Folcwalding
the Frisians' race;
Sigehere longest
rul'd *the* Sea-Danes;
Hnæf *the* Hokings,
Helm *the* Wulfings,
Wald *the* Woings,
Wod *the* Thyrings,
Sæferth *the* Sycs,
the Swedes Ongendtheow,
Sceafthere *the* Ymbers,
Sceafa *the* Longbeards,
Hun *the* Hætweras,
and Holen *the* Wrosns,
Hringweald wæs hight
the Herefaras king;
Offa rul'd Angeln,
Alewih *the* Danes,
who of those men was
of all proudest,
yet not over Offa he
supremacy effected;

ac Offa geslōg,	for Offa won in battle,
ǣrest monna,	earliest of men,
cniht wesende,	when *still a* boy,
cyne-rīca mæst,	kingdoms most,
nǣnig æfen-eald him	none of like age with him
eorlscipe māran	dominion greater
on-orette,	in contest gain'd,
āne sweorde ;	by *his* single sword ;
merce gemǣrde	*his* march *he* enlarged
wið Myrgingum,	towards *the* Myrgings,
bi Fifel-dore.	by Fifel-dor.
Heoldon forð-siþþan,	Continued thenceforth
Engle and Swǣfe,	Angles and Swæfs,
swā hit Offa geslōg.	as Offa it had won.
Hrōþwulf and Hrōðgār	Hrothwulf and Hrothgar
heoldon lengest	longest held
sibbe ætsomne,	peace together,
suhtor-fædran,	*the* paternal-cousins,
siþþan hȳ forwrǣcon,	after they had expel'd
wicinga cynn,	*the* race of vikings,
and Ingeldes	and Ingeld's
ord forbigdan,	point had bent,
forheōwan æt Heorote	slaughter'd at Heorot
Heaðo-beardna þrym.	*the* host of Heathobeards.
Swā ic geond-ferde fela	Thus I travers'd many
fremdra londa,	foreign lands
geond ginne grund ;	over *the* spacious earth ;
gōdes and yfles	good and evil
þær ic cunnade,	there I prov'd,
cnosle bidǣled,	of *my* offspring depriv'd,
freō-magum feor,	from *my* dear kindred far,
folgade wīde ;	*I* follow'd widely ;
forþon ic mæg singan,	therefore I can sing,

107. MS. freo-mægum.

and secgan spell,	and *a* tale recite,
mǽnan fore mengo,	recount before *the* many,
in meodu-healle,	in *the* mead-hall,
hú me cyne-góde	how me *the* noble of race
cystum dóhton.	bounteously treated.
Ic wæs mid Hunum,	I was with *the* Huns,
and mid Hreð-Gotum,	and with *the* Hreth-Goths,
mid Sweóm and mid Geátum,	with *the* Swedes and with *the* Geats,
and mid Súð-Denum;	and with *the* South Danes;
mid Wenlum ic wæs and mid Wærnum,	with *the* Wenlas I was and with *the* Wærnas,
and mid wicingum;	and with *the* vikings;
mid Gefðum ic wæs and mid Winedum,	with *the* Gefthas I was and with *the* Winedas,
and mid Gefflegum;	and with *the* Gefflegas;
mid Englum ic wæs and mid Swǽfum,	with *the* Angles I was and with *the* Swæfs,
and mid Ænenum;	and with *the* Ænenas;
mid Seaxum ic wæs and mid Sycgum,	with *the* Saxons I was and with *the* Sycgs,
and mid Sweord-werum;	and with *the* Sweord-weras;
mid Hrónum ic wæs and mid Deánum,	with *the* Hrons I was and with *the* Deans,
and mid Heaþo-Reamum;	and with *the* Heatho-Reamas;
mid Þyringum ic wæs,	with *the* Thyrings I was,
and mid Þrowendum,	and with *the* Throwends,
and mid Burgendum;	and with *the* Burgundians;
þær ic beág geþáh;	there I *a* ring receiv'd;
me þær Gúðhere forgeaf	there me Guthhere gave
glædlícne maþþum,	*a* welcome present,
songes tó leáne:	in reward of song:
næs þæt sǽne cyning.	that was no sluggish king.

114. MS. dohten.

Mid Froncum ic wæs and mid Frysum,
and mid Frumtingum;
mid Rugum ic wæs and mid Glommum,
and mid Rúm-Walum;
swylce ic wæs on Eatule,
mid Ælfwine,
se hæfde mon-cynnes,
mîne gefrǽge,
leohteste hond
lófes tó wyrcenne,
heortan unhneáweste
hringa gedáles;
beorhtra beága,
bearn Eádwines.
Mid Sercingum ic wæs,
and mid Seringum;
mid Creacum ic wæs and mid Finnum,
and mid Cásere,
se þe win-burga
geweald âhte,
Wiolane and Wilna,
and Wala rîces.
Mid Scottum ic wæs and mid Peohtum,
and mid Scride-Finnum;
mid Lid-wicingum ic wæs and mid Leonum,
and mid Long-beardum;
mid Hǽðnum ic wæs and mid Hæleþum,
and mid Hundingum;

With *the* Franks I was and with *the* Frisians,
and with *the* Frumtings;
with *the* Rugs I was and with *the* Gloms,
and with *the* Rum-Wealhs;
also I was in Italy,
with Ælfwine,
who had of *all* mankind,
as I have heard,
the readiest hand
praise to call forth,
the most liberal heart
in *the* distribution of rings;
bright collars,
the son of Eadwine.
With *the* Serkings I was,
and with *the* Serings;
with *the* Greeks I was and with *the* Fins,
and with Cæsar,
who o'er *the* joyous cities
had sway,
Wiolane and Wilna,
and of *the* Walas' realm.
With *the* Scots I was and with *the* Picts,
and with *the* Scrid-Fins;
with *the* Lid-vikings I was and with *the* Leons,
and with *the* Lombards;
with Hæthens I was and with Hæleths,
and with *the* Hundings;

mid Israhelum ic wæs,	with *the* Israelites I was,
and mid Ex-Syringum ;	and with *the* Ex-Syrings ;
mid Ebreum and mid Indeum,	with *the* Hebrews and with *the* Indians,
and mid Egyptum ;	and with *the* Egyptians ;
mid Moidum ic wæs and mid Persum,	with *the* Medes I was and with *the* Persians,
and mid Myrgingum,	and with *the* Myrgings,
and Mofdingum,	and *the* Mofdings,
and ongend Myrgingum,	and again with *the* Myrgings,
and mid Amothingum ;	and with *the* Amothings ;
mid East-Đyringum ic wæs and mid Eolum,	with *the* East Thyrings I was and with *the* Eols,
and mid Istum,	and with *the* Istas,
and Idumingum ;	and *the* Idumingas ;
and ic wæs mid Eormanríce ;	and I was with Eormanric ;
ealle þrage	all *which* time
þær me Gotena cyning	there me *the* Goths' king,
góde dohte,	well treated,
se me beág forgeaf,	he me *a* collar gave,
burg-warena fruma,	*the* chieftain of *his* citizens,
on þâm siex hund wæs	on which six hundred were
smǽtes goldes	of beaten gold
gescýred sceatta,	sceats scor'd,
scilling-ríme,	in skillings reckon'd,
þone ic Eádgilse	which I to Eadgils
on æht sealde,	in possession gave,
mínum hleó dryhtne,	my patron lord,
þá ic to hâm bicwom,	when to *my* home I came,
leófum tó leâne,	in requital to *my* friend,
þæs þe he me lond forgeaf,	because he had given me land,
mínes fæder-éþel,	my paternal heritage,
freá Myrginga ;	*the* Myrgings prince ;
and me þá Ealhhild	and to me then Ealhhild

oþerne forgeaf,
dryht-cwên duguðe,
dohtor Eádwines:
hyre lôf lengde
geond londa fela,
þonne ic be songe
secgan sceolde
hwær ic under swegle
sêlest wisse
gold-hrodene cwên
giefa bryttian.
Ðonne wit Scilling,
scíran reorde,
for uncrum sige-dryhtne
song ahófan,
hlûde bi hearpan
hleóþor swinsade,
þonne monige men,
môdum wlonce,
wordum sprecan,
þa þe wel cuþan,
þæt hí næfre song
sêllan ne hýrdon.
Ðonan ic ealne geond-hwearf
êþel Gotena.
Sôhte ic â siþa
þa sêlestan;
þæt wæs inn-weorud
Eormanríces.

another gave,
noble queen of chieftains,
Eadwine's daughter:
I her praise extended
over many lands,
when I by song
had to say
where I under heaven
knew *a* most excellent
gold-adorn'd queen
gifts dispensing.
When I and Skilling,
with clear voice,
for our victorious lord
rais'd *the* song,
loud to *the* harp
our voice resounded,
then many men,
haughty of mood,
said in words,
those who well knew,
that they never song
better had heard.
Thence I travers'd all
the country of *the* Goths.
Of courses I ever sought
the best;
that was *the* household band
of Eormanric.

196. oþerne, i.e. éðel.
203. MS. swegl.
204. MS. selast.
206. MS. giefe.
207. For this construction see note on Beowulf, 4009.
224. MS. Earmanríces.

Heðcan sôhte ic and Beâdecan,	Hethca I sought and Beadeca,
and Herelingas;	and *the* Herelings;
Emercan sôhte ic and Fridlan,	Emerca I sought and Fridla,
and Eâst-Gotan,	and *the* East Goth,
frôdne and gôdne,	sage and good,
fæder Unwenes;	*the* father of Unwen;
Seccan sôhte ic and Beccan,	Secca I sought and Becca,
Seafolan and Ðeôdríc,	Seafola and Theodric,
Heaþoric and Sifecan,	Heathoric and Sifeca,
Hliþe and Incgenþeôw;	Hlithe and Incgentheow;
Eâdwine sôhte ic and Elsan,	Eadwine I sought and Elsa,
Ægelmund and Hungâr,	Ægelmund and Hungar,
and þa wloncan gedryht	and the proud bands
Wið-Myrginga;	of *the* With-Myrgings;
Wulfhere sôhte ic and Wyrmhere:	Wulfhere I sought and Wyrmhere:
ful oft þær wíg ne alæg,	full oft there war ceas'd not
þonne Hræda here,	when *the* Hræd's army,
heardum sweordum,	with hard swords,
ymb Wistla-wudu,	about Vistula-wood,
wergan sceoldon	had to defend
ealdne êþel-stôl	*their* ancient native seat
Ætlan leôdum.	from *the* folks of Attila.
Rǽdhere sôhte ic and Rondhere,	Rædhere I sought and Rondhere,
Rûmstân and Gíslhere,	Rumstan and Gislhere,
Wiþergield and Freoþeríc.	Withergield and Freotheric,
Wudgan and Haman:	Wudga and Hama:
ne wǽron þæt gesiþa	they were of comrades not
þa sǽmestan;	*the* worst;
þeâh þe ic hŷ â nyhst	though I them ever last
nemnan sceolde.	should name.

Ful oft of þâm heâpe	Full oft from that band
hwínende fleág	whining flew
giellende gâr	*the* yelling shaft
on grome þeóde,	on *the* fierce nation,
wræccan þær weoldan	where would avenge
wundnan golde	*the chiefs* gold adorn'd
werum and wífum,	*their* men and women,
Wudga and Hama.	Wudga and Hama.
Swâ ic þæt symle onfond,	Thus have I ever found,
on þǽre feringe,	in that journeying,
þæt se bíþ leófast	that he is dearest
lond búendum,	to *the* land dwellers,
se þe him God syleð	to whom God gives
gumena ríce	empire over men
tó gehealdenne,	to hold,
þenden he her leofað.	while he here lives.
Swâ scríþende,	Thus roving,
gesceapum hweorfað	with *their* devices wander
gleómen gumena	*the* gleemen of men
geond grunda fela,	through many lands,
þearfe secgað,	*their* need express,
þonc-word sprecað,	words of thanks utter,
simle súð oþþe norð	ever south or north
sumne gemêtað	find one
gydda gleáwne,	knowing in songs,
geofum unhneáwne,	liberal of gifts,
se þe fore duguþe wile	who before *his* court desires
dôm arǽran,	*his* grandeur to exalt,
eorlscipe æfnan,	valorous deeds achieve,
oþþæt eal scaceð	until all departs
leóht and líf somod.	light and life together.
Lóf se gewyrceð,	He who works praise,
hafað under heofonum	has under heaven
heáh-fæstne dóm.	exalted glory.

THE FIGHT AT FINNESBURGH.

A FRAGMENT[a].

* * *

* nas byrnað næfre.
Hleoþrode þá
heaþo-geong cyning:
Ne ðis ne dagað eástan,
ne her draca ne fleógeð,
ne her þisse healle
horn næs ne byrnað;
ac her forð bernð;
fugelas singað,
gylleð græg-hama,
gûð-wudu hlynneð,
scyld scefte oncwyð.
Nû scýneð ðes mona
waþol under wolcnum,
nû arísað weá-dǽda,
ðe ðisne folces níð

* * *

* never burn.
Cried aloud then
the warlike young king:
"This dawns not from *the* east,
nor flies *a* dragon here,
nor of this hall here
are *the* cressets burning;
but here *it* burns forth;
the birds sing,
the cricket chirps,
the war-wood resounds,
shield to shaft responds.
Now shines the moon
wandering amid clouds,
now arise woful deeds,
that this hatred of *the* people

[a] The fragment, as far as I can judge, begins with a speech of Fin, the Frisian prince, on seeing a glare of light in his palace, which has been fired by the Danish invaders, in an attack by night.

3. Hickes hearo.

4. this, i.e. *this light.*

5. A fiery one. For these light-bearing dragons see North. Myth. ii. p. 31. and iii. p. 155.

7. H. hornas ne.

8. berað.

9. believing it to be daylight.

10. on seeing the fire-light.

11. the spear.

fremman willað.	will promote.
Ac onwacnigeað nū,	But wake up now,
wīgend mīne,	my warriors !
habbāð eowre land,	preserve your lands,
hicgeað on ellen,	be mindful of valour,
winnað on orde.	fight in front,
wesað ānmōde.	be unanimous."
* * *	* * *
Ðā arās monig	Then arose many
gold-hroden þegn,	*a* gold-decorated thane,
gyrde hine his swurde ;	girded him with his sword ;
þā tō dura eōdon	then to *the* door went
drihtlīce cempan,	*the* noble warriors,
Sigeferð and Eaha,	Sigeferth and Eaha,
hyra sweord getugon ;	*they* drew their swords ;
and æt oðrum durum,	and at *the* other doors,
Ordlāf and Gūðlāf,	Ordlaf and Guthlaf,
and Hengest sylf,	and Hengest himself,
hwearf him on laste.	turn'd on their track.
Ðā gyt Gārulf	Then yet Garulf
Gūðere styrode,	Guthere reproach'd,
þæt he swā freolīc-feorh	that he *a* soul so joyous,
forman siðe	at *the* first moment,
tō ðære healle durum	to the hall's doors
hyrsta ne bære	bore not arms,
nū hie nīða heard	now them *a* fierce enemy
animan wolde ;	would take.
ac he frægn ofer eal	But he, above all, inquir'd
undearninga,	openly,

20. H. landa. 22. H. windað. 23. H. on mode.
24. The line alliterating with this is wanting.
26. H. hladen.
38—43. These lines are particularly obscure. 41. H. bæran.
42. H. hyt. 43. H. any man. 44. H. fragn.

deór-mód hæleð,	*the* fierce warrior,
hwá ða duru heolde.	who the door held?
Sigeferð is min nama, cwæð he,	Sigeferth is my name, quoth he,
ic eom Secgena leód,	I am *the* Secgas' lord,
wrecca wíde cúð;	*a* warrior widely known;
fela ic weána gebád,	many woes have I sustain'd,
heardra hilda;	hard battles;
ðe is gyt her witod	for thee is yet here decreed
swæper ðú sylf tó me	whichever thou thyself from me
sécean wylle.	wilt seek.
Ðá wæs on healle	Then was in *the* hall
wæl slihta gehlyn,	the din of slaughter,
sceolde nalæs bord	*the* shield might not
genumen handa	*be* in hand taken,
bán-helm berstan;	*the* bone-helm they lack'd;
buruh-ðelu dynede,	*the* burgh-floor resounded,
oð æt þǽre gúðe	until in the conflict
Gárulf gecrang,	Garulf fell,
ealra ǽrest	earliest of all
eorð-búendra,	*those* earth dwellers,
Gúðláfes sunu;	Guthlaf's son,
ymb hyne gódra fela hwearf	surrounded him of many good
láðra hræw,	foes *the* corpses;
hræfen wandrode,	the raven wander'd
sweart and sealo-brún;	swart and sallow-brown;
swurd-leóma stód,	*the* sword-gleam stood,
swylce eal Finns buruh	as if all Fin's castle

50. H. wrecten.

54. swæ þer.

58. H. celæs borð. So great was the hurry and confusion consequent on the surprise, that the Frisians had no time to take their shields.

59. H. genumon.

60. bone-helm, i.e. shield.

68. H. lacrà hrær.

fýrenu wǽre.	were on fire.
Ne gefrægn ic næfre wurð-lícor,	Never have I heard more worthily,
æt wera hilde,	in *a* conflict of men,
sixtig sige-beorna	sixty conquering heroes
sêl gebǽran,	better behave,
ne næfre sang ne hwītne, medu	nor ever song or bright mead
sêl forgyldan,	better requite,
þonne Hnæfe guldon	than to Hnæf requited
his hægstealdas.	his young warriors.
Hīg fuhton fīf dagas	They fought five days,
swâ hyra nân ne feol	so that none of them fell
driht-gesiða;	of *the* associates;
ac hīg ða duru heoldon.	but they the door held.
Ða gewât him wund hæleð	Then *the* hero wounded went
on weg gangan,	walking away,
sǽde þæt his byrne	*he* said that his byrnie
abrocen wǽre,	was broken,
here-sceorp unhrór,	*his* war-garb weak,
and eâc wæs his helm ðyrl.	and also *that* his helm was pierced,
Ðá hine sona frægn	Then him quickly ask'd
folces hyrde,	*the* people's guardian,
hû ðá wīgend hyra	how the warriors their
wunda genǽson,	wounds had recovered from?
oððe hwæþer þǽra hyssa	or whether of the young men
* * *	* * *
* * *	* * *

78. H. swa noc. By song and mead are meant the joys of Hnæf's hall.

86. hæleð, i.e. Hnæf.

87. H. on wæg.

90. H. sceorpum hror.

93. Hengest.

Breda's market in winter. Painting by Dio Rovers.

In the Shadow of the Cathedral

D1219690

In the Shadow of the Cathedral

Growing up in Holland during WW II

Titia Bozuwa

Triple Tulip Press
Sanbornville, N.H.

Published by Triple Tulip Press
2717 Wakefield Road
Sanbornville, N.H.03872

In the interest of protecting the privacy of individuals whose real identities are not central to the story told here, certain names have been altered in several instances.

ISBN 0-9754825-0-5 (hardcover)
ISBN 0-9754825-1-3 (paperback)

LCCN 2004094084

Printing: Capital City Press, Montpelier, VT
Cover design: Jo Higgins and Herman Wetselaar
Pictures of war scenes were supplied by NIOD – Nederlands Instituut voor Orlogsdocumentatie in Amsterdam.

For:
Johanna
Alexandra
Sarah

So they may know

In memory of my parents
And Hans

Also by Titia Bozuwa

Joan, A Mother's Memoir

Acknowledgements

First and foremost, I am forever grateful to my parents who guided their children through the war years with wisdom and love.

The idea for this book sprouted up during a workshop with Sue Wheeler at Twin Farms Writers Workshops in Wakefield, N.H. Sue advised me all the way through and selflessly gave many hours of her time to keep me on track. I am thankful for her friendship and expertise.

Elizabeth Barrett did a thorough job editing my manuscript line by line. Her mother, Martha Barrett, my creative writing teacher at U.N.H. and friend, provided many helpful insights as well.

Without my brother Herman, I would not have been able to get all the facts of the war years straight. He tirelessly researched the backdrop to our shared youth. As a result of the many telephone calls, e-mails and the cooperation on choosing the right pictures and designing the cover we grew even closer.

My family on this side of the Atlantic Ocean was equally involved and supportive. I am immensely grateful to my husband Gijs for giving me the freedom to pursue my goal of writing this memoir and for his enduring love while I spent long hours behind the computer.

My son Paul guided me through the intricacies of the printing process and helped me to get the manuscript from my computer to the printer. Likewise, his wife Colleen used her considerable talents to help me think through certain aspects of the book and to write the synopsis for the cover. I thank both of them for their love, help and support.

Maybe most delicious of all was the involvement of my grandchildren. Johanna read parts of the manuscript over time and both she and Alexandra gave original input for the cover design.

Herman and I enjoyed working with Jo Higgins on the cover. Her computer expertise opened a world of possibilities and she worked tirelessly to get it just right.

Last but not least, I would like to thank my fellow work shoppers for their encouragement, as well as my wonderful reader/friends: Mary and Paul Avery, Helen Bradley, Beryl Donovan, Jane Howe, Becky Keating, Judy Nelson and Ine Vermaas. Their enthusiasm brought me to the finish line.

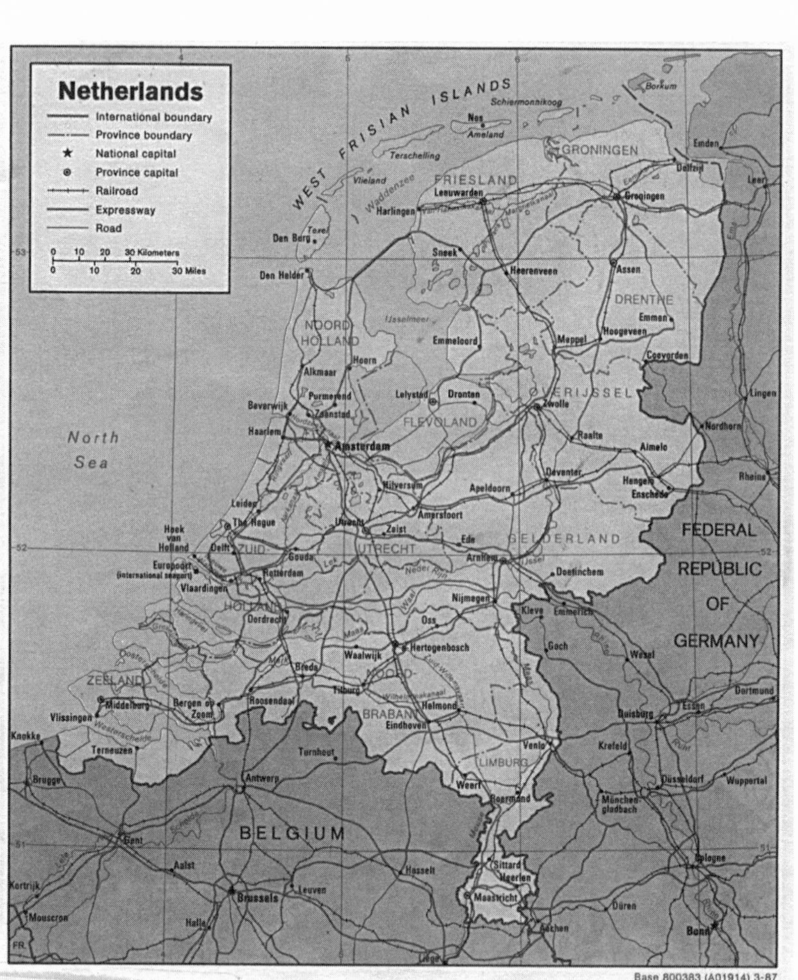

Base 800383 (A01914) 3-87

Glossary

Nederland, Holland, the Netherlands, Dutch—what are they?

The country's official name is the Kingdom of the Netherlands. *Netherlands* literally means Low Lands. The French translate it as *les Pays-Bas.*

It wasn't always a kingdom. In its long history to free itself from foreign rule (Roman, German, Spanish, French) two provinces were dominant and instrumental in turning the low lands into a republic. They were North Holland and South Holland. Therefore, the country is often referred to as Holland.

The word Dutch is rooted in *Deutsch,* the name of the German language that ours is related to. The word is now used as an adjective to denote our language, and collectively the people and culture of the Netherlands.

Some Dutch words used in this book:
Apotheek = pharmacy (de apotheek = the pharmacy)
Boer = farmer
De = the
Het = the
Juffrouw = Miss
Mevrouw = Mrs.
Mijnheer = Mr.
Markt = Market (de markt = the market)
Mammie = Mummy
Oma = Grandma
Oom = Uncle
Opa = Grandpa
Pappie = Daddy
Sint Nicolaas/Sinterklaas/Sint = Saint Nicholas/Santa Claus
Vrouw = farmers wife

Prologue

April 1984, Frankfurt, Germany

Push, push. You have to get to Holland. Keep moving.

A long corridor before me. Plain cement walls on either side of me. Here and there a dim, utilitarian light. The signs to the rental car parking lot are in German.

A car stops at the red barrier right in front of me. A man in uniform steps out of the sentry box.

Where are my papers? Where is my stamkaart? I will not be allowed to pass without it. It holds the information the German wants: Aryan or Jew.

In an instant, for an instant, I am again a child living in German occupied Holland, more afraid than I knew to be then. Afraid I will not get to my mother's side because a man in uniform can stop me.

Chapter 1

- ❖ **September 1, 1939: Germany invades Poland. England and France declare war on Germany in solidarity with Poland.**
- ❖ **September 17, 1939: Russia invades Poland from the east.**
- ❖ **September 27, 1939: Poland capitulates. It is divided between Russia and Germany.**
- ❖ **Friday, May 10, 1940: Germany invades the Kingdom of the Netherlands.**

My father came running up the stairs, three treads at a time, shouting *"Oorlog."* War! My two older brothers and I stomped down from our bedrooms. We hadn't left for school yet. People came running from all sides. Our maid, the eight pharmacy assistants in their white laboratory coats, the bookkeeper, as well as the bottle washer flooded into our living room and gathered around the radio, a German made Telefunken. A hush fell over the room as we listened to the emergency broadcast. A solemn voice announced that the Germans had invaded our country during the night without warning or provocation. Two airfields, Waalhaven and Bergen, were bombed. Parachutists surrounded Rotterdam. Heavy fighting went on in the Grebbenberg, a strategic area close to Germany.

One of my father's assistants started to cry. Her brother was in the army. My mother drew her to her ample bosom. The tight lips and somber looks around me portrayed dread.

War! The word exploded in my seven-year-old mind. I looked at the adults who stood as if a bolt of lightning had struck them mute and all the window shades had come crashing down. I wondered what would happen next.

I didn't have to wonder long, because a moment later my quick-witted father ordered his personnel to go back to their posts. *De apotheek* needed to be closed and buttoned up. The fighting could come to Breda, or we might be forced to evacuate, he said. His voice was calm but urgent. As if he'd shaken them awake, the pharmacy assistants filed out of our living room in a hurry. There was no talk of us going to school. Mammie opened the drawers of her desk to hunt for passports, and before we could even ask what we should be doing, my brothers and I were given large leather shopping bags and told to go out and hoard food.

The blond heads of my brothers quickly disappeared into the crowd outside our house. We'd each been given a purse heavy with silver guilders and mine pulled on the pocket of my cotton flowered dress, making it sag to one side. I lingered in front of my father's pharmacy on the market square – *de markt* – in the shadow of the Gothic cathedral, which was the very center of my existence, the symbol of an infinite and peaceful world. But the anxious looks on the faces of the hurrying pedestrians mirrored a frightening world. The one I'd felt happy and secure in seemed to have vanished. I'd never given it a thought that the world might harbor a people who were hostile to us and who wanted to devour our country.

Men in uniform were everywhere. Breda was situated in the southern part of Holland, not far from the Belgian border. It was a military city. Around the corner from our house and surrounded by a moat, stood the medieval castle, home to the Royal Military Academy. I was used to the sight of officers walking over *de markt* in front of our house on their way to one of the many cafes in de markt. Some of them were my parents' friends. On a warm day, they would sit on the cafe terraces in wicker chairs and wave at me, a glass of beer in their hands. Ever since the mobilization a year earlier there had been more military than usual. Today, the men marched over the cobblestone streets with heavy backpacks and rifles slung over their shoulders. The wicker chairs were empty.

Panicked housewives were rushing from store to store. They shouted to get me out of their way and bumped me off the sidewalk. I turned onto a side street. The first store I came to was the candy store. Stoppered bottles with brightly colored candies stared at me from behind the window. It was eerily quiet when I stepped inside, as if somebody had snuck cotton balls into my ears. The store lady asked what I wanted. I pointed at the red sour balls. How much, she asked. I pointed at a large size bag. A frown appeared on her forehead. That much? I took out the purse with the money.

"Did your mother send you out to buy candy?" she asked, when she saw how many silver guilders were stacked inside.

I turned red and shrugged my shoulders.

"I'll sell you a small bag, but you better go out and get what she told you to buy!" the lady said.

I was back on the street. Mammie hadn't told us exactly what to get. "Go out and buy food." I wondered how long she thought the war would last.

Soon I found Herman. I stuck with him. He was only two years older, but no irate housewife was going to snatch his turn at the counter. We wormed our way into "De Gruyter", the grocery store. In contrast to the quiet in the candy store, the noise in the grocery store was intimidating. Women were yelling at each other and at the poor grocer who couldn't fill their orders fast enough. He would have needed ten hands to scoop the sugar, the flour, the beans, and the rice out of large barrels, then weigh them and ease them into paper bags.

A woman with a mouth comparable to the size of her stout body tried to elbow me away from the counter, but Herman put her in her place. "It's our turn," he said firmly and ignored her while he ordered bags of rice and flour from the exhausted store clerk, but I could feel her hot breath on my neck.

We bought as much as we could carry. Mammie was impressed. I looked like a hero with my bulging bag that trailed over the carpet as I dragged it into the living room. Herman and I couldn't stop talking about how people had yelled at the butcher, the baker, and the grocer. The world seemed like a sweet dog turned ugly. Hans, four years older than I, came back almost empty handed. The hoarding housewives had overwhelmed him.

Mammie and Net, our maid, were on the third floor hastily packing clothes. Before the war had jumped on us like a sly cat, we'd been preparing to move to the country for the summer months, to our small house at Overa, an hour's bike ride away. The winter clothes had been put in trunks with mothballs, the summer clothes taken out and aired on our roof garden. With today's turn of events, our move was put into fast-forward. My parents had decided we might be safer at Overa.

Mammie's face glistened with perspiration. More short tempered than usual, she ordered Net around and shooed us out of the way. The suitcases, she realized too late, would never fit on the narrow luggage carriers of our bikes, so our clothes needed to be repacked into smaller cases. Ruthlessly, she eliminated what she'd deemed essential just a day earlier. Hans, Herman and I could not bring toys, we were told, but I snuck a bag with marbles into the suitcase with my clothes while nobody was looking. The small bag with the candies I'd bought for myself sat next to it.

We hadn't seen my father since the radio broadcast. He was downstairs preparing the pharmacy for the worst. While Mammie and Net raced around to secure windows and lock doors, my brothers and I spent the rest of the day looking out the dining room window. Our house stood across from the city hall, where life throbbed at an accelerated pace. Civilians and military personnel raced in and out through the heavy oak doors. Herman was actually enjoying himself, taking in the unusually busy scene below. Curious and observant by nature, he pointed at cars that drove by, packed tight with household belongings, some even carrying boxes on top, hastily tied down with ropes. "They're fleeing," he said matter-of-factly. Hans didn't say much, but he couldn't sit still, and kept anxiously rubbing his hands together. I looked in amazement at the people scurrying by, like animals who know a storm is coming.

I felt a hand on my shoulder. It was Mammie's. She looked tired, but I saw the first smile on her face since we'd listened to the radio.

"Let's have a bite to eat." It was late in the afternoon and we'd forgotten about food. "We won't wait for Pappie," she said. "He's too busy. But you must be starved!" I hadn't noticed that she'd set the table behind our backs while we looked out on de markt. A kind of normalcy returned to our home as Mammie, the pivot of our family, sat down and passed around the breadbasket.

"What is going to happen, Mammie?" I asked. It was my biggest concern. What was going to happen next?

"We'll go to Overa. We'll be safe there." She sounded sure of herself. The prospect of being in the country, away from this hectic place, was soothing.

The next morning, my father's delivery boys filled the wide reed baskets strapped to their bikes' handlebars with the food we'd bought the day before, and together we headed towards the countryside. Pappie stayed behind for the time being and Net hurried back to the village she came from. We peddled through the city, which was busier than usual. Every citizen was on the move. When we stopped at my grandmother's apartment to say we were going to Overa and that she should go there as well, she immediately put together a small bag with her jewelry and one change of clothes and started walking. She was my mother's mother, and she had just turned sixty-nine.

We met French troops on our way. They had come to help us. Unlike our own country, France had declared war on Germany when Poland was invaded. Most Dutchmen clung to the hope that Holland could stay neutral, as it had in the First World War. Besides, Hitler had made a solemn promise to our Queen he would never invade her country. Yesterday morning, those hopes had gone up in smoke.

In the gardens that lined our way to Overa, blossoming fruit trees looked like brides with colorful bouquets of tulips at their feet, a sight hard to reconcile with the notion of war. So far life was more exciting than going to school, but the expression on Mammie's face concerned me. It was set in taut lines as she biked beside me without saying much. She was not her cheerful self, and that worried me. I was in the habit of gauging her moods, because she could suddenly erupt when her patience gave out. But this mood I was unfamiliar with. She was my rock, my weather vane, and it unsettled me that I couldn't reach her.

Finally – it seemed to have taken longer than usual – we saw our house at the edge of the forest. The delivery boys quickly unloaded the food and returned to the city. The house, with its red-tiled, slanted roof, was a welcome sight, as were the cows in the fields. They looked pleasantly unconcerned while grazing on the luscious new grass. I filled my lungs with the mellow country air and looked around the familiar surroundings. A false sense of security took hold of me. I found my bag with marbles, dug a hole in the sandy soil and enticed Herman to come out and play.

Pappie had said he would join us as soon as he could; he stumbled in just before dawn. The French soldiers had stopped him at the edge of the forest, asked for his passport, and had forbidden him to go farther because they had placed mines along the edge of the woods. Pappie had pleaded with them in French.

"My family is on the other side of the forest, I have to get to them." The soldiers were not swayed. Orders were orders. But besides a quick mind, Pappie had an alert guardian angel. He pointed to some homes. "Look at that! Those people haven't closed their curtains."

The French general who had taken over the command of our city had ordered a total blackout. While the soldiers turned their backs on him, Pappie threw his motorcycle into the ditch alongside the road, jumped over it, and crawled into the underbrush. Then he ran as fast as he could. By the time the soldiers came back from checking the homes with the open curtains, their man had disappeared. They shouted and leveled searchlights into the woods. Pappie lay flat on the ground. The French soldiers weren't about to go after him in the dark woods they'd just turned into a minefield. They gave up. Pappie struggled to find his way through the woods without a light to guide him and terrified he might step on a land mine. Low branches ripped his clothes and bruised his face. Weeks later we saw an exploded German tank only a yard from the spot where he had leaped over the ditch. His motorcycle was gone.

Pappie told us the French general had ordered the evacuation of Breda's entire population. Overa was located on the outskirts of Breda and on the side closest to Belgium. When Boer Jansen, the farmer who lived across the dirt road, sauntered over to see what my parents were up to, he shook his head and said, *"Mens, ge zijt gek!"* No Frenchman was going to tell him to get off his land! Mammie paid him no heed as she fastened pots and pans, blankets and duffel bags to our bicycles. I was told to go play, so I walked down the path to the road and positioned myself on a knoll. Across from where I sat, a stream of strangers was emerging from the woods. An old man pushed a stroller stuffed with blankets. It kept getting stuck in the big wagon wheel ruts that were spaced wider than the tiny wheels on his stroller. Behind him, a mother dragged her crying son forward. He was about my age and wore a heavy overcoat. People kept coming out of the woods like ants out of an anthill.

The day we were forced to evacuate was a Sunday, Mother's Day and Pentecost all combined. The war was in its third day. Early in the morning we started out on foot. My parents and my brothers pushed their bicycles. The bikes were our pack mules. Rolled-up blankets hung from the handlebars and bags had been fastened to the carriers with leather straps. I was glad we'd left most pots and pans behind, because the few we did bring clanged loudly with every move. We each carried a rucksack with a change of clothes, except for my grandmother who was dressed in a gray ankle length dress and black leather shoes. Her broad-brimmed straw hat, also black, sat fastened to her white hair with a dainty pin. She and I closed the ranks. I slipped my hand into hers and never let go of it. I was her namesake: Titia.

The food we'd bought two days before was left behind, as was everything else we owned. Boer Jansen and his family stood in the doorway of their small farm and shook their heads as they waved good-bye. I noticed my mother was acting like herself again. There was nothing more she could do to prepare for the eventualities of war and evacuation. As she closed the door of our house, she took a deep breath and said, with resignation and energy, "Let's go." She didn't look back.

We followed the cobblestone road Napoleon had built during another war, in another century, to move his troops. In those days, the French soldiers had marched in to conquer. This time they came to protect. Their tiny Renaults, hastily painted green, were totally unimpressive. They looked like dinghies being rowed upstream on a river of human beings. More and more people funneled into the road to Belgium. A couple with five children, the three oldest each with a heavy rucksack, walked ahead of us. The youngest child was a baby. I couldn't see it, but such loud wailing came from underneath the bags and blankets piled in the baby carriage, I had no doubt a baby was tucked somewhere in there.

When I think back on that day sixty years later, I can still smell the sweat that clung to my cotton dress and mixed with the aroma of spring flowers and pungent pine trees. I feel the safe grip of my grandmother's hand that urged me on, even though it was hot, and dusty, and scary. I see people carrying their belongings on their backs, others driving horse-drawn carts bulging with beds and bedding, a teenager whipping his poor goat to pull an overloaded kid-cart, cars stranded by the side of the road, unable to move an inch in the frantic congestion. I taste again my parched tongue that would only be relieved by an occasional peppermint from my grandmother. I hear the sound of a strange language shouted at us by the frustrated French soldiers who wanted us off the road even though they were the ones who'd told us to evacuate. I feel the earth underneath my belly and the weight of my grandmother on top of me when bullets came whistling by from German planes overhead and we had to seek cover in the ditches by the side of the road. The sounds of machine guns…blood gushing from wounds…shrieking…moaning…bodies lying motionless…the noise…the bewilderment…the awful fear…

Repeatedly, the German airplanes came back and rumbled toward the exodus that moved like a slow stream of lava. The French soldiers and refugees alike were easy targets. It wasn't safe anymore to walk on the road, so we pushed forward through the woods beside it, diving into a ditch each time we heard planes coming.

We almost made it to Belgium that day. When it got dark we stopped in Achtmalen, a tiny village on the Dutch side of the border, and we asked a farmer if we could spend the night. "For a sum," he said. He let the refugees sleep in his cow barn, as many as it would hold. Fresh straw was spread over the uneven brick floor that reeked of a winter's worth of manure. The cows stood gawking at us over the barbed wire fence of their pasture. Supper was a plate of boiled potatoes.

On the coarse straw stranger touched stranger. I lay wedged between Oma and Mammie. We felt more displaced than we had walking all day. Sleep wouldn't come. There was no sense in asking where we would sleep tomorrow night or what would become of us. Yet those questions went around and around in my head, and I could tell the same questions kept my parents from sleeping. Before we took off on this march, my father had asked my mother to tuck our passports inside her generous bra. He carried the papers that proved he was a pharmacist and had his Ph.D. in chemistry under his shirt. He'd lost his temper when he saw my mother hang pots and pans from our bicycles. "Hannie," he'd cried out, "for God's sake! The only things we really need are these papers." The pots and pans were left behind. The passports and diplomas were taken. It was a sure sign they didn't expect to get back to Breda. Now I heard them whisper to each other, worrying about what lay ahead.

The night was long and restless. A dentist – my parents knew him well – had a terrible nightmare. He screamed, "Annie, Annie, stay with me!" But many who lay on the straw with him, including his wife, knew his wife's name wasn't Annie. It was the name of his mistress. The man was awakened by laughter. Hans, Herman and I wanted to know what was so funny, but we weren't told until the war was over.

The morning sunlight peeked through the cracks of the crudely constructed roof in so many places, I felt like I sat beneath an upside-down colander. As everyone clustered around the well, waiting for a turn to let an empty bucket down and pull it back up with water so we could at least wipe our faces, the topic was escape routes. What would happen to Belgium? Would it be better to push on to Portugal, a neutral country? The strangers around the well felt the bond of having a common enemy. They shared whatever information they had until a young man ran into the barnyard, waving his arms and shouting "Germans!"

"Are you sure? How do you know?" people asked.

"The farmer next door saw them with his own eyes. The French turned back during the night."

For the next five years, this was how news traveled.

My father went to check it out – he was curious by nature – and returned with rumors of Holland's surrender. There had been a devastating bombardment north of the great rivers, *de Rijn* and *de Maas.* Queen Wilhelmina had left the country. This news had a great impact on my parents and, of course, on everyone else in the barn. Leaving our homes behind, stepping into a vacuum, hadn't been easy. But to face defeat was worse. Our Queen, the symbol of our country, had fled. German occupation was now a certainty. All the adults were faced with the same decision: Should we press on? Was there a safe place left we could walk to?

Naturally, the facts behind these rumors eluded us. We could not know the Germans had bombed Rotterdam, and in the process had destroyed 26,000 homes, 13 hospitals, and 24 churches. The body count ran into the hundreds. Hitler had delivered his message: capitulate or we'll bomb you to bits. Holland capitulated.

My parents decided to return home. They figured Belgium would have no choice but to surrender as well. The Belgians would give up before they could get their family with three children and an elderly mother across to France. Some people decided to try anyway. Most of the refugees turned back.

The roads were clogged with traffic going in both directions. If this had been a movie, Chopin's funeral march would have been appropriate background music, emphasizing the heavy-hearted feeling that we had lost a very precious thing. Our independence. A different urgency moved us forward, because we were really going backward. When we'd taken off on our flight we hadn't known what was ahead of us. Now we wondered what was still standing of what we'd left behind. I remember walking in a mass of people, feeling hot, my summer dress sticking to my back like honey. Cars honked their horns, bicycle bells rang furiously, dogs barked, horses whinnied, kids cried, grown-ups screamed. I wondered if the world had gone mad when I saw our milkman urging on his loyal German shepherd that pulled his cart filled with a mattress and blankets instead of the usual bottles of milk.

We hadn't traveled far when Pappie saw one of his patients driving his horse and cart in the direction of Breda.

"Piet," he called to the man, "can you take Mevrouw Ament back to town?"

"Sure, but this is no carriage, you know!"

They hoisted my grandmother up and placed her on the wooden bench next to the driver. Good-natured as she was, she laughed, but when I saw Oma disappear in the unruly traffic my hand felt lonely for hers.

Suddenly, a shiver went through the trudging crowd. Germans! We gawked at the strange vehicles that rolled toward us like caterpillars, their treads screeching over the cobblestones. We'd never seen anything like these big tanks before. Commanding them were military men in black uniforms with the threatening insignia of crossed bones and a skull on their caps: the feared SS troops. Closely behind came the *Nachschub*, the part of the army that would make quarters for the troops and take control of the conquered territory. Petrified, we jumped out of their way.

I thought we'd never reach home. We walked in a cloud of dust and it took hours to cover one mile. When we finally reached our house in Overa we were greeted by empty wine bottles on the lawn, left as taunting evidence of a presence we could only guess at. They could have been French soldiers or retreating Dutch soldiers. But my parents had a hard time believing that soldiers on the run, be they Dutch, French or German, had drunk all that wine in only two days. But that's what happened, so the farmers said. Pappie thought it more likely the farmers had had themselves a party after we left, thinking we would be gone for a good long time or maybe would never come back. Mammie defended the farmers, but I could tell she had her doubts. Inside the house the beds had obviously been slept in. A stethoscope lay on the kitchen counter. Hans noticed my father's Paillard movie camera hanging by its strap from the coat rack, but when he took it down it was light as a feather. The mechanism had been removed from its casing.

We took the blankets off our bicycles and biked to Breda. On the way over, my father casually mentioned that before he'd left, he'd let some Dutch soldiers into our house.

"Gerard, how could you?" my mother said. She was still recovering from finding the empty wine bottles on the lawn.

"We're in a war, you know," Pappie said. "I thought I should help our own soldiers."

Hardly a stone was out of place in the city. De apotheek stood as it always had. Our home hadn't suffered a bomb shell or pilfering. My two dolls sat in their miniature cradle waiting for me.

The evacuation left a bitter taste. Around one hundred of Breda's citizens had died. The help from the French had been chaotic. The evacuation they'd ordered had only brought misery. My parents vowed never to leave their home again on command.

We watched the German army walk in on their stubby black boots with irons nailed under the heels. Clack, clack, as they hit the cobblestones in perfect step. They sang *"Und wir fahren gegen Engeland"* as they marched by in their drab gray uniforms, wearing helmets that turned their youthful faces into squares. My brother Hans said it meant they would sail to England.

De markt below our windows filled with soldiers. We'd watched many Dutch military parades before from our wonderful perch, but they'd looked more like a scene from Tchaikovsky's *Nutcracker Suite.* How could an army with an entire brass band on bicycles, their elbows resting in cups mounted to their handle bars, have beaten back this monolithic army equipped with tanks instead of horses and bicycles? Truck after truck with the angry swastika signs painted on their sides brought soldiers who sat like statues, each with a gun resting on his thigh. Their fingers were on the triggers.

Chapter 2

- ❖ **May 14, 1940: The Kingdom of the Netherlands capitulates. Hitler appoints Arthur Seyss- Inquart as its High Commissioner.**
- ❖ **May 28, 1940: King Leopold III of Belgium surrenders.**

It took days and weeks before the people who'd been ordered to evacuate were accounted for. Some had tried to reach Portugal but didn't get farther than the south of France when they realized they'd never make it over the Pyrenees. It had been hard getting back, they said. My father's brother Henri, a dentist, didn't return for almost two weeks. He'd taken his wife and four children into Belgium on bicycles, traveling through the woods, so they couldn't be seen from the air. Once there, they heard the Germans had not yet reached the most southern part of Zeeuws Vlaanderen. They took a small rowboat, filled it with their bicycles and the stuff they'd taken with them, and rowed over the Schelde River from Antwerp to a place where one of Oom Henri's patients had a farm. There they slept in the hayloft and stayed until it was obvious that they might as well go home. My cousin Rob would always remember how sore his bottom was after all that biking.

De apotheek became a depository for evacuation stories. Pappie, a good listener, gathered the tales and brought them upstairs for lunch or dinner. Jokes about the war were macabre with little humor in them that I could tell. The Germans would be the fools, of course, and we, the oppressed, were the heroes. While everyone laughed, I often wondered what was so funny. Like the grandmother story. When Pappie started in on that one, Mammie admonished him to "mind the children." She said this in English, which my brothers and I could not understand yet, but Pappie was so caught up in the times we lived in, he told it anyway. It went something like this: As a family was fleeing to France during the evacuation, the grandmother died of a heart attack, sitting between her grandchildren in the back seat of the car driven by her son-in-law. What to do with

Grandma? The parents rolled her into the Oriental rug they'd taken with them, put it on the roof of the car and tied it down securely. When they stopped to eat at a café somewhere in Belgium, the rug was stolen.

Was that funny? My own grandmother had covered me with her body when the Germans shot at us from the air. What if Oma had died during the evacuation? While the others laughed at what the thief's face must have looked like when he found Grandma inside his loot, I sat quietly because I didn't want to seem stupid. I was the youngest. But the joke didn't make me laugh.

The dead were buried. People returned from their forced excursions. Daily routines were picked up again. My father continued working in de apotheek. My mother resumed packing for the summer move to the country house, and every morning I walked between Hans and Herman to school. Each of us blue-eyed towheads carried a leather bag with our books. We walked back again for lunch at noon, then off to school once more for the afternoon session until four o'clock. It took us through the center of town four times a day, except on Wednesdays and Saturdays when we had the afternoon off.

On our walks back and forth to school over de markt and through the long Ginneken straat with shops on both sides, we noticed subtle changes that confirmed the occupied territory status of our country. The German soldiers wore somber uniforms and they always belted out songs as they marched. Dutchmen in black uniforms appeared in the streets selling their newspaper *Volk en Vaderland.* Passers-by gave them dirty looks or laughed at them outright. They inspired a song with a catchy tune:

Op de hoek van de straat staat een NSB-er
't is geen mens, 't is geen dier, het is een fariseer.

("On the corner of the street stands an NSB-er, he is not a man, he is not an animal, he is a Pharisee").

We sang it in the schoolyard even though I didn't have a notion what a Pharisee was, nor, for that matter, an NSB-er. When I asked Hans about it on our way to school one morning, he told me they belong to the *Nationaal Socialistische Beweging.* Then he said, *"Ein Volk, Ein Reich, Ein Führer,"* looking smug because he knew I didn't understand German.

"It's German for "One People, One country, One leader," Herman said. "Don't let him get to you."

"What's so bad about that?" I wanted to know.

"Hitler wants to be our *führer,* our leader," Hans said, "And God help you if you don't have blue eyes and blond hair. That's what he means by One People."

Members of NSB selling their propaganda newspapers. Courtesy of NIOD.

Mammie didn't like Hitler. One day we heard him over the radio. He had yelled and screamed, and Mammie had put her hands over her ears, a look of disgust on her face.

"Is a Pharisee and an NSBer the same thing?" I asked.

"A Pharisee betrays," Herman said. "A traitor betrays his country. We're Dutch. The NSB guys are on the Germans' side. They tell on us."

"Not every member of the NSB is a traitor," Hans said.

"Go on," Herman said. "They would be happy to give our country to Hitler as a present."

"Do you think of Opa Wetselaar that way?" Hans asked in a smart-alecky tone. "Opa and Oma Wetselaar belong to the NSB you know!"

"You're kidding me," Herman said in disbelief.

"No, I'm not," Hans said. "When I was visiting them with Mammie during Easter vacation I overheard them arguing about it."

Herman and I were silent. Hans was often a pain in the neck. We fought him all the time, about nothing really. It was just the way he said things, did things. I teased him a lot. I was as much a pain in the neck to him as he was to me. But one thing was clear: he might not be fun to play with, but he was very smart and usually right. He seemed to have an entire encyclopedia stored up there in his brains. So when Hans said that our own grandparents, Pappie's parents, belonged to the NSB, we believed him, even when it seemed totally unbelievable.

"How could Opa be an NSB-er?" Herman wondered out loud. "He's got his toilet seat rigged to play *het Wilhelmus.*" *Het Wilhelmus* was our national anthem.

Herman didn't mean to be funny, although it was very funny when we first found it out. Our cousins Marnix and Robbie had stood on the hall side of the bathroom door and told me I should stand up when our national anthem was being played. I'd wet my pants laughing.

"I don't know," Hans said. "Opa just thinks National Socialism is a good thing. A lot of Dutch people think that way."

We walked on in silence, trying to digest what Hans had just told us. We'd reached another wide marketplace. We crossed diagonally over the cobblestones to get to the newer part of town where the concert hall took up almost an entire block.

Herman changed the subject. "Did you know Mijnheer en Mevrouw de Groot were found dead?" They were friends of our parents. "Mevrouw Badon Ghijben told Mammie they found them in bed with swords crossed over their bodies. They'd left a note saying they didn't want to live in Holland under Hitler."

I'd never heard of anyone taking his own life. Death had looked awful to me on our evacuation walk to Belgium. What was there to fear more than death?

We crossed the bridge and walked by the canal to our school. Hans and Herman went upstairs, Hans to the sixth grade classroom, Herman to the fourth. I was downstairs in the second. It was our first year in a brand new building with lots of glass and central heating. When we sat at our benches – two to a bench – we could see the schoolyard with the river and meadows behind it through a glass wall.

My brothers and I at school in 1940.

The year before we'd been in a very old, dark building around the corner from our house. The windows were placed up so high we only saw rooftops outside. The classroom had been cold and damp with a coal stove in the winter that never completely took the chill off. But the teacher had been nice. On my first day in school, Juffrouw Winkel was called out of the room by the principal. We were told to sit still with our arms crossed. I decided to get up. I walked over to the blackboard and put on the teacher's hat she'd hung on a peg on the wall. It was a black thing that looked like an upside down kettle. As I stood facing the other children with the hat pulled over my eyes, Juffrouw Winkel walked back in. Without a word she took the hat off my head and told me to switch places with the girl up front. I stayed in that bench the rest of the year. She didn't punish me. She ignored me. I had to work very hard to return to her good graces.

Now we had another teacher. Juffrouw Boon. When I arrived at school that day, Madeleen, my best friend, already sat in the bench we shared. Sometimes I was invited to her house, a very different one from ours. Her father was a judge who worked in the largest room of their home. It was dark in there with a pervasive pipe tobacco smell. My father's office was cheerful with white walls and modern steel furniture. Madeleen and I usually played in the garden where they kept a goat. Her mother milked the goat and they drank its milk. When I asked her once if they'd taken the goat with them when they evacuated, Madeleen said they'd left it behind. Her father had refused to walk to Belgium with a goat on a leash.

I settled into our shared bench. The sun filtered over the pots of red geraniums in the window. Cheerful posters on the walls depicted Holland's agricultural life: farmers cutting wheat with a scythe, women binding the bundles of stalks into sheaves. The posters reminded me of Overa. Soon we would be going there for the whole summer.

My mind veered off to what Hans had told us on the way to school. It was so hard to believe that Opa was a member of the NSB. When we belted out songs about NSB-ers as despicable people, I'd had no idea my own grandparents belonged to them. Even though I wasn't as close to them as my other grandmother, the news unsettled me.

Mammie didn't talk the same way about Opa Wetselaar as she did about her own father, who'd died when I was four. When Opa Wetselaar's gravelly voice preceded him as he mounted the staircase to our living quarters, I could see my mother take a deep breath. Opa cut a ramrod straight figure, as if a lead pipe had been tied to his spine under his immaculate gray suit, a handsome man with a trimmed moustache that tickled when he smacked a noisy kiss close to my ear. Opa's voice was loud. Before I was born, an explosion in a shop he'd walked by had deafened him. He would cup his ear to hear you. Now that I'd found out he belonged to the NSB, I realized I didn't know much about my grandfather beyond the fact he'd owned the pharmacy my father worked in and our house above it. Opa and Oma had long since moved to Overveen, north of the great rivers.

The teacher told us to get out our workbooks and start copying difficult spelling words. I put my workbook on my desk and dipped my pen in the ink well. I stared at the blackboard but my mind was still overwhelmed by the shock of discovering my grandparents were like those people we saw on the street on the way to school. It was hard to think of them standing on a street corner in a black uniform while passers-by laughed at them.

"Titia." The teacher tapped my pencil with her ruler. "Wake up!"

Chapter 3

- **June 10, 1940: Italy takes the German side in the war.**
- **June 22, 1940: France capitulates.**
- **August 19, 1940: Italy occupies British Somalia.**
- **September 1940: Italy opens an offensive against Egypt.**

If war meant fighting, bombing, shooting and taking prisoners, then the war was behind us. At least in Holland. Daily life had resumed. Officers and soldiers in the streets wore gray uniforms instead of the green ones I'd grown up with, and that was the most obvious change. The Germans were boss, but it didn't make much difference in my life.

War or no war, my mother was going to move to the country, to our house at Overa. And she would take her piano with her. A horse and wagon driven by Kiske van Rooy, a neighbor at Overa, materialized in front of our house on de markt.

One June morning, I did the forbidden thing: I opened the window of the boys' bedroom on the third floor and leaned my upper body out. Kiske rang the bell. My mother appeared. As they talked they both gestured and pointed to the long bed of the farmer's wagon and then to the first floor. The window below me opened. A massive package appeared, wrapped up in blankets, a thick rope tied around it four ways. Hendrick, my father's bottle washer, and another worker labored to let the wrapped piano down slowly. A small crowd had gathered in front of de apotheek, and even my father's assistants in their starched white aprons came out to watch.

The big Belgian pulling horse was getting restless on the hard pavement of the sidewalk. Just when the piano was ready to settle on the wooden bed of the wagon, the horse jumped, gave the piano a jolt, and moved the cart ahead of its precious load. The watching crowd gasped as the piano swung toward the large window of the barbershop next door, where customers were sitting comfortably on raised chairs, being treated to a haircut or lathered up for a shave.

My mother.

Mr. Bakx's heart stopped, so he said later, as he saw our piano head toward his store window. He watched helplessly as the glass shattered at his feet. Kiske van Rooy yelled at his horse. The bystanders ducked. Somehow Hendrik held on to the rope. Some strong men in the crowd came forward to steady the wildly swinging piano as the farmer lined up his wagon just right. Once the piano was safely in the wagon bed, Kiske didn't waste a moment to "giddy up" his horse and get out of the city as fast as he could.

It was the last time our own piano was transported to Overa. My father paid for the window replacement and figured it would be cheaper to rent a piano for the summer from now on.

We soon followed the piano. Every year, as soon as the weather allowed, we moved to Overa, even though school didn't get out till the middle of July.

Mammie didn't like the idea of the three of us biking to school through the woods that separated Overa from the city. She feared German soldiers might harm us. A taxi would take us back and forth. Every morning a black Dodge appeared. The driver's name was Klaas. Sometimes Klaas came to pick us up in a limousine that still had garlands of white carnations fastened to the window frames from a wedding the day before.

Absolutely nobody came to school in an automobile, but that summer my brothers and I looked like royalty when Klaas pulled up to the curb of the schoolyard and opened the doors for us. It lasted only one season. In the following years no gas was left for taxis bringing children to school. We bicycled and hoped for the best.

Overa was my delight and had been since I was three years old, when Mammie persuaded my father to build a house in the country. She was an islander who had found herself in the middle of a city without a garden. Her ears were like conch shells: the wind and the sea still rushed in them. Mammie got her way and a sand-colored brick house materialized at the edge of the woods, with a steep-sloped, red-tiled roof that looked like the pointed hat of a gnome. The sounds of farm land surrounded our house: a mooing cow, a horse drawn cart rumbling over the bumpy dirt road in a stillness as yet unspoiled by the sounds of tractors or chain saws.

Our house at Overa.

The war felt different here. The farmers went about their business as if nothing had happened. Boer Jansen had been proven right in his decision not to leave his land when the French general had ordered the evacuation. Overa was a haven, and would become more so as the Germans gradually intruded on our private lives by taking things away from us. But here people lived simple lives and there wasn't much the Germans could take away. As children we almost forgot a war was going on, although our parents told us that Belgium and France had fallen. A bad omen, they said to each other, but they didn't give us any details. We had no electricity, no telephone and no radio at Overa. The news came with my father who biked back and forth to de apotheek every day.

Pappie had built the house strictly for his family, not for himself. He didn't remember much about the place where he was born, the island of Java in the Indian Ocean. He'd been sent away to Holland with his twin brother Max when he was five years old to join his older brother Henri who was already going to school there. His parents would return to Breda to settle after my grandfather's tour of military duty in an outpost of the Dutch East Indies was fulfilled. Pappie and his two brothers lived with a teacher's family in Breda while he attended first and second grade. His only good memories were of chasing a hoop down the city streets with a stick. Coming from a tropical climate where Javanese servants had doted on him to the dampness of Holland and the rigidity of a teacher's household was not a memory he relished. He got to know every nook and cranny of Breda and became a city mouse as much as my mother was a country mouse at heart. I never saw him with a spade or a hoe in his hands.

The first morning of my summer vacation, I dressed quickly before the rest of the family was up and snuck out. The moisture in the air was draped over the fields like a white shawl. I loved the intimacy of daybreak. For a precious hour I had the world to myself.

Where the dirt road met our land was a knoll covered with low oak shrubbery. It was a spot where I could see and not be seen. Three roads converged at that point. A tiny farmhouse stood in the triangle they created. It belonged to Boer and Vrouw Jansen.

I watched a hen emerge from behind the barn, scratching the earth to look for worms in the moist soil around the well. A flock of screeching little chicks noisily crowded around her feet. When they came too close to the road, the mother hen spread her wings and drove them under a bush, back to her own territory.

Beside the low door I counted only one pair of *klompen*. I concluded that Vrouw Jansen must be alone. I could always tell how many people were home from the wooden shoes parked by that door. The house had only one small window. It looked dark inside. The Germans had ordered a total blackout, but that didn't make any difference for the farmers around here. Right now, in July, it was light till after ten at night. Having no electricity didn't matter in the summer.

The thatched roof looked like a warm fur hat that covered the farm the way my mother's tea cozy rested on her ceramic teapot. Watching from my knoll I was filled with curiosity. Hans, Herman and I were not encouraged to visit there, but I was dying to find out what the inside of that little house looked like. Vrouw Jansen stepped outside and stuck her feet into the wooden shoes beside the door. She walked over to the well to haul up water with a bucket dangling from a hook on the end of a long pole. It hit the cement sides on its way down, and I could hear the ghostly metal sound echoing in the deep hollow. When she turned around, my first reaction was to shrink into the leaves, but my curiosity got the better of me and I decided to leap out. It got her attention. She waved. That was all I needed. Knowing full well that I was told not to cross the intersection I ran over, a delicious sense of adventure egging me on. What I really wanted was to go inside. The best way to go about it, I decided, was to ask.

"Vrouw Jansen, may I come in?"

She looked at me and seemed to weigh my request. Did she feel I didn't belong there because I was a city kid? Our house and her farm were merely eighty yards apart, but a wide river without a bridge might as well have separated them. I could tell her that I felt like a country kid, that I loved the chickens, their white horse, and the smell of the crops in the fields. But I didn't know how to say it.

"Kom," she said. I followed her into the farmhouse, into a dim space. Against the small window stood a large table with a circle of straight-backed chairs, the only pieces of furniture I could see. Vrouw Jansen put a pitcher she'd filled with well water on top of the wood stove. She poked the fire and added a few sticks. It was going in spite of this being a summer day.

"They'll come in soon for *de schaft*," she said, "I'll make some coffee."

"Schaft" was not a word we used at home. I assumed it meant coffee break or breakfast. It was all so wonderfully strange. Vrouw Jansen wore a black cotton skirt that fell down to her ankles, and her small waist was accentuated by the strings of her faded blue apron, rather dull compared to the cheerful silks my mother wore. She wore only black woolen socks on her feet. Though her whole face resembled a prune with the dirt permanently grooved into the deep wrinkles around her eyes, she had a friendly look about her.

I heard the hollow clatter of wooden shoes being kicked off outside. Boer Jansen walked in with his two sons and two daughters, surrounding me with the smell of earth and sweat, a vigorous presence that intimidated me. Boer Jansen didn't seem surprised to see me in his house and lifted me up on his knee. He took off his cap and hung it from the knob of his chair. The sun had darkened the skin of his face up to where the rim of his cap grooved itself into a distinct line. After everyone was seated around the table they bowed their heads and mumbled a few words that ended with "Amen." They crossed themselves the way our maid did, even when she was eating alone in our kitchen. It was the difference between being Roman Catholic and Protestant, Mammie had told me. We were Protestant.

Boer Jansen in his yard. I'm up on his horse.

The talk around the table was about the strawberry picking they'd done. Their last pick for the year. Too ripe to bring to market. Meanwhile, Vrouw Jansen picked up a round loaf of bread, held it against her apron, spread it with lard, sprinkled sugar over it, and then took a knife and sliced the sprinkled top off. The knife came dangerously close to her belly button. Boer Jansen reached for the coffee pot. Holding it with his wide, callused hand he tipped the spout up to his mouth and took a sip. It seemed like the most natural thing in the world when he held the pot out to me.

"Want a sip?" he asked. The spout was an inch away from my mouth. All eyes were on me. I obliged and swallowed the bitter liquid I'd never tasted before. My hair would turn red and I would stay small if I drank coffee before I was a grown-up, Mammie had said. But what was I to do? They loved it. Laughter and knee slapping filled the room. The coffee pot passed around the table. Everyone got a turn.

I sat on Boer Jansen's knee as if he were Saint Nicholas, not saying a word but seeing plenty. On the table were crumbs but no plates, or knives, or forks, or cups. As they chewed the dark bread, I could see many teeth were missing or were partly gone. Boer Jansen had only a few left and they were as brown as the tobacco I'd seen him chew. Often he had a lump in his cheek and then, all of a sudden, a jet of brown liquid shot out of his mouth and hit the ground. Under the table I noticed holes in the black woolen socks everyone wore. These people were different from my parents and their friends, yet, somehow, I felt at home.

"Want to hear what happened to Boer van Poppel?" the son named Koos asked.

"What?" his sister Bep said. Everyone looked at Koos.

"Well, you know he didn't go on the flight like most others did." He quickly looked at me, knowing full well that my family had decided to obey the order to evacuate.

"Yeah, what of it?" Boer Jansen said.

"Well, he stayed inside and placed himself next to a window so he could see what was coming down the road. Then he saw some German soldiers enter his yard. They had guns over their shoulders. Poppel didn't move a muscle but he kept looking through the lace of his curtains."

"What happened?" Bep asked.

"They were heading for his door, but one of them had to take a leak. While he was standing there splattering away the dog leaped out of his doghouse and jumped on him from the rear and got a hold of his pants. You know, snarling at the stranger! The soldier didn't have time to button up his pants. He ran, trying to hold on to his falling pants and his gun at the same time. The dog chased him all the way down the road. Poppel said it was just the best show he'd seen in a long time!"

"I would've liked to see that!" Bep said.

"Yeah, I bet you would," Koos said and they all started to tease her until she turned red in the face.

The family went back outside to work and Vrouw Jansen mopped the crumbs off the table.

When I left to go home, I saw Herman sitting on the knoll. He was very excited because, while I had been inside the farmhouse, a troop of Germans had marched by on their way to the heather fields to do war exercises. He'd wanted to follow them, but Mammie had caught him. He warned me Mammie was annoyed that she couldn't find me. Rules she thought were well established had been defied. When I entered the house, I got a dark look and a stern warning.

At lunch, my brothers were curious about my morning at Boer Jansen, but ready to disbelieve me. My best defense, I decided, was to feed their curiosity. I told them what that little house looked like on the inside, how Vrouw Jansen had shown me where they slept. In closets, would you believe, two by two with the doors closed in the winter to stay warm? That kind of closet was called a *bedstee*, Mammie said. That's what farmers slept in. When I came to the part about drinking coffee and sucking it down from the spout that everyone else had put his lips to, my mother was shocked. I was told never to do that again.

"What's wrong with that?" I asked.

"It could make you sick," Mammie said. Sick? All of them around that table, the women as well as the men, had looked rugged to me. Their complexion was ruddy, their muscles bulging under their shirtsleeves. How could Mammie think those people were sick? It didn't have to do with how people looked, she said. Germs were invisible and they could make you very, very sick.

But I sensed her secret delight in my adventure. She did not forbid me to go there again. Over the weeks that followed, Herman and I crossed the dirt road many times. When food was scarce towards the end of the war, our bond became a lifeline. The grocery stores were as good as empty, but Boer Jansen still had eggs.

For as long as anyone could remember, at least as far back as 1890, summers ended on the 31st of August, the Queen's birthday. Just as Labor Day is the signal for Americans to go back to school, so my brothers and I knew it was time to pack up and return to the city.

This year the usual celebrations were cancelled. By decree from the *Orts Commandantur* it was strictly forbidden to fly the Dutch flag. Ours stayed in a trunk with mothballs in its folds. We thought we could get away with wearing a small orange sash, or even an orange-colored blouse, since orange was the color of the House of Orange, but the Germans were not color blind and had patrols watching out for our sneaky ways of showing patriotic feelings. Rumors flew that some people had been picked up and brought to the police station. There was no sense in provoking the Germans, Mammie said. Wearing an orange sash wasn't going to make the Germans disappear. Yet I remember my mother sewing an orange jumpsuit for me…but that was later in the war. She cut it from one of her before-the-war dresses.

The summer had pushed the war to the back of my mind. Not that I hadn't overheard heated discussions among the grown-ups. When Seyss-Inquart, Hitler's commissioner for the Netherlands, sent the members of our parliament on a permanent vacation, my father was very upset. Also, the NSB was growing by leaps and bounds, from 30,000 members to an appalling 80,000. What was wrong with his countrymen? Did they really think the war had no other purpose than to spread National Socialism? Pappie regarded them as cowards who had quickly sided with the winner. And to top it all off, an ex-prime minister, Mr. Colijn, had the audacity to write a paper titled Between Two Worlds. Resisting the Germans was futile, he wrote, not even desirable. He envisioned a peaceful alliance of the occupied countries led by a strong Germany. In his view of the world France was down and out, powerless from here on in. England would soon follow. Accommodation was the operative word. My father was livid.

I heard but didn't listen. I was more interested in trying to convince Boer Jansen to let me go with him when he took his horse and wagon to collect milk cans from all the farms in the neighborhood and then bring them to the dairy co-op in town. While drastic changes were reshaping the political realities of the day, I explored the natural world as it unfolded over the seasons, as the wheat in the neighboring field was harvested, and the apples turned from mere blossoms when the war had started into juicy red fruit.

Chapter 4

❖ **October 1940: Civil servants are ordered to declare they are of Aryan descent. All Jewish civil servants are dismissed. Dutch churches and students protest.**

After the summer vacation, I was back in my room on the third floor of our home on de markt. I looked through iron bars and chicken wire at a jumble of red-tiled roofs and the soaring spire of the Gothic cathedral. The reason for the bars and the wire was to protect the glass roof that capped the laboratory below on the ground floor. My father needed daylight for his research work.

My room looked like an afterthought because it had been partitioned off from the bathroom. Its walls were shiny white and blue tiles. That I might be an afterthought as well, evidenced by my rather sterile room, never occurred to me. It seemed logical a new room was needed since the other bedrooms were already taken. My brothers shared one. The other one, way in the back of the house, was for the maid. Half of the bathroom was all that was left. I understood perfectly: my parents created the room and God created me.

There wasn't much in my room to keep me occupied, in spite of the cute little table and chairs, painted in the same white and light blue colors of the tiles. I had been given doll sized cups and saucers for my last birthday, and for a while I poured make-believe tea for my small collection of dolls. But I gravitated toward my brothers' large room where Herman had spread an impressive array of trains and tracks on the green linoleum. Every cent he saved from his weekly allowance was spent on expanding his imaginary world, which was gradually transforming from a peaceful scene before the war into a battlefield.

Birthday gifts for Herman now were toy soldiers – standing up, lying down, all with their fingers on the trigger of miniscule guns – army ambulances with a red cross painted on the sides, miniature cannons. There were orderlies carrying victims on stretchers, officers on horseback, and tanks. Impressive battles took place in that room, orchestrated by my brothers who treated the floor like a chessboard on which they advanced or retreated battalions. The only trouble for me was the two-sidedness of the game. Two brothers, two armies. I wanted part of the action.

One morning, up earlier than the rest of the family, I sneaked across the hallway and opened the door of my brothers' bedroom just a crack to see if they were still asleep. When I was sure they were, I crawled over to the great battlefield. Like a general planning a surprise attack, I surreptitiously moved the soldiers on Herman's side so they surrounded the army Hans had lined up on the other. A cardboard box served as a mass grave. One by one Hans's soldiers disappeared into it. Just as the thought occurred to me that I should create a hospital so I could use the orderlies with their neat stretchers, Hans stirred. Totally absorbed in my masterful strokes against the toy-sized enemy, I'd conveniently forgotten that neither army belonged to me. Hans sat up straight in his bed and screamed.

"What are you doing, Titia?"

"I'm playing."

"Those are our soldiers and you're messing them up. Get out! Get out of this room! You have no business being here."

Hans was getting very agitated. I looked over at Herman for help. He shrugged his shoulders. He couldn't find a good argument to defend me. After all, it was true. I had messed up their game.

"Get out of our bedroom!" Hans screamed.

"No," I said and froze myself in the middle of the battlefield.

"I'll call Mammie," Hans threatened, whipping off his blankets.

Clearly, I would lose the argument. Before I left the room I swung my foot and sent the armies flying. Hans stormed after me and burst into my parents' bedroom. Soon afterwards, I was summoned and lectured on how to behave. There was no excuse for kicking someone else's toys. Punishment: stay in your room until supper. And we hadn't even had breakfast yet.

We had a no-nonsense mother. There was no room for negotiation, and even if she hadn't uttered a word her very presence was enough to shrink me when I saw her deep blue eyes harden like pieces of black coal. Mammie had the advantage – though she didn't think of it that way herself – of being large and tall. When she was in a good mood, I loved to snuggle up to her roundness, but this morning the curves looked sharp.

So, off I went to my room to contemplate my vengeful behavior. I pitied myself for being the third and last child. In most games there were two sides, and the third party got ignored or absorbed by one of the two main players. There was no advantage to being a girl either. Boys didn't have to climb trees in skirts.

Not only was I the youngest and a girl, I was also small for my age. Herman was lean and lanky, well on his way to becoming as tall and elegant as our grandfather

Wetselaar. Hans was tall as well, but his frame forecast a heavy-set man prone to weight problems. And I was small. Very small. Every time my tante Jeanne, Oom Henri's wife, came to visit us at Overa she called me *zusje*. She didn't endear herself by calling me "little sister." There was some consolation in knowing she was the least favorite aunt in our family, someone who had made life miserable for my mother when she came to Breda as a bride. Tante Jeanne, who was herself small, had teased my mother with presents that were without exception shaped like a pig. Chocolate pigs, sugar pigs, pig ornaments, whatever she could find in the way of pigs. I didn't know that detail at the time, but it was clear to me that not much love was lost between the two sisters-in-law. After one of her visits when I cried about her always calling me *zusje*, my father – also short – consoled me. *"Klein maar dapper,"* he said. That slogan got him through. Small, but brimming with courage.

There was a soft knock on my door and Herman appeared with some bread. He sat down on my bed and said not to worry; he would let me play with the soldiers. He was too loyal to say, "When Hans isn't there," but I knew that's what he meant. None of the soldiers I'd kicked were broken, he reported.

In the middle of the morning Mammie opened the door. I adored my mother. Mammie was the most beautiful woman I knew. My father told me many times he'd fallen in love with those blue eyes and braids of blond hair that reached to her hips. The braids were gone, the hair had darkened, but the eyes were still as clear as crystal.

"So, Titia, why did you disturb their toys?"

"They never let me touch them!"

"You have your own toys."

"I don't like my own toys. I wish we were back at Overa."

"Maybe if you ask Herman first he will let you play," Mammie said, and I understood she had talked with him.

"It was Hans who screamed at me," I said, still feeling the sting of his tattletaling.

"I'm sure if you go about it the right way, you can play in their room."

To give Hans and myself an opportunity to forgive each other, my mother sent us on a mission. The Germans had issued a new decree. All radios had to be turned in.

"Amme nooit niet," said the defiant part of the Dutch population. Never! Yet we watched many obedient people walk across de markt with radios under their arms on their way to a department store on the Brugstraat behind our house. Most people had no other choice. Their house was either too small to hide a radio – the mechanism for a radio in 1940 took up more room than in today's

radios – or they had been forced to give German officers a room to live in. While soldiers lived in the barracks, officers selected nice homes and ordered the owners to give up the room of the officer's choice – usually the largest one – though certain conditions were taken into account. Doctors and pharmacists, for instance, were exempted.

Mammie told us we had to hand in our radio. Instead of directing us to the new Telefunken on the bookcase in the living room, she showed us one I'd never seen before. Somehow it had materialized on our dining room table. It was made of dark mahogany and upholstered with silk behind the cut outs where the speaker resided. The pink silk looked a lot like a blouse my mother often wore. Something was up.

Hans nodded in the direction of the Telefunken, a questioning look on his face, but Mammie looked sternly at him and said, "Never mind." We were shoved out the door and told to come back with proof of turning it in.

Hans and I walked awkwardly on the sidewalk with the radio between us, ducking on-coming pedestrians. At the department store an elevator took us to the third floor. As soon as the doors opened, we saw German soldiers stacking radios. Not quite throwing them. Three quarters of the entire third floor, almost up to the ceiling, were taken up by radios of various makes and shapes. Grown-ups stood in line like obedient children.

This was our first close-up view of German soldiers. It wasn't as if I'd never seen men in uniform before. After all, we lived in a military city. I'd sat on the knees of my parents' officer friends, who'd often come by for a cup of coffee on their way home from the Military Academy. The soft green-gray gabardine material from which their uniforms were cut had been intimately familiar to me. I had traced the gold stars on their stiff, high collars with my fingers. I had secretly taken their tall caps from the coat rack in our hall and tried them on.

Now I took in the details of the German uniform made from a heavy wool fabric that looked terribly drab. The color of lead. Rectangular patches of black and white stripes, outlined by a heavy black band, were stitched onto their collars. They weren't quite as sinister as the crossed bones and skull on the SS uniforms, but even so those black and white stripes stood out starkly against their ruddy faces.

Hans handed the radio to a soldier and bravely said, *"Certificat, Bitte."* He was asked for his name. It was written on a form, dated and stamped.

Minutes later we were back on the street.

"Why did we have to do that?" I asked.

"The Germans don't want us to listen to the B.B.C. in England." I knew our Queen was in England.

"Why?"

"This way we can only listen to distribution radio. They pipe it in over telephone wires," Hans said. "What they really want is to be the only ones to give us the news, the way they want us to believe it."

"It was our radio! What right do they have to take our things?"

"They have all the rights. We don't," Hans said.

"But what are they going to do with all those radios?" I had visions of a big locomotive pulling a hundred freight wagons loaded with our radios to Germany.

"I think they'll smash them. The whole point is, they don't want anybody to listen to them. Not their own people, not Belgians, French, whatever. This way they can take radios off the market."

We went directly home and handed the proof of our deed to Mammie.

Years later, Hans told me the radio we gave to the Germans hadn't worked. It just looked nice with its pink silk, cut from Mammie's blouse, behind the dark woodwork. My father had taken out all the essential parts and replaced them with spent ones. He foresaw that radio parts would be unavailable later in the war. Nor did he want to part with his brand new Telefunken. I'm still in awe of his foresight, especially because he was all thumbs when it came to gadgets. Maybe he'd had the help of the mechanic in the hardware store around the corner.

My parents took a calculated risk by sending Hans and myself to deliver the radio. Pappie had walked over to the department store to observe how the Germans went about gathering the radios, and he noticed most citizens brought them during their lunch hour. The soldiers didn't have time to check if the radios worked. He also noticed people were handed back a certificate which only stated they'd turned in their radio, not what kind of radio. Once it had been added to the heap there was no telling whom it had belonged to or if it was in working condition. He had drawn the right conclusions.

Chapter 5

❖ **October 28, 1940: Italy attacks Greece.**

Opa and Oma Wetselaar were coming to visit, we were told at breakfast. We should hurry back from school in time for tea. Tension hung in the air. Ever since the war broke out, Opa and Oma hadn't been part of our daily conversation. Our parents probably weren't even aware we knew what they tried hard not to tell us.

"I wonder what it will be like to have Opa and Oma over for tea," I said to my brothers, as we rounded the corner of de markt on our way to school.

"What do you mean?" Herman asked.

"Well, you know, the whole NSB thing."

"Maybe they won't bring it up," Herman said,

But Hans said, "Opa likes to talk about it because he's sure he's right."

"What if Mammie also thinks she's right? Will they fight?" I asked.

"I doubt it. She'll let Pappie do the arguing," Hans said. "She wouldn't oppose him in his own home. Opa still owns the house and de apotheek, you know."

My mother was never hard-pressed to enumerate the disadvantages of our house on de markt. It met very few of her sensibilities. In the middle of a city, one in a row of buildings, without a garden, the house made her feel hemmed in by bricks and neighbors. She had good reasons to dislike its impractical layout as well. The square footage of the hallways and staircases taken together exceeded all the rooms combined. Opa Wetselaar had bought the pharmacy and the property beside it after he returned from the East Indies. He combined the two and gave a modern facelift to the facade by installing large windows on the ground floor, surrounded by glazed tiles, very modern for its day.

Pappie worked for his father. The lawyer who'd drawn up the contract between father and son had called it immoral. Knowing this and seeing her husband work long hours, Mammie was irritated that a large – and in her eyes disproportionate – share of the profits went to her father-in-law for his retirement. At regular intervals we received postcards from various parts of Europe and the

Middle East. We saw pictures of Opa and Oma on a camel next to a pyramid in Egypt. I had dolls in local costume from Poland and Lapland. Opa and Oma had moved to Overveen, a fancy suburb of Haarlem, and bought a beautiful, modern house. When Mammie wanted to teach us the necessity, the virtue even, of thriftiness, she used as an example how she had turned over every cent in the first years of their marriage. As children we knew by heart what eggs and apples had cost before we were born.

The house was like a heart with arteries and veins leading in and out, up and down, wide ones and narrow ones. Herman and I invited our friends to come and play hide and seek on the Sundays the pharmacy was closed. It could take an hour to find someone, lost in the maze of connections between the pharmacy, the laboratory, the attic filled with cotton balls and bandages, the alleys that led to other businesses and ultimately to the side street on the backside of the buildings. It was endless, the places you could hide or ways you could run while someone was in hot pursuit, the perfect place to play cops and robbers. Toward the end of the occupation, we pretended the cops were the German SS soldiers and the robbers were the illegal Underground workers.

The laboratory was the most tempting to sneak into. Spacious and bright, it held mysterious equipment. I liked to yank the leather belt around the axle of the wide centrifuge. The harder I pulled the faster it went, building up to a satisfying high-pitched noise, like a car accelerating from first to second gear. Sometimes Pappie would take time to demonstrate what is was used for, how he spun down a urine or blood sample, then put a tiny drop of the separated fluid between glass slides and placed the sandwiched specimen under the microscope to identify any bacteria. He did research for several industries and the lab work for two hospitals, the Protestant one and the Catholic one. For his doctoral thesis he had invented a special process for making beer, which was still used by Pilsner beer factories in Czechoslovakia. I can still see him standing at the large wooden counter and pouring some fluid into a tube with a steady hand, then shaking it around while holding it up to the light from the glass ceiling. From the closet over the sink he would take a bottle marked "tincture." There was tincture of this and tincture of that, Latin names for stuff that could perform miracles. Just a few drops would turn plain water, or that's what it looked like, into red, or orange or blue.

But the core of the building was de apotheek. That's where people came and went, where the action was, where ten pharmacy assistants stood behind a long counter to fill prescriptions by making them from scratch. Each had a fine brass scale in a mahogany case in front of them. Behind them, along the entire length

My father. Charcoal by Dio Rovers.

of the pharmacy, were oak shelves with Delft ceramic pots and brown glass bottles with the ingredients they needed. After school I hung around with the assistants to watch them make pills.

But not this afternoon. Mammie had ironed the dress she wanted me to wear and sent me upstairs. It was not a good idea to be underfoot when my mother was getting ready to receive company. It made her nervous. More often than not, though, it was my father who got on her nerves. She was so used to his habit of being late, that whether or not he lived up to his reputation, she began to fume about his anticipated lateness before the guests arrived. My brothers and I waited in our rooms on the third floor till Mammie beat the copper gong in the hallway, the sign for us to come down.

Apparently Opa and Oma had been there a while. They were sitting with both our parents in the living room having a cup of tea. We let ourselves be kissed. Mammie was her charming self again. That was the amazing thing about her. Just as you expected an eruption, she turned a secret knob. It lit up her face with a smile. Not a fake one. The real thing.

Oma pulled me toward her and asked how old I was and what grade I was in now. I inhaled her Madame Rochas perfume and studied how her pince-nez stuck to the bridge of her nose. There was an aura of elegance about her, the way she dressed in fine silk. Her white hair lay in careful waves away from her friendly face. Mammie signaled that I shouldn't just stand there and stare, taking in the perfume and the black velvet band that held the folds of her neck together.

Opa gave me his usual smacker close to my left ear. My brothers and I were allowed to have lemonade and a *taartje*, a treat usually reserved for birthdays. Oma, my mother often told us, was a fine cook and loved good food. The wide array of individual cakes had been delivered in a beautiful wooden box with the name of the best baker in town painted in gold letters on top.

The conversation wasn't flowing easily. Although Pappie and his mother shared a gift for telling jokes, they were holding back. Usually, a good portion of their get-togethers was devoted to exchanging the best of their extensive repertoires.

Opa and Oma Wetselaar.

My brothers and I drifted over to the windows that were like running movie screens. No matter how bored you might feel, looking out helped you over it instantly. Many hours of my youth were whiled away with my elbows on the windowsill as I studied the bustling market. I could tell anyone who would listen what kinds of cars were parked there in double rows: Chevrolet, Packard, Citroen, Fiat, Mercedes, Ford. Often, I even knew whom they belonged to.

"Look," Herman said, pointing to the left.

A platoon of German soldiers had appeared around the bend of the Gothic Church. We could hear their singing over the click-clack of the irons under the heels of their boots.

"Look, Opa," Herman called out. "Look at the parade!"

The adults joined us at the windows to take in the sight of Germans carrying gear and guns, coming from their quarters at the Royal Military Academy. They marched smartly and at a good clip. Seen from above and taken together they resembled a grey snake that wound its way fearlessly over the cobblestones of de markt.

Opa beamed. "Look at them." he said, "Now that is marching!"

Pappie, who reached to just below his father's shoulder, remained silent.

"The German military have superb discipline," Opa stated.

"I would rather see our own soldiers, Pa," my father said.

Opa liked order, and he expected his environment to maintain it. Everyone complied. Except for the birds. They drove him to distraction early in the morning with their senseless chirruping, the more so because he couldn't think of a way to stop them. The only blessing of having become deaf, he often said, was not hearing the birds sing before the sun came up.

"Our soldiers were no match for Hitler's army," Opa said. My father didn't respond.

"Really, Gerard, believe me, it's time for a change."

"We'll see," Pappie said.

It was hard on him, this conversation. One did not speak against one's elders. My father had wanted to become a doctor, he'd told us once, but Opa thought otherwise. One of his sons should take over his pharmacy. Pappie was the smallest of the three sons. His twin brother had been the first to see daylight at birth and from that start remained the taller one. Oom Max studied economics. Oom Henri became a dentist. I don't know how my father wound up studying pharmacology and chemistry. He never complained about it, never blamed his father for the course his life had taken, but my mother reminded my brothers and I of it when our turn came to make career decisions. I'm convinced my father would have made a terrific doctor.

"Do you really think Holland is ready for National Socialism?" my father asked. Oma gently touched Opa's sleeve, as if to implore him not to drive his notions too far. Mammie had cleared the side tables to make room for something stronger than tea. The adults went back to their seats while we kept looking at de markt through the windows of the dining room, which was connected to the living room by an archway.

"Hitler's ideas are timely, Gerard," I heard Opa say. It was the opening salvo to a discussion that has taken me many years of adult life to fully understand. The child I was then heard strange words like Bolshevism, liberalism, and other "isms" I'd never heard of. They were part of a purely intellectual debate, although it heated up as Pappie kept filling the little shotglasses with *jenever* from a *kruik*, an earthen bottle he kept on the carpet next to his chair, while the women ladled *advocaat* – somewhat like eggnog – from more shapely glasses with small silver spoons. They stayed out of the discussion.

The fundamental differences in views of the world – *weltanschauung* Hitler called it – were laid bare by the war. Equality, brotherhood, and liberty were deeply held convictions that had shaped the Netherlands into a constitutional monarchy. Many political parties, at least twelve, shared in the task of governing. The result was usually compromise. The haggling it took to come up with a reasonable compromise was exactly what Opa abhorred. *"Dat gezeur en gezwam van die mensen,"* he would sigh. The lack of authority and order, of a unified vision, had caused Western Europe to become decadent, was Opa's opinion and that of many others. Europe had strayed from the laws of nature with its self-evident order, where strong was strong, an animal an animal, a human a human.

"Take the paintings of Picasso," Opa said. "He paints people in chunks. People don't look like that. It's unnatural. And contemporary music! It hurts your ears. There's no harmony in it whatsoever." He seemed to be personally insulted by these manifestations of decadent society.

National Socialism emphasized the people as a whole. *Das Volk.* The individual was subordinate to the state. People were not equal. The strong had a right to rule over the weak. The Teutonic race was the most creative, the purest, and the salvation of the world. The Dutch people were descended from the same blood and would be brought back to their roots. Voluntarily, Hitler suggested, because it was evident that man was inescapably determined by his roots. Pure logic.

Pure nonsense, my father thought.

"How can you believe such propaganda, Pa?"

"Propaganda?" Opa retorted. "You wait! The new regime will clean up a lot of this wishy-washy, back-and-forth debating we've had to endure here."

"I think the Nazi ideals are a convenient license to do away with anything and anyone they don't agree with," Pappie said.

At this point my mother drew the heavy curtains shut between the living room and the dining room, where Hans had spread out the Monopoly game out on the round mahogany table. The voices, predominantly of father and son, were muffled by cloth. We concentrated on knocking each other's real estate off Bond Street, or Piccadilly, or better yet: send the other player to jail!

Absorbed in our game, we were surprised when the curtains were drawn back a half hour later. It was time to say good-bye. Whatever difference of opinion had raged, it seemed set-aside for now. We all embraced each other warmly and promised to stay in touch.

Hans had questions.

"Opa is an NSBer, isn't he? Are you?"

"No, I'm not," Pappie said.

"How come? If Opa thinks it's a good idea, then why don't you?" Hans loved to be the devil's advocate. He was very good at setting up tensions.

"Opa thinks the Germans will force changes for the good."

"What kind of things?"

"Like national health care and better conditions for the working class."

"Are you against that?"

"No, but I don't think the Germans invaded our country because they wanted to make things better for us. Hitler makes it sound that way, but I don't believe for a moment that he doesn't put his own interests first. Holland has a lot to offer the Germans, like our harbors, our industries."

"But Opa doesn't see it that way?" Hans asked. He was struggling to understand how two men he respected could disagree so fundamentally.

"Your grandfather is an idealist. I know you think of NSBers as traitors, and you're right. Many of them are. They are the opportunists who think they can make some big money by lining up with the ones who have the power now. Your grandfather is not one of them. He doesn't expect financial gain. That isn't the point for him. He wants things better for people who can't pay their doctor's bills for instance. For as long as I can remember he's always been for the underdog."

"Are you an idealist?" Hans asked.

"Hmmm. I certainly have ideals and, for that matter, many of the same ones Opa has. But I'm more a realist than an idealist. Where we don't agree is on strategy. A dictatorship is not a form of government I can accept."

By this time we were eating dinner. Mammie reached for the silver bell that buzzed the maid to come and take the soup plates away.

"Shhh," she said, and brought her fingers to her lips. "Let's not discuss this in front of Net."

After Net had come and gone with the rest of the meal, Pappie told us not to discuss with our friends or anyone else that our grandparents were NSBers. Times were strange and dangerous, he said. People might be quick to conclude that we were NSBers as well, and such a label might be hard to undo.

"Will we see Opa and Oma again?" Herman asked.

"Yes, but not often," Mammie said.

We now had a big secret to carry around. If people asked us about our grandparents we would say they lived far away and we didn't see them all that much. Bland statements about our closest relatives. Strange. Should I hate them? Should I love them?

"I respect my father," Pappie had said. "I think he's misguided, but he's still my father."

And he was still my grandfather.

Chapter 6

- **February 1941: Germany intervenes in North Africa under the command of General Rommel.**
- **February 25-28, 1941: Laborers in Amsterdam go on strike to protest the persecution of Jews.**
- **April 6-27, 1941: Hitler conquers Greece and Yugoslavia.**

Herman and I overheard a conversation between Net and her fiancé while putting the washed and wiped dishes away on the pantry shelves in the kitchen. Sitting by the stove, Henk told about a strike in Amsterdam. Trams had been sabotaged in protest of what the Germans were doing to the Jews, paralyzing traffic. Many laborers were out of work and thousands of people had filled the streets in protest, and not only in support of the Jewish population. There was unease as well about unemployed men being carted off to Germany and put to work in factories there. After two days, the *Totenkopf* infantry regiment put a quick end to the uprising. Henk told Net that laborers like him were getting worried about being taken to Germany.

We liked Henk. What if the Germans took him? He still had work, but what if he got laid off? Could the Germans just take him away? Herman and I looked at each other in alarm. We had to find a hiding place for him. Herman whispered to me, "Our cellars!" The next day, after school, we set out to explore.

This must be the way Alice in Wonderland felt in the rabbit hole, I thought as I descended into a dark well.

"Hold on tight," I yelled to Herman. Unlike Alice in Wonderland, I'd given some thought to how I would get out again and had tied a rope around my middle before jumping in. Herman was holding on to the other end.

Our house had two very large cellars. One was under de apotheek, the other under our home. My grandfather had connected the two properties above the ground but not below it. As we didn't have a refrigerator, one cellar was used for food supplies and for my father's wine collection. The other stored coal for the many stoves in our home, various sizes of medicine bottles, wicker bottles with rubbing alcohol and all the prescriptions that needed to be kept for at least ten years. The assistants stuck every doctor's prescription on a pin after they'd filled it. At night, after de apotheek closed, my father would review them one by one and string them together with a crooked needle that was threaded with a thin rope. When the prescriptions reached the length of a garland, they got thrown down in a well in the cellar. This had been the custom even before my father took over de apotheek.

"What do you see?" Herman called. He was standing at the bottom of the brick steps that led to the hole I'd jumped into.

"Not much. It's dark here."

"Do you think there's a door?" Herman asked.

We'd decided to look for a hiding place in the cellars because Pappie had told us once that our house was very, very old, and that the underground parts were the oldest of all. Our cellars dated from the early fourteen hundreds as part of *de Grote Kerk*, the gothic cathedral that rose up majestically on de markt and dominated the houses next to it. Pappie had also talked about tunnels that connected to the church. We were mystified. Where were these tunnels and what were they for? Hans speculated that our house had been part of a monastery. That made sense. Several recesses in the brick walls of the cellars were shaped in the pointed gothic motif and could have held statues of saints. The arched ceilings evoked images of friars in heavy garb. Once we let our minds wander in that direction, we decided it was entirely possible that those tunnels had been built for the monks to flee from one place to another. Many wars had raged through Holland over the centuries.

We hadn't found any sign of a tunnel in our own cellar. Herman and I sneaked into the one under de apotheek. As we went down the curved staircase, we'd looked into the hole off to the right of the brick steps where the prescriptions got dumped. We'd seen it before but not with the same eyes. Was there a false bottom underneath? A trap door? How deep would it be?

I had volunteered to find out as long as Herman would stand guard. Most probably we weren't allowed to go in there. It seemed better not to ask for permission and spoil our adventure. Now I was up to my neck in garlands of white paper. From this close up they seemed like magnum necklaces. The hole was as wide as Boer Jansen's well at Overa and it had the same dank smell.

"Say something!" Herman called down. "Are you still there?"

"Yes, but I'm stuck. I can't move."

Beside me and below me was paper. I was standing on the treatments of several generations of sick people. Hopefully, they'd fared better than the small pieces of paper their doctors had prescribed their pills on.

"Shall I throw you a flashlight? I can get one from upstairs." Herman said.

"No! Don't let go of that rope!"

My eyes were adjusting to the darkness, but there wasn't much to see beside a brick wall and paper. I'd hoped for remnants of the past, at least an ancient prayer book. Something more exciting than paper, paper, paper. Still, I had to find out if this was indeed a tunnel and if so, where it led. I gingerly moved my foot around and suddenly I was jerked down, as if I'd hit an air pocket. The paper reached up to my eyebrows and still I had no solid footing.

"Help!" I cried, but my voice was muffled.

"Titia, where are you?"

Herman's voice sounded far away. I panicked. The rope tugged at me. He must have heard me. *God, I have to get out of here.* With my arms flailing wildly I located a brick in the wall that was protruding. I held on to it for dear life. I could breathe again, but I was petrified.

"Pull me up!" I yelled.

Herman was alarmed. I could feel it in the tugging of the rope that cut sharply into my sides. He got me up a little ways and I found a sturdier brick to hold. But apparently Herman couldn't pull me all the way out.

"Can you hold on?" he called down. "I'm going to get Hendrick."

The minutes I spent until Herman returned with Hendrick seemed like an eternity. Gone were my dreams of secret tunnels, of finding a hidden bag of golden coins from the middle ages.

Everything about Hendrick was big, even more so when viewed from below: his red nose, his bloodshot eyes and the enormous leather apron that reached from his chin to his ankles. He was the jack-of-all-trades in de apotheek and in our house. Seeing him above me, kneeling next to Herman's spindly legs, I thought he looked like an angel. Immediately he took charge of the rope Herman had abandoned and pulled it up firmly until I was within his grasp. Hendrick's hands equaled the size of the shovel he used to take the ashes out of our stoves. Despite the roughness of his calloused skin, I was surprised by the gentleness with which he grasped my shoulders.

I was hauled back on to the bricks from where I had started, shaking and not much wiser. Hendrick went back to work. We asked him not to tell on us. Although feeling deflated we were still convinced the wide hole wasn't just a hole, but the beginning of a tunnel. An aura of mystery hung over it, undoubtedly enhanced by stories about the dowser who'd finally pinpointed – only a year or so ago – the entrance to the vault in the cathedral where members of the royal family had been buried. According to the royal archives Anna van Buren, the first wife of William of Orange, had been buried in the cathedral, but once the crypt was opened it had to be determined, beyond any doubt, that what was found there was indeed a human heart. In his laboratory my father proved that even after 380 years, the embalmed heart still reacted to the tests he submitted it to. Queen Wilhelmina had written a letter to thank my father for his research.

There had to be a way to find out if there was a tunnel. Why not start from the other end, we thought. The cathedral end? From the cellar we ran down the dark hall that led to the room where Hendrick was busy cleaning bottles by placing them on a specially designed spout that let the water out under great pressure. On weekends we often had water fights there, drenching the ceiling and each other by pushing on the spout without a bottle on it.

It was only a few steps to the alley that led to the side street facing the church, which was clothed in scaffolding and had been that way for as long as I could remember. Dio Rovers, a friend of my parents, was in charge of the restoration – one of the few activities the Germans didn't interfere with.

We stepped into the churchyard where stonecutters chiseled massive pieces of sandstone. The decorative parts of the church that had fallen off or been nibbled at by the tooth of time needed to be replaced. Dio Rovers made the designs that guided the stonecutters' hands. His studio was part of the make-shift yard.

I can't think of a more amiable face than Dio's. Its texture was all wrinkles, but not the way they made Vrouw Jansen's look like a prune. They'd been etched around his eyes and on his forehead by a very fine artist's pen. His curls lay like a wreath around his balding head. He glanced up at us over the rim of his glasses, an amused, inquisitive look in his blue eyes. Dio took you in as if you were a special gift, searching your face for possibilities. Later, during several sittings for a portrait, I realized he followed the light to transpose what he saw onto canvas, thereby revealing your soul.

We stood before him, fidgeting. Would we say: "We're here to look for a tunnel to our house?" It might not be smart to tell him that. One whole year of occupation had put a clamp on directness. Most probably Dio Rovers was not an NSBer, but Mammie had warned us to always assume people, even the ones we knew from before the war, might be Nazi sympathizers. That way you would be safe. There's a lot at stake, she'd said. We might hurt not only ourselves, but also other people. At the time it had felt like a very vague guideline. Today, we understood. It would be better for Dio not to know we were trying to hide Henk from the Germans.

Herman was the diplomat. He used the indirect way.

"May we climb the tower, Mijnheer Rovers?"

"Well sure," Dio said.

He showed us where the staircase began.

"Come back here to tell me you made it safely down again. No foolishness, right?"

We promised.

The church dated from 1410. The work on the tower had begun sixty-two years later. Nobody had to convince me it had taken half a century to complete it. As we labored up the stone steps, the idea that someone had even come up with the notion of building a staircase to heaven was astounding. A heavy rope served as a railing and guided us through the dimness. What had it been like to carry these heavy blocks of stone up, I wondered. This type of stone was not found around here. It must have been brought on wagons, pulled by strong horses, from faraway quarries. The energies expended by men and animals had been nothing short of monumental. What had driven them?

When we'd satisfied our curiosity to see what our house looked like from above, we turned around and slid from the narrow confines of the tower into the overwhelming spaciousness of the church, where the columns and ribs that upheld the vaulted ceilings seemed as tall as the tower we'd just climbed. Our eyes adjusted to the muted light from the windows. Enveloped by pervasive silence and majestic vastness, we stood still, feeling overwhelmed. Our family regularly attended a church that was more like a pocket in a man's suit compared to this cathedral. I felt like a particle of dust swept up by a powerful force. Strange. Feeling small usually bothered me, especially when people made me feel small, but in this place I felt small in a different way. Maybe the surging power of this place was awe, that word my mother sometimes used. I had often wondered what she meant by it. A light switched on in her eyes – a light from within – when she used the word, when my parents discussed the sermon over a cup of coffee after church. My father would listen intently, but he never showed the same rapture. He didn't seem to have that light.

We got startled out of our wits when the organ pipes filled with air, a rumbling sound at first, then clarifying into deep tones. It sounded like the Bach cantata my mother played on the piano. Herman jumped. Obviously, we weren't alone. I looked up to see if there was a mirror above the keyboard so the organist could follow what was going on below. Indeed there was. The face I saw reflected in the mirror looked fully concentrated. Maybe the man was too absorbed in his music to notice us. It wasn't that we weren't allowed in the church, but we weren't sure. Although it was also Protestant, this was not the church my parents belonged to. Some churches you were allowed to go in, others not. We knew our Catholic friends at school weren't allowed to go into Protestant churches. That was the rule, they said. We assumed we weren't allowed in theirs.

"Do you think the tunnel ends up here somewhere?" Herman whispered.

"I hope not," I whispered back as I noticed names and dates that had been chiseled into the stones under our feet.

"Pappie says the royals are buried in a sort of cellar," Herman said. He obviously had some macabre thoughts. What kind of cellar was ours connected to?

"A grave is not a tunnel!" I said with as much aplomb as I could muster.

"You never know," Herman whispered.

A dowser had found the crypt of the royals. Without such an uncommon tool at our disposal our chances of finding the other end of the tunnel were narrowing, and Herman's hint that the whole adventure might end us up in a crypt with dead bodies was cooling our enthusiasm. Without admitting that to each other we kept on walking. The granite floor of the cathedral was itself a graveyard. We were walking over cracked and sagging stones with impressive coats of arms, over engraved words, over the bodies of people about whose lives we knew nothing except that they were long gone. The length of their days didn't matter. They were old, old, old. Not in any way connected to the world we were a part of.

The organist's mirror was slanted toward the nave, so we stayed out of his line of vision by quietly walking under the lower arches of the aisles. It wasn't logical for a tunnel to end in the transept, in full view of the chancel and the congregation.

The cathedral had many nooks and crannies, some similar to the niches in our own cellar that had housed statues before iconoclastic fury in the sixteenth century had removed them for good. When we had gone around the aisles twice without finding a trace of a secret door, we came upon the one piece of art that had escaped the crazed mob of religious protesters. Every citizen of Breda knew it was listed as the second most important monument in the Netherlands, after Rembrandt's famous *Night Watch.*

Light from the tall, pointed windows laid a pattern of slender fingers over the mausoleum, as if a hand were holding this massive structure in a protective grip. It was so big and so beautiful that we stood still before it. At first, I avoided looking at the life size bodies of a man and a woman, carved in a white stone that lay atop a slab of a darker stone. Instead, I concentrated on the carved sword displayed on the slab that created a roof over them that was held up by a soldier on each corner.

No matter how hard I tried, my eyes could no longer avoid the bodies. I looked them over carefully. The woman intrigued me. Her semblance was carved in a seemingly transparent stone, her features so authentic it was hard not to think of her as real. Dead to be sure, but real all the same. She was incredibly beautiful in her flowing gown and head shawl. Above all, she appeared at peace. What was it like to be dead? So far, what I'd seen of death was the blood and horror on the road to Belgium when the Germans shot at us from the air. Had this lady traveled to a place of peace? Maybe it was the same place my Opa Ament had gone to.

Every Sunday, my brothers and I went to Sunday school in an old, dark building where a lady with gray hair done up in a bun and a dress down to her ankles, showed us etchings of Bible scenes. Juffrouw Mercier told stories about the people in the pictures who were all dressed in nightgowns. It was about God, she said in her velvet voice, but in fact it was about people who lived long ago and did horrible things to each other. Those Sunday morning lessons didn't make me feel God. I never made the connection.

But today was different. The organ music, the mysteriously fragmented light from the stained windows, the upward sweep of the columns, all combined to do what Juffrouw Mercier could not. They made me believe in something that could only be felt. Something that could not be seen or gleaned from a picture. That invisible thing must be the awe my mother talked about. It must be what had driven the people to build this cathedral. It must be God.

"Beautiful, isn't it?" The voice from behind made us jump. I don't know how long we'd stood there. Neither one of us had heard footsteps. It was Dio. Would he be mad at us for having gone into the church?

"This was made more than four centuries ago by an Italian sculptor," Dio said.

"Who were they?" Herman asked.

"Count Engelbert II and his wife." Dio's mind didn't seem to be on us climbing the tower.

"How did she die?" I asked.

"Of sleeping sickness."

"Is that why she looks so peaceful?"

Dio smiled. "Maybe, but you're looking at more than someone just sleeping." That was all Dio said. Then he walked on.

More than sleeping. What did he mean by that?

Herman nudged me. "Let's go home. There's no way into the tunnel."

"There must be."

"Yes, but we can't find it." Herman had a way of resolutely stating a simple truth.

"How about Henk? How are we going to hide him?" I asked, not willing to give up on our adventure.

"He'll have to find another place." Herman was shifting the responsibility. "Maybe it would be better for him to hide around the town where he lives and not in the middle of the city."

That evening at the dinner table, we tried to find out from my father if he was sure there were tunnels between the houses and the church. We avoided being specific.

"Long ago," Pappie said, "like hundreds of years ago, there were connections, but now tunnels don't make sense. We wouldn't like it if our neighbors could walk into our cellar..."

"And take a few bottles of your wine," Hans piped in.

"Right," Pappie said. "So the tunnels may still be there but they've been cemented shut."

Herman and I looked at each other over the table. We could have saved ourselves a lot of trouble had we known that. But I wasn't sorry. I kept thinking about that benign expression on the face of the lady in the church. Something I couldn't put into words had entered my inner world. I never would have believed that an alabaster carving could have given me such a warm, trusting feeling inside.

When the pharmacy was sold in 1962 to a Chinese man who wanted to make a restaurant out of it, an amazing discovery was made. Underneath the countless garlands of prescriptions was a concrete floor and several containers filled with mustard gas. They must have been put there during the First World War.

What to do with mustard gas? It was totally illegal to own such a poison, even for a pharmacist. It was turned over to the military authorities of Breda.

Chapter 7

❖ **April 1941: All cinemas and cafes are ordered to display a sign that Jews are not welcome.**

❖ **June 22, 1941: Germany invades Russia.**

Today was market day and long before my brothers and I rounded the corner of de markt on our way home from school, we heard the happy tunes from the cathedral's carillon, which the *beiaardier* showered over the inner city.

As we passed a vegetable stand we heard him ring out a national song. *"Piet Hein, Piet Hein, Piet Hein zijn naam is klein, zijn daden benne groot, hij heeft gewonnen de zilveren vloot."* People behind and in front of the crates with cabbages chuckled. Piet Hein had captured the silver fleet in 1628. As the song said, his name was small, but his deeds were great. His name was synonymous with victory.

It was forbidden to play the national anthem or our patriotic songs, just as it was forbidden to fly our flag or wear the color orange. In concert halls music by Felix Mendelssohn was banned. Dead for a whole century, to the Nazis he was still a Jew. Of course, the Germans patrolling de markt didn't know what they were listening to. How long before some NSBer would tell on the *beiaardier*? My romantic ideas about the man in the cathedral's tower increased by leaps. He could sabotage the Germans and remain invisible. Imagine!

The invisible man in the tower was a source of my fantasies. When he played the carillon, I could see the bells move from my bedroom window. I imagined him hopping up and down, frantically pulling on this and that rope to keep up with the notes. If the carillon had as many bells as our piano had keys, then he must be exhausted and totally drenched after the half-hour concert he gave every market day.

As we got closer to de apotheek, we saw the farmers were loading the crates back on their wagons. They'd been there since sunrise. Still in bed, we'd listened to the familiar clatter of the city crew dropping off the hardware for the stands onto the cobblestones. During breakfast the fishmongers, flower merchants, and farmers had set up shop. By the time we left for school women, holding large leather or straw bags, walked by the stands and critically evaluated the wares. Now it was almost over and the city crew would come and clear the market of garbage and horse droppings. Their grand finale was the water truck that sprayed the cobblestones, followed by men in high rubber boots who scrubbed them clean with tall brooms. Every Tuesday and Friday we watched this ritual. No fail. The German occupation hadn't changed that part of our daily life.

If it hadn't been for the strange uniforms that dotted the milling crowd, one might have thought it was still peacetime, but there were subtle changes. What you didn't see was what made the difference. Where were the cheerful colors of the oranges and lemons, the yellow bananas and grapefruits? Most chickens had been slaughtered, so there were no eggs. No sausages either, because the pigs had been slaughtered as well, all in an effort to save the grain for making bread instead of animal feed. Fish was in short supply, as the North Sea had become prohibited territory for fishermen. At least there would always be bright colored flowers.

A small crowd of people waiting their turn at the counter of the apotheek blocked our way inside. The farmers who brought their wares to market did their errands afterwards. Filling prescriptions was one of them. Opa Wetselaar, in his days as the pharmacist, had done more than fill their prescriptions. He'd talked to them, listened to them, and helped them. To Oma he would fume about how these dirt-poor farmers didn't have the money to see a doctor. If a farmer told him his wife was sick but he couldn't afford to call a doctor, Opa would take his bike to their home and help them out as best he could. His concerns had driven him into politics. He served on the city council but left Breda when the other members couldn't be moved to institute some form of health care. He had more compassion than patience and the times weren't ripe for his compassion.

Hans, Herman and I wormed our way through. At the other end of de apotheek my father stood talking to a man I'd never seen before. He aroused my curiosity. His oversized, gaudy watch made me decide he wasn't a family friend. His clothes were too refined for him to be a farmer. So if he wasn't a friend or a farmer, why wasn't he standing in line like the others patients that picked up their prescriptions? My father stooped down to give me a kiss and told the man I was his daughter. The man smiled and patted my hair and I didn't like it. He was a fake, I thought, who was acting too nice, as if he wanted something that was hard to get. My brothers slipped by. They weren't about to have their hair stroked.

"Who was that guy?" Herman asked as we dropped our schoolbags at the foot of the stairs and hung our coats.

"No idea. A drug salesman maybe." Hans shrugged.

Toos, one of my father's assistants, in front of the pharmacy.

We went to wash our hands and took our seats at the dining room table. Net came in to pour milk into our glasses while Mammie cut bread slices and arranged them in a basket.

"Where is Pappie?" she asked. This question was put to us at every meal, because my father hardly ever appeared on time, in spite of my mother's pleadings. Maybe he felt he had a reputation to live up to.

"He was talking to a man in de apotheek," Hans said.

"Someone I know?" Mammie asked.

"I don't think so," Herman said. "I'd never seen him before."

"I didn't like him," I said.

"Why not?" Mammie asked.

"I don't know. I just didn't. He wore a big gold watch on his wrist and he stroked my hair."

Mammie could see trouble brewing and asked me to go find Pappie. I ran down the stairs, but my father wasn't where I'd last seen him.

"Hij is op de markt," Truus, his bookkeeper, said.

What was my father doing, going to the market just before lunch? Yet I knew that was a silly question. My father could be any place at any time. And this time he was in front of de apotheek talking to a man called Kees who had his cheese stand there. I sidled up to them.

"So where did you go when the war started, Kees?" my father asked.

"I hid in the church," Kees said with a wicked smile.

Pappie chuckled. "I bet!"

"Well, my French isn't too good, and with all these French soldiers around…I thought I'd better not mess with them."

Kees was a sight to behold. His ears stood at acute angles to his head and his eyes looked in opposite directions, positioned at the extreme outsides of their sockets. The only thing his eyes had in common with each other was that they bulged. They weren't even the same color. I wondered how he could see me when I stood in front of him, but Pappie had told me not to worry, Kees saw well enough to get his hands into everything, even things that didn't belong to him. He lived in a village nearby, where the police didn't dare enter. The village of Putten had only one religion and that was crime.

If that was so, then Kees was the most charming thief I would ever meet. Even though not much could be said for his looks – along with his ears and eyes living at odd angles, his head was the shape of a triangle with his hair plastered on its flat top and parted in the middle – he had a way about him that was more charming than threatening.

He took my hand and stood me in front of his cart where big wheels of cheese were stacked up, some cut in half with their velvety texture exposed. His was the best farmer's cheese on the market, Mammie said. Store cheese couldn't stand up to it. Kees sliced off a piece for me to taste.

"This was your Opa's favorite," he said. I took it from his hand and prayed he wouldn't ask questions about my grandfather.

"I'll give you a piece to take home," he added and took a bigger knife to slice off a good chunk, at least a pound.

"I can still give a piece for tasting to my good customers," he said with a wink to my father. "No need to ask for distribution coupons for every piece I slice."

Kees wrapped the cheese in a piece of newspaper. When we were inside I gave it to my father.

"You better give this to Mammie," I told him. "She doesn't like it when you're late."

With a triumphant gesture, he placed it beside my mother's plate and gave her a kiss.

"A little present from Kees." I could see her struggle to keep her face set in its angry lines. There was no use. Pappie always won.

"What did you do for him?" she asked.

"Oh, I helped him with some medicine for his father," Pappie said as he unfolded his napkin and took a slice of bread. He held it up to the light from the window.

"The color is getting grayer by the week. I wonder what they put in it," he said. "When the government gets into the business of making bread, it starts to look like something baked by a committee!"

"Who were you seeing in de apotheek?" Mammie asked.

"Oh, that was van Dijk," Pappie said, "He wants me to help him make a surrogate tea."

Pappie explained that the Germans had taken most of the tea the Dutch government had stockpiled before the war. First they took all our coffee and now they were taking all the tea they could find. Soon there would be no more tea, he predicted. Coffee, tea, tobacco, it all came from the same place, our East Indies. Mijnheer van Dijk saw the shortage coming and he knew no Dutchman could start the day without a cup of tea.

"Isn't tea a leaf? It must grow on a plant," Hans said.

"It grows on a shrub," Pappie said. "Van Dijk asked me to make something in my laboratory that will taste like tea."

I thought of the many bottles with strange names in the laboratory downstairs. Could he make tea out of those?

"Will he pay you for that?" Mammie asked.

"I'll first have to make it!" Pappie said, and I could see he was intrigued with the project. But I could also see that my mother had her doubts. Her husband was innovative and hard working. But was he a good businessman? Would he just give away an invention? It didn't seem unlikely to her. I was sure they would have more conversation about it when we weren't around.

Herman changed the subject. "I have a boy in my class. His name is Pietje Ruedesueli. His parents are NSBers. You know what he did today? He came to school in the uniform of their youth group. The teacher called the headmaster in. He was sent home. Mijnheer Broekhuizen said nobody could come to school in a uniform."

"Serves him right," Hans said, "One boy in my class, Bram Jacobi, he is Jewish. His family is having a hard time. His father worked at City Hall, but now he can't work there anymore, because the Germans said only people who are not Jewish could work there. I don't think that's fair."

My parents looked at each other, but didn't comment.

"I thought Jews were people of the Bible," I said. "Juffrouw Mercier always talks about them in Sunday School. Those people are all dead, you know."

"Jesus Christ was a Jew," Hans said.

"He's also dead," Herman said.

"That's not true!" I said. "He rose again. Dominee Toxopeus said so himself." I was sure I'd heard the minister say at the Easter Service that Jesus had risen from the dead and we should be glad.

"All of you are right," my mother said. She launched into a small lecture about the Old Testament, how that was the history book of the Jewish people, and about the New Testament, which was the history book of Jesus's life and teachings.

"Yes, but what does that have to do with today?" I asked. "Abraham and Moses lived a long time ago. I don't get it. Why can't Bram Jacobi's father work at the City Hall?"

"Because he is a Jew!" Hans said. "Abraham and Moses and David had children you know. And their children had children and so forth. All of them are Abraham's children. All of them are Jews. Right up till now."

My mother could see I was confused. "They are of the Jewish race," she explained. "In the Bible it speaks of Jews and gentiles. We are the gentiles."

"The girl who sits behind you in class is Jewish," Hans said.

"Carrie Goldstein?"

"Yes. Carrie Goldstein."

That afternoon, back on my school bench, I took a good look at Carrie. What was different about her? How could anyone tell she was a Jew? And why did that matter? She had black, curly hair, a pointed nose, and brown eyes. She was short like me. I'd always liked her, but now I felt a little strange. Talking about her at lunchtime had set her apart. Was her family also having a hard time, like the Jacobis? Should I've been nicer to her?

First on left on first row is Bertha, second is Titia, third is Madeleen. Carrie Goldstein is third girl from right.

Our school stood in a meadow next to the Mark River. No matter where you lived, first you had to walk along the waterside before you chose to go left or right to find your way home. When school was let out, little groups formed. Some stayed in the schoolyard and played soccer. The rest of us progressed along the river in bunches. It was a moment of truth. Did you belong to a group or did you have to go it alone? I usually walked with my friends Bertha and Madeleen. Martha tried to join us, but we found ways to ignore her. She was bossy.

That day I noticed Carrie Goldstein walked by herself. I broke away from my regular group and asked if she would let me walk with her. She looked at me in great surprise. She would love to, she said. We trailed behind the others and sat down in the grass next to the river. I wanted to ask her if it was true she was a Jew, but decided against it. What if that was an insult? Something dark was attached to being a Jew. Also, she didn't ask me if I was a gentile, so why should I ask her if she was a Jew? I didn't want to hurt her, but all the same, I was curious.

"Where do you live?" I asked her. Better to stay neutral.

"On *de singel.* You know where the hospital is?

"You mean *het Diaconessen Huis?*"

"No. That's the Protestant one. I mean the Catholic one. *Het Sint Ignatius Ziekenhuis.*"

"Oh yes, I know. That's farther down."

"Well, I live in between the two," Carrie said.

I wanted to ask if her father was still allowed to work and much more, but while I was trying to figure out how to phrase my probing, two German soldiers walked up behind us. Carrie froze and kept looking straight ahead of her, staring into the muddy water of the river. When I turned around, the soldiers were leisurely sauntering along the path, laughing like the men on their way out of the cafes on de markt.

The soldiers stopped. They shouted and laughed at each other, and their speech was slurred. Then one reached inside his long overcoat and pulled out a hand grenade. My heart was pounding in my throat. What were they up to? But before I could even start guessing, he pulled the pin and threw the grenade in the river. A fountain of dark water welled up and when it settled dozens of dead fish had risen to the surface, belly up. I grabbed Carrie's hand.

"Stay! Don't move," I whispered to her.

She gingerly turned her head toward me. I'll never forget that look in her eyes. So afraid. So sad. As if she were one of those fish that had been killed for no good reason, that now floated on top of the water, lifeless and futile.

"They'll go away," I said in a low voice. Carrie didn't move a muscle. Talk with her, I thought. We have to act as though throwing grenades in the river is something we watch every day. Those soldiers shouldn't be aware we're both shaking like reeds. We won't give them anything to gloat about.

The soldiers moved on, still laughing. When we were sure they were going to keep moving in the opposite direction, we got up and ran to the bridge at the end of the path.

That evening, when my mother put me to bed, I told her what had happened after school.

"I hate the Germans," I said. *"Die rot moffen!"* A *mof* was a fat cookie the shape of a pig. All over Holland *mof* was the preferred nickname for a German, and *"rot mof"* made it sound even better. A rotten cookie!

"It's not a good thing to hate, Titia."

"Don't you hate the Germans?"

"I'm not keen on some of them, but hating? No," Mammie said.

I was incredulous. They bombed and killed. Every night we heard their bombers fly over on their way to England. They took our food, they…

"Hating only makes things worse," Mammie said. She sat down on my bed. I asked her why the Germans hated the Jews so much and she tried to explain that Jew-hating went all the way back to the Bible, where it tells us Jews are God's chosen people. Many Christians, Mammie said, are angry with the Jews because they killed Jesus.

"But Mammie, that's so long ago! Carrie Goldstein didn't kill Jesus!" I said.

My mother laughed. "Maybe the real problem is they're a very smart race."

"Carrie is smart. She's the smartest kid in our class. I never knew Carrie was Jewish until Hans told me."

"Knowing she is Jewish didn't make any difference, did it?" my mother said. "There is one thing you need to understand, Titia. Hating is like killing with your mind."

"But Mammie, how can I like the Germans when they do such awful things?"

"You don't have to like them! There's a big difference between disliking and hating," She looked very thoughtful. She folded her hands, prayerlike, and rested them in her lap.

"On the one hand, we have to stand up for what we believe is right. On the other hand, there's no sense in provoking the Germans. The Germans have made themselves our boss. That's the problem right now. But we'll find ways to stand up for what we believe in."

She must be right, but I didn't understand all she said. How could I have stood up to those drunken soldiers? It was all easier said than done. What exactly was the difference between provoking a German and standing up to him?

My mother sighed as she got up from the bed. "Now you must go to sleep."

Chapter 8

❖ **August 12, 1941: President Roosevelt and Prime Minister Churchill meet secretly in Placentia Bay, Newfoundland, to draft the Atlantic Charter.**

Back from summer vacation, I looked forward to seeing my friends again. We'd last been together in July when I turned nine and Mammie surprised me by having the *paardentram* pick us up at school. My friends and I filled the whole tram. Two horses pulled us through the woods to our summerhouse at Overa, where our big picnic table was loaded with lemonade and cake. A treasure hunt led us through a maze of *akkers* – fields with crops of strawberries, white asparagus, and wheat around our house – to the orchard of Boer van Beek, where we climbed the cherry trees and ate as many cherries as we could reach.

We'd moved up a grade and settled ourselves into a new classroom with a different teacher. Madeleen was there, and Bertha Bicknese. Unfortunately, so was Martha, the bossy one. I looked around for Carrie Goldstein. She wasn't there. The next day she wasn't there either, and not the next. A week went by. No Carrie. Madeleen and Bertha didn't seem to know where Carrie was or what might have happened to her, and Martha said she didn't care. I was getting anxious. At Overa I'd lost track of what was happening in the city. War, Germans, Jews, it had all faded to the back of my mind. Still, I'd heard the adults whisper about things they didn't want us children to know.

My mother waited for us after school – her daily ritual – with a plate of cookies next to the familiar teapot covered by an embroidered cozy. While folding the laundered clothes and checking them for tears, she would listen to our tales.

"Carrie Goldstein hasn't come back to school," I said. Mammie kept folding.

"Bram Jacobi didn't come back either," Hans said. "The teacher didn't want to say why. He sort of glossed it over."

Mammie neatly stacked the pillowcases in the blue *linnenbak* on a small side table next to her chair. Then she said, "Jewish children are not allowed to attend public or private schools anymore." It sounded like a headline in the newspaper. I could tell she had dreaded having to tell us this. Her eyes held a look both of tenderness and concern.

"What?" Hans exclaimed. "Is that one of their bright, new ideas? It's none of their business where we go to school!" We didn't question anymore who "they" were. Who else but the Germans would think of such a rule? When Hans got excited, a small mound of spittle formed on his bottom lip. "This is a free country!" As soon as he said it, I could see he realized that freedom was a thing of the past.

"What can we do?" I asked. "Carrie was the smartest kid in our class."

"Only Jewish teachers can teach them," Mammie said. "I'm sure something has been worked out so they can go on learning. Carrie is probably going to school in her own house."

"Can I go visit her?"

Mammie sighed. "I'm afraid not," she said.

"Why not? She's my friend."

"She's not allowed to mix with non-Jewish children."

Now that was really the limit! Mammie told us of even more ways the Nazis were persecuting the Jews. They were no longer allowed to go to the beach, or to swimming pools, or to race tracks, or sit on benches in public parks. They could not use public libraries. The most serious edicts Mammie didn't tell us about. Those appeared exclusively in the Jewish Weekly. That way it wasn't out in the open. Only if you had a Jewish friend did you know of these strangling measures. Professional men – doctors, dentists, pharmacists, and architects – weren't allowed to serve non-Jewish patients or clients any longer. Jews could not be appointed as teachers or professors. The bank accounts of all Jews were frozen.

"Bram Jacobi told me once he couldn't keep his pigeons any longer," Hans said.

"What are they afraid of?" Herman asked, "That they're going to send the pigeon with a message to England? 'Please, Mr. Churchill, come help us'?"

The steaming cups of tea and the tray with cookies had lost their attraction. All I could see before me was the face of Carrie Goldstein when she'd sat next to me on the bank of the Mark River, and the drunken soldiers had come upon us. How different that moment must have been for her than it had been for me. She already knew she belonged to a different race, to a people who were being shut out by Hitler. The sadness I'd seen in her brown eyes had revealed knowledge of something I'd never imagined for myself. As if she knew she had an engine inside of her whose fuel supply had been irrevocably cut off.

"Time to do your homework," Mammie announced.

She kept a close check on the work we brought home. Hans seemed to breeze through it. Herman took longer. Mammie had him sit at the table in front of the window and helped him. Not with arithmetic. He had that down pat. Languages were another matter. As my assignments were still small, I had more time to play before dinnertime. I walked up the steep staircase to my room on the top floor, and sat down at the table that served as a desk. I emptied my leather school bag and looked at the sheet of French words I had to learn by heart. Mijnheer Snijders had carefully pronounced the words and we had to say them after him. Again and again, till we got it right. Pronunciation was everything, he said.

"Le chien et le chat," I said out loud and instantly felt foolish, sitting in my own room, listening to myself speaking in a strange language. Enough of that. Restless, I walked over to the window and through the iron bars noticed our neighbor, Mevrouw Backx, hanging out her laundry on the ropes that criss-crossed her tiny balcony, not any bigger than the flatbed of a farmer's wagon.

The church bell gave five strokes. I looked up at the clock's huge brass arms and numbers that were attached to the side of the tower, just below the top that had been nicknamed "the pepper shaker" because of its odd shape. An hour left before the gong in the hallway would be struck for dinner. Maybe Herman was done with his homework. I went downstairs and peeked into the dining room. Herman was still sitting by the window, but he was looking at traffic on de markt. Mammie must have gone to the kitchen in the back of the house.

"Pssst!"

Herman looked up. "What?"

"Let's go outside," I enticed him. Herman closed his textbook.

We ran down the staircase, avoiding the kitchen, and walked through our father's lab to a small yard with an open shed for bicycles. From there the alleyways pointed in all directions. The whole complex resembled an octopus. Our home and the pharmacy formed the body and the alleyways were the sucking-bearing arms.

We lingered in front of the washroom for a while and watched Hendrick clean bottles. The alleyway leading to the side street was built like our cellars with the bricks leaning into each other, creating a roof just tall enough for a man to walk through without hitting his head. Its walls smelled of dried urine. Men full of beer considered it their *urinoir.* The heavy door to the street was left open for the pharmacy assistants to move in and out with their bicycles. Once, I had come in with my bike and found a German soldier with his fly open, relieving himself. I'd dropped my bike and run. After that incident, we brought our bikes in through the front door and leaned them against the wainscoting of the hall, under a large painting of my great-grandfather, posed in his captain's uniform with gold epaulettes and colorful decorations on his chest.

Without any thought to where we were headed, we sauntered through the dark alley toward the light of the road, the foul smell of sin – as we understood it – penetrating our nostrils. We looked up and down the funnel-shaped street. At its widest part an armored vehicle rose above the parked passenger cars. German soldiers were inside the cafe on the corner, easy to pick out in their gray uniforms as they stood at the bar, drinking beer. Anger rose in my chest. Carrie Goldstein was virtually a prisoner in her own home and these were the men who laid down the stupid laws she had to live by. There they stood, careless, drinking, singing, and arrogant. I looked over at their vehicle on the other side of the street, the very symbol of their power. One of the boys in my class had told me that if you put water in the gas tank of a car, it couldn't go anywhere. I nudged Herman.

"We should go back to Hendrick and pick out a bottle," I whispered, "fill it with water and return." He raised his eyebrows. In a low voice, even though the German soldiers were separated from us by glass, I explained that the water would disable the motor. "Serve them right," I added. Herman thought for a moment, but didn't argue with me. He had a gift for correctly guessing people's motives.

We didn't run. Slowly, as if we'd been called away, we turned and walked back to the alley. Hendrick was sorting bottles by color and size. I casually picked up one with a long neck and filled it with water from the spout, while Herman kept Hendrick's attention away from what I was doing. The bottle fitted nicely in the pocket of Herman's jacket. Walking slowly, so as not to spill the water, we returned to the darkening street. No one was about. Because of the total blackout order since the war had started, people were in the habit of trying to get home before nightfall. Streetlights were dimmed. The day was receding into dusk, and ghostly shadows fell over the cobblestone street. The parked cars were becoming just gray outlines without detail.

We walked toward the pantzerwagen, approaching it from the backside. It was parked out of view of the soldiers who were still in the cafe, still drinking and singing. Herman located the cap to the gas tank behind the driver's door.

"I'll open it, you pour in the water," he said, and handed me the bottle. The cap came off easily. I stuck the neck of the bottle inside the hole and heard the water gurgle down. The seconds it took seemed like minutes. When the bottle was empty, Herman twisted the gas cap back on. My heart was beating in my throat. With all the calm we could muster, we turned back. Our impulse was to run, although we didn't see anybody moving in the darkening street. The moment we reached the gate of our alleyway, we slipped in, closed the heavy door, and leaned against the stinky wall to catch our breath, even though we hadn't been running. Our entire operation had been perfectly synchronized without a premeditated plan.

At suppertime that night, I strained my ears for any sounds from the street. Not until we were ready for bed did we hear the shouting outdoors. Herman came into my bedroom with its one window facing the backsides of other houses. Because of the blackout we couldn't lift the curtains on the front side of our house, where the boys' room was, but in my room we could push aside the shade, pry open the window and listen. Loud German swear words rose over the roofs.

"They're good and mad," Herman said.

Once in bed, under the heavy covers of before-the-war wool blankets, I began to think about what we'd done. Our deed, or rather our misdeed, loomed larger in the dark. I'd never done such a brazen thing. What had possessed me? The scene played itself backward and forward, again and again. I couldn't avoid it and sleep wouldn't come to take me away from myself. It probably would be easier if I told Mammie. Up to that point in my life, all my deliberate acts of insubordination had been found out, confessed, and reconciled. This was different. It wasn't like stealing licorice, for which I had a great weakness, from de apotheek.

Pouring the water down the gas tank had been more satisfying than tasting stolen candy. There was something righteous about it, and something very thrilling. Deep down I knew I'd done it not just for what had been taken away from Carrie Goldstein, although that had been foremost in my mind. It was for all the little things the Germans did to us, like telling us we couldn't fly our own flag, wear an orange sash, sing our own songs; like taking away our radios, our butter and our best cheese. It was for the very fact they gave themselves the right to tell us what to do and what not to do. The soldiers in the cafe on the corner, taking over the bar while the Dutch people sank away to the dark corners, had stood in for Hitler and Seyss Inquart, the only Nazis I knew by name.

I shifted uncomfortably under the sheets. How could Mammie say she didn't hate the Germans? Was hating really such a bad thing? The Germans made us hate them. So it was their own fault if our people did things to them.

Still… It's not right to hate, Mammie had said, because it's like killing with your mind. But she also said you had to stand up for what is right. Was what Herman and I had done hating or standing up? How could you tell the difference?

The next day after school, Herman and I saw the armored car being towed away. We'd entered the bookstore of Mr. Harthoorn, which was immediately to the right of our alleyway. Through the window we had a clear view of the street. Pretending to look at a book together, we saw a wrecker truck back up, attach a chain to the pantzerwagen's back bumper, and haul the disabled vehicle off. The angry swastika sign on its side had been reduced to sheer mockery. We winked at each other and put the book back on the table.

Herman went back to the house to do his homework, but I lingered outside, savoring the moment. Then I walked across the street and let myself into the stone cutting yard at the cathedral. I was pulled into the church as if it were a huge magnet and I a tiny nail. As soon as I stepped inside immense silence and space settled over me like a wide cape.

I walked straight to the place that had intrigued me when Herman and I were here last, looking for a tunnel to our cellar. The tomb caught the light in a different way than it had in late February. The sun's rays barely raked over Count Engelbert's armor displayed on top of the mausoleum. The sculptor had carved the bodies with uncanny precision. The features in the count's face were sunken, his ribs and bones sticking out. I wondered what had happened to him before he died. How mysterious, to stand next to a body carved in stone of someone who had died centuries ago, yet who looked as if he had just died yesterday. But if it had happened yesterday, I would have known what he died of, what kind of a man he was, if he had been in pain, or in peace, or both. None of that I could know by just looking at his likeness in stone.

Four men, one at each corner, upheld the heavy top slab with the armor. Had Count Engelbert been a noble kind of warrior? Was there such a thing? My mind flooded with the same confusion I had felt last night in bed. I walked around to the other side where the lady, his wife, lay with almost a smile on her face. I didn't know a good word for her expression, but it was exquisite, whatever it was. It was something you wanted to stand close to, something that was hard to grasp, yet here it was for the taking, miles and miles away from hate. Mammie had talked about hate as a very ugly thing. It wouldn't be like this lady's smile.

It seemed almost too much of a coincidence for Dio Rovers to walk by as I was – again – looking at this part of the monument, and to have him say exactly the same words he'd said the last time.

"Beautiful, isn't it?"

"Yes."

"Serenely beautiful," he added. That was probably the word I'd been looking for.

"It's the alabaster stone that gives that translucent quality," Dio said. "These four men at the corners are cut from the same stone. They represent courage, nobility, perseverance and caution."

"Did Count Engelbert die in a war?" I asked.

"No, he died of consumption. That's why he looks so emaciated."

"Then why did they put his sword on top, if he didn't die fighting?"

"Hmmm." Dio brought his hand to his chin in a thoughtful gesture. "In those days men wanted to be thought of as courageous warriors."

"I don't like soldiers," I said. "They kill and do mean things."

"War is ugly, isn't it? But weapons have to be used sometimes to defend ourselves, or to defend ideals."

"Are the Germans defending their ideals?" I asked. I immediately regretted having asked that question. Mammie said it was better these days not to put people in difficult positions. This might be one of those times.

"We have to defend ours." Dio's twinkling eyes seemed to say "Don't ask me how." He turned and walked toward his studio, leaving me standing there. His footsteps sounded hollow on the granite slabs and I could follow his progress by their echo.

What were the ideals we had to defend? I'd never thought about the war in that way before. It had seemed to me the Germans wanted to have things like our land, our food, our people to work for them. Did they want to have our ideals too? Was that what it was all about: we shouldn't let the Germans take our ideals away from us? I had a hard time wrapping my mind around this new discovery, and sat down in one of the wooden chairs that stood below the chancel. Serenity. Dio had given me the word for what I'd felt, serenity was what I wanted to take away from here and keep in a safe place.

Once outside, I let the steady light from my newfound treasure – serenity – point the way in the darkness of the falling night.

Chapter 9

- ❖ **December 7, 1941: Japan attacks the American Pacific Fleet at Pearl Harbor.**
- ❖ **December 11, 1941: Hitler declares war on America.**

If the Germans didn't allow us to celebrate the Queen's birthday, would they forbid celebrating Saint Nicholas's birthday as well? I worried about this as the sixth of December approached. But Pappie assured me that if the Germans wanted to befriend us, they'd better not take away all of our revered traditions. He predicted they wouldn't dare. Although Dutch fishermen weren't allowed to fish the North Sea, the Germans would guide *Sinterklaas'* steamboat through the maze of U-boats between Spain and Holland. His analysis put my worries to rest, and I was relieved to see my mother take out the season's songbooks.

From my window I watched the wind chase clouds as black as ink blots through the darkening autumn sky. Randomly shaped and huge, they played hide-and-seek with the moon. The days were growing shorter, the nights endless. The weather's mood was perfect for the arrival of *Sinterklaas.* Certainties and mysteries don't mix very well, but for Saint Nicholas the sober Dutch make a rare exception: the last week of November and the first week of December are given over eagerly to believing the unbelievable.

On a Sunday afternoon two weeks before December fifth, our whole family walked to the harbor after church. Though large outdoor gatherings were prohibited, we ignored the patrolling German soldiers whose barracks stood next to the small harbor. When the "Spanish" ship came into view, a ripple of excitement went through the crowd. Fathers hoisted their toddlers onto their shoulders; everyone else craned their necks to get a good look. *Sint* was easy to spot in his floor length red velvet robe and snow-white beard. Long white hair fell over his shoulders from under his miter, which was embroidered with a golden cross. His black helpers, *Zwarte Pieten,* surrounded the holy man and shook their switches at us. A band struck up and together we sang *"Zie ginds komt de stoomboot uit Spanje weer aan."* We belted out the traditional song with the same vigor we used to sing the one that was taken away from us: our national anthem.

A spirited horse waited on the quay to take the bishop through our city, followed on foot by the Black Peters. The Spanish noblemen who accompanied the bishop mounted chestnut steeds and their ladies, in long velvet dresses, climbed into the waiting carriages. It was all a sight to behold.

As soon as *Sint* had mounted his white horse, we hurried back home, ahead of the crowd. From our living room windows we watched the mayor emerge from the heavy oak doors of the City Hall to hand *Sinterklaas* the key to the city. For one whole week he would reign over Breda. For one whole week we could take a vacation from the war, though not from school.

Every evening, my brothers and I stuffed our shoes with carrots for the white horse that carried *Sinterklaas* sure-footedly over the roofs of our homes in the dark of the night. We placed them in front of the coal stove in the living room and sang. *"Sinterklaas kapoentje, doe wat in mijn schoentje."* Surely he would hear our plea. Every morning the carrots were gone, replaced by sweets, which was doubly miraculous since sugar was getting scarce and sweets were available only with distribution coupons.

For me the truth separated from the legend when I came home from school for lunch one day, and happened upon *Sinterklaas* in our own house, in broad daylight, a few days before the sixth. He was in his red robe but without a miter. I would have been willing to believe, as my mother hinted, that the bishop had come to have a conference about our good and bad behavior, had I not noticed his regular haircut and the obviously uneven shoulders under the red robe. There was no mistaking them. They clearly belonged to the body of a very good friend of the family, Mijnheer Lykles, who had been born that way. Even though my mother spirited him in a flash into the pantry, I'd seen enough.

I concluded my brothers must also know this truth. What would happen now that all three of us knew? Would it be over? Would my parents stop playing these games? I went to de apotheek and told my father what I'd seen. He gave me a long look.

"Now you're a part of the Saint Nicholas story as well!" he said.

He explained the legend. A man named Nicholas had really lived in Asia Minor, a far-away country, in the fourth or fifth century. He had been born to great wealth and became a bishop. Every year, on the night preceding his birthday, he left gifts on the doorsteps of poor people's homes. He'd been declared a saint after his death, and people all over kept on giving to the poor in his memory. Because he left the gifts the night before his birthday, gifts are now exchanged in the evening of the fifth of December. The legend had evolved differently in various countries. In Holland, maybe because of our eighty-year war with Spain during the Reformation, he was placed in Spain, surrounded by Spanish nobility. His helpers were black, probably originating from Morocco or Ethiopia. If you were good, you received rewards; if you were bad you got a licking from Black Peter's switch, or worse, you were taken to Spain in the burlap bag Black Peter always carried over his shoulder.

It was exciting to be grown up enough to help carry on the legend, but this required work and especially creativity. *Sinterklaas* never gave a gift without a rhyme. He was known for his moralizing wit. But when Mammie saw my brothers and myself sneak through the house with packages in weird shapes, she set us down and warned us not to pull each other's legs too hard.

"*Sinterklaas* was a very good-hearted man or the church would never have made a saint out of him," she said. "You can joke all you want, but leave the moralizing to me."

That advice came just in time, because I had been scheming how I could tease Hans about how he always looked for excuses not to go to school. My father, at times, was enraged by this habit. One terrible morning, Hans locked himself in the bathroom when it was time to go to school. Pappie told him to come out, but he wouldn't and it became quite a scene. Herman and I were thoroughly convinced Hans faked being sick, but Mammie seemed to take his complaints seriously. She was caught between a hard working, ambitious father and a son who, for all outside appearances, was lazy. I hadn't decided yet how I was going to tease Hans with it, but my thoughts had wandered to stealing a medicine bottle from Hendricks's washroom, putting some wicked-tasting stuff in it, and calling it a cure. After Mammie's sermon I dropped my plan. Instead, I took one of my sweaters that was too small for me, unraveled it – wool was scarce – and rewound part of the curly thread around a piece of paper. On it I wrote, "Follow this thread." The rest of the thread led to the boys' bedroom and on to Hans's bed where I placed a fuzzy toy mouse between the sheets.

Our house quivered with anticipation. Oma Ament came to spend the night. With her coat barely off, she dove into the kitchen to make the traditional bishop's wine, a spiced wine for the adults, and hot chocolate for us. Both kettles were placed on top of the coal stove. We gathered around the dining room table. Mammie went to the piano and played the traditional songs. As we were singing *"Rommel-de-bommel, wat een gestommel,"'* a hard knock on the door stopped us. The door opened, a black hand appeared and before we knew it, we were pelted with *pepernoten,* small button like ginger cookies. While we scrambled to gather them up, a large laundry basket with gifts was shoved inside the doorway. By the time we straightened up from having crawled all over the carpet, *Sinterklaas,* in red robe and red miter, presided at the head of our table. He had the same crooked shoulders I'd observed a week earlier. I'd always wondered how *Sinterklaas* got into our house. Now I knew. He had the key. Mijnheer Lykles was a trusted friend.

Sinterklaas opened up an imposing leather-bound book and called us forward one by one. My father was first.

"I hear, Mijnheer Wetselaar," *Sinterklaas* intoned, "that someone found your key in the lock of your front door. And I see it noted here that your ring with all of your keys, even the one to your safe, was attached to it. You were extremely lucky that it was a friend who found this out or you might never have seen them back!"

"Yes, *Sinterklaas,*" my father said in a meek voice.

We all chuckled. It was Mijnheer Lykles who'd found the keys.

"Well, I would advise you to pay more attention in the future. You don't want to give some German officer the opportunity to check if you've turned in your radio, because I notice you still have your Telefunken in the living room!"

Everyone got a turn. The butterflies in my stomach began to flutter. Even though I knew it was Mijnheer Lykles who sat there, the solemnity with which my parents answered him, and the seriousness of their trespasses, were shifting me back to the view I'd held of *Sinterklaas* all the years before: *Sinterklaas* knew everything. Did he know I had put water in the gas tank of a pantzerwagen? Did he know I had stolen *griotten,* my favorite kind of licorice, from the apotheek more than once?

"Titia!" Oh brother, this was it. I got up and stood next to his chair.

"I hear you give your brothers a hard time. Be kind. Think before you speak." Hans stuck out his tongue at me. "Otherwise, you're a cheerful presence. Keep it up. There's enough gloom around."

Good! He didn't know that much after all.

For an hour we forgot we were in a war. *Sinterklaas* was a far more important authority to heed than Hitler. We were blissfully unaware that in two days the war would take a drastic turn; that unimaginable suffering would be inflicted on people who lived on the other side of the earth.

Sinterklaas got up to leave. Mammie played the traditional farewell song *"Dag Sinterklaasje, daaag!"* and we waved until he disappeared from sight.

True to tradition, we hadn't opened a single gift during *Sint's* visit. Mammie began to hand them out, one by one, from the wicker basket next to her chair. I was given a heavy package with a long rhyme attached. I recognized Hans's handwriting, and if that wasn't enough of a give away, the message was: I shouldn't play with the toys that belonged to Herman and Hans. As it was obvious I didn't like typical girl toys, *Sint* would give me something different. I unwrapped the newspaper – special wrapping paper didn't exist – and found a book titled *Hopla*. This was an expensive gift. Hans had paid for it with his allowance. The book was filled with fun things to make, tricks to perform, magic. Its physical weight matched its weight in guilt. Just thinking about the little mouse that awaited Hans in his bed made me cringe.

Two days later, as we played with our new toys, tried on the socks Oma had knitted, ate the last of the candies we'd found in our shoes, we were jolted by news from the forbidden BBC through the equally forbidden Telefunken. Our parents looked as shocked as when we'd stood around the radio, a year ago on the tenth of May, and heard that German troops had entered our country. This time it was the Japanese who'd made a sneak attack. Pearl Harbor, in Hawaii, from now on would not be remembered for its pearls. Its romantic name had been tainted by Japanese bombs, sunken ships, and drowned sailors.

My father kept shaking his head. America was now at war with Japan. The Netherlands and England were America's allies, so they would automatically declare war on Japan. What would this mean for our East Indies? And what about England? She would have to defend her colonies in the Far East, as well as in North Africa, while at the same time Hitler threatened to invade her homeland. England was stretched to the limit.

Two days later, Hitler declared war on America.

"My God," Pappie said when he heard it. "Hitler has gone mad. How many young Germans is he willing to sacrifice? For what? But there's hope. America is now involved with Europe, as well as with the Pacific. This could be a turning point."

The war expanded my concept of how immense the world was. Every morning, for almost two years now, German soldiers had marched by our house on their way to war exercises outside the city, singing of sailing to England. If it were that hard to cross the North Sea, how hard must it be to cross the Atlantic Ocean? How could America ever hope to land enough troops in Europe to wrest our country from the grip of these single-minded Germans, and at the same time free Asia from the Japanese? When I twirled the globe on my father's desk to locate our own city of Breda, Holland was just a speck. Even the North Sea wasn't any wider than my middle finger. But when I placed my hand on the Atlantic Ocean, it didn't cover all of it. I couldn't understand how my parents expected such a faraway land to come to our rescue, how its people could be motivated to cross an ocean for a country so small, it vanished under the smallest part of my smallest finger.

Musing about the big world and the tiny spot I occupied in it, I let the globe twirl around and around. Whole continents flew by. The globe wound itself down to the part that was mostly all blue, to where the Pacific and Indian Oceans met, to the Dutch East Indies where my mother's brother lived on the island of Java. We had a picture of him in shorts, a rifle in his hand, and a dead tiger at his feet, his face hidden by a wide tropical hat. Continents, countries, I'd never paid attention to or knew about, broadened my horizon, places like Singapore, the Philippines, Libya, the Balkans, and Washington. Our fate now hinged on the vision of Prime Minister Churchill and President Roosevelt.

It had been nineteen months since the Germans had invaded our country. It was like a wild dog had chased us, got a hold of our clothing so we couldn't get away, and now was starting to dig his teeth into our flesh, a little bit deeper every time the news from the war front was bad. The worst was still to come, but we didn't know it. The future was opaque. We turned to the bright light of Christmas.

The house was decorated with fresh boughs of spruce. A Christmas tree, bought on market day, stood in a corner of the living room, dressed up with red balls, silver garlands and angel hair. Wax candles in holders sat pinched on the branches waiting to be lit on Christmas Day when Mammie would read from the Bible. The pungent aroma of greens permeated our home, as did my mother's determination to make this time of the year festive, no matter the circumstances. Looking back, it is not the lack of food or gifts that stand out for me. It is Mammie's zest for life, her anticipation of the mystery of something precious entering our lives. Mammie's certainty of faith allowed the light of Christmas to shine in our home and she accomplished it without a lot of props.

For Herman and myself there was another reason to remember that Christmas. Juffrouw Mercier, the old lady of the Sunday School, herded us into the Lutheran Church. We were made to sit, as a group, in the front pews, under the rather prominent nose of Dominee Toxopeus, the minister, who to my mind could have walked straight out of the Bible with his parchmentlike skin and voice of doom. We sat in our very best clothes on our very best behavior, at least on the outside. On the inside, we waited for the moment Lientje Vrooms would wet her pants. She was an only child with the face of a lamb, in a frilly dress. We had learned to leave a gap between her and the next person, because as surely as Christmas came every year, so would a rivulet appear on the wooden bench that soon would swell to a river. Anticipating this happening is surely the reason I can't remember a thing about what was said during the Christmas Eve service. I only have visual memories: the solemn interior of white-washed walls, a huge brass candelabra with real candles overhead, the austere minister in his black gown with a white front piece that looked like a baby's bib, the dark woolen clothes of the parishioners, the black gloved hands of the deacons who collected our money, the aroma of greens, the wrinkled face of Juffrouw Mercier who looked up in adoration at the minister, the faces of my fellow Sunday school students who, like me, had a hard time concentrating on the spoken word. There is nothing more distracting than the anticipation of someone next to you wetting her pants. Poor Lientje. Just knowing that nobody wanted to sit next to her may have been enough reason to have the dreaded thing happen. I understand that now. Then it was just hilarious.

Christmas 1941 didn't bring peace, but it was memorable for its warmth.

Chapter 10

❖ **May 1942: Dutch officers are rounded up and sent to concentration camps in Germany.**

❖ **May 2, 1942: A yellow Star of David has to be worn by all Jews on their outer clothing.**

Jews who lived in towns around Amsterdam were ordered to move to the city. It was an abrupt order that didn't leave them time to secure their possessions. In a hurry they had to turn off gas, electricity and water, then hand over the keys to their homes to the police. Homeless, with no more belongings than the things they could carry, they were herded into the *Hollandse Schouwburg*, a theater in the middle of Amsterdam. Nobody knew for sure what was next.

The rest of the country was hardly aware of this new twist. Most of it happened out of view and wasn't reported. But my father heard about it through the grapevine that de apotheek had become. Two years into the war, our parents were more willing to discuss in front of my brothers and me the events that Pappie brought to the dining room table. There was more danger in us not knowing the facts. Better to filter what we heard in the street.

But who could reasonably explain what was happening to the Jews who lived in our midst? Almost immediately after the occupation, the targeting had begun. I knew only too well through Carrie Goldstein how this strategy to discredit Jews had eaten away at their rights. They couldn't ride streetcars, go to a theater, or use a library to name just a few of the restrictions imposed on them. The Jews were being stifled, unable to make a living or lead a normal life. To what end?

One day in May, my father came upstairs fuming. He sat down at the head of the table and unfolded his napkin. "From now on Jews have to wear a yellow star with a black J. They have to give up one textile stamp for it and pay four cents."

We sat in silence, stunned.

"In Amsterdam," he went on, "Christians started to wear yellow flowers, and some even yellow stars, but anyone who helps Jews will go to prison."

"Why are they picking on the Jews more than on us?" Herman asked.

"They want us to think of them as their brothers. Blue eyes, blond hair. Same race."

"Hitler has dark hair," Hans countered.

"You're right. And gray eyes," Pappie said, "He knows Jew-hating is as old as the world. He found a common enemy in the Jews and used it for his own purposes. Jews have been persecuted for so long, they've learned to stick together."

"I can see why you'd want to stick together when everybody is against you," Hans said.

"Does Opa hate the Jews, Pappie?" I asked.

"I don't think so," Pappie said. "Opa became a member of the NSB mostly because he thought the Germans would bring medical insurance to the poor."

"But does Opa like what they're doing to the Jewish people?" I wanted to know.

Pappie sighed. "He thinks we're misinformed."

It was time to go to school again. The three of us walked through the Ginnekestraat, but the lunch conversation was still on our minds.

"Maybe the Jews should hide. Then the Germans can't get at them," I said.

"That's what they're doing," Hans said.

"Where could they hide?"

"Probably with people they know."

"Do you think Pappie and Mammie would hide the Goldsteins?" I asked.

"They can't," Hans said.

"Our house isn't safe," Herman said. "Can you think of one place in our house where Hendrick wouldn't come? And we have a hotel next door. The neighbors watch our house from the back. Too many eyes." Herman was always practical.

"Hendrick didn't tell on us! Why would he tell on the Goldsteins?"

"Hendrick is an alcoholic," Hans said. "Pappie has to watch him all the time. He's not allowed in the cellar because he'll drink the stuff that's in those big bottles. It's pure alcohol."

"Are you kidding?" I said, but I remembered Herman telling me that he'd had to really talk Hendrick into coming down to the cellar when I was drowning in "the tunnel."

"Then why does Pappie keep that stuff if it isn't good for Hendrick?" I asked.

Herman and Hans laughed. "Because he needs it for making medicine, dummy! I'm sure if Pappie caught Hendrick drinking it again, he'd fire him on the spot!" Herman said.

"You never know what somebody might do," Hans said. "Pappie can't be sure that the people who work for him aren't Nazi sympathizers."

"Fem, or Lies, or Renne? I can't believe that."

"Believing isn't enough," Hans said.

We arrived in the schoolyard. Clusters of pupils had formed while waiting for the school doors to open. Martha was at the nucleus of one. As I walked by, I felt hostile stares fastened on my back. Martha always seemed to attract rowdy boys. She wasn't part of the circle of girls I felt comfortable with like Madeleen and Bertha. I could feel her directing unnerving attention toward me.

The school bell rang and we thronged into the long corridors, hung our coats and took our seats on the wooden benches. Martha was seated in the back of the classroom, outside my line of vision, and I forgot about her until I remembered I had a piano lesson after school. I wasn't crazy about piano lessons, but what made me dread them now was to have to walk by Martha's house to get there. Martha lived on the canal, just a few houses before the one where Mevrouw van Nieuwenhoven, my piano teacher, lived. There was no way around it. I had to walk the whole row of houses before I could ring the big brass bell and wait for Mevrouw van Nieuwenhoven to pull the rope at the head of her staircase to open the front door.

I gathered up my homework and stuffed it with the piano book in my leather school bag. Bertha and Madeleen waited for me and together we walked along the canal. At the bridge they said good-bye and took a right. I went left and crossed the bridge to get to the other side. Martha and her gang were right behind me. I quickened my step. So did they. How could I shake them loose?

I felt a rush of air, and they all ran past me. In front of Martha's house they lined up and waited for me to come by. My school bag felt like it had stones in it instead of paper, pulling me down, slowing my tread. I could feel the prickling sensation that comes with breaking out in a sweat. I kept going.

Martha stood in the middle of her gang, an evil queen surrounded by her bodyguards. I looked into her round freckly face, framed by straight red hair. Her eyes taunted. What was she thinking? What had I done to her?

I had to get by there and not show how their hostility unnerved me. I looked away from their stares, squared my shoulders and walked on. Each step seemed to measure a mile, but I got to the door without incident.

The piano lesson went badly. My hands were shaking and my fingers didn't want to land on the right keys. I felt dwarfed by Mevrouw van Nieuwenhoven's large body sitting beside me on the bench in front of the baby grand. Her directions were commands like the ones I heard German sergeants bark at their soldiers as they marched by our house, but this perception was probably influenced by the knowledge that she was German by birth. For an hour I ran the same scale over and over, until it began to sound like a motor that didn't want to start. Mammie and Hans were very good piano players who never had to fasten their eyes on the keys. They took lessons from Mijnheer van Nieuwenhoven, my teacher's very gentle husband. Herman and I, less gifted, were stuck with his sergeant.

On the way home I tried to think of reasons why Martha had turned against me, why she was targeting me. Did she think my family was NSB? Did people in Breda know about Opa Wetselaar? Or if it was perhaps jealousy that made her so hostile, then what was she jealous of? She could at least give me a reason for setting others up against me. I had to stop this. Mammie said you have to stand up for what's right.

I enlisted Herman to help me out of my predicament. He said he'd round up his friends and walk back with me after school the following day. I could always count on Herman's loyalty. First, though, I should find out what this was all about.

The next day during recess, I walked up to Martha before she could gather her bodyguards and asked why she was acting so strange. What was up? She looked to see where her friends were, but I pressed on. But she only stuck her tongue out at me and walked away.

"What's going on?" Madeleen asked.

"I wish I knew," I said.

"She's bossy, but so are you sometimes," Madeleen said.

After school, Martha was ready for me and I was ready for her. Madeleen and Bertha said they'd walk with me till the bridge, and Froukje, who lived close to de markt, said she'd go all the way. Herman had told me he would keep an eye on how things developed. So my friends and I set out along the canal. Martha and her gang had walked ahead of us. We'd lost sight of them until, all of a sudden, they jumped into our path from a driveway. They'd been waiting. Their slingshots were aimed at us. We stood frozen on the sidewalk. I slowly walked up to one of the boys and looked him in the eye.

"I dare you!"

He stared at me briefly, his slingshot still aimed at me, the elastic taut in his right hand. There was no stone in it. This was all a bluff. Martha and the boys ran away when they saw Herman approaching with his friends, all of them two years older than they were. The boy in front of me dropped his slingshot and ran too.

Madeleen and Bertha took a right to go home, shaken. Froukje Dorsman, Herman, his friends and I ran in pursuit of *de rotzakken*, over the bridge, down the wide Wilhelminastraat where it was hard to hide. We saw them diving into *de Passage*, a covered shopping center, then lost sight of them. Martha knew this part of the city better. We decided to catch our breath and walk to the inner city, our own stomping ground.

It became a game of peek-a-boo, spying and running, either in pursuit or fleeing. We almost forgot what had gotten us into this in the first place. We'd see Martha standing at the corner of an alley, motioning to her friends. Then they'd run. Now we were in de Ginnekestraat, weaving in and out of the constant stream of pedestrians. Martha's gang turned up ahead of us.

As we were running after them, we saw Martha come to an abrupt halt, talk briefly to her gang and take a sharp right into the tiny medieval chapel we passed every day. The heavy oak door was always open. We stopped and looked into the very dark and mysterious space. The light from the burning candles in front of the Virgin Mary's statue threw ghostly shadows on the chalk-white walls. On the wooden benches sat our "enemies" among women praying on their knees, their hands holding rosaries. Martha looked around at us and stuck out her tongue. Her favorite gesture.

None of us was Catholic. We couldn't go in, or at least we were convinced we couldn't. It seemed like a brilliant stroke on Martha's part. We couldn't get at them and she knew it. The game was over, but who had won? We felt awkward standing there, on the threshold, smelling unfamiliar incense, hearing the soft, repetitious mumbling of the praying women. Every once in a while another person came in, or one went out. This was a busier place than I'd realized.

"We have them corralled!" Herman said triumphantly. "We can't go in, but they can't get out!"

"What shall we do?" Froukje asked.

"We'll stay here till they feel it," Herman said.

It was an excellent strategy. After fifteen minutes or so, Martha's bodyguards began to squirm. They turned around from time to time to see if we were still standing in the open doorway, then whispered to each other.

"O.K. we can go home now. We've made our point," Herman said.

He resolutely walked off, leading the way to de markt, never looking back, confident he wouldn't be followed.

Looking back on this little episode, I realize we were acting out the times we lived in. The world was clearly divided into opposing camps. One half persecuted the other. Rumors about people hiding, fleeing, of innovative ways to trick the Germans fluttered around us. And truth be told, Martha and I were both bossy, ready to lead others. On the one hand, we were just kids playing games that forecast the roles we would take on later in life; on the other hand, the German occupation had set us up to mimic the tensions we so keenly felt in those days. Martha never gave me a reason for her sudden animosity, but for the rest of grade school we were friends. We lost sight of each other when we went to different high schools.

I walked Froukje to her home. Her father had a bookstore in de Veemarktstraat, just a few houses from my uncle's dentist office. I'd never been inside. The space was small with hardly enough room to turn around without knocking over a stack of books. Both Froukje's parents worked there. Walking through a store to go upstairs to the living quarters felt familiar, but what took me by surprise was their living room. Unlike ours with comfortable fauteuils and tasteful objects d'art, this room looked like a church. And it was! On one side was an altar covered by an embroidered white cloth that reminded me of the little chapel we'd just come from. A big Bible lay open next to a wooden carved cross, large candle sticks and other things that looked church like, but whose use I didn't know. The smell of incense made me feel ill at ease.

"Is this your home?" I asked.

"My father is a priest," Froukje said matter-of-factly while she pulled open the sliding doors to the dining room.

"A priest?"

"It's with a small group."

Before she closed the sliding doors with their colored, opaque glass, I looked back once more and noticed a peg on the wall opposite the altar. A white robe and other paraphernalia hung from it.

"Do people go to church here?" I asked.

"Yes, every Sunday and some evenings."

Only one girl in my class, Bertha, lived like I did, above a pharmacy. I'd never thought much about what other fathers might do for a living. Madeleen's father was a judge, Anneke's father was a Dutch army officer.

A little while later, Froukje's mother came upstairs. She seemed relieved to find us in the dining room looking out the window at the traffic, but there was a look of worry that seemed to be permanent. Froukje's father had quite a different aura about him, an other-worldly quality, as if he saw – or wanted to see – only beautiful things.

When I came home, I told my mother about the church in Froukje's living room. She was more concerned than surprised.

"It's probably better not to talk about what you saw."

"Why?"

"It's really nobody's business but their own. People should be free to profess their faith the way they see fit, but not everybody agrees on that."

"I don't understand."

"Have you learned about the Eighty Year War in school yet?"

"The one against the Spanish?"

"Yes. Well, that war was about religion. There were people who didn't like the way the church was run, so they broke away from it. That's why we now have Catholics and Protestants. The Protestants were the people who protested."

"Is Froukje's father protesting?"

"He probably is. I don't know what his group is called, or which church it turned away from. My own father didn't agree with the Dutch Reformed Church on the island where I was born, even though he played the organ there."

"Was the church mad at him? Did they punish him?"

"No, nothing like that. The Protestant Church is used to disagreement. There are many different Protestant churches. Like the Lutheran Church we went to on Christmas Eve. The big church next door is Dutch Reformed. Then there is Doopsgezind and Remonstrant. I'm sure there are even more."

"You forgot Catholic," I said.

"No, I didn't forget. They are one big church with a Pope in Rome. That's why they're called Roman Catholics. All the Roman Catholics in the world answer to the Pope. He is their spiritual leader."

"Like Hitler is the leader of the Nazis?"

"Yes and no. Hitler doesn't want to have anything to do with a church. He's a political leader."

"Would the Germans do something to Froukje's father if they knew he was a priest?"

"No. Hitler hasn't dared close the churches. That's not what the war is about. But if her father was once a Roman Catholic, that might be a problem for other Catholics. Since we don't know, it's better not to talk about it. I tell you, Titia, if you only know half-truths or if you only suspect but do not know for sure, it's wiser to keep quiet. You wouldn't want to cause difficult situations for others. Remember that. It's the basis for gossip and gossip can ruin a person's life."

Life, I realized, was full of secrets and riddles.

After dinner my father fell asleep in his armchair next to the stove with the newspaper on his lap. Mammie cleared the table. Net took the dishes to the kitchen and we helped her carry them through the long, unheated corridors. When we were all done with our chores and my father had woken up from his nap and gone to one of his many meetings, Mammie gathered my brothers and me on the couch. She read from Helma Lagerlof's wonderful book about a boy named Niels, who escaped the bleakness of his own backyard by flying on the wings of a goose. It was our favorite book, translated from Swedish.

Mammie's voice could carry you anywhere, like the goose that carried Niels. I let myself fly away on her words, away from Breda, over the fields around our house at Overa, away from Mevrouw van Nieuwenhoven, from Martha, from the war. Where would I land? Where would I want to land? Was there a place without mean piano teachers, without troublemakers, without hate? If there were such a place, I would put Carrie Goldstein on the wings of the goose that sent Niels on his travels around the world. That would be the perfect place for her to hide.

My thoughts wandered off to my "Martha problem" and what I should do about it. Or should I do nothing? Herman had walked away from the chapel without fear. That had been impressive. What was there to fear anyway? If she didn't have the guts to tell me why she had set others up against me, then maybe she was the one with fear. Carrie Goldstein couldn't walk away from the people who threatened her. I'd seen the fear in her eyes when the soldiers killed the fish in the river with a hand grenade. She couldn't walk up to a German soldier with a big yellow star on her coat and say, "Why do I have to wear this stupid thing?"

Niels's adventures were alluring in the pleasant rhythm of Mammie's voice. To fly away, to soar over the earth, to be free! If only human minds could soar like that instead of throwing up barriers.

Chapter 11

- **March 6, 1942: The Dutch East Indies are conquered by Japanese troops.**
- **Late May 1942: The BBC announces the first bombing mission over Germany.**

As I biked along de Wilhelminastraat to het Engelbert van Nassau Plein on my way to visit Oma Ament, I marveled that the Germans hadn't changed the street names honoring members of the House of Orange. Maybe they hadn't got to it yet; too busy scanning our textbooks for ideas that veered from their ideology, especially history books unkind to Germany. At school we were told to remove a page from our French textbook per order of the Nazis. It contained the words *La Reine Wilhelmina.* We were given a corrected page to paste in its place. A popular children's book was taken off the market because a character named Adolf had been given an unflattering role. Adolf fell in the canal...pushed by Willem.

I'd been sent on a mission to cheer up Oma Ament. Oom Tjalling, her oldest son, worked on a plantation on the island of Java. A few days earlier, the Japanese had invaded Java and most of the Dutch East Indies. I'd never met this uncle. I only knew him from the photograph on my mother's desk, the one of him kneeling beside the tiger. It stood next to a picture of his father who looked at me with his lucid, stern eyes. Forever. Strange thing with photographs, I thought, they allow you to meet people you could never shake hands with because they are dead or inaccessible like my uncle or the royal family. Yet they remain two-dimensional, frozen for all time into a split-second pose. It left me wondering if my uncle was really that fearless, my grandfather that handsome in his dark suit, and Queen Wilhelmina that regal with a tiara crowning her hair.

Oma Ament rented rooms in a house halfway between de markt and our house at Overa. She seemed as content there as could be expected after moving from the northern Dutch province of Friesland, where large bodies of water and flat

Oma Ament.

pastures make up the landscape, interrupted only by rows of tall poplars, their crowns leaning away from the prevailing wind. Friesians pride themselves on their authentic language, which set them apart from the other ten provinces where a variety of Dutch dialects are spoken. The way Friesland was described to me made the contrast with my own province of Brabant sound like the difference between Vermont and Louisiana, not because of the climate but because of the character of its people. Friesians are reserved, Brabanders ebullient. One of my goals for after the war was to go to Friesland and see for myself.

Oma had seen me coming and welcomed me at the top of the stairs. I felt intimidated by the task at hand. How could I console a woman seven times my own age? Oma didn't look any different than she had a week ago. Her eyes weren't red from crying, as I had feared. Blue and steady like my mother's, they related the everyday wisdom she'd gained over her years. Oma wasn't fancy. Her clothes were plain, her hair pulled back in a bun, her body heavy-boned and solid, the body I'd felt on top of me when the Germans shot at us from their Messerschmitt.

She offered to make some tea.

"Real tea?" I asked.

"No. I save real tea for special occasions."

"Do you have some lemonade, Oma? I hate that surrogate stuff."

Oma laughed. "Your own father invented it."

"I know. Mijnheer van Dijk comes in de apotheek all the time to talk to Pappie about it. Mammie says Mijnheer van Dijk is getting rich from Pappie's tea. I don't think she likes him."

Oma didn't respond. She put a glass of lemonade and a cookie before me on the Oriental rug that covered the table. It was not a cheerful room. The curtains and upholstery were cut from deep burgundy and dark green plush; the furniture was of solid mahogany. The walls with their somber wallpaper closed in on me as if I were sitting inside a box, but I tried hard not to let the room's heavy feeling influence my mood. My task was to bring cheer.

"Oma, do you have a picture of Oom Tjalling?"

She went to a closet, took out a leather bound album and spread it open on the table. Tall palm trees, lush undergrowth and mountains looming in the distance formed the background to Oom Tjalling's life in the Dutch East Indies. Picture after picture showed a bespectacled man, surrounded by short, dark skinned people among tall stalks of plants unlike any I'd seen at Overa.

"What does he do there?"

"He manages a sugar plantation."

"What will happen now?"

"That's hard to know. The ships that used to carry the mail don't run anymore. I haven't heard from Tjalling and his wife since the war broke out. All I know is the news that comes over the radio and that's censured by the Germans and the Japanese." Oma folded her hands in her lap in a gesture of resignation. "Tjalling must worry about us as much as we worry about him, but that must be the same for many other families. So many people have relatives who work on Java."

I looked at the handsome man in white shorts and knee socks and tried to see him not as a total stranger, but as a brother to my mother and a son to Oma. What if Herman would go to Java and we wouldn't hear from him anymore? Mammie knew from one moment to the next where we were and what we were up to. For Oma it must have been the same when Oom Tjalling was growing up. By the hour she knew where he was and now she had been cut off from him.

"What was it like in the first World War, Oma?"

"Nothing like the one we're in now. We read about the war in the papers, because Holland managed to stay out of it. We didn't have a radio yet, you see. There were no airplanes on bombing missions flying overhead. It wasn't a war about ideas like this one. It was about power and conquering territory. We had to buy a new atlas when it was all over. New frontiers were drawn between countries. Several empires disappeared. Kaiser Wilhelm, who'd started the war, lost his crown and fled to Holland."

"To Holland? Does he still live here?"

"As far as I know he does. Queen Wilhelmina had little choice. He was a distant cousin to her. She allowed him to buy an estate near Utrecht."

"Did you see war movies back then?"

"Sometimes we saw movies, but they were hysterical!" Oma laughed. "You would see soldiers on the screen who looked like your brothers' toy soldiers and moved like they were wound up. Kaiser Wilhelm inspected his troops in one of those silent movies, and he kept touching his cap in salute, his arm going up and down like the puppet that pops out of the street organ."

"Were you still living on the island then?"

"No, we'd moved. Your mother had to go to high school, so we moved back to the mainland."

I loved the way Oma could make history come alive, creating pictures in my mind that illustrated the dates in our textbook. Through her stories I learned about the island where my mother was born. The fact that Mammie was born on a small island was important to me. None of my friends' mothers had lived on an island. Oma described Vlieland as a huge sandbank in the middle of the North Sea. She had arrived there as a bride. Opa Ament had been called to do government service as the doctor for a series of islands that swept out from the mainland like a dog's tail. Vlieland sat halfway up the tail. It was as remarkable for the things it lacked as for what it offered. No trees, no telephone, no electricity, no running water, no radio. The five hundred or so inhabitants made do with one bakery and one dry goods store. Meat was a rarity. People ate the fish they caught. Goats walked in the street and during the summer months most people went barefoot. There was one street and the only trees on the island lined it. Opa ferried between the islands to see patients. Oma put up food, canned beans or covered carrots and potatoes in the root cellar.

"Didn't you get bored?" I asked.

"We were too busy to be bored," Oma said.

Opa, in his free time, played piano or chess by mail with the national champion, Dr. Euwe. It apparently didn't matter that they made, at the most, one move a week. If the weather was bad, it could take up to a month before the next move arrived by mail from his invisible partner.

Before the war, I'd visited Vlieland with my family. It had taken two days to get there; the first by train, the second by boat. In the middle of the sea we changed ferries, and stepped from one boat to another over a narrow plank with the water fifteen feet below. We played on spectacularly wide beaches and built a magnificent sand castle. My romantic notions about Vlieland resemble the features of that castle, its finer details eroded by the tides that washed over it. Years later, when I followed in Oma's footsteps and found myself as a doctor's wife in a small faraway village, I derived strength from her tales. The washed-over castle became a firm foundation for my own life.

Oma spun a thread that linked me to her own history and to my mother's.

When I came back to de markt, I leaned my bike against the house. My brothers and I didn't have a house key. Our routine was to walk in through de apotheek and my father's private office to the front door, then we would carry our bikes into the front hall and lean them against the wall under my great-grandparents' portraits. Today as I walked by Truus, the bookkeeper, I noticed she was agitated. Color rose easily to her cheeks, but at the moment she was flushed from the top button of her dress to her hairline. She looked like she was going to say something when I put my hand on the doorknob to my father's office, so I hesitated. When she put her nose back into her accounting books, I opened the door and understood immediately why she'd appeared agitated. There, in my own father's office, stood a German officer. I was shocked. Had Pappie done something wrong? Would he be taken away? I was gripped by fear and completely flustered.

In German my father said to the officer, "This is my daughter." The man offered his hand and I had no choice but to shake it. It was like the time I was introduced to Mijnheer van Dijk, except then I took an immediate dislike. This man appeared more likable with his beautiful blue eyes and wavy blond hair. He held his officer's cap under one arm. Nothing about him was even remotely threatening, and Pappie didn't seem to be in a panic. What was going on? Should I walk away? Put my bike inside and flee upstairs to tell Mammie? I didn't do any of those things. I just stood there.

In Dutch my father told me that Herr Von der Hoevel was a pharmacist. Then he told me to get my bike inside and I was dismissed. I realized I was witnessing something very unusual and shouldn't go out and tell the world about it. No wonder Truus had been upset. She must have wondered why her boss had taken a German officer behind closed doors. I wondered about it too. I'd learned enough in the past two years to know that people were ready to declare someone a Nazi sympathizer with only vague evidence, a label that could be hard to undo. Why was Pappie taking the risk? I asked him at the dinner table that night.

"Herr Von der Hoevel is an Austrian," he answered.

"Does that make a difference?"

"A big difference," Pappie said. He explained that Hitler had annexed Austria. The Austrians had been forced to enlist in the army.

"Herr Von der Hoevel had to give up his pharmacy. He's homesick for his wife and their baby."

I was astounded. Men in gray uniforms were German Nazis. I had lumped them all together as our enemy. To think that some of these men who raised their arm in a *"Heil Hitler"* salute could be homesick seemed preposterous. Forced to serve a regime they didn't agree with? Could this be true?

"Do you like him or do you feel sorry for him?" Hans asked.

The idea you could feel sorry for a German officer was a new concept as well.

"Both," Pappie said. "He works as a pharmacist in the *Wehrmacht.* He came in for some drug information and we got talking. That was a few months ago. He kept coming. After a while I realized this young man was terribly lonely."

"Isn't that dangerous?" Herman asked.

"Yes, I suppose it could be. There are always people who're out to dupe you. Don't worry, I'm careful."

"How about Truus?" I asked. "She looked very nervous."

"Truus is also Austrian," Pappie said. "She understands Herr Von der Hoevel's position very well."

"Then why was she so nervous?"

"Because she's protective. She was afraid others might draw the wrong conclusions."

Truus had worked for Opa Wetselaar and now for my father. She was a fixture in de apotheek. Even though she spoke with a slight accent I'd never connected her with a foreign country.

"How did she get here?" I asked.

"On a train from Vienna during the first world war," Mammie said. "Her family had put her on the train because they had no food. I remember we read about trains from Austria every day. People here in Holland adopted those children."

So that was Truus's story. Many people seemed to have hidden stories. My uncle who'd shot the tiger in the Indies had also, by mistake, shot an arrow in the eye of their maid on the island when he was a young boy. The woman lost her eye, Oma had told me. Then there was Juffrouw Berlioz, the peculiar lady who jaywalked over de markt every day on her way to the library where she worked. She was thought to be the granddaughter of the famous French composer in a funny way that wasn't clear to me, but apparently was understood by the adults. Same as with the woman who walked our streets in a floor length coat and white fur hat, like the Queen, and who told everyone who wanted to listen that she was the Queen's sister. The adults chuckled and said it was possible, but I couldn't see how, since Wilhelmina was an only child.

"Should we greet Herr Von der Hoevel as your friend when we see him?" Hans asked. There was a hint of sarcasm in his tone.

"I don't think you'll run into him very often," Pappie said. "Be yourself, Hans. I know the world looks to you as if it's bad people against good people, but it's not that clear-cut. You're seeing Herr Von der Hoevel as one of Hitler's soldiers. Period. But he's also a decent man."

We sat silently around our dining room table. This was a sermon and we understood what we'd been given to think about. It would be hard to see the German soldiers as human beings instead of *"die rotmoffen."* My father had thrown a beam of light into a dark corner. It was easier to equate a gray uniform with evil, to see every soldier as an extension of Adolph Hitler. The occupation had taught us to be wary of all people. How do you look for the good in someone you're suspicious of? Try anyway, our parents seemed to say.

What I grappled most with was that this Austrian officer had no choice but to serve in Hitler's army, while my grandfather clearly did have a choice and became a Nazi sympathizer all the same. My father supported both of them.

Chapter 12

- **July 3, 1942: German troops are halted outside Stalingrad.**
- **Autumn, 1942: American and British forces attempt to push German and Italian troops out of French North Africa, including Tunis.**

Time crept along as slow as a turtle between Christmas and June. Overa and the joys of summer seemed years away and there wasn't much to do but go to school. Distractions were mostly offered by our occupiers. Each new edict caused a stir, as when all Dutch military officers who'd initially been free to return home after our country capitulated, were rounded up one day and taken to concentration camps in Germany. The Nazis, after two years of occupation, realized they had failed to capture our imaginations, let alone our loyalty. Better to prevent a revolt by removing potential leaders. Several of my parents' friends were officers, so Mammie had a new task. She consoled the wives left behind.

Life for the Jewish population became unbearable. Carrie Goldstein could not visit me and I couldn't go to her house. Jews were not allowed to mix with Christians. Where did the Germans find the license to treat perfectly good people as if they were trash? When I asked my mother about it, she answered that something that is unreasonable can never be explained, because it is so totally wrong to begin with. And in this case it was evil as well. The Germans had drawn a distinction between Carrie and myself. A distinction I'd never felt before and couldn't see any reason for now.

Carrie, as a Jew, was under constant threat. Her movements were restricted. She couldn't go to school. Marked by blue eyes and blond hair I was not likely to be stopped and questioned by German soldiers, unless I did something stupid like publicly insulting them. I was free to move around, but life was rather dull. Before the war my brothers had been scouts and I a brownie, but Hitler had outlawed the organizations because they had been the idea of an Englishman.

Movies weren't an option. If it lacked the NSB stamp of approval it was banned. For four years American and English movies weren't screened. German propaganda seeped out of every mode of entertainment. The radio programs were entirely run by Nazi sympathizers with German officials controlling them. To fill the void, we put on our own little shows. We invited our best friends to be part of our theater troupe. The dining room table was shoved against the wall and the heavy curtain that hung on a rod between our living room and dining room, created a stage of sorts. Our first play was about King Bluebeard. Hans, with a paper crown and a blanket for a long mantle, played the king. Our friends' parents were invited to sit in our living room on Sunday afternoons during the long winter months.

We also embarked on an enterprise we thought might make us some money, even though money wasn't what we were looking for. There wasn't much we could buy with our weekly allowance. Not sweets, for instance, because Mammie held onto the coupons we needed for anything made with sugar. We started the enterprise because it was something to do, and money made it look more serious.

Since Pappie had succeeded in creating a surrogate tea from a combination of herbs and heaven knows what else, we thought we might try our hand at some substitute for Virginia tobacco. Good tobacco was rare, available only on the black market. With Herman's friend Ronnie van der Elst, whose father was one of the officers taken to Germany, we set up shop in my brothers' bedroom. We clipped a hedge in Ronnie's garden and put the cuttings between newspapers. Every day we checked if the leaves were sufficiently dry so we could shred them into something that looked like pipe tobacco. After ten days we decided we'd waited long enough. From de apotheek we stole *puntzakken* used for packaging licorice candies. Hans could draw well and he designed an impressive label. It stated "Dutch tobacco" as the content. We didn't name it after the hedge, because we didn't know its name. The price, we agreed, would be twenty-five cents per bag.

Now we needed customers! For a start, Herman and I volunteered to peddle our wares to the husband of our cleaning lady. After school we walked over to his house. Invited into their small kitchen, we gave our sales pitch. Jan generously pulled a quarter out of his pocket. We insisted he put the tobacco in his pipe and smoke it. I noticed he'd been quicker to reach for his money than his pipe. Seeing that we were anxious for him to try it, he laboriously filled his pipe, lit it, and puffed on it. A horrible smell filled our nostrils and the tiny kitchen. Marie opened all the windows. Herman and I apologized profusely and offered to give him back his quarter, but Jan said "Keep it."

In the evenings after dinner, when my brothers had to do homework, and Pappie was napping in the big chair next to the coal stove, and Mammie was puttering in the dining room, I often sneaked out to de apotheek. When one assistant had night duty, I loved to hang out there. Fem Oorthuizen was my favorite. Unmarried, and probably in her forties, with a sweet, untouched quality about her, she appealed to my need for safety during those dark evenings when we heard the constant drone of English bombers on their way to Germany. With the window shades down because of the blackout and Fem behind the long black counter preparing prescriptions, de apotheek felt snug in spite of its large size. The aroma of herbs, stored in oak drawers labeled with black letters on white enamel plaques, mixed with the antiseptic smell of denatured alcohol, added to the mystery of my father's apotheek. Quiet, snug, and mysterious, that's how I remember those evenings.

The long counter was shielded from public view by opaque glass. Each of the eight working stations was outfitted with a scale beside a mahogany block with brass weights. I loved to watch the prescriptions being filled. It took absolute precision and specific skill. Take pill making. The assistants would carefully weigh the ingredients on the brass scale, then mix them in a mortar and form them into a ball. The ball was divided into parts and the parts were rolled into strings. The strings were then laid on a board with a corrugated copper plate. The assistant placed a paddle with a handle on each end over the board and pressed hard. The result, when the paddle was lifted, was comparable to feed pellets. The pellets were transferred to another wooden board, and rolled with a paddle until they were perfectly round. Powder was sprinkled over them so they wouldn't stick together, then the plug was pulled from a round hole in the board and all the little balls fell into a round box.

What I liked most was watching Fem prepare *poeders.* After the war, *poeders* became tablets. But during the war Fem would lay thin paper wrappers on the counter in a pattern similar to laying out cards for a game of solitaire. She overlapped the wrappers, leaving enough space uncovered so she could plop the powdery substance onto each paper with a long-handled spoon. The skill was in putting the exact same amount of powder on each paper. Fem then folded the paper into neat packets. Sometimes she allowed me to help her: make a fold in the middle lengthwise, fold over the extra part on the top twice, then fold both sides to the middle, so the powder was securely sealed inside.

There wasn't much else I could do to pass the time. Sports weren't part of the school curriculum. There were clubs that organized matches in soccer and field hockey on the weekends. Only boys played soccer, and I was too young to play field hockey. Of course there was tennis. My father was the city's champion.

Before the war, he'd made it to the semi-finals of our whole country in doubles with his twin brother Max. He had a smashing backhand and was quick on his feet. Whenever his opponents lobbed the ball over his head, he'd turn on a dime from his net position to run and hit it back. It was nerve-wracking to watch him do it.

My brothers and I hated tennis. None of us seemed to have inherited his uncanny eye for the ball. We tried to please my father, but he was an impatient teacher. Mammie thought she could solve the problem by setting up lessons with a trainer, but our hearts weren't in it. Part of going to the tennis club meant being constantly asked if we had become as good at it as our dad. Of course we hadn't, far from it. But the worst of tennis in our lives was when competitions were being played on Sunday afternoons. We went with Mammie and sat on the bleachers watching our father play. He usually won, but once, when he lost, he disgraced us by throwing his racket on the ground. After that I never went to watch him play in competition again. I absolutely refused.

Even if I would have liked to play tennis, I couldn't do it in the winter. After school, I had friends over or I walked home with Bertha Bicknese. Her father was also a pharmacist. Her family lived over the pharmacy, just like mine. One day, we were playing in their garden. One of her older siblings was raking the gravel path while Bertha and I played a game of leapfrog. We went around the circular border till Bertha lost her balance and I dove onto the gravel. A sharp pain drove into the palm of my left hand. I landed on the rake her brother had left on the path with the points facing up. Bertha took me into their pharmacy. Her father cleaned off the blood and put a bandage over the puncture wound.

It was just a small accident. Nothing new. I was perpetually decorated with bandages on my knees and elbows, always dare-deviling on my bike to see how close I could ride to the edge of the canal without falling into it. Just before I'd get too close I'd jump off onto the cobblestones. The fun was well worth the scrapes. Getting a small puncture wound by falling on a rake wasn't half as spectacular. But the next day my hand felt sore and began to swell. I complained about it when Mammie tucked me in that night. She took one look at my red hand and sent me to de apotheek in my nightgown. My father asked if Mr. Bicknese had put iodine on it. He hadn't, I said, and Pappie exploded. The next morning he took me to his friend, Dokter van Hilten, who stated the obvious. My hand was infected. With a surgical knife he slit the side of my palm so the pus could find a way out.

Herman offered to swap beds when he saw me shivering and shaking all over. My room lacked a coal stove like the one that kept the boys' room warm. Once I was settled in bed, I thought Hendrick had fired the stove up to its max. My hand throbbed, and now my head was throbbing as well. The light from the windows pierced my eyes like well-aimed arrows. Mammie drew the curtains and sat next to the bed, cooling my forehead with wet towels. Apparently, she had nothing else to do that day, for she sat beside me the entire time. Not talking. Just being.

My father came upstairs to check the wound. A red line was creeping under my skin from my wrist up the inside of my arm like a burrowing worm. My temperature was taken. An alarm bell sounded. I heard it clearly though I seemed to float under water. The sounds of the world were muffled and I only caught snatches of what my parents were talking about. What came next was a blur. I found myself in the operating room of *het Diaconessenhuis.* Somehow they'd gotten me there. Who'd dressed me? Did they take me on the back of a bicycle? We didn't own a car. But here I was, on a stretcher with Doctor van Hilten at my side. A nurse approached with a mask. A whiff of ether took me away into nothingness. When I woke up in a different room with a big bandage around my left hand, I wondered where I'd been.

The foot of my bed had a frame of steel tubes. All around me was white, like snow: the bedding, the walls, the curtains. A picture of Jesus hung on the opposite wall. His right arm was raised as if to say "hello." It was definitely more cheerful than seeing him hanging from a wooden cross with blood dripping from his palms.

Mammie came in and took my good hand in hers. Doctor van Hilten had made an incision an inch long on the top of my left hand to let more pus out, she said. She had to go home now to feed the rest of the family. She would be back soon.

"Will you put on your red silk dress, Mammie?" I asked. This took her back a bit, but she promised she would. I closed my eyes again and for the next hour – maybe it was the whole night – I had delirious dreams about my mother in her party dress. I saw my parents coming into my room to say good night before they went off to a formal dinner. Pappie looking dapper in his tuxedo and Mammie queenly with her hair done up in a roll and jewelry shining from her neck, her wrist, and her ring finger. She twirled, which made the skirt of her dress swoop out. The deep red burgundy silk spurted around her like blood and together with her radiant smile she changed into a spectacular sunset. I reached for it, but it sank into the horizon. No matter how hard I ran I couldn't reach it before it had completely vanished.

I woke up in a panic, feeling hot and exhausted from running. A deaconess stood over me with a thermometer.

"*Dag,* Titia," she said with a lovely smile. "I am Zuster Arja." Her hair was kept back from her face with a heavily starched cap, white like her apron and like everything else in the room.

"Where's Mammie?" I asked.

Before she could answer, I'd sunk back into another world where I saw the palms of Jesus's hands dripping with blood. Drip, drip, until there was no blood left. I opened my eyes and looked at the picture of Jesus waving at me.

"He didn't die," I said to Zuster Arja, who read the thermometer and took my pulse. While she counted my heartbeats her gaze followed mine to the picture on the wall.

"That's right. He's with us still and he's looking over you."

If Jesus hadn't died from his bleeding palms, maybe I wouldn't either. I had entered the portal of death. Strangely, it didn't scare me. The woman cut from alabaster who lay in the big church didn't look scared. "Beautiful," Dio Rovers had called her. I was back in the cathedral. Deep vibrations from the organ pipes swept me up as they'd done when Herman and I were exploring for the entrance to the tunnel. I swam in the majesty of the columned vastness. A feeling of love lifted me into its endless space.

When I opened my eyes again, my entire family stood at the other side of the steel tubes at the foot of my hospital bed. My mother in her beautiful dress, my father in a suit, my two brothers in knit pullovers. Everyone looked helpless, devastated. I sensed they had come to say good-bye. How could I tell them not to worry? I was safe. It was all right.

Doctor van Hilten, dressed in a white coat, walked over to me and rolled up the sleeve of a loosely fitting garment they must have put on me in the operating room. The worm in my arm had morphed into a snake. A poisonous snake was eating my blood! Horror filled my father's eyes. Zuster Arja, my father, the doctor, all three knew what the thick red cord in my arm meant. I closed my eyes and floated off.

That I didn't float off to a place from which no human returns, I owe to my father. When Dokter van Hilten told him there was nothing more to do than pray, Pappie wouldn't accept the verdict. He told his friend that the Germans had recently come up with a sulfa drug that was extremely effective in treating bacterial infections.

Doctors don't want to be told by pharmacists how to treat their patients. Each preferred the other to stay in his own territory, with the doctors claiming the high ground. They were, after all, closer to the patient. It was a relationship full of friction, needing careful stepping around. Dokter van Hilten wasn't convinced the sulfa drug would help, and anyway, the Germans were keeping the good stuff to themselves, he said. It simply wasn't available.

Pappie sought the help from Herr Von der Hoevel. How he managed it, I do not know. Did he go to the Military Academy in the castle and ask for him, exposing himself and his Austrian friend? What I do know is that I returned from delirious heights because the man in the German uniform had produced a bottle of Prontosil, the miracle sulfa drug. The surgeon hated to admit it. Not his scalpel but a pill had saved his patient's life.

I could eat and drink again, laugh again. I waved back at the picture of Jesus on the wall. Neither of us had succumbed to the puncture wound in the palm of our hands.

A very lively boy shared the room with me. He must have been there all along, but I had no memory of seeing him before. It was a mystery what ailed him. He had no bandages and didn't look sick. Acting as the nurses' helper he could jump in and out of his bed at will, walk the halls and do all sorts of things I wasn't allowed. His name was Peter.

Mammie came in with a nice present for me: a fancy album with blank pages for people to write messages in. She called it a *poezie* album, a poetry album. I asked Zuster Arja to write in it. She pasted a picture of Jesus on the opposite page of some thoughtful words to remember her by. Peter asked if he could write in it too. He wrote, "I wish you will always be happy and will read this to remember the days you had to be in the hospital. When you are big, then you will think: Then I was small." He signed it Hartog Cohen. It seemed odd he didn't use his own name. Many years later, I realized that a boy with the last name of Cohen had to have been Jewish. Of course! The deaconesses had hidden him from the Germans! My mother must have realized the hospital's secret at the time, but when I'd told her that Peter had not signed with his own name she'd shrugged and said nothing. She also didn't tell me how ridiculous she'd felt coming into the hospital in her party dress.

When I returned from the hospital Herr Von der Hoevel came to see me one evening. My father brought him upstairs to our living room. Before he left, Herman went downstairs to check the street to see if it was safe for him to leave. It was bizarre. Neither an Austrian officer in Nazi uniform, nor us, could be seen fraternizing.

While I was in the hospital, the advance into Russia had been halted, I was told. The winter was brutal there, so we were very concerned when Herr Von der Hoevel announced he would be transferred to the Russian front. He visited several times until he left. From the front he wrote us a few letters. After the war we received a picture of himself with his wife and son. He had survived his ordeal.

Chapter 13

- **July 1942: Jews have to turn in their bicycles to the German authorities.**
- **August 11-13, 1942: Allied merchant ships, on their way to Malta, are attacked by German U-boats. Five of the fourteen ships get through. 350 men are lost at sea.**

Maybe because they'd almost lost me, my parents asked Dio Rovers to paint my portrait. I was told to bike over to his house after school. My mother picked out a blouse with a small round collar and a natural sheep's wool sweater for me to wear. The choice wasn't hard to make. My wardrobe was limited. I wore the same skirt day in, day out. Over the next few weeks, as soon as the school bell rang, I did as I was told, got on my bike and pointed it in the opposite direction of de markt.

Dio's house stood in a quiet neighborhood with small gardens front and back. The woman who answered the door wore her reddish blond hair in a roll that covered the back of her neck from ear to ear. She told me to go up two flights, to the attic. Dio would be waiting for me.

The attic was different from any I'd ever seen. The light was even. It created no shadows. A large piece of glass, set into the slope of the roof, was its source. Dio was busy squeezing small ribbons of paint on his palette. I looked around while he screwed the tops back on the lead tubes. A few chairs, a large easel, and canvasses of all sizes took up most of the space.

Dio was one of the kindest people I knew. It couldn't be hard to spend time with him. But now that I stood in the middle of his studio, I felt intimidated. Was it the smell?

My father's working space smelled of ether. The minute you stepped into it you knew it had to do with illness. Dio's studio smelled of linseed oil and turpentine. It called up something distinctly different that I couldn't put into words.

"Hallo, Titia," Dio said. "Are you ready for this?"

"Yes," I said, although I wondered what I should have done to prepare myself.

"Let's have you sit over here." Dio pointed to a low-backed chair on a raised platform. It faced the back of his easel.

"Look at me," he said. A tall square table held the things he would need: a pitcher with brushes of all lengths, a jar with oil and a heap of rags. He picked out a long brush and held it at arm's length while looking over at me. With one eye closed he seemed to measure my face by moving the handle up and down.

'Yes, that's good. Keep looking at the easel, Titia."

I sat with my hands in my lap and stared at the wooden tripod. Dio took up a pencil and made some quick strokes on the canvas. I wondered if he would let me see what he'd done afterwards and how long I would have to sit still like this. Dio looked at me the same way he had when Herman and I had walked into his studio at the church, as if searching for something that lay behind the skin of my face. Did I have secrets that he could reveal with his brush and paint? What had I done that nobody should know about? Put water in the gas tank of a German car? It was the war that made me do that. Part of what we thought was right. But then...why hadn't I told my mother? Well, it wasn't the kind of thing you tell your mother. No way would she have condoned our act. Would she have punished us? On the one hand she told us to stand up for what's right, on the other she said it was foolish to provoke a powerful enemy. Where was the line?

Dio picked up the palette and looked over at me, taking me in. We were in this together, I realized. It was my job to surrender, secrets and all. His job was to catch what I was willing to give. We shared a goal and this created a feeling of intimacy. I think we were both aware of it.

Sitting with my hands in my lap and nothing to do, I discovered it was impossible to think about nothing. Images of the summer just past floated in like cheerful, high summer clouds, such as when I'd helped Boer van Schaik cut white asparagus from his raised bed. My job had been to find the purple tops when they cracked the soil, reaching for the sun. Boer van Schaik then carefully used his fingers to dig down and expose the white stalk underneath. He snipped it from its root with a forked knife. I wasn't allowed to touch them. They were too costly for children's fingers, he'd said.

I saw baskets full of cherries we'd picked in Boer van Beek's orchard, saw Boer Jansen cutting the ripened wheat with his sharp scythe, Vrouw Jansen and their daughters right behind him, bundling the loose stalks in sheaves. Three sheaves were made to lean into each other, and then they were bound at the top. Afterwards, the field next to our house looked like a camping ground with yellow tents. While they soaked up the sun and dried out, we played hide and seek in them.

Playing with my brothers in the wheat field.

"Over here," Dio said. My eyes had wandered off. He smiled, and as he did his face was like an open window. "Just straighten up a bit, Titia. Yes, that's good."

The brush in his right hand was suspended in the air while he looked in my direction with great intensity. He looking at the light, I thought, the way it falls on my face. It was as if I wasn't even there.

My mind went back to Overa. It had been a great summer away from the penned-up feeling of total blackout every night. Some things you never get used to. In the country we didn't have to go through the nightly ritual of closing the curtains. There weren't any. The walls of the living area were all glass, turning the wide landscape into a part of our space. The sun went down at ten when we were already in bed. Sometimes Mammie read by the gas light over the dining room table, waiting for my father to return from de apotheek.

The summer had flown by too fast. Overa had a way of taking me in her arms and enveloping me. Every morning I awakened to the birds in the tall pine trees next to my window, singing their little hears out. How could Opa Wetselaar get angry with them? What harm was there in serenading the new day?

"I think this will do for today, Titia," Dio said. "Did you find it hard to sit still?"

"Not really."

"Can you come back tomorrow after school?"

I peddled home on my bike and passed a troop of soldiers who marched to the rhythm of songs they belted. Germans were more pleasant to listen to when they sang.

On Friday, I pulled on the big brass bell and the lady with the wiry reddish hair opened the door. I had asked my mother if she was Dio's wife.

"Who did you think it was?" Mammie had asked me.

"His housekeeper."

"She's his wife," Mammie said.

I had a hard time putting the two of them together as a couple. Dio was gentle, and even though his wife had done no more than tell me to climb two flights of stairs, my impression was of a cold woman. Mammie just shrugged and said, *"Les extremes se touchent."* I didn't like it when she used another language to explain something. "It means," Mammie said, "opposites attract each other."

I wondered if that was true for my own parents. Mammie was tall, Pappie a head shorter, a contrast that made people giggle. Pappie was thin and athletic. Mammie was definitely overweight. You couldn't imagine my mother doing a pirouette. Mammie had a short fuse. My father took a long time before he let himself boil over, but if he did you'd better watch out. Hans had found that out more than once. What they had in common was a delicious sense of humor.

"*Dag,* Dio," I announced. It was probably brash to call him by his first name, but it was out before I knew it. At home we talked about Dio.

"*Dag,* Titia," he answered, as a smile played over his face. "Ready for another bout of sitting still?"

"Sure," I said. "Can I look at it?"

"Not yet. You might not like it and then I would have to paint an unhappy face!"

I went over to my spot, inhaling again the smell of oil and turpentine that had seemed so strange to me the first time.

"Turn a little more to the right, Titia. That's enough. Remember to look over here at the side of the easel," Dio instructed.

There I sat again, with my hands in my lap. The long handle of Dio's brush moved up and down. When it stopped, he squinted his eyes to take in whatever he'd put on the canvas, and then he looked back at me. Once more I had the distinct feeling he didn't see me at all.

We'd only been back at de markt for a few weeks but my mind was still at Overa. While there, Mammie had agreed to let me keep two rabbits with white and black fur. She wasn't keen on animals and I was only allowed to keep the rabbits if I let them be slaughtered at the end of the summer. Boer Jansen would do it for us. As long as I don't have to eat them, I'd said. Our seamstress would make a nice winter hat and mittens out of their skins. Walking around inside my rabbits seemed a strange prospect, but I knew wool was scarce. We had to be practical, Mammie said. It was wartime. At least I'd been able to keep animals. When I was four, we had kept a goat. He jumped on the kitchen counter and left proof of his presence. He was sent back to his previous owner. Pronto!

Dio put his brush down, stood up and stretched, which made his artist's frock stand out like a skirt blowing in a breeze.

"Can you come back on Monday?" he asked.

My parents celebrated both their birthdays on that weekend between the painting sessions. Their friends came over for drinks before dinner. My part in the festivities was to pass the modest fare around, crackers and small chunks of cheese with a piece of candied ginger on top. The women talked about how to deal with the shortage of textiles and the things that used to be imported like coffee, tea, tobacco and peanuts. Two years ago those items had been considered daily necessities. Now their pretty containers were only reminders of a once abundant life.

The men discussed how the Germans wanted to force all the doctors to belong to an organization called *"De Artsenkamer."* It would be fashioned after the German model in which doctors were expected to put the Aryan race and *das Reich* first, the individual last. The Dutch doctors had responded by writing to the High Commissioner that National Socialism differed from their own views. They roundly refused to let considerations other than their own conscience and sense of duty interfere with how they practiced medicine. It hadn't worked. The Germans kept pressuring the doctors. Now everyone waited for what would come next. Fines? Jail? Taking away the license to practice? What was the right choice to make?

I only half understood what the issue was. Some said it had to do with the Jews and retarded people. It was scary to hear them say the Nazis regarded the Jews, gypsies, and retarded people as inferior to the Aryan race and that those people should be put behind bars. The issue was hotly debated that evening.

My father, I noticed, was an excellent debater. He didn't smack down an opinion the way he would smash a tennis ball into his opponent's court. The choice the doctors faced was a deeply serious matter, he said. Their professional honor and their Hippocratic oath were at stake. But it might turn out that their very ability to practice would be taken away if they didn't comply.

While I passed crackers, I listened. Some of the men seemed stuck in their own opinion, stating it over and over again. Maybe it was the Dutch gin that made them so vehement.

"Of course they should refuse!" Mijnheer Broers said. "It's so obvious. It's not even a choice!"

"That's easy for you to say," Mijnheer Lykles said. "You're not a doctor. If they take your license away, you've let down your patients and you've lost your way to make a living."

"Those are practical considerations," Mijnheer Broers retorted. "Everything Holland has ever fought for and stood for, liberty, personal freedom, is being attacked. We can't let Germany get away with it."

"How will you feel when you can't see your doctor, because he isn't allowed to practice?"

The gin made their faces red, but it was the angry argument that contorted them. The party left a lasting impression on me.

Apparently, it showed when I went back to Dio's studio on Monday.

"What are you thinking about, Titia?" Dio asked as he was painting.

Oh dear, what was I to say? It was the first time he'd spoken to me during a sitting.

"We had a party at our house for my parents' birthdays," I said.

"Does a birthday party make you mad?" Dio asked.

Uh, no, well…I was just thinking about all the arguing," I blurted.

"What about?"

"Something about if doctors should join an organization the Germans want them to. Some of the guests thought they should, but others thought they shouldn't."

"What did your father think?"

"He said it was a hard choice, but that they shouldn't." Should I have said that? If it had to do with the Germans you had to watch your words.

"You haven't told me yet why this made you look so serious," Dio said.

"I hate the way people carried on about it. They looked ugly," I said.

Dio laughed and I was mortified. It would have been better to keep that thought to myself.

"I love it," Dio said. "You're right. People in protest get carried away."

I was much relieved. At least I hadn't made a fool of myself.

"Opposition in itself isn't a bad thing," Dio said. "What if we would let the Germans walk all over us? But it's the quiet people who are the most effective. You would probably call them the beautiful people, but you're not likely to know who they are. They have to work very carefully. Out of sight."

I was dumbfounded. Dio was referring to the people in the underground movement who did all sorts of wicked things, like blowing up bridges or stealing important files from City Hall.

Dio picked up his brush again, squinting at the painting and then at me. I straightened up a bit and wondered if all my thoughts had shown on my face.

Maybe that was the real difference between a painting and a snapshot. Over the course of the week my face must have reflected different moods, different thoughts. Did Dio choose which mood he liked best, or did he combine them? I became even more curious to know what it looked like on the side of the canvas I couldn't see.

"All right, we're done for today," Dio said. "I will need you to come one more time and then you may look at it."

For the last time, I climbed the staircases and entered the studio. I'd grown fond of Dio's studio. Even though it had been dull to sit still, not talk and look at the back of an easel, what made it special was the absence of things. No noise, no limits, no interference. In class and at Sunday school something was always asked of you: to learn, to understand, to accept what you're told. Being at home was also a task: live by the rules, pull your part of the load, get along with your siblings. You could think here, let your mind wander. A plant could grow here just by absorbing the even light.

I went over to the platform and sat down. Dio pulled his paint-stained smock over his head. There was a familiarity to his motions. I could anticipate the squinting look, the sound of the brush dabbing at the paint, mixing it, stroking the canvas. Layers and layers of paint must have been put on it by now.

At last he stood up, stepped back from the easel, turned his head this way and that and put his brush down.

"Would you like to see it?"

The big moment had arrived. I walked over slowly, almost afraid. What if I didn't like it? It had to satisfy my parents. That was the most important, of course, but it would also be nice if I could stand to look at it as well since it would be hanging over the piano.

What did I see? Titia Wetselaar jumping right off the canvas into the room, into the world. The front view he'd chosen gave immediacy to the painting, as if I had asked a question and was expecting an answer.

Chapter 14

- **February 2, 1943: The German army is defeated at Stalingrad. Ninety thousand Germans are taken prisoner.**
- **May 1943: The Allies rule the seas after clearing the Atlantic Ocean and the Mediterranean Sea of German U-boats.**

Historians would write: 'The capitulation of the German army at Stalingrad on the second day of February in 1943, was the turning point in favor of the Allies.'

What historians could see in retrospect, we experienced first hand. In Holland we didn't need to be told something had turned around, but not for the better from our point of view. When the Nazis lost their prized role of victors, their behavior changed from a friendly neighbor, who only wanted us to acknowledge our Aryan roots, to a greedy wolf. Germany became hungry. Hungry for our bicycles, our horses, our rails, and even our church bells. Coal, meat, cheese, it was all carted off to the *Heimat.* Hitler's wrath after his first major defeat came down on us like an arctic weather front.

The Germans wanted not only commodities like potatoes and coals. They needed to replace the soldiers who were away at the front. Hitler dipped into the pool of men in the occupied territories, effectively turning it into another commodity he could haul off to keep his war machine chugging.

Every day, on our way back from school, my brothers and I stopped at *de Bredase Courant* to look at the latest news. I was almost eleven years old now and halfway through the fifth grade. My horizon had widened enough to take in the headlines about new ordinances and battles in far-away places.

One day in March, I read about the doctors. As I'd learned at my parents' birthday party in September, they were being forced to join a medical society – *de Artsenkamer* – the German authorities had organized for them. Only a small number had come forward to claim membership. At regular intervals Pappie's doctor friends received a letter to remind them of their duty to present themselves. If they didn't, they would be fined one thousand guilders. If they still didn't respond within fourteen days, the fine would be doubled. Still, very few had come forward.

On this day, March 24th, the paper headlined that 5,300 doctors had, individually but simultaneously, sent a registered letter to the president of the *Artsenkamer* to announce they were giving up their right to practice medicine. What they did next wagged many tongues in Holland: the doctors covered the word ARTS behind their names on their shingles with a piece of tape, disclaiming their M.D. title.

Herman and I bicycled through town to see if this was indeed so. Pappie's friend, Dokter Wijnen, had used orange tape to cover the credential behind his name on the plaque nailed to the brick facade of his house. It still listed his office hours and patients were coming and going through his front door. The *Artsenkamer* had been effectively sabotaged. We biked by every doctor's house in town. Without exception they had taped their M.D. out of sight.

Likewise, university students were forced to sign "a statement of loyalty" which meant they had to promise to follow all regulations the occupying authorities imposed: curfews, no lights on in the evening, et cetera. More rules would undoubtedly be added to the list. Seventy-five percent of the students flatly refused to sign. The Germans made it clear that anyone who refused would be sent to a labor camp in Germany. The threat motivated every university president in the country to close their doors in solidarity with their students. No more classes were held or exams taken after April 11, 1943.

The Germans rounded up as many students as they could find and put them behind barbed wire in Vught, a town in our province that was rapidly becoming infamous as a human dumping place. A score of the students were executed on the spot to impress on the rest what the Germans thought of their insubordination. Others were sent to concentration camps or put to work in factories. Most students went into hiding. We called them *onderduikers.* The only students I knew well were two of Oom Henri's sons. They disappeared. We had no idea where they were and we knew better than to ask.

Laborers didn't fare much better. A system called *Arbeitseinsatz* had been instituted. Initially the Germans said it was voluntary. But all too soon it turned out that *Arbeitseinsatz* was the German euphemism for forced labor. Men out of work had been the first to go to factories in Germany. Now, employed or not, men in their twenties had to present themselves for a physical examination. Doctors wrote exemptions wherever they could with little or no indication of disease. Strapping young men suddenly complained of flat feet, poor vision, and other imaginary ailments.

Political prisoners and Jews are taken to the railroad station on their way to concentration camps. Photo courtesy of NIOD.

Hitler's appetite for making war was insatiable. He needed more soldiers to replace the casualties his troops had suffered. He needed more bullets, tanks, guns, submarines and planes. There weren't enough Germans left inside Germany's borders to feed his war machine.

It hit our country like a bombshell when a new decree was posted. One day in May, my father came upstairs to have lunch with us and we could tell right away something was wrong.

"This is the limit!" he fumed. "All our soldiers are retaken as prisoners of war."

"What?" my mother said. With a quick gesture she brought her hand to her face. "How can they do that?"

"They do what they want," my father said with bitterness in his voice. Hitler, in a magnanimous gesture, had allowed Dutch soldiers to return to their homes after Holland's capitulation in 1940. But that had been when he wanted to please us. The Dutch would come around, he was convinced, and become his "Aryan brothers." Three years into the war, he had failed to realize his vision.

"Do you realize what this means?" Pappie asked, more of himself than of us. "This means hundreds of thousands of workers will have to leave their jobs. Whole factories will be emptied out. My God, what have we come to?"

"Does anyone in de apotheek have to go?" Hans asked.

"No, I employ mostly women. But some have relatives who'll have to go."

Strikes broke out over the next ten days. Work at the biggest factories stopped entirely. People were in uproar. Of course, it didn't take long before the Germans took countermeasures. Shots were heard all over the country. Eighty men were executed without due process. In total two hundred people died and the Germans won the argument. They had the guns and the bullets. We worried about Henk, Net's fiancé, and Jan, the one who'd choked on our surrogate tobacco, but they both survived the crisis.

Putting down revolts carried a price. It encouraged underground resistance. There was hardly a family left that hadn't been affected in some way by the decrees. Parents of students had rushed to Vught after the universities closed and frantically looked for their children. As it stood now, a family with children between eighteen and twenty-five had at least one child in mortal danger. Either a son had been executed, or been sent to a labor camp, or, worse, to a concentration camp. He could be hiding or working for the underground, or both. So far, girls hadn't been sent to labor camps, but many were doing dangerous work as couriers. A weird, secretive atmosphere took hold of our country. Parents didn't know the whereabouts of their children. Wives of the soldiers, retaken as P.O.W.s had to fend for themselves without money coming in. The brave people who were giving shelter to *onderduikers* put their lives on the line. The anti-German sentiment was growing so strong, many who had not done so before began to take risks.

Again and again, our parents impressed upon us that we could not take anyone's loyalty to Holland for granted. They assumed Hans, Herman and I were aware of what was happening around us, even as they tried to keep the worst from us, especially names of specific people. What we were most aware of was the fact that our grandparents belonged to the hated N.S.B. party. We didn't talk much about Opa and Oma in our home. It was the uncomfortable family secret. During the last summer vacation we'd gone up to Overveen to visit them. Hans and Herman had spied their N.S.B. uniforms in the hall closet. When Oma insisted we meet some of the "very nice" children of their "comrades," our parents spirited us away to visit our cousins in Bloemendaal, the neighboring town. I knew my father was very sad, but also angry at his father's stubborn attitude. Opa simply denied the facts my father held out to him. Everything German was great and everything English was abominable. No matter how hard Pappie and his brothers tried, they couldn't change their father's mind.

Chapter 15

- **Spring 1943: Russian troops push the German army back.**
- **July 1943: American and British troops capture Sicily.**
- **September 1943: American and British troops land in Southern Italy.**

One day in late May, we had a great surprise. My father came upstairs with Carrie Goldstein, whom I'd seen just a few times since the summer of 1941, when the Germans decreed that Jewish children could only be taught by Jewish teachers.

"*Dag*, Carrie," I said.

I felt very awkward. What was she doing here? She wasn't allowed to be with Christians. What if they found out? The yellow Star of David on her jacket threw me as well. I'd seen it before, sewn on coats of strangers. But Carrie…?

"Mijnheer Goldstein is downstairs in de apotheek," my father said. "He needs some medicines for their trip." He gave a hinting look at my mother and then he left.

"*Dag*, Carrie," my mother said, and gave her a big hug. "Sit down and tell us how you are."

"We're going on a trip. We have to leave our house tomorrow. First we go to Amsterdam and from there to Westerbork."

When my mother heard Westerbork, she winced. It was a small town on the border with Germany in the province of Drente.

"Can you take things with you, Carrie?"

I thought this was an odd question. Of course, you take with you what you need.

"In the notice we got it said just a small suitcase. I wondered if you would have a thermos I could take."

Mammie immediately told me to go upstairs and get my field bottle and to ask Hans and Herman to do the same. I ran up the staircase to the boys' room.

"Does she need all three?" Hans asked.

"She has a sister and parents."

We went looking in our closets. It was a prize possession, this aluminum can with a screw top, a green jacket around it and a leather shoulder strap. We looked at each other, our field bottle in our hands. It is one of the most distinct memories I have of the war: us standing there at the top of the staircase, about to part with something we valued and knowing there was no way out.

"I hope she appreciates it," Herman said.

The three of us went downstairs. Mammie had put together some candies and cookies for Carrie to take on her trip.

"How are Bertha and Madeleen?" Carrie asked me.

"Oh, they're fine. Mijnheer Brens is our teacher this year."

"Do you like him?" Carrie asked.

"Yes, he's allright. Who's your teacher?"

"I don't have one. At first we had school with different parents teaching us, but now most are gone."

I was sorry I'd asked. Carrie was taller than I remembered her, but her face had the same sweet, shy smile. My father came back into the living room to say Carrie's father was waiting for her. We had to say good-bye. Carrie thanked us for letting us use our field bottles. She would bring them back after the war was over, she said. An ominous silence followed her words, as if a lumpy stone had settled itself in our throats. Pappie broke through it by taking Carrie's hand. Mammie hugged her and I saw tears in her eyes. My brothers shook her hand and I kissed her cheek.

"Stay in touch," I told her. "If you know where you'll be, send me your address and I can write to you."

"I will," Carrie said, and followed my father out the door.

Mammie made us sit. Tears were streaming down her face. We sensed something was very wrong for Carrie and her family.

"Why is she going to Westerbork?" Herman asked.

"Hundreds and hundreds of Jews are taken there from Amsterdam during the night when it is dark. The Germans hope that by transporting them during the night we won't know what they're doing," Mammie said.

"Then what are they doing?" I wanted to know.

Mammie sighed and wiped the tears from her face. She folded her hands in her lap and stared at them, something she often did when she wanted to think before she spoke.

"They are rounding up all the Jews and taking them from Westerbork eastward."

"Eastward? To Germany?" Herman asked.

"We really don't know exactly. But people say they bring them to Poland."

"To do what?" I asked.

"We don't know. Nobody has come back from there yet. But we think they're brought to concentration camps."

"But what has Carrie done wrong?"

"She was born a Jew," Mammie said.

Of course, we'd discussed this several times at our table. No matter how many times it came up, I just couldn't understand why the Germans were picking on the Jews. Even if it were the Jews who killed Jesus, it didn't make sense. Jesus had been a Jew himself. Besides, that had happened almost two thousand years ago and Hitler was not religious. So what did he care?

Pappie explained it to me this way: "When someone calls a beautiful vase ugly and he is persistent enough and convincing, then sooner or later people will drop their own judgment and believe the beautiful vase is indeed ugly."

The full impact of Carrie leaving came slowly, as if we could postpone it, or fend it off, by not giving in to the obvious truth: Carrie and her sister and her parents were going on a trip from which they might not return. I nestled myself next to my mother on the couch and started to cry. The boys were blowing hard into their handkerchiefs. It was the saddest moment of the war. And what made it worse was realizing we'd hesitated to give her our prized thermos bottles. We were angry with the Germans and ashamed of ourselves.

After Carrie left and my brothers had gone back upstairs to do homework, I walked aimlessly through the living room, picked up a book Mammie had left on the coffee table and put it back without looking at it. A gloomy feeling pulled my body down into a chair beside the window. It looked out over de markt, yet what I saw was projected on a screen in my head. There I watched Carrie, the way she'd come in with my father, how my mother had embraced her and how foolish I'd felt seeing her after such a long time. It wasn't as if I'd never thought of her. When Herman and I put water in the German pantzerwagen, I'd really done it in revenge for her. Every time I saw somebody with the yellow Star of David, I thought of Carrie. But then, when she stood in the middle of our own living room, totally unexpected, I'd had a hard time putting it all together. She looked familiar and yet like a stranger, as if something had drawn a line between us that we couldn't cross.

I sat with my head in my hands in front of the window, following the motions of Gerritje, the funny little man who guarded the bikes of shoppers, who paid him a dime for the service. He was proud of the big bicycle rack the town allowed him to use and he polished it with a rag. He'd fashioned himself some sort of uniform with a visered cap. Whenever he received his dime from a customer, he touched his cap in an almost military salute. Gerritje was simple, happy just to be and to serve. He didn't do anybody any harm. The Germans would never take a person like him to a labor camp. But they would take Carrie. What harm could she possibly do?

"When the war is over I'll bring them back," she'd said when she took our thermos bottles. But would the war ever be over? I felt a dread I had not felt before.

Queen Wilhelmina, speaking over *Radio Oranje*, convinced us she had never doubted, and still didn't doubt, the outcome of this war. Never had she considered surrendering to Hitler. In that way she was like Winston Churchill who'd growled into the microphone, after his troops had been pushed into the North Sea at Duinkerken, "We shall fight on the beaches, we shall fight in the fields and in the streets, we shall fight in the hills; we shall never surrender." Even though I didn't understand English, his voice had been enough to make me stand up straight. It had given my mother goose bumps. Churchill had remained true to his word.

It was a dreary day and the cobblestones glistened from the moisture in the air. De markt had become as colorless as the people. Their clothes were threadbare and faded. Being the youngest of three, I wore my brothers' clothes. Herman's jacket had been remade to fit me. The whole winter I'd worn a coat Hans and Herman had worn before me. My father joked it was a good thing he'd always had expensive taste. His suits never wore out. The material from which they were cut was indestructible, woven with iron thread. To dress well was harder for my mother. She was fashion conscious, but like with so many other things, the Germans had picked over the best dresses and sent them home to their lonely wives. She made do by adding a bow and new buttons, a flourish here and a colorful pin there. When we came home from school she was often sitting at the dining room table with the sewing machine, trying to patch up our clothes and the bed sheets. At night she darned socks next to the coal stove.

It was too awful to think about people being taken away from their homes. Would Carrie have to work in a factory? Would they put children to work making bullets? Questions, questions. There were no answers to so many questions. For instance, what if we had offered for Carrie's family to come live with us? There was a lot of talk about people going into hiding. Pappie knew who some of the *onderduikers* were. He didn't give names, of course, but patients told him stories about narrow escapes. Once he told us about a man who had five sons. One had already been sent to Germany. The others were hiding. The Germans were continually searching for them, but he had good neighbors who warned when they saw a German patrol coming. His youngest son quickly put on his sister's dress, a wig to cover his hair and took to the street in high heels, right under the nose of the German Polizei, while another son was climbing out of the attic window on the other side of their house. So far they'd been lucky.

Our house was big enough to hold four more people. Room was not the problem though. Our house was too open, too many people coming and going. Just recently, Pappie had had to fire a young woman because she'd stolen money and other things. He wasn't so much worried about the money but that she was the sneaky type. Our house at Overa would have been ideal to hide people if it didn't have so many windows. Four people couldn't move around in it without being seen from the road. And what would the farmers think when they knew we stayed in the city during the winter months?

It had started to rain. The two Belgian pulling horses in front of the van Gendt & Loos delivery wagon were getting soaked. Their blond coats steamed. They worked hard these days. For lack of gas, live horses almost exclusively provided horsepower. When a car went by you could be sure a German or an NSBer was behind the wheel. Doctors and other lucky people whose cars hadn't been taken yet had rigged up furnaces on the cars' rear bumpers that they stoked with coal. When that became scarce as well, they used wood. Cars weren't the only means of transportation the Germans had their eyes on. First they'd had the Jews hand in their bikes. Then they randomly made all people give up their bicycles. The chance you might have to walk back from wherever you went on your bike was real. It got to the point that we hid our bikes most of the time. Children's bikes weren't in demand. All through the occupation I rode around on a model that was very adequate for a seven-year-old. Eventually, the tires wore out. The irony was that when the war broke out, my father had bought extra tires. They hung from the ceiling in the attic, where they would probably be crumbled from the heat by the end of the war. But it would be folly to use them now, a sure invitation to take them away from us. We became experts at fixing flat tires. Each of us had a little pouch with emergency repair equipment under our saddle, attached with two tiny leather straps.

So much had changed. Even I, although I'd been only seven years old at the time, could remember how different de markt had looked before the Germans came. It had always been a constant bustle of cars and delivery trucks, and Dutch officers on horseback with soldiers marching behind them on their way to the shooting ranges outside the city. Well-dressed pedestrians walked on the wide sidewalks; bicyclists weaved their way through the traffic of cars and horse-drawn wagons. On market day a bright quilted blanket was laid out for us over the cobblestones with colorful flowers, orange and red-white-and-blue flags snapped in the wind from *de haringkarren*, where fresh herring was prepared on the spot for the customer, who would grab it by the tail and lower the delicacy slowly onto his tongue. No matter where you directed your eyes, they were met by abundance. Overflowing crates with tomatoes, strawberries, apples, spinach, Brussels endives wrapped in royal blue tissue paper; stands under white canvas roofs, where people ordered big chunks of cheese or bags full of fresh fish. Every Tuesday and Friday, my world had looked colorful, plentiful and cheerful. By the hour I'd sat and watched. I had taken that happy scene for granted. Sometimes it was hard to discern what was lacking in the scene below our window, but not today. Life had become lackluster and shabby.

"Titia! It's time to set the table," Mammie called.

Her voice shook me awake and I was glad. Too many gloomy thoughts. Hans helped me drape the pink tablecloth over the round table and I took out the pretty china. Mammie insisted on a festive table every night, no matter how meager the meal. At times, I thought it preposterous to bring out the crystal and polished silver. What we got to eat could be put into a small bowl: potatoes without jus and every once in a while a small piece of meat. Plenty of vegetables though. For dessert something I truly hated: *watergruel*, a gray, unattractive porridge made of pearl barley. The recipe called for raisins – not available any more – and lemon peels, equally unavailable. A red fruit sauce made it some what palatable.

We waited for Pappie to come upstairs from de apotheek. Herman and I killed the time by looking out at the parked cars on de markt and naming the brands: Dodge, Citroen, Peugeot, Ford, Rover, Vauxhall, Opel, each one showing fatigue. There was no such thing as a new car.

The minute my father stepped into the dining room, we could tell what kind of news he'd just heard. It was practically written on his face. If it was a good joke his eyes twinkled. The other day he'd had us doubled over with one about a German officer who entered a bakery and greeted the baker with, *"Heil Hitler."* The baker responded, "*Heil* Rembrandt." The officer asked what that was all about. The baker answered, "We only honor our painters after they've died."

But tonight we could tell we weren't going to hear a joke.

"They've taken Dokter Wijnen away," Pappie said as he sat down and unfolded his linen napkin.

"Where to?" my mother asked.

"To Amersfoort."

"My God!" Mammie said.

Amersfoort was a city in the province of Utrecht. During the war, if somebody was taken to Amersfoort, it meant he was taken to the infamous prison there. Most underground workers and others who didn't cooperate with the Nazi regime were taken either to Vught, Scheveningen (dubbed *het Oranje Hotel*), or Amersfoort. Those lucky enough to make it out of there told horrifying tales about executions on the spot, men sent on to concentration camps in Germany, or wasting away. Amersfoort had taken on the sound of horror.

"Why Dokter Wijnen?" Hans asked.

"He's not alone. About half of all doctors in Holland have been taken there."

"Will they let them out?" Herman asked.

"Not until they sign up for *de Artsenkamer.*"

"Do you think they'll hang tough?" Hans asked.

"We'll see," Pappie said, and picked up his knife and fork.

Four days later, most doctors returned to their patients. They'd had no choice but to sign up. The Germans, once again, had let it be known they could settle any argument or punish any insubordination with brute force.

Chapter 16

- **February through April, 1944: The Allied Forces are stalled around the monastery in Cassino, Italy.**
- **May 11, 1944: The battle around Cassino ends in favor of the Allied Forces.**
- **June 5, 1944: Rome falls into Allied hands.**
- **June 6, 1944: D-Day. Allied Forces land in Normandy, France.**

There is hope! They have landed in France.

My father was out of breath from running up the stairs. He had heard the news from a friend who'd had it whispered into his ear by the baker.

"Unbelievable!" he said, still out of breath. "The coast of Normandy! Incredible!"

It was lunchtime and my brothers and I had just come home from school. Mammie sat in stunned silence with her hands pressed together on her bosom. Nobody asked my father who had landed. We'd prayed for it daily. It had become a sport to guess at what spot the Allied Forces would land. From Denmark to Holland, all the way down to the part of France that faced the Atlantic Ocean, the coastline had been reinforced with bunkers. The Germans were waiting. My father's excited reaction proved not many had given credence to a landing in Normandy with its steep cliffs.

"Are you surprised they picked Normandy?" Hans asked.

"You bet I am!" Pappie said.

Herman ran upstairs to get his atlas while we cleared some dishes to make room on the table. He flipped through the pages as if he had to catch a train and had only two minutes to check the schedules. Standing elbow to elbow we looked down at the map of France. Pappie pointed to the area where the Allies had landed at dawn. Thousands and thousands of men, he told us, had come across the English Channel.

"Calais would have been easier," he said. "The channel narrows here, see, and the shore area is flat. The Germans must have been shocked." Then he pointed out how far it was from Normandy to where we lived, below the Rhine River.

"Don't expect them to come here anytime soon. Maybe they'll make a straight line to Germany and pass us by."

"Those poor souls in Alsace," Mammie said, looking at the map. " Every time Germany and France take up the sword, they swing it over their heads."

"Now listen carefully, all of you," my father said. He deliberately made eye contact with each of us. "We are not supposed to know this, because nobody is supposed to have a radio. This news didn't come over distribution radio! So, no matter how excited you are, don't say anything that makes the Germans suspicious that we know."

Pappie left the room with a light tread. Mammie cleared the dishes. My brothers left for their respective schools; Hans to *het Gymnasium* – Latin School – and Herman to the H.B.S. where he was taught everything his older brother was except for the classics. I was still in grade school, closer by, so I had some time left. The atlas still lay open to the map of France. Rivers bubbled up and mountains rose from its flat surface, three-dimensional in the magic of the moment. My imagination whirled in a way it never had in class where our teacher used a canvas map of the world to hammer into our memories, with the force of repetition, the names of countries, rivers, mountains. Mijnheer Brens would point a long stick to a particular place on the map and we were supposed to give the correct name in unison, the same way we'd learned the multiplication tables.

I looked at where my father's finger had rested, to where soldiers had poured out of boats onto beaches, a tiny spot that was no longer just a name on a piece of paper. Pappie had said there were cliffs. The Germans would have the vantage point of a rooftop, like when Herman and I stood on our roof garden and looked down at the bicycle yard. From there we shot at rats with an air rifle. It was so easy! We didn't have to look them in the eye. Easy to spot, clustered around the rim of a drainpipe. We hardly ever missed. Pappie knew what we were doing, because the bicycle yard was behind his lab. He warned us to be careful not to shoot the windows. Rats, he said, were good things to get rid of. They spread disease.

But aiming at people? I wondered what it felt like to step onto a beach and see a steep wall ahead that you knew you had to climb while sharpshooters hid overhead. I hoped that after the war we would know what the landing had looked like. The Germans certainly weren't going to provide us with photos of Allies landing on their continent.

When we met for dinner, Herman and Hans told about the whisperings at school in the corridors and the clusters of people on every street corner on their way home.

"The war hasn't been won yet," Pappie warned.

"Can't we celebrate just a little bit?" Herman asked.

"What do we celebrate with?" Mammie wondered, looking down on her plate of potatoes and cauliflower.

"I'll make a toast with water and save my last bottle of French wine for our liberation," Pappie said, and we raised our glasses of water while he intoned in an unusually serious voice, "May they soon be here. God be with all the fighting men." It was more a prayer than a toast.

"Allies and Germans?" Hans asked.

"Yes, Allies and Germans. They've all been sent into war by Hitler, if you come right down to it."

I supposed you couldn't very well ask God to help just the Allies. God was supposed to be with everyone, good or bad, English or German, although, if I were God, I'd help the Allies more than the Germans.

"And let's pray the Germans won't act like cornered cats," my mother added.

"What do you mean by that, Mammie?" I asked.

"The Germans may lash out, be stricter with their rules," she answered. While I tried to think of rules they could hurt us with, I noticed Hans looking over to the living room.

"Pappie, what happened to our radio?" He asked with a sly smile.

"I don't know," Pappie answered, straight faced. "It just disappeared one day. Good thing too! They're getting serious about seizing radios. I wouldn't like to wind up in jail."

"I take it then that our Telefunken is not in our home anymore?" Hans asked, hoping to egg Pappie on.

"That's right. It is not in this house anymore. Don't worry about it."

We didn't believe him. If he'd had to give up the radio to the Germans, we would have heard about it. And it would have been too risky to give it to someone else. He must have hidden it in the house somewhere. Under his bed? In one of the cellars? There wasn't a place we didn't look, but it was gone. We hated to admit it, but we couldn't locate our trusted before-the-war Telefunken. Yet my father never failed to tell us news that wasn't printed in the papers. Every night, our meager meal was garnished with tales of the Allies' progress. How did he know? We learned new words like beachhead, amphibious operations and airborne divisions. Names of strange places became as familiar as the salt and pepper shakers on the table: Bayeux, Ste. Mere Eglise and Cherbourg. It was an exciting way to learn geography. Always we were warned not to talk about these things. I suppose my father told us because it was history in the making. At school it was hard to know if others were as informed as we were, because we were all being careful with the news we heard. You didn't go up to a friend and ask:" Did you hear?" unless it was printed in the newspaper.

The one piece of news the Germans were eager to share with us was the use of their newest invention: the V1, a small pilotless plane flown at high speed on a predetermined course. Loaded with explosives, it detonated on impact. The city of London was its target.

There were plenty of other things to think about that June, such as getting ready to go to Overa to spend the summer months, unaware it would be the last time. I also had to do my entrance exam to *het Gymnasium* where Hans was. With a group of students my own age, most of whom I didn't know, I was tested on history, geography, the Dutch and French languages and, unfortunately, math. "If the train leaves the station at 5.20, arrives at 12.15 at its destination, and has to travel 200 miles, at what speed does the train travel?" To my great surprise I passed. At the end of the summer, I would go to a different school in a different neighborhood.

At Overa we only occasionally saw men in uniform. We were surrounded instead by life bursting forth from plants bearing juicy red berries, by fields of wheat, still green and young and reaching for the sun. At Overa, people concerned themselves with the harvest, with their animals, with each other. Yet the war had found its way into this pastoral existence. In the middle of my mother's flower garden a gaping hole welcomed us to our summer vacation. Shocked, we stared down at a hole big enough to bury a horse in. Somebody had dug deep and thrown the dirt up and around the hole to form a rim. Mammie stared in disbelief at her vandalized borders. Who had done this?

The mystery was quickly solved. The hole in our yard wasn't the only one in the neighborhood. The Germans had ordered their Dutch "slaves" to dig trenches and traps for tanks in places with strategic value to them, be it in a flower garden, a precious asparagus bed or a meadow for cattle. It had been a total surprise to our neighbors when a crew of men with shovels had shown up and started to dig. The farmers had protested to no avail.

My mother swiftly regained her composure. "If this is the worst that happens to us, then we should get down on our knees and thank the Lord."

Herman saw possibilities in this new configuration of the flower border. He carried to the garden his toy soldiers, tanks, wagons, trucks, everything he'd bought over time with his allowance and birthday money. Tunnels were dug, while other areas were flattened for battlefields. As soon as breakfast, lunch or dinner was over, Herman dashed out to *de kuil.* He lived in his own creation, in a war of his own making, one he could direct and endure. Whenever German trucks came down the country road loaded with soldiers on their way to train on the heather fields nearby, Herman would follow their actions like a hawk. A whistle would go off, he told us, when allied planes flew over, a signal that the soldiers should get out of plain sight. One of them had quickly disappeared into a haystack. When he jumped back out, he broke his leg. Herman saw things I wasn't on the outlook for. Much about the war fascinated him.

Meanwhile, the real war's outcome was at the mercy of rough terrain in France and the stamina of enlisted men. It was a toss-up who would emerge as the undisputed victor.

Chapter 17

- **July 2, 1944: One million Allies have landed in Normandy.**
- **July 29, 1944: The Polish Underground Forces begin a general uprising in Warsaw.**
- **August 1, 1944: "Dragoon" assault on Saint Tropez, France.**
- **August 28, 1944: Allies take Marseille.**

My parents had built the house at Overa to provide a break from our life in the center of the city, to breathe in country air, to see things grow. It had fulfilled all these functions, but during the war, especially the last years of the war, it lent the extra benefit of putting the war at arm's length. Yes, we heard the same sounds from bombers on their way to Germany, and yes, we saw German soldiers once in a while marching to the heather fields close by, but there were fewer reminders a war was going on. We could play outdoors, visit the farmers and help raise vegetables. Only Herman stayed in "war mode", playing with his toy soldiers or marching with a gun he'd fashioned from a branch and a rope.

With the fragrant air of the farmland drifting through the wide-open windows, I listened to the deep silence, punctuated by the occasional mooing of a cow that begged to be milked or the grinding of wagon wheels over the gravel road. The rhythmic klippety-klop of horses' hooves assured me God was the ruler yet. And even though my father came home daily with news from the front, the Normandy beaches seemed far, far away.

One aspect of the war we couldn't get away from was the increasing scarcity of food. My brothers and I also noticed that our parents were less patient with us. Even for minor infractions we were punished by having to pump water. There was no electricity at Overa to power the pump, so we had to crank a wooden handle back and forth to build the pressure up. For twenty minutes at a minimum. We spent more time than we liked in the small closet next to the

Herman playing soldier.

sweating water tank, feeling sorry for ourselves as though we were Roman slaves pulling the oars of the emperor's vessel, back and forth, back and forth. In the summer of 1944, it wasn't hard to be relegated to the water tank closet.

I found ways to stay out of trouble. I'd looked forward to getting up early, skipping over to Boer Jansen's to join him on his milk route. Although my city life wasn't dull, riding in the crude wagon and having Boer Jansen show me how to get his loyal gray to do what I wanted topped doing stunts on my bicycle next to the canal. On the first morning of my vacation, I stood at his door at five o'clock. We led the workhorse out of his pasture as the sun peeked over the horizon. Boer Jansen threw the heavy collar over the horse's neck, eased the snaffle bit into his mouth, and I was allowed to back Lies up to the shafts of the wagon. Around us the fields were draped in moist air. We seemed to conspire with nature to remain unseen in the low and misty morning light, as if Boer Jansen and I were on a secret mission. The rest of the world was still in slumber, except for the roaming chickens and the pigs lazing in a corner of their muddy pen.

While the Allies and Germans fought each other in Normandy, turning the countryside around Falaise into a wasteland that General Eisenhower later compared to Dante's Inferno, I watched the wheat turn from green to a luscious golden yellow. While precious young blood soaked the fertile farm land of France, I sat on a grass knoll next to Boer Jansen as he sharpened his scythe in preparation for cutting the wheat. While French farmers listened to the firing of cannons, I heard the steady pounding of Boer Jansen's hammer on his scythe, patiently straightening the dents on the blade where it had met up with tough stems. Around me was the promise of a harvest. I watched the scythe lay the ripened wheat, bunch by bunch, row after row, with the swing of Boer Jansen's strong arm, its steady rhythm both calming and reassuringly down-to-earth.

Herman and I helped to thrash the wheat. The dried sheaves had been laid out on the dirt floor of the Jansen's barn, and we beat them with a *vlegel*, two sticks, each as tall as we were, connected by a complicated knot of leather straps. We could have easily killed each other as we swung the flying stick to the ground. We survived because Boer Jansen insisted we take turns. The straw was kept for bedding, the grain was swept up, dirt and all.

Boer Jansen allowed us to pick up the ears of wheat left behind on the field next to our house. Every ear counted. With the borrowed *vlegel* we beat the devil out of the ears in our sandy driveway between the house and the shed while Mammie was out on an errand. We didn't want Boer Jansen to get in trouble for teaching us how to use this murderous tool. After a day of reaping and thrashing we had a coffee can's worth of kernels that we ground with a meat grinder. The maid showed us how to make dough. When all was said and done, we had two tiny loaves of dark brown bread, which we cooked in small tins in a pan with boiling water, for lack of an oven.

Though we lived next to farmers who liked us, food was hard to come by. Each farmer's livestock was counted by Nazi agents who visited regularly to make sure the products made it to market, except for the twenty percent farmers were allowed to keep for themselves. Fifteen chickens were allowed per farm. The agents determined how many pigs could be raised at one farm depending on how much garbage was available for their feed. Grain wasn't to be wasted on chickens and pigs. Each pig got earmarked. It seemed a sure-proof way to prevent a flourishing black market in bacon and ham, but, of course, the farmers found ways around handing over all they should. To get a share of the illegal goods one had to be on good terms with the farmers or offer something valuable in return. The Germans were aware they hadn't been able to wipe out the underground trade. At any time a bicycler with a large package could be stopped for inspection. If he didn't have a watertight explanation for owning and transporting a staple – more than could be bought with distribution coupons – the goods were confiscated.

My father had a plan. With sugar available to the pharmacy for the preparation of cough syrup and other medicines, he could trade it for meat, eggs, flour and bacon. Instead of carrying the sugar in a big bag, he stuffed his knickerbockers – very fashionable at the time – with small bags around his knees where the pants puffed out. He could hardly walk, but he could bike. Carefully, as though he were riding over a road paved with eggs, he made his way to Overa, passing several checkpoints without being stopped or suspected. My mother soon had enough small bags of sugar to barter for the rest of the summer.

My father had another staple to barter. In his laboratory he concocted a decent brand of Dutch gin from alcohol and juniper berries. Divided into small medicine bottles they were bartered for cheese and eggs.

Soap was unavailable. Money couldn't buy it. Even offering jewels wouldn't get you a bar of soap, the smooth soft kind we remembered from before the war. What we used instead resembled a hunk of clay. It scratched, didn't produce suds, nor did it clean. The missing ingredient was oil derived from olives, palm seeds, coconut or cottonseed. None of these plants and trees grew in our climate. Desperate housewives tried to substitute pure lye for it with the unwanted result of burning their own skin. Our clothes were never really clean. My mother put the soiled laundry in a big kettle with water and let it boil for hours on the stove to at least kill the germs. It took her a full day. The kettle had to cool before the clothes could be handled. With wooden tongs she deposited the dripping linens in the kitchen sink for rinsing. On laundry day we were banned from the kitchen. The danger of getting burned by hot cloth in transit from kettle to sink was not imaginary. We didn't need to be convinced anyhow. We'd been sent off too often to pump water.

The last summer of the war was also memorable for the unwelcome company of head lice. They burrowed deeply into our dirty hair. We scratched and scratched. Mammie bought us very fine-toothed combs, and Herman and I combed each other's hair. Every morning, seated on a stool in the garden, we looked like monkeys in the zoo, counting each little critter, not bigger than a fleck of dust. Each louse was squashed between our fingernails. The soft sound when the tiny body snapped was deliciously satisfying.

At least we didn't have scabies like kids we saw around the local swimming pool. We were sorry when we mentioned it at home, because we couldn't go swimming for the rest of the summer. But when I saw huge tapeworms crawling out of my body one day when I went to the bathroom, I was filled with horror. They looked a mile long, at least three times the length of the worms the crows pulled out of my mother's flower border. Only then did I understand our parents' concerns. Tape worms, round worms, lice, I got to know them all that summer.

On the first Saturday in August, my father brought to Overa a map of Western Europe. With so many windows in the living room, he decided the only blank wall he could display the map on was in my parents' bedroom. We crowded in to watch him fasten it to the cement wall with *pleisters* (like band-aids). My mother produced different color threads and a pincushion. From a bunch of scrap papers Pappie read the names of places he knew the Allies had taken from listening to *Radio Oranje*. We still didn't know how and where he heard *Radio Oranje,* but we didn't ask. As he listed the names of towns and villages – Caen, Caumont, Avranches, Saint Malo, Rennes – Mammie pushed a pin at each point on the detailed map.

"What's the thread for?" I asked.

"To see how the armies are moving," Pappie said. "We still don't know which way they want to go. They're having a hard time breaking out of their beachhead."

"Could the Germans push them back into the sea?" Hans asked.

"I don't think so."

In the weeks that followed we crowded around the map every night as soon as Pappie came back home with names. Mammie had to get more pins to keep up. By the twelfth of August, Brittany had been secured and a new invasion, this time from the Mediterranean Sea, was launched. Mammie put a pin on Saint Tropez. Carefully studying the map, Pappie concluded the Allies were pushing toward Germany from three sides: through Italy, the south of France, and through the middle of France. Holland and Belgium had to wait. That's what it looked like.

At the beginning of our summer vacation, I'd pushed thoughts of war, of men dying on beaches, as far out of my mind as I could, but as I saw on the map how the Allies were fighting their way toward Germany, I got as excited as my parents. They had made the progress visible.

One day, on our way back to Overa after a dentist appointment with Oom Henri, my brothers and I came upon a crowd. An accident? A large, open truck with a swastika sign painted on the side stood parked in the middle of a square, het van Coothplein. A German soldier with a gun slung over his shoulder was checking a *stamkaart*. Men in civilian clothes stood in a line with soldiers behind them, their guns pointed at the men.

We got off our bicycles and mingled with the crowd.

"A *razzia*," Hans whispered to me. My brothers kept me between them.

"What will they do?" I whispered.

"They're looking for Jews. Or they'll send men to work in Germany."

We stood close by, facing the row of men, all of them young. The German checking *de stamkaart* shouted like a barking dog. One very young man, the age of my cousins, was called forward to show his *stamkaart*. His blue eyes blazed with defiance. He held his body perfectly erect, as if he wanted to tower over the soldier. They were of equal size. The German hardly looked at his identification card. Shoved toward the truck bed with the butt of a gun against his ribcage, the young man was forced to climb in.

"Let's get out of here," Herman said.

We jumped on our bicycles and sped away, and almost bumped an elderly man off his feet. He was hurrying around the corner to signal a young man who was approaching on the sidewalk. The young man immediately turned on his heels and raced into a side street.

We spurted down the Wilhelmina straat, faster than we needed to. Adrenaline pumped our pedals. When we reached the Baronielaan we slowed down.

"What will they do to him?" I finally burst out.

"He didn't look like a Jew to me," Hans said. "They'll probably make him work in Germany, unless he works for the Underground."

"How will his family know?"

"Maybe there was somebody in the crowd who knew him."

"But if there wasn't, how will they know?"

"They'll hear about the *razzia.* News like that travels fast."

Except for the early days of the war when we'd had to flee, what I knew about the occupation had come to me indirectly. I'd overheard many adult discussions, and of course Germans were all around. The lack of food and clothing was real, but being thrust into the role of witness brought me painfully close to what others suffered. The two men, one a soldier, the other maybe a student, both of the same age, same height and with the same blue eyes preyed on my mind. The one in uniform had clearly won. Just because he had a gun and a swastika sign on the buckle of his belt. It seemed it was all he needed for barking like a dog, for poking a man in his ribs. For taking Carrie away.

I came home with many questions.

"What right did he have to take that man?"

"He was following orders," Mammie said.

"Couldn't the soldier just look the other way?"

"When you wear a uniform you have to do what you're told by your commander. That includes arresting people."

"Who commands the commander?"

"Hitler. All the soldiers and officers have to swear allegiance to Hitler. Some are in love with the power of the uniform," Mammie said. "If you're not powerful yourself, it's tempting to borrow power from a uniform and a gun. Hitler empowers them."

Not all leaders were brutal like Hitler. Mammie used Queen Wilhelmina to illustrate proper authority and the color orange as its symbol. That was why people wanted to wear it in defiance. Our country, she assured me, would not allow a leader to turn into a runaway dictator like Hitler. Our Constitution would prevent it. Authority, Mammie stressed, needed to be balanced with humility, but arrogance often got in the way.

"And that," she said, "goes for all of us."

A week before it was time to head back to the city, Mammie could finally use thread to loop around the pinheads on the map of France to show how the Allies were advancing. We decided on the color orange for the advance toward the Seine. Red was chosen for the movements upward from Marseille, and blue for the advance through France's middle toward the infamous Siegfried Line along the Rhine River. That line extended from the German city of Trier to the Dutch city of Nijmegen.

We were beside ourselves when Paris fell on the twenty-fifth of August. Were Belgium and Holland next? My father reasoned the Allies would want to capture the harbors of Antwerp and Rotterdam so they could bring supplies to their troops. The advance from their beachhead in Normandy had been agonizingly slow, but now they were moving with the speed of a snowball rolling down a slope. Would we live to see the day Allied soldiers walked on de markt instead of Germans? Who would liberate us? English, Americans, Canadians?

When we packed up to go back to school, I went to say good-bye to Boer and Vrouw Jansen.

"See you after the war," I said and waved at them from my bicycle.

Had I known what was ahead, I probably would have cried. The next time I set foot in our house at Overa, I had my own baby in my arms. Boer Jansen's farm had been erased. A modern house had sprouted up on exactly the same spot, much like a mushroom appears after a good night's rain. The faithful workhorse was no longer part of the landscape. Neither were pigs and chickens. Saddest of all: I never saw Boer and Vrouw Jansen again. I hadn't realized how old they were when I was young. They had seemed ageless, full of energy, working, working, always working. For retirement, they went to live with one of their children in another town. They faded out of my life, but never out of my mind.

The reason we couldn't return to Overa had everything to do with the way the war developed. General Montgomery captured Antwerp on September fourth, as my father had predicted. Securing the estuary of the Schelde River, however, took a long and hard fight. Belgium was on one side of the river, Holland on the other. The Germans made a stand at the island of Walcheren in Holland. They'd used the four years of our occupation to dig bunkers in the dunes. Walcheren had been turned into a fortress. With German guns aimed at the river, no Allied ship could get through.

The island is shaped like a saucer. Sandy dunes constitute the rim. The hinterland is low and fertile, dotted with prosperous farms. But at the western edge, at Westkapelle, was a gap where a dike one hundred feet wide and thirty feet high held the sea back. A garrison of about 10,000 Germans was entrenched behind it. In early October, the RAF struck a hole in the dike and created a gap four hundred yards wide. The salty water of the sea streamed in and inundated the low-lying land. The German defense behind the dunes was flooded, but so was the rich farmland. It took till November third before Walcheren became allied territory. History would record the battle as one of the toughest the Allies encountered in Europe, with 27,633 casualties, more than it had taken to capture Sicily.

When the island was flooded, the farmers were stranded on the top of their roofs. They took what they could carry of their belongings and rowed eastward, toward our city of Breda. For many years, ribbons of salt lay in the furrows of the rich clay and made the island look like a poorly decorated cake. My parents offered our house at Overa to one of the many displaced families. Not long after they were resettled a terrible storm in 1954 broke through the gap at Westkapelle again. It was a replay of what had happened nine years earlier. A second flow of refugees streamed eastward and another family took up residence in our house at Overa.

My parents didn't take possession of Overa again until 1960, when I had already lived in America for three years.

Chapter 18

- **September 5, 1944: General Patton's Third Army crosses the Mosel River in Germany.**
- **September 17, 1944: Operation "Market Garden" is launched to make a bridgehead over the Rhine River at Arnhem, the Netherlands.**

The war was all we could think about now. Entering my new school was a non-event, and learning Latin was no match for the excitement of moving threads on the map of Europe. If Antwerp had been taken, then Breda could be next. Antwerp was barely two hours away. My father came upstairs from de apotheek at night with news that moved the pins ahead, closer and closer to us. The Allies' march through Belgium had been more like an army exercise than a real war. After Paris fell, the Germans went on the run. Their losses were catastrophic. Several of their commanders had died. General Rommel was seriously wounded. Like a broom the Allies pushed their enemies ahead of their advance.

When I came out of school on Tuesday, the fifth of September, a crowd had gathered in front of the building. I cringed at the idea of having to witness another *razzia*, so I waited for Hans. Our school was located on a canal. All eyes, we saw, were fixed on the other side of the water. The silence was eerie.

Herman, whose school was next to ours, was in the crowd. Hans, Herman and I ran over to the bridge to get a closer look. Disheveled German soldiers walked by us: dirty, their uniforms unbuttoned and torn, somber and silent as if in a funeral procession. I thought back to the beginning of the war, how beaten we'd felt returning to Breda from the evacuation. I almost felt sorry for these soldiers. Tired horses pulled farmers' wagons, stuffed with household goods, a far cry from the day the soldiers had driven into our city in tanks and pantzerwagens, the victors.

German soldiers, stationed in Breda, stood among us to look at the sorry retreat of their comrades. They were as bewildered as we were. It was hard not to laugh out loud when a soldier came by pushing a baby carriage filled with pots and pans, but we didn't dare make a fool of him. A cornered cat will scratch, Mammie had warned us.

I couldn't stop looking at the faces. Taken together they were a beaten army, but individually their defeat took on a tragic air. Had it been worth it to fight for the Führer? Their country was being bombed every night. Was anything left standing that would make it worthwhile to return to? What had happened to their families while they fought at the front?

Women walked among the soldiers. Children even. Goats. Dogs. This was an army without weapons. These were soldiers on crutches, or with an arm in a dirty sling, or with bloody bandages wrapped around wounds. I was torn between compassion and ebullience. Being small, I'd wormed my way to the front of the crowd to be close to this fantastic parade. I could see their boots hit the cobblestones. Click, click. Muddied and worn. Very tired boots.

An old Renault truck, probably confiscated along the way, came by. A bandaged soldier on a gurney lay on its bed. His leg was in a splint and a bandage was wound around his head. Only his blue eyes were showing. The truck crept along to keep pace with the walkers. The soldier made eye contact with me, as if he was beyond shame, unlike the others who looked down at the cobblestones. In that split second the true picture of war drove itself into me. Hurting and getting hurt, that's what it was all about. Every time we moved a pin on Europe's map, people had died, got wounded, lost their home and God knows what else.

Watching these beaten soldiers brought home how unfair making war is. As Mammie said, these soldiers had acted on the authority of a horrible man. I hated Hitler for what he'd done to us and to his own people. Yet at the same time, I hoped we would be liberated, even if it took more suffering. We deserved to be free. Four-and-a-half years of brutal occupation had brought nothing but loss. But I didn't dare think about what suffering it would take to set us free.

When we got home and told about what we'd seen, Mammie ordered us not to go back to the canal. Later we heard shots. Frustrated Germans had shot randomly at bystanders who'd snickered at the retreating troops.

The fifth of September 1944 would go down in Dutch history as *Dolle Dinsdag*, Crazy Tuesday. Pappie said the soldiers had been given orders to present themselves in Breda for regrouping. *Sammelstelle*, it was called in German. Instead they'd asked local people for directions toward the East, toward their *Heimat*. Never mind regrouping.

My father told us that *Radio Oranje* had broadcast that Breda was now in Allied hands. Of course, we only had to look out the window to know we were not liberated. Germans still walked on de markt. But stories circulated about Nazi sympathizers, NSBers, and German military in other towns who'd also listened to the broadcast and who had decided to flee. It took a week for our occupiers to reestablish their authority over their own and over us.

On September 17, 1944, the sun sparkled on the tile roof of the city hall and there wasn't a cloud to throw a shadow. Just home from school, sitting with a cup of tea in front of our living room window, I noticed that people on de markt stood as if nailed to the sidewalk and staring at the sky. Even Germans soldiers. I ran downstairs and joined them. The air was saturated with a steady drone. A German officer came out of our neighbor's barbershop and said to no one in particular, *"Ach mein lieber Gott, was ist los?"* Like an invasion of noisy sparrows, bombers with gliders in tow blanketed the brilliant blue sky. They were headed in a northeasterly direction, leaving white vapor trails. Small white puffs of smoke from German anti-aircraft artillery surrounded some planes, but the steel blanket that was being pulled over our heads seemed impenetrable.

The constant humming drowned out all other sound. When the last one had passed over, it turned eerily quiet. Then they came back, this time without the gliders.

We were as dumbstruck as the biblical shepherds must have been when the sky opened and the angel Gabriel appeared. Was this a sign the war would soon be over? Where had the gliders been dropped and what was in them? Soldiers? Guns? Ammunition? We all agreed it was the most mysterious sight we'd seen during the war.

At the breakfast table the next morning, my father told us that what we'd seen was called Operation Market Garden. Three Airborne divisions had been dropped at Arnhem, a Dutch city on the Rhine. My father had disappeared the night before after supper for an hour or so, as he did every evening. Where to we didn't know and we'd learned not to ask. But he always came back with news about the war.

A few days after Operation Market Garden began, my father came home from his nightly outing looking as white as a ghost.

"My God, Gerard, what happened?" my mother asked.

"All pharmacists have to report to the headquarters of the *Grüne Polizei* tomorrow," he said.

"Where did you hear that?' Mammie asked.

"Over the radio."

"What do they want from pharmacists?"

"Bring us to Germany."

Not at any time during the war had I seen my father so distraught. He paced up and down the living room, naming all the things he'd have to do before leaving. We stood frozen in fear and panic, except my mother. She amazed me when she, as if she didn't care, slipped out of the room while Pappie started to feverishly write down orders for the pharmacy assistants.

Fifteen minutes later there was a knock on the door. The door opened and there was Mammie with our neighbor, the barber.

"Mijnheer Bakx has a message for you, Gerard," she said.

Mijnheer Bakx, usually a jolly, friendly man, looked most uncomfortable.

"It was only a joke, Mijnheer Wetselaar."

"A joke!"

"Mijnheer Sol rigged the wires. The message you heard over the radio was read into the microphone in the next room by his son."

"What?" my father cried out.

"I'm sorry, Mijnheer Wetselaar, but it was just a joke. We didn't think you'd take it seriously."

So, that was where he went every night! To Mijnheer Sol, who had a hardware store around the corner? Through the network of alleys behind our house, Pappie could walk over there without being seen. He had brought our radio there and they'd hidden it behind boxes with hammers and nails. Mammie, of course, knew he went there every evening to listen to the BBC with the barber, the printer, the baker, the fish store owner, the liquor store owner and the inn keeper, the neighbors in our city block. She also knew the Germans didn't give orders like that over the radio. They picked people up from the street or hauled them out of their homes.

My father opened a bottle of *jenever* – the Dutch gin he brewed in his own laboratory – and they laughed their fears away into the night.

September was birthday month for three members of our family: both of my parents and Herman. The war was the only topic at the birthday party that year. The adults sat around in a wide circle in our living room and commiserated about the ill fate of the airdrop at Arnhem. The weather had turned bad. The Allies had not succeeded in making a bridgehead over the Rhine.

My brothers and I served whatever snacks my mother had been able to come up with to go with my father's laboratory *jenever.* We soon got bored. Herman took up his favorite pastime of marching up and down our long corridor with his air gun slung over his shoulder. Hans entertained me with stories about English parachutists. Kids at school had seen planes being shot down in the area. The pilots had bailed out of their planes. Others had been dropped as spies. It was a problem for the farmers because the Germans had made it clear they would kill on the spot anyone who hid a parachutist.

"Do you know of anybody who's hiding one?" I asked.

"Are you kidding? The Germans would kill him if they found out!"

"If you knew, would you tell me?"

"You'd be the last person I would tell," Hans said.

"Thanks!"

The idea of English soldiers crawling around the woods and fields near our city was fascinating.

"I wonder what English soldiers look like," I mused.

"People say they wear leather jackets and leather caps."

That gave me a thought. I ran downstairs. Next to my father's office was a coat rack. Behind his winter coat and his raincoat hung the leather jacket he'd used on his motorcycle before the war. I opened a drawer of the antique closet in the entrance hall and underneath some tennis rackets found his leather cap with a fur lining. Goggles lay next to it. I called Hans and Herman. Together we sneaked into de apotheek. We found a cork and located a box of matches. Hans burned the top of the cork and with the black end we created a moustache on Herman's slightly fuzzy upper lip. He'd just turned fourteen and was tall for his age, already taller than my father. The leather coat fit him well. He pulled on the cap and then the goggles. We didn't know what English soldiers looked like, but nobody else did either. We could have fun with this. I was chosen to go into the living room and take my father aside.

I took a deep breath and opened the door. The cacophony of voices rushed over me as if I'd let hot air out of an oven. I tapped my father on the shoulder and whispered in his ear.

"Pappie, there's an English parachutist in the hallway. He came through the alley. What do we do?"

His body stiffened under my hand. He jumped up and followed me out. There stood Herman: tall, erect and unrecognizable behind his goggles and under the tight-fitting cap.

My father took a long look and we saw his brain working furiously. He looked Herman up and down twice, and then his gaze rested on the leather coat. After a second he burst into laughter, but quickly stifled it.

"Herman, you look terrific," he said. "Stand by the door until I motion you to come in. Don't say a word or they'll know who you are." Herman didn't speak English, of course.

Pappie went through the door of the adjoining dining room and left it open. He managed to get everyone's attention. An awesome silence sank into the room, as if someone had turned off a loud radio. He explained the situation and motioned for Herman to come forward. A gasp. Silence. My uncle,

Oom Henri, was the first one to recover his wits and asked Herman a question in English.

"Where are you from?"

Herman didn't say a word. The question was repeated. No answer.

The uneasiness in the room was audible. Chairs creaked as bodies shifted around in them. My mother startled everyone by getting up and walking over to Herman. She took a good look at him and undid the cap's chinstrap.

"Hallo, Herman!" she said.

The guests laughed until they cried.

It was obvious that Pappie had talked about the joke his neighbors had played on him a few nights earlier, because the conversation quickly veered to a scheme for revenge. Oom Henri told Herman all he had to do to speak make-believe English was talk Dutch as if he had a hot potato in his mouth. Nobody would notice the difference, he said. The gin and the relief worked wonders. By the end of the party the scheme had been well honed.

The next day, when it was time to listen to *Radio Oranje* over the BBC at the hardware store, Herman followed our father through the back alley. We'd all had a hand in dressing him up. Mammie had fashioned an impressive fake moustache and pasted it on. She taught him a few phrases in English. We debated if he should take his air gun, but Hans said that parachutists were unarmed. Herman stuck my father's pre-war passport in the pocket of the leather coat for identification.

They left. Finally, it seemed like forever, they stumbled up the back stairs. It had worked! Herman had worried beforehand that he would be recognized right off. However, at the sight of him in his parachutist outfit, the radio friends had panicked.

My father had explained to them that this man had shown up in our back alley and that he'd given him shelter for the last twenty-four hours, but now he wanted their advice on what to do with him. Did anybody have a good idea? The other men were stunned into silence. Was Mijnheer Wetselaar sure he was English? one asked. My father turned to Herman and asked him something in English. Herman made some of his "English sounds." However, none of the others spoke English so they couldn't verify his accent.

"Mijnheer Wetselaar, how can you be sure he's not a German spy in disguise?" the baker asked. At that moment the young man who'd rigged the radio and spoken the joke-message into the microphone turned white. Herman told us he actually had foam on his lips. Pappie asked Herman to identify himself. Herman produced his father's passport. Everyone gathered in a circle around Herman. The looks on their faces attested to their panic, and the pressure got too much for the young man. He fainted.

In English, Pappie asked Herman again to show his identification. Herman opened it up to the page where my father's picture was. Nobody recognized it.

The neighbors had become very frightened, shifting around nervously, wringing their hands, each waiting for the person next to him to speak first. How could they be sure they weren't walking into a terrible trap? Even if this man was indeed a genuine English parachutist and not a German spy, what were they going to do with him?

Pappie asked Mijnheer Bakx, the barber, to step forward. He came up to Herman, who told us later he was beginning to feel very uncomfortable. Pappie took the passport out of Herman's hand and brought it right up to the barber's nose.

Silence.

To my father's utter amazement, Mijnheer Bakx still didn't recognize the picture. Pappie gave him a while. Then he pointed his finger at the picture. Everybody had crowded around them. Very slowly, a look of recognition came over the barber's face, but also disbelief. He looked at my father, then at Herman, but not until my father did what my mother had done, undoing the chin strap and removing the cap, did the man realize he was looking at the boy whose hair he clipped once a month. He'd thrown back his head and laughed uncontrollably.

Chapter 19

- **October 2, 1944: The Polish Underground Forces surrender to the Germans in Warsaw.**
- **October 21, 1944: The German city of Aachen falls into Allied hands after a bitter fight.**

Operation Market Garden had failed. The casualties ran into the thousands, and for the people who lived close to the river it had been a nightmare. Their homes were in shambles. For miles around windows were shattered. Most people upped and left their ruins to find shelter elsewhere. I found it depressing to stand in front of the map in the boys' room and not be able to move threads and pins like we had toward the end of August. Closer to their own country, the Germans were putting up a hard fight. Liberation wasn't as near as we'd hoped. Yet there were signs Breda wasn't forgotten. Every night bombers flew over – we'd gotten used to that – but Breda hadn't been the target. This changed. In preparation for taking our city, the Allies needed to demolish vital railroad crossings. Breda was like a spider in the center of her web of roads and rails, linking the ocean to the hinterland and the north to the south. Belgium was practically our backyard and any troops wanting to cross the wide rivers just north of us would have to come through our city.

The first time the alarm went off we were at the dining room table. Oma Ament had moved in with us, because my parents wanted her to be under the same roof when the fighting started, like we'd been at the beginning of the war. The routine of what to do when the sirens sounded had been drilled into us: run to the long corridor to the kitchen and lean against the wall. The walls might still be standing after a direct hit and there were no windows that could shatter.

When the sirens started to wail, we pushed our chairs back and ran. Oma first. Herman and I last. The sirens had gone from a low wail to full blast, an enervating, high-pitched sound, by the time we passed the stairway. Since we were last, Herman and I looked at each other for just a moment and then, instead of following the others to the corridor, we ran up the stairs to the attic, and out the door to the roof garden. From there we worked ourselves via the gutters onto the flat roof that topped our house. Three stories separated us from the cobblestones below. The screaming sirens, only one block away on top of a department store, pierced our eardrums. Moments later – we were still out of breath from climbing up the roof – three small bombers swooped over us like swallows catching flies. We clearly saw a white star painted on the underside of each wing. We'd never seen this sign before, but we knew German planes bore the swastika. Their bellies opened and bombs fell onto the railroad station, barely a mile to the north. It was a spectacular sight, the explosions loud and terrifying, over in less than a minute. The planes pulled away with their wings dipping into a sharp curve. We could see flames and smoke rise up. So much damage in such a short time, it was awesome.

We didn't find a welcoming committee when we came back down. Mammie stood at the bottom of the staircase, fuming. Herman and I got house arrest for the entire weekend and a load of algebra problems to solve. We didn't care. It had been worth it.

Over the next few weeks, we could hear the war move closer. In the distance, artillery fire rumbled like an approaching thunderstorm. It was time to make preparations for when the fighting would break out in Breda. Workmen came to slash openings through the brick walls that had separated the various cellars in our city block since the thirteenth century. It was a tedious and dusty job to connect to our neighbors on both sides. When it was done, my father said he could walk a circle underneath our entire block, but he wouldn't allow us to do it. Only in case of emergency, he said. After the openings were made – large enough for a child to walk through – tree trunks were placed in our cellars to support the floors in case the house above came down.

My mother outfitted one of our cellars for living, the other one as an improvised toilet and washing up area. The shelves that ordinarily stored the medicine bottles were converted to sleeping bunks. Other shelves groaned under rows of canned vegetables. The propane gas stove and our mattresses were brought from Overa. Big bottles with drinking water stood waiting for us. We were ready to be liberated.

Around the middle of October, we heard a very strange roar during the night. I was in bed and tightened into a ball under the covers. This was definitely not a plane. But if not a plane, what? The next day, Pappie came home with the answer: the Germans had started their attack on the harbor of Antwerp with their latest invention called the V II. It was a self-propelled bomb, programmed to go off at a set distance. As long as it made its whistling, roaring sound it would keep going. When it stopped, it would come down in a count of six and explode.

Every night, I lay petrified as soon as I heard the roar, clutching my blanket and praying for the whistling not to stop. But it stopped more than once. Around our home at Overa, which was in a direct line with Antwerp, were several craters, and one night almost all the windows were broken. A friendly farmer came to the city to describe what had happened. After we the liberation Pappie went over to see the damage. The house looked frightening, he said, without windows and glass shards strewn about, inside and out. It took a long time before it could be repaired because glass was scarce as a result of the war.

Up to this point we'd led relatively normal lives: we went to school, my father worked, my mother ran the household. We played with friends. People came to visit. But after Crazy Tuesday, the day we watched the German army retreat through our city, the familiar pattern fell apart. It took more time and energy to do ordinary chores like laundry without decent soap; or to buy anything. First we had to stand in line to receive coupons for everything we needed – from food to fuel to textiles – and then to shop for these items. Mammie divided tasks. Hans, Herman and I took turns standing in line at the grocery store, armed with the coupons and a large leather shopping bag. Two or three people at a time were let in to get orders filled. It took forever to have the flour, the sugar, the lard carefully weighed and packaged.

Although our grocery store was around the corner from the SS Headquarters, standing in line for hours was the way to find out what was going on in town. People were less afraid to talk than they had been at the beginning of the war.

"Did you hear what happened last night? Twenty-one were executed at de Vloeiweide! On the spot! Worked for the Underground, of course. Some bastard betrayed them."

The news traveled down the line. Somebody else had seen a group of English soldiers, POWs, being marched through de Ginnekenstraat. They wore a uniform the color of sand, or maybe more like pea soup. Yet another knew somebody who'd seen a strange-looking vehicle with a white star painted on the hood. Thus we passed the hours, waiting our turn, shuffling forward inch by inch on shoes that hadn't seen new soles in years. We were beyond apologizing for the way we looked or the way we smelled. The lack of soap was quite evident. I was wearing a boy's jacket over a cotton dress made from one of my mother's before-the-war dresses. My neighbor in line, a gentleman with an old felt hat, had elbow patches on his faded raincoat.

During lunch hour one day when it was my turn to stand in line at the grocery store, the sirens went off. Instant panic. A man with an armband on his overcoat – he looked like an official – tried to herd us across the street and told us to get inside a house and stand against the wall. At the same time, I heard airplanes screaming toward our street. The SS Headquarters! The man with the official armband grabbed my wrist and pulled me over to a house, but I worked myself loose. All I could think of was that I would get buried under the rubble. The roar of the airplanes became louder. I ran into the middle of the street. I heard bombs explode, then I heard screams from inside the houses behind me. I ran as fast as I could toward the end of the street. Out of breath I fell into my father's arms, then jumped on the luggage carrier of his bike and put my arms around his waist as he raced away from the scene. It all happened so fast, I didn't even question how my father could have been there, at the right spot at the right time, but he'd grabbed his bicycle when the sirens went off, knowing where I was. He must have flown.

The SS Headquarters were hit, but so were the homes across from the grocery store, the very ones the well-meaning man had wanted me to go into for shelter…

This picture reminds me of the bombardment I witnessed. Courtesy of NIOD.

The next time the sirens went off, I was home. Herman and I knew better than to climb on the roof again. My instincts told me to run outside, but I did what I was told: stand against the wall of the kitchen corridor. Oma stood between Hans and Herman. Mammie wrapped her arms around me. I tightened against her solid body. Planes were screeching overhead and all the while the sirens blared. My mother's hand stroked my hair with amazing calm and assurance, as if that alone would keep harm away. I felt her marvelous confidence and clung to it the way I had when I was sick. The planes roared, and we heard bombs explode at some distance.

This time, the English pilots miscalculated. Instead of hitting the living quarters of the German Army Commander, they bombed the nursing home adjacent to it. Twenty-nine residents died. Oma's sister, Tante Anna Halbertsma, was one of the surviving residents. My parents arranged for her to live in *het Diaconessenhuis*, the hospital where I'd survived my blood poisoning and where the young Jewish boy whiled away his days in hiding.

It seemed as if we'd been placed under a shower head that kept pouring out shocking events. At each meal my father dished out more stories than my mother could dish out food. The Germans were becoming hysterical, he said. They entered homes and ordered people to give up their blankets. The very last passenger cars on the road were taken and converted into transport vehicles by cutting off the back half, so six soldiers could sit in the trunk. Obviously, they were preparing for their getaway. The big bell of the Catholic Church on de Baronielaan was lowered to the street and hauled off to be turned into bullets. People were digging holes in their backyards to hide their brass candlesticks, another item on the Germans' wish list. A curfew was ordered. After six o'clock we weren't allowed on the streets and at night the electricity got cut off.

Back when we had returned from Overa after our summer vacation, my brothers and I found the door to the guestroom locked. At first, we were convinced the radio was behind that locked door, but then we found out it was hidden at the hardware store. Our guestroom, we were finally told, had been turned into a depot of vital medical supplies for all of Western Brabant. Ever since the Allies landed in Normandy, my father had been spiriting away medicines and bandaging materials from de apotheek to upstairs. Since the Germans took whatever they could put their hands on, my father had set aside drugs like insulin and digitalis for when there would be a shortage. It was his contribution to the work of the Underground.

On one of the last days before the fighting began around our city, a friendly German officer warned Pappie de apotheek would be raided within hours. Like Herr Von der Hoevel, he was an enlisted man but not a Nazi. When we came home from school to have lunch, we found everyone in a panic. We were told to stuff our school bags, our rucksacks and bicycle bags with as much bandaging material and medicines as we could carry. Pappie warned us to bring them only to people we could trust.

Where would I bring these precious things, I wondered out loud. Never mind, Herman said, get on your bike and go! We sped away and peddled through the streets where SS troops, who'd recently arrived in town as reinforcement, were guarding important intersections and setting up machine guns in dark alleys. Our bulging bags were so obviously not filled with schoolbooks that we decided to go our separate ways. I'd been furiously thinking about all the people I knew I could trust and who lived close by. My instincts led me to the house of Mimi van Hoegaarden, a classmate at my new school. Our parents were good acquaintances. I liked her mother a lot. She seemed like a sensible person, too down-to-earth to belong to the NSB. That's where I went. Mevrouw van Hoegaarden immediately understood the dilemma and wasted no time. She emptied my bags and sent me off to get more.

I never made it back that day. A German officer had just arrived when I returned home. He demanded to be brought to every room in the house. My mother was showing him around while my father was keeping another officer occupied in de apotheek. On this unusual tour of our home, I walked a few steps behind my mother. I couldn't believe my eyes when I saw Oma Ament in bed in the room where the assistant on night-duty usually slept. There wasn't much furniture in it, just a chair and a stand with a washing basin. Oma lay in the wide, old-fashioned bed that featured heavy mahogany boards at both ends. She wore a crocheted bonnet over her sparse hair.

"Who is this?" the German officer asked. His tone was threatening and I shrank.

"This is my mother. She is sick with tuberculosis," my mother said.

The officer turned on his heels and left the room with my mother in tow. Every German soldier dreaded contagious diseases. I stayed behind and looked at Oma who put her fingers to her lips, warning me to be quiet. From the gleam in her eyes I could tell she was about to burst into laughter. As soon as we heard the officer's boots descend the back stairs and the door to the laboratory slam shut, she motioned me to come over to the bed.

"Feel my cap," she whispered.

I put my hand over her cap. Hard things were inside of it.

"What's in there, Oma?" I asked.

In a last desperate attempt to hide things, Mammie had suggested they put Oma in bed and stuff as much as possible around her body under the covers and the most crucial vials with injectables inside her bonnet. Not enough time was left for Oma to climb the stairs to her own room. The pharmacy assistant's bedroom had been the closest. Oma told me all this with a wicked smile on her beautiful face. She'd enjoyed the whole charade.

Downstairs, meanwhile, my father had to part with an antique pharmaceutical scale, a beauty with brass scales hanging from delicate chains and encased in an exquisitely crafted mahogany closet. It broke his heart to see it go out the door under the arm of a German officer, but he realized the German wasn't going to leave empty- handed. Better a scale than all the medicines.

Twenty years after the war was over and my friend's family moved to another house, bandages and medicine I'd brought there were found in their attic behind a wall. My brothers and I had tried to remember where we'd brought what, but so much happened in the days that followed that neither the trusted friends nor we knew exactly in what secret places the stuff had been stowed.

Chapter 20

- ❖ **October 12, 1944: German troops evacuate Athens, Greece.**
- ❖ **October 22, 1944: Operation "Pheasant" is put into motion. British and Canadian troops cross the border between Belgium and Holland.**

A few days after the German visit to de apotheek, we had another scare. For an hour – or maybe it seemed that long because it was so terrifying – we sat in the living room as far away from the windows as we could, covering our ears. *Boom! Boom!* No sirens. No low flying aircraft, just one explosion after another. When it was over, the sidewalks on de markt were littered with shards of glass. Some stores around us had had all of their windows blown out, others not one. Sound waves had moved like hard ivory billiard balls through the streets, bouncing off from this side, and then that side, leaving a curious pattern of broken glass. De apotheek was spared, but a fancy curved window at a clothing store had become a pile of sharp-edged debris. The Germans had blown up their ammunition depot at the airport near Gilze-Rijen.

On October 27, the *Ortskommandant*, the *Grüne Polizei* and the *Sicherheitsdienst* packed up after ruling our city for four-and-a-half years. We would have loved to see the SS depart as well, but they stayed to defend the inner city.

From my room that evening, I looked up at the cathedral. She'd been brought about by thousands of God-fearing hands. Was it her inner serenity that made her stand so tall and incorruptible? During the Inquisition, citizens had stormed her in fury and smashed her prized art inside. It had disgraced her, but it had not taken her down. Tall and slender, she stood as a symbol of survival, rising above the human strife around her foundation. Living in her shadow had shaped my sense of reverence.

But then, I had the sudden devastating insight that this beautiful cathedral didn't stand there just by the grace of God, but because planes with bombs hadn't yet been invented when other wars raged. If she were to be bombed, those carved stones would crash down on us. In my Latin class we'd translated a story about a man being stoned. I'd asked what that meant. "Being killed by stones," the teacher answered.

I didn't dare speak this scary thought or ask for reassurance from my mother. My parents were very preoccupied these days. Conversations were whispered between them, with Mammie's voice the soothing one and my father acting nervous and distracted. It was many, many years later – I was already married – when I found out from Herman what my father had been so upset about in those weeks. On Crazy Tuesday, the 5th of September, the Underground in our area had brazenly arrested eighty prominent collaborators and German officers, convinced the end of the war was near and they would simply pass them onto the Allies. As it turned out, the Allies had their hands full with securing Antwerp's harbor and regrouping after the failure at Arnhem. Breda had to wait.

For the Underground to hide their "catch" in our city, under the nose of the *Grüne Polizei*, was dangerous. They transported their captives to the Biesbosch, a network of waterways and inlets that were part of the great rivers. There they put them on a boat and anchored it in a cove. As the liberation wasn't as close at hand as they'd hoped and it became harder and harder to feed those eighty men and maintain order aboard, the Underground approached my father and begged him to provide a lethal dose to kill them all. It was a lot to ask. Their dilemma was clear, but to kill prisoners of war was against the rules of the Geneva Convention. Above all, my father had never killed more than a fly in his life. He decided not to fill their request, but he agonized over who would be killed first: the POWs or the Underground workers. The liberation came in time. All eighty men were handed over to the Allies. Alive.

The rumble of artillery fire grew closer. Rumors that the Allies were closing in on Breda convinced my parents it was time to move to our shelter. We gathered the blankets from our beds, put underwear and sweaters in rucksacks, collected our toothbrushes and took one last look around our home. Before he left his room, Herman put a pin on the map and extended an orange thread from the Belgian border to our own city.

Mammie led the way into the cellar with a *knijpkat*, a flashlight that fit in the palm of her hand. I could not see her but I heard her kneading the small dynamo inside the gadget. Oma was right behind, resting one hand on Mammie's shoulder as her feet felt around for the uneven stone steps. Closing the door behind us had a dreadful finality to it. We'd turned ourselves into cave dwellers.

Pappie struck a match. Our dark shadows fell on the brick walls. As we moved, they moved, hovering over us like ghosts. The gas lamp, brought over from Overa, was lit and its familiar bluish-tinted light was reassuring, but its hissing sound echoed against the walls, as if we'd entered a well. The cellar had the same dank smell as the well Vrouw Jansen hauled her water from. Each of us was assigned a shelf for a place to sit, as well as to eat and sleep since we hadn't brought furniture. Mammie started to heat some of the canned vegetables in her makeshift kitchen while my father, never one to sit still for long, looked in on our neighbors. Oma Ament started to read to us from her shelf below, but we couldn't concentrate.

I climbed down from my bunk and peeked into the gap that led to the innkeepers' cellar. I didn't know those neighbors as well as the ones on the other side. The innkeeper and his wife huddled in the middle of their cellar around a lantern. The wife sat in her fur coat on a wooden kitchen chair, her hands fumbling with a rosary while she mumbled her prayers. When a shot sounded outside, she raised her voice –"Lord, have mercy" – as if to drown out the loud bang. For all the days and nights we spent in the cellars, she sat on her straight-backed chair and prayed.

My father came back from his patrol and I overheard him saying that Mevrouw Bakx, the barber's wife, was very pregnant. They'd asked for his help in case the baby came.

To save on gas and candles we went to sleep. The adults had taken the wider bunks below, the children the upper ones. These must be the storage shelves for the smallest bottles, I thought, as I wedged myself between the plank and the curve of the brick arch above me. Wrapped up in our blankets and being cautious not to move, we looked like Egyptian mummies. We listened to the rumbling of heavy artillery in the distance and the scurrying feet of a family of rats whose space we had invaded. It was cold and damp in the cellar and I was glad I'd kept my sweater on. It was my favorite one, worn out at the elbows and the sleeves too short for me, but still my favorite. I willed my mind to travel to Overa. Herman had described how, when he'd biked over once after we'd left there, he'd seen that the Germans had used our lawn to build a *tobruk*, a round platform for a machine gun. Rather than imagining how they would shoot at Allies, exposed in the open fields while they themselves were protected by the pine trees around our house, I let my thoughts wander to the early morning hours of summer when I had been present for the wonder of the rising sun, for when its first rays refracted the night's dampness and veiled the fields. I let my mind gorge on the sounds of waking birds, on the promise of the day, on the growth of juicy strawberries protected by tough leaves. Finally, I slept.

Narrow strips of light filtered in through the cracks around the steel bulkhead. We'd made it to another day. No footsteps could be heard on the sidewalk above, no familiar traffic noises. The city lay in wait. The constant rumbling of artillery fire drew closer. From which direction? We couldn't tell for sure. To pass the time Hans fashioned a table out of planks, spreading them over a few large wicker bottles, and started a game of Monopoly. He'd brought his favorite game with him. We found crates to sit on, but we didn't get very far into the game. Just a few houses and one hotel had been placed on the board when we heard a loud bang from nearby. We quickly crowded together on one bunk, straining to hear the sounds of airplane engines. We heard none.

"They say the Americans bomb a city before they move in," my father said. "The British use artillery. God, I hope we're being liberated by the British!"

When no more loud explosions were heard, Pappie went over to the other cellars to see if anyone knew what was going on over our heads.

"The Germans blew up the bridge over *de singel*," he said when he returned.

"Which one?" Herman asked.

"The one at de Wilhelminastraat," Pappie said.

I gasped. That's where my friend Bertha Bicknese lived. Her father's pharmacy stood on the corner.

A second BOOM sounded.

"Must be the other bridge," Hans said.

Playing Monopoly was becoming too realistic. We swiped our opponent's houses off their lots, sent a player to jail. It was too close to what was going on in our own neighborhood. We switched to playing cards.

The fall of night blended itself with the day. Except for the hands of the clock we couldn't tell the difference. The following day, our third as cave dwellers, was announced by running feet outside. The iron under the heels of German boots clashed with the steel of our bulkhead. A familiar sound. The sound of artillery got closer to us.

"I wish they'd stop. I want to sleep," Hans said.

"Put your fingers in your ears," Herman said, and swung his long legs over the side of the bunk. He winked at me.

"I'll take a stroll."

"Where to?" Hans asked.

"First I'll go to the bathroom and wash up."

"We'll have breakfast in a minute," Mammie said.

"Don't worry, I'll be there. Think of it, I'm already dressed!"

"Don't you dare open the door, Herman," Pappie called after him.

Calling the other cellar a bathroom was a laugh. Mammie had sectioned off a part with a heavy curtain and placed a potty-chair in one corner and a large slop-jar next to it, as well as an old-fashioned basin on a crate for washing up. The slop-jar would hold for only a few days, and after that? We couldn't go upstairs to empty it. When challenged on the subject Mammie simply answered, *"Geen zorgen over de dag van morgen."* But as the smell from that section grew stronger we did worry about tomorrow and the day after. There was no telling how long we would have to stay down here.

Mammie ordered me to get some eggs out of storage. I reached my hands into the large brown crock holding Boer Jansen's eggs, afloat in white stuff that looked like wallpaper paste. It was called *waterglas.* In the darkness I couldn't tell the difference between the white of the eggshell and the preservative. Feeling around in the slimy paste felt like reaching directly into the chicken to steal her egg. But it was war and I washed the egg down with Pappie's surrogate tea and some claylike bread.

Mijnheer Bakx, the barber, ran in to tell Pappie the baby was announcing itself. What was he to do? Seeing that Pappie was in a panic at the thought of having to deliver a baby, Mammie immediately volunteered to go over. She'd brought three children into the world, she told Mijnheer Bakx. It should give her some authority.

Not to worry, she told us when she came back. The labor pains were just starting. How could she be so lighthearted, I wondered. The prospect of giving birth in a cellar without a doctor was enough to make me feel weak, but it only seemed to stimulate my mother to be the eye of the storm.

It was now noon on Sunday, the twenty-ninth of October. Terrifically loud explosions sounded as if they were happening directly above us. Gun smoke seeped through the cracks of the bulkhead and we heard stones crash onto the pavement. It was de markt's turn to be targeted. Mortars whistled outside and exploded nearby. We sat huddled together on Oma's bunk, silently, each mind racing through the possibilities: our home, the City Hall, or the cathedral, God forbid. I admired the foresight of my parents to put tree trunks, bark and all, in the cellar for support. They were a comfort while outside the world was being blown to bits. A frightful force was overwhelming us. We could hear and smell it, but we couldn't see it.

Again the rushing of feet, but this time not the harsh sound of iron scraping over the bulkhead. Yet we heard voices shouting in German, *"Kommen sie mal 'raus."* Who was shouting at whom? We didn't dare move.

Mijnheer Bakx came running in, breathing hard from pure excitement. "The Brits are here!"

We didn't dare believe him. Hadn't we just heard German voices? But our neighbor swore up and down he'd seen them himself. Pappie thanked him for the news, but he told us to stay put. "Snipers kill more people than bombs," he added.

At around three o'clock we heard what sounded exactly like what we remembered from the beginning of the war more than four years ago: the screeching of tanks over cobblestones. Pappie went around the block through the joined cellars to separate fact from rumor. He fell over his own words when he came back to tell us the tanks we'd heard belonged indeed to the Allies.

"They're still fighting, so we should stay put," he said, but I could tell he could barely contain himself. After an hour it became too much to just sit there. The great moment had arrived. Mammie and Oma went to sit with Mevrouw Bakx, whose labor pains were coming more frequently now. The rest of us ventured upstairs.

After living for three days in darkness, the light blinded us when Pappie opened the door. He stuck his head out, looked left and right into the long corridor that led to de apotheek. He motioned us to follow him. Gingerly he turned the handle on his office door. Everything seemed in order. We went up the staircase, expecting the worst, but not a window was broken in our entire house. Across the street the military tailor's shop had been hit. Heavy stitching machines lay spread out over the sidewalk as if they were toys a child had thrown down in a temper tantrum. We could see the sky through the devastated roof. Parts of it still clung helplessly to its sides. I ran to the window in my own room to check if the cathedral was still standing. She was, but had been hit in many places.

As we stood in front of the dining room window surveying the damage, a big Sherman tank came by. On top of it, in a blue overall, a helmet on his head and a gun in his hands, sat our own cousin Rob Wetselaar. We couldn't believe our eyes. So he was also part of the Underground…and that's why we hadn't seen him for quite a while! Oom Henry's children were a few years older than we were, except for Mietsie who was about my age. Mammie had often said: Small children, small worries; big children, big worries. I wondered where Bu and Liesje had disappeared to. They were the oldest children in that family and had evaporated from sight as well. Rob was eighteen years old and I was proud of my cousin, who looked like a hero to me. Later he told me he'd been ordered to show the Allies the way to the Military Academy.

Pappie told us to go downstairs and tell Oma and Mammie our house was still standing. As we turned to go, shots rang from the corner of de markt and de Veemarkt straat. We couldn't help it. We ran back to the window to see what happened. Two people lay dead on the cobblestones. Pappie yanked us away from the window.

"Snipers! Get back here! Quick."

Back in the cellar we gave our mixed report, but news had traveled even faster below the ground. Mijnheer Bakx said our liberators weren't British but Polish.

"Polish?"

"Yes, Polish. It says Poland on their uniforms. Those voices we heard outside were of Polish soldiers. They were cleaning the area of snipers."

"They didn't get them all," Hans said. "We saw two people shot."

"Those were Jews. Isn't that awful?" Mijnheer Bakx said. "They'd been hiding in that corner house for years. They got so excited, they ran out."

My head was spinning. Contrary feelings fought each other. So much news, so fast. I couldn't process it all. Our family was lucky. Our house stood. Those Jewish people were dead. Our neighbor's house across the street was shot to pieces. The cathedral still stood. We were rid of the Germans, or almost. Now we had Polish. What would it mean to live under Polish and British? How long would it take before we could go outside without being afraid?

Chapter 21

- ❖ **October 20, 1944: Belgrade, the capital of Yugoslavia, is liberated by Russian troops.**
- ❖ **November 9, 1944: The Allies drive the Germans over het Hollands Diep, north of Breda.**

After spending another night in the safety of the cellar, we couldn't stand to think of ourselves as scared rabbits any longer. We crawled out of our hole. Mammie had sat through the night with Mevrouw Bakx, whose labor pains had come more forcefully. A doctor was reached and Mevrouw Bakx delivered her baby in her own bed. Upstairs. In daylight.

Exhausted though she must have been, my mother mounted the staircase with a light tread and went directly to the chest where she'd kept our red, white and blue flag. Mothballs had guarded it for four-and-a-half years, dousing it in such thoroughly pervasive camphor smell that no moth had dared come close. Whenever I smell mothballs now, I remember how my mother ceremoniously flattened the wrinkles; how Pappie fastened the flag to the mast and lowered it out the window; how a mild breeze caught the heavy cloth and unfurled it gracefully; and how tears streamed down my mother's cheeks.

Below us on de markt, armored vehicles displaying a striking white star headed in the direction of the castle. Soldiers in black berets and pea soup-colored uniforms – later we learned that color was called khaki – tried to get people out of the way. The battle wasn't over yet, they warned. But the people danced and sang in the streets, grabbing every soldier they could get a hold of. Drowning out close artillery fire they sang, *"Oranje boven, Oranje boven, Leve de Koningin."* We joined in from the windows at the top of our lungs, serenading our Queen, the symbol of our country as we remembered it.

Our celebrating fervor was premature. In the center of the city as we were we didn't know about the fierce fighting in the outskirts. The SS troops battled with tenacity. They weren't about to give up. A lot was at stake for them. If the

Allies could drive them with their backs to the great rivers, the entire province of Brabant would be lost. On the first of November, the situation was still very critical, and while people danced under our windows on de markt, fifty of our citizens were killed by German artillery fire. Finally, after thirteen days of intense fighting, the Polish troops pushed the Germans over the widest part of the river at Moerdijk. When the losses were tallied up, 3,000 German prisoners had been taken and the Poles counted 800 wounded and 200 dead.

The eleventh of November, we learned, was Poland's National Independence Day. Having put the Germans at a comfortable distance, the Polish troops were ready for a moment of respite. The welcome in Breda had outdone anything they'd experienced on their long run from Normandy, they said. To celebrate their country and the hard-won victories, as well as to thank the city of Breda for its warm hospitality, they put on a parade.

The sidewalks were packed with Breda's citizens. Everywhere I looked, the color orange dominated. Faded silk ribbons were pinned onto worn-out winter coats or woven into braids. *Holland's glorie*, the red, white and blue flag joined with an orange banner, flew from homes and buildings, most looking like ours: wrinkled. The church bells that had escaped the German war machine rang for hours. Whatever was left of the carillon in the cathedral rang out national songs, and high up in the pepper shaker-like tip of its tower the streaming flags faced north, south, east and west. Child or adult, we were all intoxicated with the cleared air, with the triumphant ringing of the church bells, with the sight of our own national colors. Tears of joy for regained freedom, tears of sadness for those who hadn't lived to see it, flowed freely and mirrored the true meaning of this day. It was like attending a wedding and a funeral at the same time.

Our house on de markt was ideally situated for watching parades. From our first-row-place, we'd seen Dutch parades before the war and German parades during the occupation. But today, I didn't want to watch from a window. I wanted to feel the joy that foamed like a freshly opened bottle of champagne. I wanted to dance in the streets, join arms with all those celebrating strangers. My father, Herman and I stood on the sidewalk in de Eindstraat, packed in tight among an exhilarated crowd. Far down the street we heard the screeching of steel tracks on the cobblestones. All necks were craned in the same direction. I tried to look over the hats of gentlemen taller than I, and when that didn't work I wormed my way to the front. Herman and Pappie, who wasn't that much taller, had also worked themselves to the front by the time the first troop of soldiers came by who proudly carried their regimental colors up front. The Polish soldiers with helmets and in khaki battle dress stepped out smartly. Together they presented a picture of discipline. A very different one from the

Germans: no clicking of iron heels, no arrogant goose-stepping, no somber gray uniforms buttoned up to the neck under stiff collars.

Now the heavier materiel approached. Low tanks (Bren Gun Carriers, a man next to us said) headed the column. I was so excited, I waved at the helmeted men who stood proudly at attention in them. Suddenly, one tank stopped at exactly the spot where I was standing. I felt myself lifted up and put on the front of the tank. I looked up into the face of an officer. Under his helmet his blue eyes were filled with tears. He reached inside his breast pocket and pulled out a string of beads with a cross. He put it around my neck.

"For you," he said in English, and to my father, who was shocked at first, he said, "She looks just like my daughter."

He kissed me on both cheeks, and I was lowered to the pavement. Before I could thank him, the carrier had moved on. Dazed, I felt around for the beads. I'd seen a rosary in the hands of our neighbor, Mevrouw Mol, but I'd never held one.

The rest of the parade went by in a fog. With my heart beating furiously and too many thoughts swirling in my head for me to focus on the columns of soldiers that marched by, I had only one thought: go home and show Mammie this treasure.

Parade of Polish Brigade in Breda.

Pappie was just as excited as I was, and the three of us worked ourselves through the milling crowds, back to de markt. When Pappie told her the story and I showed her the rosary, Mammie took me in her arms and I could feel her thoughts. Here we were, liberated, all of us spared, our home undamaged, my father able to work. How did that compare with worrying about a wife and children who'd been thrown to the German and Russian wolves? How many times had this officer prayed with the rosary in his hands before going into battle? Had his wife given it to him as he left to fight the Germans in his homeland, before working his way to England so he could fight his way back? What had gone through his mind when he saw a girl in the crowd who looked like his own child?

Before going to bed that night, I examined my face in the mirror and wondered what that Polish officer had seen that caused him to cry. Mammie said it was my blond hair and my blue eyes, but most of all my high cheekbones. Even so, I was mystified. The rosary was beautiful, made of silver. How would he feel if he knew he'd given it to a Protestant girl who didn't know the right prayers? When I was at the small chapel that time when Martha hid on us with her buddies, several women had been praying with rosaries in their hands, but their words had been indistinct. Once in a while I heard "Hail Mary." That was all I could make out. The beads made me feel guilty. Should I learn to say the right prayers from Net? She was Roman Catholic. Her brother was even becoming a priest. Our whole family had visited Theo at the seminary where he was studying. The church was a miniature of the grand Saint Peter Church in Rome, a very impressive building. Tall candles burned on the marble altar, but a peculiar smell had put me off. I liked Theo, but I hadn't felt at home in his church.

I got into bed and took the rosary with me under the covers. How do I deal with this, I wondered. Maybe God didn't care whether I was Protestant or Catholic. I fumbled with the beads and asked God to keep the officer safe and to protect his soldiers and his family, especially his daughter. The next morning, I woke up with the beads on my pillow.

The bed I woke up in wasn't my own. My room had been given to Lieutenant Leftley, the boys' room to Captain Binns, both British officers who were billeted with us. During the occupation my parents had always been able to claim an exception for having to give up rooms for German officers because of de apotheek. The same reasoning didn't seem to apply when it came to our liberators. My parents had gone out of their way to open their home to them. Mattresses were put on the floor next to my parents' bed for Hans and Herman. Oma and I occupied the guest room, which had ceased to serve as the secret depot for medicines. I didn't get back to my own room till the following summer. English and Canadian officers came and went.

Nobody talked about going to school, and I was just as glad because there was so much going on. On a spot exactly in the middle between the City Hall and our house, crude scaffolding was hastily hammered together from unmatched pieces of lumber. A big crowd gathered around it. We looked on from our windows as a woman was shoved onto the rough podium. A barber with clippers in his right hand grabbed her by the elbow with his left and proceeded to take off her hair until she was completely bald. The crowd was howling and hissing, and again and again they howled, as one woman after another was shaven.

"This is medieval," Pappie said.

The podium looked like a busy barbershop, the planks littered with curls and strands of hair. When a row of ten women had been shaved, the barber stuck a small Dutch flag on a stick into the collar of their coats and handed them over to men who paraded them around de markt.

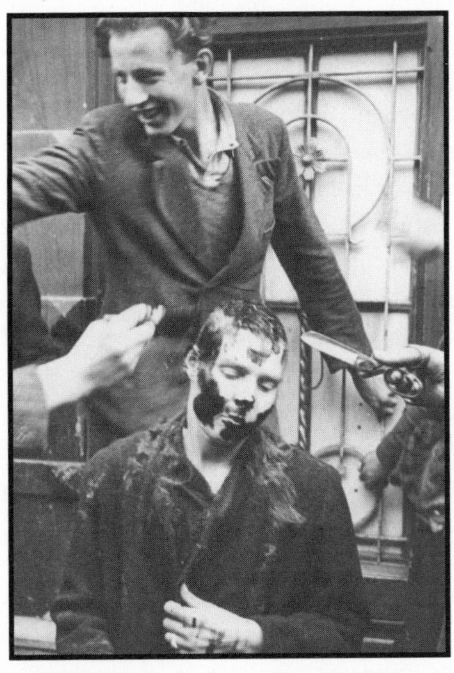

A young woman being shaved bald and tarred in punishment of her involvement with German soldiers. Photo courtesy of NIOD.

At first I didn't know what to make of it. Hans said the women had been too kind to the German officers and soldiers. Still, I didn't get it.

"Were they traitors?" I asked.

"Something like that," Hans said with mischief in his eyes.

Mammie, who overheard us, told me these women had been unfaithful to their country.

It was a horrible sight and it reminded me of my parents' birthday party a year earlier, when I'd concluded that angry people look ugly. This hissing and spitting crowd looked even worse. As the women were marched around, the sun turned their bald heads into polished billiard balls. From close up under our window their faces looked agonized and shamed. Looks I would never forget.

"Why are they doing this?" I asked my mother.

"People want to take revenge."

"Will they do this to Opa and Oma Wetselaar?" As soon as I said it, I was sorry, but of course, we were all thinking of them.

"I hope not," was all Mammie said.

During the next days and weeks, members of the Underground – recognizable now by their blue overalls, armbands and black helmets – walked over de markt pushing a man or a woman on their way to jail. All were NSBers. The release from more than four years of suffering acted like sugar on yeast, feeding on itself, ballooning the need for revenge. But it wasn't a pretty sight.

Twenty years later, when I returned to Holland for the first time after emigration, I went to a hairdresser on de markt. I recognized the woman who did my hair as one whose hair had been clipped under our window. How ironic she became hairdresser, I thought. While she set my hair in curlers, I studied her face in the mirror, looking for inner scars in her eyes. But she seemed completely at ease. A wedding band told me a man had taken her as his wife in spite of her dark history. Maybe that was why she seemed at peace. She'd been forgiven, and wasn't that the basis of our Christian faith?

What she had done during the war was wrong, of course, but I wasn't so sure that the punishment she received, to be publicly taunted and despised, wasn't equally disgusting. The crowds had taken justice into their own hands. Pushed too long and too hard, they hadn't been in a forgiving mood. Their own homes might have been bombed. Maybe they'd lost a husband, a son, or a way to make a living. Irreplaceable losses I couldn't identify with. Where was the line between taking revenge and administering punishment based on our common laws? The scenes in front of our house had not represented a moment of civilization. What I'd witnessed had been fueled by basic instincts.

As if scenes like shaving women bald in public weren't enough to make us worry about Opa and Oma Wetselaar, an unexpected happening foretold what was in store for them. The day after we watched the shaving spectacle, my mother asked me to take care of a baby.

"A baby?" I asked. "The neighbors'?"

"No, not that baby," Mammie said. She wasn't in the mood to tell me more.

Moments later, a man and two women came up the staircase from de apotheek. The older of the two women, probably the grandmother to judge by her gray hair, held a baby boy in her arms. He seemed more a toddler than a baby. Mammie squeezed his round cheek, but I could tell she hadn't been at all prepared for this invasion. From the conversation I gathered the adults wouldn't be staying, but the baby was. A bag with clothes and toys was handed over.

Where to put the child? Every room in our house was taken and we didn't have a crib. The bewildered boy was set in our bathtub with a folded blanket under and over him, a pillow behind him. The strangers were on the verge of tears. I was told to sit with the boy, entertain him. Being the youngest in my family and without cousins in that age group, I was at a loss what to do with a small child in a bathtub. Not for a second did I take my eyes from him. What if he turned on the tap?

The man and the two women left. In all, they'd been in our house for ten minutes at the most. I never saw them again. Mammie told us they were distant relatives of my father. If they lived in Breda, then why hadn't we ever met them before? Hans wanted to know. Because they were members of the NSB, was the answer. When the Underground picked them up, they'd pleaded and got permission to bring the child to de apotheek. Pappie had seen their desperation and Mammie had risen to the task of harboring the boy. His name was Herman, and when my brother came home after school, Hans opened the front door and said, "We have a little brother, Herman, and you know what his name is? Herman!"

We all pitched in to take care of our little brother. Little Herman, luckily, was a sweet boy. We played with him till he was exhausted and then we put him back in the bathtub and waited till he fell asleep. He never did find out what the tap was for. One day – he'd been with us for only a short time – he was gone when we came home from school. Mammie told us not to worry. He was safe. They had survived their ordeal was all I knew about him and his parents, let go by the authorities because they hadn't done anything demonstrably unpatriotic during the war, except becoming members of the NSB. At the time, so much was going on, the incident was put on the back burner of my consciousness.

Captain Binns and Major Leftley moved on to another part of the front. Major Corcoran and Captain Dobbs took their place. I had picked up a few English words to try out on them. Awake before anyone else in the house, I positioned myself on the staircase so I could be sure to see the two officers leave their rooms to go to work.

"Good morning, Captain Dobbs, cold day," I would say, or, "Good morning, Major Corcoran, rain in night."

There was something magical about having English officers live in our home. Everything about them fascinated me. For one, the delicious aroma of aftershave. My father had run out of such luxuries long ago. I fell in love with their immaculate uniforms, and even with the khaki color. The brass buttons on their jackets were always shiny, their brown shoes spit polished. A shiny leather strap ran diagonally across their chests, front and back. It attached to a wide belt around their jackets. I loved every part of their appearance. The man who kept them looking so spiffy was called Mac. In the evening, Mac came to the kitchen and polished the shoes and every bit of brass on the uniform jackets. He wore a wide beret with a red pom-pom on top. Mac was a Scot and spoke a different kind of English than the officers. The only one who could understand and converse with him was Mammie. Much to her surprise she found that his language resembled and somehow was related to the language she'd grown up with as a child: Friesian. Mammie could understand Mac better than even his own superiors.

After dinner, when I knew he sat near the warm stove while Net cleaned up the dishes, I slipped out to watch Mac. Although Net didn't speak English at all, and I only a few words, we had a wonderful time together, gesturing if we didn't know a word or, as a last resort, drawing a picture. Mac taught me how to polish the brass buttons without getting the uniform dirty and how to clean a sten gun. Within a week, I was totally familiar with its parts and could take the gun apart and put it back together again. I had to promise not to tell Major Corcoran.

My mother spoke English fluently since she'd lived in London as a young woman and she was well acquainted with English literature. In the evenings, after they'd had dinner at the officers' mess, our guests were invited into our living room where they had lively discussions with my parents. My brothers and I soaked it all in. If we didn't have a clue what was being said, Mammie would fill in with translation. With the fall and rise of the officers' voices we absorbed their language. I didn't know then that, over the course of my life, I would speak more English than Dutch.

Captain Dobbs was a career officer. Major Corcoran had been drafted. Their task was to get cities up and running again after the German occupation. They worked directly under a Canadian officer who replaced the *Orts Commandantur*, his German counterpart who'd fled the day before our liberation. Breda now had a Canadian mayor as well as a Dutch one.

In the streets we saw Poles, Brits (we called them Tommies) and Canadians. No Americans, because they were busy liberating the eastern part of Brabant. Yet before the war was over, I saw my first flesh-and-blood American on a blistery day in November. I thought he should have been riding in on a proud stallion like the one in the statue of William III of Orange that stood in front of the castle. For more than two centuries, William had sat astride the horse with his bronze arm raised in a sign of victory. But the American I saw came around the bend in an open jeep. He wore a khaki battle dress uniform with five stars. It was easy to recognize him from the pictures in the newspapers. General Dwight Eisenhower. He jumped down from the jeep with a swift, supple motion. I waved at the man who, at that moment, was close to conquering Germany. He waved back and smiled. Then he disappeared into the hotel that was used as Allied Headquarters.

I ran home to share my incredible luck. I fell over my own words trying to express how the man had impressed me. He was so friendly, I told my mother. Nothing like the German officers we used to watch as they mounted the granite steps of the city hall, their soldiers looking like statues while the officers passed by; their uniforms with the swastika cross prominently displayed below the collar and the exaggerated caps that had been tailored to impress. Nothing humble about those German officers. They were the conquerors and they'd played their role to the hilt, in appearance and in body language.

I had a new hero.

Chapter 22

- ❖ **November 20, 1944: General Patton's Third Army captures Metz.**
- ❖ **November 22, 1944: The French First Army closes in on the Rhine River in Basel.**
- ❖ **November 23, 1944: The Allies enter Strasbourg, in the Alsace.**
- ❖ **December 3, 1944: Allies reach the German Roer River.**

Being liberated didn't mean we had more food. Or electricity. Or coal. On the contrary, we had less of everything. Though some trucks came out of hiding, there weren't enough left to transport all the things we were in dire need of. The Germans had requisitioned most of them for their flight. Even if there had been enough trucks, many roads had become impassable. Blown-up bridges caused detours. The trains didn't run anymore. The Allies had all they could do to keep their troops supplied with gasoline, ammunition and food. The farther they advanced, the longer their supply lines became. The commercial transportation system was like a body with its legs cut off.

Our school closed for lack of coal. Parents like ours, with a big enough home, offered space for classes. It was the subject of my first full sentence in English. Mammie translated what I wanted to say and I learned it by heart overnight. As Captain Dobbs came down the staircase the next morning, I said, "We have school at home today."

He raised his eyebrows and asked, "Here in your home? Where?"

I didn't know the word for *eetkamer* in English, so I took him by the hand and opened the door to the dining room. He looked bemused.

Going to school now meant gulping down breakfast and clearing the dishes in a hurry. Our schedules were reduced to a bare minimum. Hans and I had classes in the dining room. Herman's class met in the boys' room where Major

Corcoran spent the night. "No problem," he said, when Mammie brought up the possibility. "I'll tell them back home I'm sharing my room with a teacher."

Major Corcoran took delight in our map of Europe with the pins and threads. We'd first thought we should move it to the hallway downstairs, now that the Germans had left and the danger of displaying what we learned from the BBC had passed. As the Allies made progress, Major Corcoran and Captain Dobbs shared in our childish delight in moving pins and threads.

To see my classmates sit around our table, which had been stretched from a circle to an oval, was bizarre. Juffrouw Moens sat in my mother's chair teaching us Latin. "*Laudo, laudas, laudat.* Repeat." Mimi van Hoegaerden, who sat next to me in Herman's chair, was very smart and gifted in languages.

"What does it mean?" I whispered to her.

"I praise, you praise, he praises."

With Mimi's help I got through my Latin homework. I had little interest in it. Why should I learn Latin when I was far more interested in learning English?

The winter turned out bitterly cold. In the morning, my bed sheet was frozen where I had breathed on it. We instituted a new household ritual. As part of preparing to go to bed, we poured hot water from a large kettle on the kitchen stove into rubber bottles and stuffed them under our covers. Once under the covers, we held the bottle in a tight embrace. It took a kind of courage to get out of bed in the morning and greet the coating of ice in the washbasin. Only the dining room, the living room and the two large bedrooms on the third floor had stoves. The kitchen was the coziest place in the house with its cooking stove as large as a man's desk. But to get there, we had to run down the long, unheated corridor. Worst of all was the icy toilet seat at the end of the same corridor.

There being hardly any school, Herman and I roamed the streets. At a garage close by, a sergeant doled out hot soup to the soldiers from a steaming kettle that took up most of the back of an army truck. If you carried some sort of container with you, you might get a handout. The soldiers freely shared their chocolate and cigarettes. I cozied up to one and got my first taste of corned beef. The cigarettes we gave to Pappie.

We studied everything from jeeps to army trucks in detail. The soldiers allowed us to gawk at their gear and their vehicles. They engaged us in conversation, taught us what their insignia and medals stood for. Each uniform had a band with letters sewn onto the top of their sleeve. It signified their regiment. I got a soldier to give me one and I stored it proudly in my jewelry box next to the rosary. But I really wanted to wear it, so I talked my mother into making her old gabardine coat over for me. Its color approximated the khaki color of the Allied uniforms. As if she had nothing else to do, she sized it down, replaced the bone buttons with brass ones and sewed on all the trophies I'd collected. I spit-polished the only pair of shoes I owned the way Mac had taught me. Herman had somehow got his hands on an old French helmet and a German hand grenade (used for practice). His latest trophy was a heavy canvas belt, part of the Allied uniform. We looked terrific, we thought, as we peeked in Mammie's tall mirror. I lived in a man's world and I wanted to look like one.

Just how much I lived in a man's world, I found out on a particularly cold day, when I spotted the old Dodge taxi that used to ferry us back and forth from our house at Overa to school. It was parked on de markt with the motor running. Even the driver looked familiar. Klaas! I knocked on the window and waved. He reached over to the passenger's side and opened the door for me.

"*Dag,* Titia, come in. It's nice and warm in here." I was flattered he even remembered my name.

"*Dag,* Klaas," I said. "How come you're wearing a uniform?"

"I'm the driver for the Canadian mayor. They gave me a uniform to wear."

"Did you drive for the Germans too?" I asked.

"Once in a while, but no way would I wear their uniform," he said with a laugh. "Why aren't you in school?"

"They closed the school."

"Which school are you going to now?" I told him I was in the first grade of *het gymnasium.*

"Well, well," Klaas said. "You're a big girl now. Quite the young lady!"

It was true. I was a head taller since he'd seen me last. I'd let my hair grow to my shoulders and I'd outgrown most of my clothes. I chuckled at being called a young lady. Far from it, I thought. A tomboy was more like it.

We talked about the weather, how glad we were to be liberated, how exciting it was to see a different army. My body was beginning to warm up. My feet had felt like blocks of ice when I'd walked outside. Now they started to tingle. It was quite cozy, and sitting in a car was exciting. I hadn't been in one since the first year of the war when Klaas drove us to and from school, but we always sat in the back seat then. Sitting in the front passenger seat, I admired the polished wood of the dashboard.

We'd run out of conversation and sat watching people going in and out of the City Hall. Then Klaas put his arm around me. It wasn't a protective gesture like one of my father's friends might have done. It was leading up to something else. I could just feel it. He pulled me toward him and kissed me, first on my neck, then on my cheek.

I didn't like it at all. I sensed this was just the beginning of his advances by the way he jerked his body around.

Our house was only a stone's throw away, behind the car, and if nothing else, I was impulsive. I pulled away, grabbed the door handle and got out as fast as I could. Feeling hot and sweaty, I ran through de apotheek, up the stairs and into the kitchen where I knew my mother would be preparing lunch with Net. The look on my face alarmed her. She took me into the living room and asked what was wrong. It wasn't easy to describe. It could have just been in my head. Maybe, Klaas hadn't meant to do anything wrong. Was this tattletaling?

"You did the right thing, Titia," my mother said when I finally got the whole story out. "I'm proud of you! If you're ever in such a situation again, do the same thing: run. Some men have ill intentions. Sitting in a car with a stranger is not a good idea."

"But Mammie, Klaas was not a stranger!"

"I know. You trusted him. You'll find that even people you think you can trust can play bad tricks."

"But how can I know who the bad people are?"

Mammie thought before she answered. She looked out the window and sighed. "There are two ways to go about it," she said. "You can either trust a stranger until proven otherwise, or you can mistrust a person until proven otherwise."

"What do you do?"

Mammie laughed. I'd put her on the spot.

"I do what you did," she said. "I use my intuition. You sensed something was wrong and you acted on it."

I wanted to know what intuition was. As I grew older I would know how to tell from the way people act, Mammie said. "The way someone looks at you, or evades looking at you, will tell you something about that person," she said. "The way some people beat around the bush instead of giving you a straight answer, the way they move or hold their hands as they speak, all these are clues to help you guess what someone's real intentions are."

Mammie took me in her arms.

"I can't give you a sure way of knowing, but you made a good start today!"

I still had questions. What were those "ill intentions" and "dirty tricks"? What had Klaas wanted to do? But only a part of me wanted to find out. With the wisdom peculiar to a child, I knew I wasn't ready for the answers. I didn't want to dwell on something that hadn't even happened while so many interesting things were going on around me.

In practical terms, the result of the incident was more homework and when I went out, Herman became my constant shadow. I never saw Klaas again. If my parents talked to him about it, they never told me.

We seemed to have more family than I ever knew. For instance, I'd never heard about the man who was introduced to me one day.

"Titia, this is your Oom Hans," Mammie said. "Oom Hans van Amstel."

Something in the way she emphasized van Amstel and the way she looked away made me suspicious. We were liberated, so why this secrecy? Or was this one of the signs that the war wasn't quite over yet?

Mammie seemed on familiar terms with this new uncle, obviously part of her side of the family. Much to my relief, he wore a captain's khaki uniform. At least not another NSB member in our family.

My brothers and I were curious how this uncle was related to us. We'd never heard the name van Amstel before. But we'd learned during the war not to ask unnecessary questions. Besides, we were more intrigued to learn this uncle served on the staff of Prince Bernhard.

"The staff of Prince Bernhard? Here in Breda?" A member of our royal family in our own city!

Herman and I soon found out where Prince Bernhard's headquarters were: just a street away from us, in a large building on the harbor, opposite the wall that surrounds the castle. It used to be the post office and was remarkable for its turn-of-the-century architecture and its extravagant little tower. We posted ourselves across the street to try to get a glimpse of the Prince. Chilled to the bone, we waited for hours, but we were rewarded. Like General Eisenhower, Prince Bernhard arrived in a jeep with himself at the steering wheel, wearing battle dress with a leather flying jacket and a silk shawl. Dashing and handsome. A white Scotch terrier sat in the back of the jeep. He lifted the dog up and took it inside under his arm. With his other arm he waved at Herman and me. I was smitten. We were the only ones on the street. Not many people knew yet about the Prince's choice of Breda as his headquarters, or for that matter, that he was Commander of *de Binnenlandse Strijdkrachten* (the Underground).

It didn't take long for other members of the Prince's staff to find their way to our house. Our uncle brought someone new every time he visited. My mother's personal warmth and hospitality worked like a magnet. My father's homemade *jenever* surely helped. In any case, at the end of their working days, English and Dutch officers filled our living room. Since more English than Dutch was now spoken at home, at least between five and seven o'clock, I learned English by osmosis. Sitting in a small leather chair in a corner, I lapped up the language of the free world. Mammie, if she was close by, helped me get the gist of the conversations. The stories were spell binding: how the landing at Normandy had been planned, how hard the fights in that area had been, and what a glorious entree they'd made into Paris. They chose their words carefully, only talking about what was behind them, and not what was immediately ahead. But we understood through their veiled remarks that the part of Holland north of the great rivers would not be liberated soon. The drive was toward Germany.

Mammie displayed limitless energy. She made the most of whatever was available to provide us with regular meals, darned socks, repaired bed sheets, and as much warmth as she could create in spite of persistent shortage of coal. Thanks to the soap the officers slipped to her, we even had cleaner clothes. My favorite sheep wool sweater went from gray back to off-white.

Only once did we refuse to eat what she served for dinner. As usual, Net came in with the serving dishes after we were seated. We might lack food, but in my mother's house we didn't lack decorum. The small silver electric bell that hung from the chandelier and was used to signal Net when we were ready for the food, which Mammie had usually prepared beforehand, accentuated this. On this day, Net brought in a steaming dish with endives in a white sauce, spruced up with grated nutmeg, and a platter with round, dark red pieces of meat. We seldom had meat and these pieces were larger than what we'd seen in quite a while. I saw that Mammie looked like she always did when she was about to tell a lie, well aware that she wasn't good at it. Only once had she fooled somebody: the German officer who believed Oma Ament had TB. When my mother tried to lie she looked self-conscious and more serious than usual, yet with a tiny smile around the corners of her mouth.

We first dug into the meat, took a bite, pushed it around with our tongue to get a better grip on what kind of meat it was. Whatever it tasted like, it looked, at closer inspection, more like a piece of chocolate cake.

"What kind of meat is this?" Hans asked.

"It is good for you," Mammie said.

"What is it called?" Hans persisted.

"Parasang."

"*Sang*. That means blood in Latin. Are we eating blood?"

Pappie saw the look on Mammie's face, close to exasperation, and said, "Yes, you're right. Very clever. It's made of oxen blood. Highly nutritious."

We looked down at our plates, where the white sauce of the endives had turned brownish-red from the *parasang*. It wasn't very appealing. We tried anyway. There wasn't a trace of fat in it to make it palatable. Finally, my father put down his knife and fork and said, "Sorry, Hannie, but I don't think we have to make ourselves eat this." And that was that. After dinner, I snuck into the kitchen to find out if our "meat" had arrived in a bottle, but Net showed me a package with powder that needed to be reconstituted with water. The box bore the logo of a drug company. Organon.

Undaunted by these little dips in the road, Mammie started to plan for the season's festivities. Breda was determined to make the most of the first Saint Nicholas celebration since the Germans had left. The Polish and British troops were curious what this Dutch tradition was like. and when the good bishop arrived from Spain in the harbor, not just children but enthusiastic soldiers greeted him. Mammie sat up for hours during the night to make rhymes in English for Captain Dobbs and Major Corcoran. Not being able to use the English language to make rhymes and there being hardly anything to buy for a present, I stuffed little things like a box with matches inside a bigger box, then another box, until the present became huge in size. On the fifth of December, we sat around our extended dining room table with Oma Ament, our new uncle, and the two English officers. Major Corcoran and Captain Dobbs didn't know what to expect, but they'd brought sweets and spent the evening chuckling at our pranks. They were in awe of my mother who, they said, had shown her grasp of the English language in the poems they'd received.

Shortly afterwards, the war took a dangerous turn. The Allies had made steady progress toward Germany since they'd landed in June. Different armies had closed in from various directions. Almost daily, we could add new pins to the map. Patton's Third army had captured Metz. The French First Army had reached the Rhine River north of Basel. On November 23, they entered Strasbourg. Virtually in a straight line from Aachen, close to Holland's most southerly border, all the way to the south of Luxembourg the Allies were poised to enter Germany. However, the same German general who had led the great attack in 1940 that eventually pushed the British forces from the Continent in Dunkirk, pounced on the Allies on December 16, in one last desperate attempt to keep them out of his country. If General Von Rundstedt could penetrate the Allies' line, he could push them back to Antwerp and wreak havoc with their logistics. Antwerp's hard-won harbor brought in their vital supplies. Breda was located in such a way that, if the Nazis succeeded, it would sit in a vice formed by Germans north of the rivers and Von Rundstedt's troops to the south. It was not a good situation. The officers that frequented our home now wore battle dress and had pistols strapped to their belts, which they put beside their chairs while they visited.

The weather wasn't cooperating. The Allied Air Force was grounded for days because of clouds and impenetrable fog. Von Rundstedt made the most of his advantages: the element of surprise and the bad weather. He broke through the Allied defense line and advanced fifty miles through Luxembourg and well into Belgium. A dangerous breach was created. The German attack gained the popular name of "The Battle of the Bulge" because of its initial rapid progress.

A small city, Bastogne, lay in the path of the German advance and it played a dramatic role, still evident when I visited there in 1961. Row upon row of white crosses dotted the green hills around the embattled town, which had finally been saved in the night of January third in 1945.

In Breda we could hear the low rumble of bombing and artillery, muffled by the great distance. People would stop in the street and say to each other, "the Ardennes," and mention of that mountain ridge evoked fear. The German attack cast a pall over our first free Christmas. The churches filled to capacity with people praying for the soldiers who had to fight in snow and freezing cold, and praying for freedom, our own as well as of the not-yet-liberated northern part of our country. It was the worst winter Europe had seen in decades. Whatever we suffered in our cold houses couldn't be compared to the news and pictures we received from the front. Not only did we have a roof over our heads, we still had enough coal so we could huddle around the stove at night.

Against this somber background we prepared for New Year's Eve. My parents had invited Oom Hans van Amstel and several members of Prince Bernhard's staff. Major Buma was a robust man, tall and straight as a tree but with a disproportionate small head. He reminded me of an asparagus. Captain Kas van der Graaf was lithe and dashing with a dark moustache and very alive eyes. Major Corcoran and Captain Dobbs had been invited, but went instead to the officers' mess to sit out the end of the turbulent year with their comrades.

We followed the Dutch tradition of playing games around the dining room table until it was almost twelve. The Dutch officers had brought champagne, which Pappie poured into crystal glasses that had spent the war years sitting in the closet. We heard Big Ben strike twelve over the BBC. The fact that our radio was back in its place was in itself worth a celebration. After the toasts and sincere wishes for an end to the war in the brand new year, the children were sent to bed. On the way, we noticed both Major Corcoran's and Captain Dobbs's shoes were outside their bedroom doors, as they always were, waiting for Mac to polish them. The Brits had already turned in.

The next morning, my parents were up unusually early, especially considering they hardly ever stayed up as late as they had the night before. A hint of worry and suspense floated in the air. Mammie told us to leave the door from the dining room to the hall open so she could catch Major Corcoran before he left for work.

When Major Corcoran came down the stairs, Mammie rushed out to meet him. She looked him over carefully, as if she expected him to be only half there. It was so unlike her. There seemed nothing unusual about the man. He was his usual courteous self.

"Good morning, Major Corcoran," Mammie said. "Are you all right?"

"Good morning, Mrs. Wetselaar. Happy New Year!"

"Are you really all right?" Mammie asked again.

"Sure, sure."

"Thank God!"

Now it was the major's turn to be curious.

"We had a guest last night," Mammie started out. "He is an officer on the Prince's staff. He took his pistol, aimed it at the ceiling and fired a bullet."

"Well, well," Major Corcoran said.

"It was meant for good luck," Mammie went on. "But it was in the dining room. Under your room!"

"It was?" Major Corcoran became animated. "Can you show me?"

Mammie took him into the dining room and showed him the perfect round hole in the ceiling. When I saw where it was, I understood my mother's agitation. The bullet had to have entered somewhere near his bed. Major Corcoran became excited like a little boy. We all followed him up the stairs. He crawled under the bed and found a bubble in the linoleum floor covering. He carefully felt around it with his fingers.

"That's a bullet under there. No question. I don't know if it will bring *you* luck, but I do know *I* was very lucky!" Major Corcoran said. He looked almost happy. I could see him storing this episode in the part of his brain where all his other war stories resided.

"You could've been killed!" Herman said. "Look, it sits right below where your pillow is."

"Lucky me!" Major Corcoran said.

Mammie stood with her hands pressed to her cheeks. She looked mortified, but Major Corcoran put his hand on her arm for reassurance.

"Every day I survive this war is a lucky one. Maybe this shot tells us the end of the war is in sight. That would be good luck indeed!" And with that chivalrous remark he turned to go to work.

Hans, Herman and I were dying to find out what exactly had happened. Captain de Graaf had come across as a dashing officer, but drawing a pistol?

Apparently, after we'd gone to bed, the war stories had come out. Kas de Graaf told how he and a friend had fled from Holland after they had liquidated an infamous member of the NSB, a dangerous collaborator with the enemy. He described their perilous flight and how they had been saved and hidden by nuns in a monastery. To show their gratitude to the nuns, he'd drawn his pistol and shot a hole in the ceiling, assuring them good fortune for twenty years.

My parents and the other guests had listened with fascination to his story, but they hadn't been prepared for what came next. Kas de Graaf got up, drew his pistol and aimed it at the ceiling. While he put his finger on the trigger he said to my parents "You have been incredibly hospitable to us and I thank you. This shot will bless this home and ensure good luck for the next twenty years."

Before Mammie could ask him to redirect his aim, he pulled the trigger and my mother cried out "Oh, my God, Major Corcoran!" instead of thanking Kas de Graaf for his blessing. My father went upstairs, saw the shoes outside the door and realized the major had come home. He debated whether he should open the door. He put his ear to it, but heard nothing. Very carefully he opened the door and peeked inside. Nothing seemed out of the ordinary. He went back downstairs and reassured everyone.

But Mammie hadn't slept a wink.

Chapter 23

- ❖ **January 12, 1945: The Russians start their offensive.**
- ❖ **February 8, 1945: General Montgomery leads assault on the Rhine River.**
- ❖ **March 25, 1945: Germany's fate is sealed. Troops cross the Rhine.**
- ❖ **April 12, 1945: President Roosevelt dies.**
- ❖ **April 25, 1945: Allied and Russian troops meet at the Elbe River.**
- ❖ **April 30, 1945: Hitler commits suicide.**
- ❖ **May 4, 1945: General Montgomery accepts the unconditional surrender of German forces in North West Germany, effective within 24 hours.**
- ❖ **May 8, 1945: Total, unconditional surrender of all German Forces is signed.**

The German retreat from the Ardennes in Belgium and Luxembourg brought immense relief. The battles from now on would be fought on German soil. The Allies concentrated on driving the Germans first over their infamous Siegfried Line of defense, and then over the Rhine River toward the heart of Germany. This left the part of our country north of the rivers in isolation. Our occupiers had discovered the Dutch centuries-old method of defense: break the dikes and flood the polders. The Allies were acutely aware of this weapon. They left Holland alone on their left flank, reasoning that if the Germans flooded the land, the Dutch population would suffer even more. Another consideration was the lack of troops to spread effectively over such a large area. Their main goal was to get to Berlin. This made strategic sense, but it rendered the severe winter of 1944-1945 nearly unbearable for the Dutch people up north. It was frustrating to work on our map on the wall, moving pins farther and farther into Germany, and see the threads by-passing our northern provinces. The rivers that served us so well in peacetime were a hindrance in war.

We hadn't received any news from Opa and Oma Wetselaar for months. The seal between north and south was as tight as the ones that topped Mammie's canned bean jars. My mother's brother Henk lived outside of Amsterdam with his large family. Her other brother, Oom Tjalling, was in a concentration camp in the Indies. My father's twin lived near Haarlem. Liesje Wetselaar, my cousin, was in Utrecht. On and on went the list of family and friends we worried about daily as grim stories managed to seep through the seal. Lack of food, fuel, electricity, transportation and security undermined many people's lives. The railroad was on strike at the urging of the Underground, so the young traveled on bicycles without tires for miles and miles to trade valuables for food with the farmers.

I considered myself lucky when we heard these rumors and I tried very hard to remember them when I shivered under my pile of blankets, when I washed myself with icy cold water without soap. Mammie fed us daily a spoonful of cod liver oil to keep us healthy. It tasted awful. But in spite of swallowing it religiously, I fell ill in the middle of the winter. Mononucleosis lurked somewhere in my surroundings and waited for my lowest point to grab me. It knocked me flat with high fevers.

There was a bright side to it. I got moved to my parents' bedroom where a stove kept me warm. I slept in Pappie's side of the bed and Pappie moved to the guest room with the boys. Major Corcoran and Captain Dobbs came to my bedside and brought oats for porridge to build me back up. After the initial high fevers, I began to enjoy my sick state. Net would come in to remake my bed while I sat wrapped in a blanket by the window. Back in Pappie's refreshed bed, with the opened windows allowing the winter air to drive out the sick room smells, I listened to the sounds rising from de markt, trying to link them to the scenes I wasn't a part of but that I knew so well.

Toward the end of the winter, Major Corcoran and Captain Dobbs left for places closer to the front, which now had moved into Germany. It was like seeing family members leave. They'd been with us for four months. My brothers sneaked into Major Corcoran's room, into his closet, and put a pillbox with the label of de apotheek in his helmet. I wrote my name and address on a piece of paper and left it on Captain Dobbs' nightstand. We were afraid they might forget us.

The boys had their room back, but mine saw a new occupant: Captain Mooney, a Canadian officer who told us he was a lawyer in his civilian life. In April, a woman officer, Eileen Fields, took his place.

Uniformed foreigners weren't the only ones who made their temporary home with us. During the late winter and early spring, several Dutchmen came and went, some for only a night, others for as long as ten days. Prince Bernhard himself dropped one once in the middle of the night. Each new arrival was introduced to us with the same last name of van Amstel. The boys and I began to ask questions. Were all these people related to us? We'd never heard the name van Amstel mentioned until Oom Hans arrived on the scene.

Mammie realized she couldn't fool us any longer. Oom Hans was indeed our uncle, but van Amstel was not his real name. He'd taken it on to protect his wife and son who were still north of the rivers. If the Germans found out he worked with Prince Bernhard for the Underground, they could take them for hostages or worse. The other men with the same last name were all "line crossers" who tried to get back and forth over the cold wide rivers on "special missions."

The last line crosser stayed with us from the end of April into May. He chain-smoked his way through the tension of waiting for the signal to undertake his mission. It never came. What came instead was the end of the war!!!

When the news was broadcast that General Montgomery had accepted the unconditional surrender of all German forces in northwest Germany, including those in Denmark and Holland, it was as if a light had switched on, a light so bright that it made every drab, familiar thing in our surroundings sparkle. City Hall suddenly looked crisp and clean as if angels had scrubbed it overnight. We were beside ourselves with joy. Short of five days, Holland had endured German occupation for five long years. People poured into the streets like captured animals whose cages had been opened. Strangers embraced and grabbed each other by the waist to dance in circles of elation.

It wasn't beer, or *jenever*, or wine that accounted for the exhilarated mood. Freedom was the tonic that gave rise to the singing, the dancing, and hugging all through the day. The weather celebrated with us. Daylight stretched into the evening, the trees leafed out, and even the birds were on cue to serenade our freedom. Mammie told us we probably wouldn't ever, in our entire lives, attend a party this spontaneous, this celebratory. She has been proven right.

It was rumored that Queen Wilhelmina had taken up residence in Anneville, a beautiful estate on the outskirts of Breda. Our exuberance channeled itself into a torchlight procession to Anneville. In the middle of a singing crowd, I walked for hours to the place where we hoped to find our Queen.

I was filled with conflicting emotions as I walked down the long lane towards the big house. Just before the war, my father's side of the family had celebrated Opa and Oma Wetselaar's fiftieth wedding anniversary there. They had been the object of our affection and admiration then. I remembered how

Mammie had bought me a fancy pink dress and shiny patent leather shoes, how all the adults were in evening gowns or tuxedos, how each of the grandchildren had to recite a poem. Much had changed since. Nobody in our immediate Wetselaar family had followed Opa into the NSB. Here I was, a torch in my hands, celebrating the defeat of a political conviction Opa had adhered to. Where was he now? And Oma, who had so faithfully followed him? I couldn't bear to think about it. At this very moment they might be in danger.

As we approached the mansion, the crowd grew quiet. There, on the granite steps, stood Queen Wilhelmina. In the pictures I'd seen of her she wore a diadem and richly embroidered gowns, but on this day of liberation she wore a simple gray suit. We stopped walking, crowded ourselves onto the spacious lawn and waited for something to happen. Dancing and singing in the streets hadn't been enough to realize we'd come full circle, from evacuation and occupation to liberation. Flying our flag and the color orange hadn't been enough to express our relief. We wanted a living symbol. Somebody in the crowd started to sing the first line of our national anthem. *"Het Wilhelmus"* never sounded more heartfelt. When the last line faded into the stillness of the night, we shouted, "Long live the Queen." The Queen bowed. Deeply satisfied, we returned home.

In the weeks that followed, news from the north dribbled in. We still weren't in communication with Opa and Oma because the Germans had dismantled the central telephone stations and taken the equipment to Germany. It was equally difficult to cross the rivers. Vital bridges had been blown up or bombed. Our infrastructure was in shambles and it would take weeks to repair. The stories that trickled down were not reassuring. Already, the months immediately behind us were being called "the hunger winter." The cold and the lack of food and fuel had cost many people their lives. The rest had survived on tulip bulbs, a not so tasty substitute for onions or potatoes.

But in Breda, life was one big party. Having the Queen, and now the crown princess as well, in our midst was special. I watched them go into the cathedral for worship on Sunday mornings, and I learned how people evaluate every little detail concerning royalty. Standing among a group of women I heard sputterings about the hint of lipstick Princess Juliana had allowed herself. The women were shocked.

My mind wasn't on school, on learning Latin, on doing algebra and geometry. Learning could wait. I wasn't about to let unique events slip by me. They couldn't be relived. The teachers agreed that my mind wasn't on learning. They had me repeat the first grade of *het Gymnasium.*

The big event that crowned all the happenings around our liberation was as resounding as the big bang at the end of a fireworks show: Eileen Fields, the young woman officer who lived in my bedroom, was going to get married in the cathedral. Her marriage to another British officer, Roy Hartnell, was the first British military wedding on the Continent, and the authorities grabbed the opportunity to have a big celebration. General Montgomery was invited. A parade would be held. Greyhounds were shipped over from England for races in the afternoon.

Being asked by Eileen to be her bridesmaid dwarfed the exciting prospect of a parade in front of our house. I'd never been anyone's bridesmaid, and to think I would be one to a British military couple took over my life. I could think of nothing else. Mammie went to work on fashioning a dress for me. For lack of material, she took one of her before-the-war dresses and remade it for me. On the navy blue material she sewed two small flags: a Dutch one over my heart, a British one on the other side.

The day of the wedding, early in June, was filled with brilliant sunshine and the air throbbed with anticipation. Strict security measures were in place around the arrival of General Montgomery. Police had cordoned off de markt for motor traffic.

I waited with Eileen in our front hall for the high-ranking officer who was to give her away at the altar. When he arrived, we walked over to the main entrance of the cathedral and met the English chaplain, who gave us the sign that the service could begin. Everyone stood up when I preceded Eileen and the tall English officer down the isle. The organ poured traditional processional music over us. My parents were hidden from view, seated somewhere behind the dignitaries. The shiny brass buttons on army uniforms twinkled like stars in the light that fell in shafts from the tall windows. Roy Hartnell stood with his best man on a raised platform, waiting for his bride. Having never attended a wedding before, I didn't realize this deviated from the Dutch tradition in which the bride and groom enter together.

The chaplain stood behind a heavy oak table with burning candles in tall candelabras and a brass bowl filled with white carnations and feathery green branches. The cathedral was familiar territory for me, but I'd never felt so small in its vastness, and yet so important. I was the only child present and I was part of the ceremony. The organ pipes looked taller and more impressive than ever. Still, the cathedral had been damaged. It had suffered thirty-six direct hits during the fighting over our city. Many windows had been broken and in the ceiling a big gaping hole looked like a human mouth.

People got up to sing a hymn, and I felt the vibrations of the organ in my chest. English words I didn't understand melded with the deep sounds from the tall pipes. They bounced off the violated ceiling. I felt as if the big mouth up there was swallowing the war's horrors, as if these voices and this mighty music could erase the fearful memories, and lift hate and revenge out of sight. As it had done so many times before, the cathedral filled me with awe.

I followed the proceedings with great curiosity, but the most lasting impression of that day was Eileen Fields' serenely happy face. In her kahki uniform, its brass buttons polished to look like gold, she was the happiest bride I'd ever seen, and I had studied many as they entered and exited the City Hall.

When we came out of the church, de markt was bustling with activity. My parents found me and we hastened home to take our seats behind our opened windows. As usual, friends rang our door bell and begged for a place at one of the four windows that looked out on de markt. There was no question about it: we had the best view, positioned directly opposite the wide steps of City Hall, where soon General Montgomery would review the parade.

In the distance we heard the rolling of drums and the rumbling of military vehicles over the rough cobblestones. Necks craned in the direction of the sounds, and I hung my upper body out the window until Pappie pulled me back. He didn't want to lose me after the war was over, he said.

The big door of the City Hall opened and General Montgomery, in battle dress and his famous black beret, stepped out. The crowd cheered for long minutes. Here was a man who'd fought for us, who'd taken incredible risks to free us. A hero.

The Allied troops marched smartly, but the Scottish bagpipers stole the show. We'd never seen anything like them. They marched back and forth in intricate patterns, weaving through one another, all the while creating a piercing, haunting sound. Their uniforms of black fur hats, skirts, and knee socks were eye-poppers. I was ready to label them ridiculous until Mammie explained, with tears in her eyes, how these bagpipers march on the battlefield among the fighting soldiers to give them heart. With the sounds of artillery fire still ringing in my ears, I looked at them with different eyes. These men in their funny skirts – kilts, Mammie called them – had seen a kind of suffering I couldn't even begin to imagine.

Soon after this exciting day, Lieutenant Eileen Fields, now Mrs. Hartnell, came to say good-bye. I was sad to see her go, the last of the officers to billet with us.

Pappie, meanwhile, had found a man willing to take him on the back of his motorbike to the north to find out what had happened to the rest of the family, especially Opa and Oma Wetselaar. We all came down early in the morning to see him off. Beneath his tarplike raincoat he carried a large rucksack with food.

We waved until they rounded the corner of de markt. His driver was a burly man and behind him Pappie looked like a dark green tent with a small head coming out at the top. He wore the fur-lined cap Herman had used to impersonate a parachutist.

A week later Pappie returned, exhausted. It had taken two days to get to Haarlem. They had had to rely on ferries to get across the wide rivers, because the main bridges were destroyed, and to circumvent the potholes they regularly had to get off the bike and walk beside it.

Once there, they found nobody home at their familiar addresses. The Underground had confiscated Opa and Oma's house in Overveen. The Allies occupied the house of Oom Max and Tante Iet. The Germans had turned them out first, using their home as their headquarters for decoding intercepted Allied messages. It had taken some detective work to locate everyone. An accidental meeting with an acquaintance of Oom Max finally led to his temporary residence.

The brothers set out to find Opa and Oma. As the armistice was signed, the Underground had loaded Opa and Oma onto a truck and taken them to the Navy Hospital in Haarlem, which was serving as a temporary jail. With persuasion and persistence, Pappie and Oom Max finally got permission to be allowed to visit their parents.

Pappie was shocked when he saw his parents. They looked gaunt. During the last part of the war, and especially during the "hunger winter," Opa and Oma had lived isolated lives. Liesje Wetselaar, their eldest grandchild, had broken her family's rule not to visit them and had gone to find out how they were during that last winter of the war. She was a student nurse in Utrecht at the time, unable to get back to liberated Breda. In spite of a disabling railroad strike she made it to Overveen when Opa and Oma still lived in their own home. It was pitiful, she told my father, to find them looking like skeletons, especially Opa. Too upright to trade on the black market, they were literally starving. But Liesje found they had sufficient heating oil to exchange for food on the black market, and although at first Opa refused, he finally gave in and she bought whatever she could find to feed them.

At the Navy Hospital, members of the Underground treated their prisoners with a vengeance. Pappie was appalled at the humiliation forced upon his mother who'd done nothing more than faithfully follow her husband. Every morning at roll call, Oma was made to march naked with other NSB women around the inner courtyard.

Opa had undeniably made a colossal mistake. All the same, the sons convinced the authorities that their father had never caused any Dutchman harm during the war. Though misguided, he couldn't be labeled a traitor, and the authorities were not able to prove he had betrayed his country. He was guilty only of becoming a member of the NSB party, convinced it would improve the quality of life for the poor.

A fine of one hundred thousand guilders set their parents free. (today one hundred thousand guilders would be equivalent to one hundred thousand euros), Opa and Oma went to live temporarily with Oom Max and his family.

The NSB label clung to the Wetselaar name for many years. Oom Henri's son Rob was the first one in the family to find this out. After serving in the Underground, Rob wanted to enlist in the American Marine Corps. He got himself to Belgium. During the screening process he was asked if he was related to Johan Dirk Wetselaar, member of the NSB.

"Yes, he is my grandfather," Rob replied.

Rob convinced them he wasn't a member of the NSB himself. On the contrary, he worked for the Underground. They took him at his word and sent him to Camp Lejeune, the Marine Corps Base in North Carolina.

Oom Max' son Robert and my brother Hans were asked the same question by their fellow students when they went to university in Amsterdam. The war had been over for several years by then, but it was still remembered that Johan Wetselaar had topped the list of NSB members in the province of North Holland, because he'd given the most money to the party.

Chapter 24

- ❖ **July 1, 1945: U.S and British Armies begin withdrawal to their allotted zones in Germany, ceding conquered territory to Russia.**
- ❖ **June 26, 1945: The San Francisco Conference to frame "The World Instrument for Peace" ends successfully and results in The United Nations.**
- ❖ **July 26, 1945: Prime Minister Winston Churchill is voted out of office in England. Mr. Atlee of the Labor Party, succeeds him.**
- ❖ **August 6, 1945: America drops the atomic bomb on Hiroshima, Japan.**

Dio Rovers's portrait, though generally admired, became an unexpected topic of conversation. A line from north to south split my face into equal parts. A raised fiber in the linen canvas ran over the middle of my forehead, down my nose and chin. Dio took the painting off the wall and made it disappear. We never saw it again. He offered to make a new one, so at the end of the summer I found myself going through the familiar routine of biking to Dio's home every day for the last week of my vacation. While my friends were at the swimming pool in the nice, warm weather, I sat inside with my hands in my lap. Though I'd tried, I didn't see a way out. Dio wanted to make good on his promise to replace the first portrait, and of course, I liked Dio a lot.

Mevrouw Rovers opened the door with a friendly smile. "You know the way," she said, and I mounted the three flights of stairs to the attic. Dio was mixing paints. *Deja vu.* It was as if nothing happened in the world since my first portrait. The low-backed chair stood in exactly the same spot, waiting to receive my body. This time Dio wanted a three-quarter view.

"Did you have a good vacation?" he asked.

I told him it had been a different kind of vacation, because we couldn't live at Overa with the refugees occupying our house, and that Herman was changing schools. He would be leaving in ten days for Baarn, in the province of Utrecht, to attend *het Baarns Lyceum.*

"To Baarn? What do you think of that?" Dio asked.

"I don't like it at all."

"You'll miss him," Dio stated as he took up a pencil.

"Yes."

While Dio concentrated on his work, I thought about Herman leaving. I could think of no bigger change in my day-to-day life. Herman was my best friend and a useful buffer between Hans and myself. A day didn't go by when Hans and I were at each other's throat, teasing unmercifully. Herman, more diplomatic, let Hans's moods slide off. In some ways Hans and I were alike. We lacked Herman's quality of letting his temper flare only if it would decisively resolve an argument. But Hans and I would just go on and on, allowing a bagatelle to grow into a row. For instance, Hans would get on my nerves when he sat at the table nervously drumming his fingers. It drove me crazy. I would ask him to stop. He wouldn't. Soon we were hurtling insults at each other, and after a while they had nothing whatsoever to do with drumming fingers. Hans would retort that I did plenty of things that irritated him.

"Like what?" I asked.

"Like coming into my room without knocking!"

"Big deal. All you do is sit behind your desk drawing pictures of houses."

"So?" Hans said.

"Why don't you go out and get some fresh air? Do something!"

At that point Herman, master at averting a pointless all-out fight, suggested we go swimming.

What Hans and I did to each other hurt more than fist fights.

When the first painting session was over, I got on my bike and went to see Oma, just to say hello. I knew she was anxious about Oom Tjalling. The Japanese had surrendered after atomic bombs had flattened two of their cities and killed thousands of people, and thus the Dutch East Indies were free. But the Red Cross had not been able to verify if Oom Tjalling and his family were still alive. Gruesome stories about cruel prison camps over there trickled down to the newspapers.

Oma was sitting on the street-side balcony in a wicker chair soaking in the late summer sun and motioned me to come upstairs. By the time I entered her room, she'd already taken out lemonade and cookies. One of the things I loved about Oma was that she had time. Mammie was always running around trying to keep our home organized, making sure we had food on the table, mending clothes, helping us with homework, telling the help what to do. Oma had probably done the same when she lived on the island and later in Friesland. But that was then. Now she only had herself to feed and two rooms to keep clean. She'd made a few friends since she'd moved here and never seemed bored, always ready to listen or play a game. After we were liberated and Breda was declared safe, she said it was time for her to move back home, and make room for the officers, and maybe she was just as glad to return to the peace of her own apartment and get out of the busy train station that our home resembled at the time.

"How is Herman?" she asked me.

"Getting ready to go to Baarn, Oma."

"You'll miss him," Oma said.

Everybody seemed to know I would miss Herman.

"Yes. I sure will. Hans and I don't get along too well."

"He may surprise you!"

"He bugs me."

"Look at it this way, Titia. The oldest child in the family has it the hardest because the parents have to learn to be parents. You were the third child and the only girl! Hans didn't have that advantage."

"Mammie says she wishes Hans could be the one to go to Baarn, but Pappie won't hear of it. He wants at least one of his sons to finish *het gymnasium.*"

"And Hans is smart enough to do it." Oma sighed. "Well, that's life."

Easy for her to say, I thought. She doesn't have to live with him.

Mammie had fought for Herman, because she was appalled with the little help the teachers at the local H.B.S. provided him. She'd sat for hours with him to help with his homework. He didn't need to be prodded; Herman was ambitious by nature. It was the reading that gave him so much trouble. Pappie wasn't close to what the three of us did at school, but Mammie persisted and convinced him to let Herman go to Baarn. If it only could be the other way around, I thought. But, as Oma said, that's life.

"You look very serious today, Titia," Dio said. I hadn't been in my chair more than five minutes for the second sitting.

"I was thinking about a Jewish girl I knew at school and I wonder if she'll come back. The people from the Agfa photography shop behind our house came back. They went underground. But we know for sure that Carrie and her family went to Westerbork."

Dio stared at what he had painted. Had he heard me?

" We thought the war was behind us when we danced in the streets, didn't we?" he said after a while. "Finding out what really happened in Germany is harder than listening to artillery fire. I'm also waiting for some people to return."

He picked up his brush, waved it briefly through the air, then dipped it into some paint and looked intently at me.

"I saw the pictures of Dachau," I blurted. "Mammie made us look at them. We should know, she said."

The brush dabbed furiously at the canvas.

"What made Hitler do that, Dio? Killing people who've done nothing wrong, I mean."

"Fear," he said.

"Fear? I thought it was the Jews who had to be afraid of the Nazis. How could it be the other way around?"

"Hitler brainwashed his country into hating the Jews because he was afraid they would rule Germany. They are a smart race. There wasn't much the Jews could do. They were in the minority."

He concentrated on painting again, looking over at me only once in a while. The week before, Mammie had made us sit down at the dining room table because, she said, she had something to show us.

"I was going to hide these from you." Her hand rested on a magazine. "But Pappie and I decided that at some point you're going to see them anyway."

Slowly, as if she really didn't want to, she opened the magazine to pictures of naked bodies thrown in a pile; a crowd of men who looked out at us from hollow eye sockets as if they were already skeletons; men with only a torn shirt on and sticklike legs; women dressed in rags, their hair disheveled, dirty and long.

We were speechless. My hands felt clammy. When Jews and young men were sent to Germany, we expected they would be in for a rough time, but this? I'd never imagined it would be this awful and I wondered if anyone else had.

"Where were these pictures taken?" Hans asked. He looked pale and shaken.

"Some in Germany, but mostly in Poland. You will hear these names mentioned often: Dachau, Bergen-Belsen, Auschwitz and many more."

"Who were these people?" Herman asked.

"Mostly Jews," Mammie said. "But also others. Hitler called them *Untermenschen.* They included gypsies, Jehovah Witnesses, colored people and retarded people. Hitler wanted to do away with anyone who didn't fit his ideal of the Aryan race."

I wondered what "doing away with" meant. These pictures were gruesome.

"Did this happen to Carrie Goldstein?" I asked. The question had been burning in my mind from the moment Mammie opened the magazine.

"We don't know. We just don't know who survived. It will take some time to sort that out. You have to prepare yourself, Titia. Carrie may not come back."

"Can we find out? Maybe she didn't go to one of those places!"

"Some day we'll know," Mammie said. "I'm showing you these pictures because it should never be forgotten that this happened."

It didn't seem likely, but Mammie said people would rather deny the past than live with an ugly truth. "If we don't want history to repeat itself, we have the duty to let the world know. That's why these pictures were taken."

The rest of the day, I struggled with the foreboding feeling that I would never see Carrie again. The thought of how she might have suffered appalled me. I felt as if I was being forced to peek inside a casket to check if a certain dead person was inside. I could never take it if Carrie had died of hunger and had looked like one of those bodies in the magazine.

Dio put his brush down and said it was enough for today. When she saw me to the door, I noticed Mevrouw Rovers was friendlier than she had been a couple of years earlier when I came for my first sitting. Maybe it was the war that had made her so curt back then. Oma Ament said my parents' generation had faced agonizing choices and the pressure of the war years had taken a toll on their health. Once she told me that it would take time for them to return to their normal selves, I noticed Pappie was perpetually tired and Mammie's fuse had shortened quite a bit. When we cranked up the old gramophone to play the exciting records Herman and I bought with our allowances, she got irritated. George Gershwin's Rhapsody in Blue was our favorite and we played it over and over again.

"Please…I've had enough!" Mammie would say.

We protested. "You don't want us to play those old records with Fritz Kreisler on the violin, do you? And we're sick of listening to Schubert's *Lieder*!"

Mammie found Gershwin's music vulgar, and she was equally disgusted with the syrupy – her word – movies with Diana Durbin and Bing Crosby. To avoid her wrath, Herman and I sneaked out to the theater at least three times a week. Herman was infatuated with Diana Durbin. The American culture washed over us and we soaked it in like sponges. Magazines like *Look* and *Life* brought America into our living room. Shiny refrigerators, sleek cars in bold colors instead of the traditional black we saw in the streets, a world left untouched by the war, people with well-fed round faces in colorful clothes amazed us and caught our fancy. We greedily leafed through the king-sized magazines, rich with advertisements of things we didn't even dream about because we didn't know they existed.

Mammie wasn't prepared for the speed with which the American culture took hold. My generation felt free and liberated. Mammie's generation was licking its wounds, trying desperately to regain its balance.

For the last painting session, I climbed onto the stool and looked out of the sky window in Dio's studio, while he put on his apron and squeezed a white thread of paint out of a lead tube. In the distance, the cathedral's pepper shaker-like tip towered over the houses. It did not look as grand from here as when I looked up at it from my window at home. Living in its shadow had allowed me a unique perspective, at once intimate and awe-inspiring. *De Grote Kerk*, as it was commonly called, was Breda's identity. Anyone returning after a long absence would know he was home when its spire came into view.

It was time to sit.

Dio chose a brush from a wide-mouthed ceramic vase and dipped it into a glob of paint.

On a table behind him charcoal sketches of the cathedral leaned against the wall. I had never seen *de Grote Kerk* the way he'd sketched it, without scaffolding and a solid fence around its base.

"Look over at me, Titia," Dio reminded me.

How many times had I heard that phrase? Making eye contact with Dio was not the thing to do. His mind wasn't on me. It was on painting me.

"Would you like to walk around a bit?" Dio asked. "Your right shoulder begins to droop!"

I got up and stretched. For a moment, I was tempted to walk over to the easel and peek at what Dio had done so far, but I knew he wouldn't approve. He'd never said so, but my intuition warned me he didn't like to talk while he painted.

"Are you glad the war is over, Titia?" he asked as I walked around.

"Yes, but sometimes I feel guilty, because in my family nobody died."

Dio wiped his brush on a rag. "But you can feel happy and sad at the same time."

"I still wonder what the war was about," I said. "Hitler was crazy, but how about all those other people who did such horrible things? Were they crazy too? It's hard to get those pictures of Dachau out of my head."

"I agree," Dio said. He squeezed more paint onto his palette. "Maybe the scariest thing of the whole war was that people could be misled to the point of making a science out of killing. Many books will be written about it, I'm sure, but I wonder if anyone can really come up with a good answer."

He motioned me to sit down again.

I enjoyed the familiar smell of turpentine and the special light from the slanted window. I sat down and took a deep breath for the next wait.

He scared me a short time later when he exclaimed, "Done!" He stepped back from the easel to take in his creation. I waited to be invited. He gestured for me to come over. I prayed I would like it, for Dio's sake more than my own.

I was lost for words. The way he had rendered my eyes startled me.

"What's the matter?"

"You made me look mad, Dio."

"You think so? Maybe you're not used to seeing yourself with a serious look on your face." Dio wasn't given to commenting on his own work. I was surprised he said anything at all.

The next week, when the finishing touches had been applied, Dio brought the painting to my parents. They liked it even more than the first, they said, and that was what counted. I didn't like it, but I'd done my part.

Dio's painting of me, dated 1945.

When I came home and walked in through de apotheek, I saw Pappie talking with Mijnheer van Dijk, the man who'd pushed my father to help him manufacture surrogate tea. He'd done exceedingly well for himself. His wife and daughters wore showy, expensive clothes and they had moved to a better neighborhood. My mother was not pleased. She resented the fact that Mijnheer van Dijk had bamboozled her husband into working out a formula he could walk off with without giving anything in return. I wondered what he wanted my father to come up with this time.

Upstairs, Herman was packing his bags. Only a few more days and he would be gone.

"Are you scared?" I asked him.

"Why would I be scared?"

"I don't know. Strange people, a new school. I would be scared to death!"

"I'm glad I don't have to go back to the H.B.S. here."

"Will you miss us?"

"I'll miss everyone but you!" he teased, but once at the station and ready to step into the hissing train, he didn't seem quite so sure of himself. After he put his suitcase on the luggage rack, he came to the window. Mammie and I wiped our tears. Herman blew his nose. Black smoke swept over us from the locomotive up front as it slowly pulled itself from the platform. Herman yanked the leather strap inside his compartment door to let the heavy window down and leaned out to wave at us. Then the train pulled around the bend and we couldn't see anything but a plume of smoke. Mammie hooked her arm through mine as we walked back through the park, a familiar route we'd often taken to school.

"This is best for him," Mammie said, as much to herself as to me.

Closure to the war years was seeing Herman off to Baarn. Life would never be the same. Already, I felt nostalgic for the time when danger was an everyday item, for the constant excitement and anticipation of that incredible day when we would be free, for the common bond we felt with our neighbors, for learning to make do with what we had. Now I felt empty.

With the war over, people were beginning to worry about the Red Danger. Major Corcoran, who'd come by on his way back to England during our summer vacation, told us how the Russians were almost impossible to deal with and that the Russian menace might replace the Nazi foe. This somber conversation was background to the delight with which Hans, Herman and I fingered the presents Major Corcoran had brought: a pistol and a copy of *Mein Kampf* with a personal inscription from Hitler for Dr. Fritz Grüne. Major Corcoran had personally confiscated these items from the doctor who had run one of the worst concentration camps in Germany. The major had talked about it with British understatement, but his eyes had brimmed with glee as he handed the historical items to my brothers as keepsakes.

School vacation was definitely over on the day we turned the calendar to the first of September, the day after Queen Wilhelmina's birthday. Tomorrow, I would be back in the school benches laboring over Latin, learning what I should have learned last year. Last year, when I'd first gone to *het gymnasium* Crazy Tuesday had exploded outside the gate. So much had happened since. I felt as though I had crawled out of a dark tunnel into a bright light. But the skies had darkened again as soon as we learned how millions had died over the entire globe as a result of the war, what atrocities had taken place, how many people had not returned from where the Germans had taken them.

Light and dark, black and white. Mixed together they result in gray.

"You can be happy and sad at the same time," Dio had said to me. But I didn't want to live in a gray world. If I had to choose, I would rather live through black to reach white.

As I put my pencils and eraser in my schoolbag, I looked up at the cathedral through my window. Its tower stood out against a cloudless blue sky, aspiring to spiritual heights not often attained from where we stood, grounded as we were in our daily existence. On impulse, I got up and walked over to the cathedral, wishing from the bottom of my heart that somehow she would impart her serenity to me.

Epilogue

When I returned to Breda as an American citizen in 1991, I remembered how I'd skipped across the street to the cathedral, the day before returning to school after the war was over. The oak door had been ajar and workmen were inside repairing the patches of plaster that had come off during the artillery barrage. The sounds of ladders scraping over the slate floor and the whooshing of spatulas applying plaster had echoed against the stone pillars.

Back in the revered place of my youth, I walked around the nave and visited the monument of Count Engelbert and his spouse. The late afternoon sun lit up their alabaster bodies and they looked peaceful and otherworldly, just as I remembered them. The surrounding walls had been repaired, the damage of thirty-six direct hits now invisible.

When I sat down in the same chair, facing the magnificent organ, I felt rejoined with the inspiration the vastness of this place had instilled in me as a thirteen-year old. I hadn't come then to look for a minister's explanation of the word of God. My bond with this church hadn't been forged by organized religion. I had befriended its awesome exterior from the window of my childhood room, admiring its graceful spires and stonework, always wondering how so many hands could have been motivated to undertake such a huge project. Men had worked on it with total dedication, day in and day out, most of them knowing they wouldn't live to see the final result.

There was bitter irony in realizing that thousands of men had labored for more than a century to erect this building to the glory of God, while within the span of five years, millions of people had died at the hands of men who had followed an earthly leader who rejected God's very existence.

The vaulted ceiling inspired awe, as if it were only incidental that human hands had created it and it was, in reality, God's protective umbrella over us. When I'd sat here last, I had contemplated the pictures of men dying in the battlefield with only the sky over them, images of emaciated POWs, of innocent children caught in crossfire or maimed under the debris of their destroyed homes. My mind had wanted to reach to the face of God, not to the face of death. I remembered agonizing over what God's role had been in the war. If we prayed to God and believed He could help us to prevent our death and destruction, we automatically assigned Him the role of magician. But life seemed to be constructed in such a way that death was an inevitable part of it. Was it reasonable to ask God to spare us from death if it was part of life?

I had been confused about what God demanded of us. Surely not killing others! What was the test? Did God exempt men like Eisenhower from taking responsibility for the deaths of many because he served the cause of liberating the oppressed, while holding Hitler accountable because his motivations were selfish and evil? Could men stand up for what was right even if it meant killing others? Since WW II, war had raged on every continent: In Korea, Eastern Europe, Vietnam, Israel, Kashmir, Nigeria, Iran and Iraq. The war machine had never stopped and I began to doubt it ever would. Every short-lived period of peace seemed to create a vacuum that sucked in the next round of violence. Was this man's destiny?

The Second World War hadn't made a pacifist out of me. I had been excited when the Allies landed in Normandy. I had cheered the Polish troops that liberated us. I had delighted in seeing the Germans being led away with their hands raised in surrender. I revered Eisenhower and Churchill as men of vision, as superb strategists who'd labored to free us from occupation.

Forty-six years ago, the world had seemed divided into good and bad. That was the way it had been played itself out before my youthful eyes. Over the years, though, I recognized the nuances and the danger of following the wrong leader. Even my own grandfather, who'd been an upright man, a smart man, had followed the wrong leader. What did it take to recognize others for what they were truly worth?

Although I couldn't fathom God's ways, I didn't question God's existence. When blood poisoning had almost taken me, He was so unquestionably present that the event had been more about experiencing love than experiencing death. Even though my family whom I loved stood at the foot of my hospital bed, I'd felt detached, swooped up by a love greater than anything I'd ever known. Of course, I was glad to come back from that lofty place to live beyond my ten years, and grateful that my father had pushed to get me the medicine that would save my life. What I took away from the hospital experience was a vague yet sure understanding that detachment was the way towards our ability to surrender our existence. Detachment from things, from people, from the lure of power.

These thoughts, seeded by the war, had taken root and guided me through the pitfalls of adult life, which is never without loss.

I looked up at the vaulted ceiling, more beautiful than I remembered it. The skirt of scaffolding had been removed from the exterior, as had Dio Rovers's studio and Dio himself, who had been such an integral part of my war experience.

The war had sliced time. We talked about "before the war" and "after the war" because nothing had seemed the same when the war was over. Not the landscape, not the composition of families, not the outlook on life. The earth had been scarred, and so were many souls. Those scars were carried in different ways and some didn't completely heal. A friend my age couldn't get through university. He'd lost his ability to concentrate during frequent bomb attacks on his city. The worst one had happened during school hours and it had changed the course of his life. Once, when I was a student driving home from a party, one of the older students in our group asked to be let out of the car. He sat by the side of the road and cried inconsolably. The vast heather field we were driving through was where the Germans had executed his buddy in the Underground.

We didn't often discuss what had happened to us during the war. We were out to have a good time. Let bygones be bygones, we thought. Only the present and the future counted. But once in a while something happened that pulled us up short. When the Hungarians revolted against the Russians in 1956, we huddled together and wondered out loud, "Could it happen again?" Thunderstorms reminded me of bomb explosions and I tended to hoard. During the oil crisis of 1973, I dreamed up a scheme to buy a car with a diesel motor and a pump on the side of our house, so we could put heating fuel into the car's gas tank.

In 1984, I found myself in a panic en route to my ailing mother. The worst snowstorm of the decade had closed Logan Airport in Boston. My husband Gijs and I lost a whole day waiting to fly to Frankfurt, where we would rent a car to get to Holland. I prayed my mother would still be alive after her heart attack.

The early morning in Frankfurt was gray. Tired passengers waddled like obedient ducks down the trunk to the terminal. Worried and tired, I let myself flow in the human stream. My husband had swooped up our bags and I trudged behind him to the car rental desk. While he negotiated about insurance and mileage, I watched people rush by, most of them German passengers, extremely well dressed, the colors of their clothes subdued grays, loden greens, muted browns, the colors of the war as I remembered it. Gijs looked at me with concern. I wasn't moving very fast. We lumbered through endless corridors. Just plain cement walls, here and there a utilitarian light.

Push! Push! I have to get to Holland. Keep moving!

Suddenly Gijs stopped.

There's a door to go through. A car comes. It stops. A man in uniform steps out of the sentry box.

"Gijs! Stop!" I yelled.

On the other side of the glass door the soldier raised the red barrier over the road. The car proceeded. *I have seen this before.*

"What's the matter?" Gijs asked.

"Where are the papers? Where's my *stamkaart*?"

"Your what? You mean your passport? We already went through customs."

He looked at me with puzzled eyes. "Titia, did you say *stamkaart*?"

And then I realized. The war was over. The days where every Dutchman had to carry an identification card were gone. A *stamkaart* gave the information the Germans wanted: what race you stemmed from. Aryan or Jew.

That temporary out-of-control feeling had been a reminder that war memories are like lodged logs. They just sit there while the river rushes over them.

I got up from the uncomfortable chair and left the cathedral. Outside the sun splashed over sleek cars, making their colors stand out against the old gray cobblestones. Bright tablecloths on the terrace tables in front of the many cafes shouted their message to the world. Colorful signs almost hid the old brick facades of new businesses. The post-war spirit of consumerism had transformed de markt. Even my father's apotheek had become a restaurant. Was this the same place where I grew up? Where we had to make do with the little we had?

The very things we'd longed for during the war: clean, new clothes, *patates frites*, at least ten varieties of bread, candies and toys, shiny cars that ran on gasoline, surrounded me wherever I looked.

Sitting in a wicker chair in front of what used to be my home, I sipped from my cup of cappuccino.

Now we have it all, I thought.

Or did we?

Post Script

What happened to the main characters?

Mammie:

Mammie threw herself into the study of art after her three children left home. She enticed a professor from Leiden University, Mr. Veldkamp, to come to Breda to teach a women's group the history of art.

When de apotheek was sold in 1962, my parents moved into an apartment and summered at Overa where Mammie created a truly magnificent garden.

Although suffering from arthritis in her knees, she remained active. She touched many lives with her love of art and literature. Her innate wisdom and spirituality were an inspiration to her four grandchildren.

Mammie died at home, a week after Pappie, on her 85th birthday in September of 1984.

Pappie:

After the war, Pappie was instrumental in starting up a government-supported health insurance system in Breda, the very thing that had eluded his father. In 1962, he sold the pharmacy and our home to a Chinese man who turned it into a restaurant. Breda's center was emptying out as residents moved to the quieter outskirts. Pappie saw the handwriting on the wall: his patients would want to switch to a pharmacy closer to their new homes.

He'd looked forward to retirement, but was hampered by severe arthritis. He switched his love for tennis to golf and became quite good at it, but eventually he had to give it up. His left leg was shorter than his right leg by several inches. Because he became almost totally deaf, he lived a rather isolated life in his last years, though he never lost his marvelous, quick wit. He died at home three days before his 86th birthday.

Oma Ament:

Oma's last years were pleasantly uneventful. She moved to a nursing home in Breda and died peacefully in her own bed in the spring of 1955. Her mind remained clear to the end.

Opa Wetselaar:

When Winston Churchill's monumental work about WW II came out in 1948, Opa read every volume cover to cover. With pencil in hand for notes and comments in the margins, he studied the facts he had previously denied. In discussions with his sons, he showed insight in his own misguided judgment.

On August 1952, at the age of 81, he slipped away in his sleep.

Oma Wetselaar:

Loyal to the end, forgiving Opa for the mistake that cost them their comfortable way of life, and retaining her gracious ways and sense of humor, Oma lived quiet years after the turmoil of the war. With Opa she moved to a private nursing home where she died at the age of 85, in 1955.

Oom Tjalling:

My uncle survived four years of Japanese prison camp. In early 1946, he repatriated with his wife and two children –Titia and Herman – and moved in with us for several months. The boys' room became their living room and all sleeping arrangements in our house were turned upside down again. Tante Iet and the children had never been in Holland and they suffered from the cold.

It was not an easy time. My mother was at the end of her rope after the strenuous war years. My uncle didn't find it easy to fill the days without having work. My aunt was caught between her husband and his older sister. The exchange of war stories often led to competition of who had endured the most, the Dutch in Holland or the Dutch in the Indies. Eventually, we all got enough of war stories.

Oom Tjalling moved back to Friesland and bought a paint factory. He died of a heart attack in 1962.

Carrie Goldstein:

As I was putting the finishing touches on the manuscript for this book, my brother Herman alerted me to an ad in Breda's newspaper asking for any information about the Goldstein family. I got in contact with Rachel van Kooy in Austria, who was the keeper of albums that belonged to the Goldstein family. Carrie's father had given them to Rachel's grandfather – who was Dutch and lived in Breda at the time – for safekeeping, but she didn't know if any of the Goldsteins had survived the Holocaust.

As a result of her probing, Rachel discovered that the Goldsteins had indeed been brought to Westerbork. On the 20th of November, 1942, Carrie, her mother and her sister Leny were deported to Auschwitz. Three days later, on Leny's birthday, they were exterminated. Their father had been transported from Westerbork a month earlier and faced the same fate.

Hans:

Hans had no difficulties finishing *het gymnasium.* He went on to study law at the University of Amsterdam. Hans was smart and verbal, but suffered from a deep fear of doing exams. Although close to getting his degree, he quit and got a position at the electricity company of the province of North Holland. He died of a massive heart attack at his desk at work in 1989, at the age of sixty. He was unmarried.

Herman:

In spite of his dyslexia, Herman fought his way up in the world. He graduated from *De Grafische School* in Amsterdam, a technological college for the graphic arts. It was his springboard for a successful career in management consulting.

In 1967, he married Marijke Verhagen. They have two daughters, Titia and Wendy.

Herman is now retired and lives with Marijke in Muiden, close to Amsterdam.

Sources

This book describes the war years in my native land as I remember them. I wrote from my own perspective, aware that other members of my extended family might color events differently, especially where it involved Opa Wetselaar and his membership in the NSB.

The cousins Wetselaar met in Friesland in September 2002, on the birthday of my father and his twin brother, to compare notes and sort out our memories of our youth. We discovered that the views we held of our grandfather were remarkably similar. Liesje Wetselaar, the eldest grandchild, wrote long letters from Australia to fill in more details.

My brother Herman helped tremendously in verifying names, dates, facts and places.

To accurately render the background against which my personal experiences played out, I consulted the following:

Crusade in Europe by Dwight D. Eisenhower, Doubleday.

The Second World War (six volumes) by Winston S. Churchill, Houghton Mifflin.

De Eeuw Van Mijn Vader, by Geert Mak, Uitgevery Atlas.

Het *Grijs Verleden*, by Chris van der Heijden, Uitgeverij Contact.

De Eerste Poolse Pantserdivisie in Nederland, by Thom Peters. Uitgeverij Brabantia Nostra.

Die *Slappe Nederlanders – of viel het toch wel mee in 1940-1945?* By Dick Verkijk, Uitgeverij Aspect.

Voedsel en Honger in Oorlogstijd 1940-1945, by Gerard Trienekens, Kosmos, Z&K Uitgevers.

Anne Frank Remembered by Miep Gies, Simon & Schuster.

Wilhelmina, by Cees Fasseur, Uitgeverij Balans.

I often consulted the *Encyclopaedia Brittannica* as well the *Dutch Winkler_Prins Encyclopaedie*, Elsevier.